Revolution and
the Historical Novel

Revolution and the Historical Novel

John McWilliams

LEXINGTON BOOKS
Lanham • Boulder • New York • London

Published by Lexington Books
An imprint of The Rowman & Littlefield Publishing Group, Inc.
4501 Forbes Boulevard, Suite 200, Lanham, Maryland 20706
www.rowman.com

Unit A, Whitacre Mews, 26–34 Stannary Street, London SE11 4AB

British Library Cataloguing in Publication Information Available

Library of Congress Cataloging-in-Publication Data

Names: McWilliams, John P., author.
Title: Revolution and the historical novel / John McWilliams.
Description: Lanham, Maryland : Lexington Books, [2017] | Includes
    bibliographical references and index.
Identifiers: LCCN 2017046217 (print) | LCCN 2017050674 (ebook) |
    ISBN 9781498503280 (Electronic) | ISBN 9781498503273 (cloth : alk. paper)
Subjects: LCSH: Historical fiction—History and criticism. | Revolutions in literature. |
    Literature and revolutions—History. | Revolutionary literature—History and criticism.
Classification: LCC PN3441 (ebook) | LCC PN3441 .M44 2017 (print) |
    DDC 809.3/81—dc23
LC record available at https://lccn.loc.gov/2017046217

Printed in the United States of America

For Mireille and for Family
Always and Forever

"Those who serve revolution plough the sea."
—Simon Bolivar, November 1830, quoted in Gabriel Garcia Marquez,
The General in His Labyrinth (1990)

Contents

ix

Permissions

A Legacy of Walter Scott

Historical Novels of Revolution and Counter-Revolution

Walter Scott	Waverley; or 'Tis Sixty Years Since	1814
	Old Mortality	1816
	Rob Roy	1817
	The Heart of Mid-Lothian	1818
	The Bride of Lammermoor	1819
	A Legend of the Wars of Montrose	1819
	Woodstock: or The Cavalier	1826
James Fenimore Cooper	The Spy	1821
	The Last of the Mohicans	1826
Honoré de Balzac	Les Chouans	1829
Alexander Pushkin	The Captain's Daughter	1836
Charles Dickens	A Tale of Two Cities	1859
Leo Tolstoy	War and Peace	1863–1869
Victor Hugo	1793	1874
Sarah Orne Jewett	The Tory Lover	1901
Anatole France	The Gods Will Have Blood	1912
Herman Melville	Billy Budd, Sailor:	
	An Inside Narrative	1892, 1924
Willa Cather	Death Comes For the Archbishop	1927
Margaret Mitchell	Gone With The Wind	1936
Boris Pasternak	Dr. Zhivago	1957
Giuseppe de Lampedusa	The Leopard	1958
Gore Vidal	Burr	1973
	1876	1976
	Lincoln	1984
	Empire	1987
Gabriel Garcia Marquez	The General In His Labyrinth	1990
Hilary Mantel	A Place of Greater Safety	1992

Foreword
A Search for Synthesis

For at least a century after the American and French Revolutions, many knowledgeable Europeans and Americans assumed that the improvements of their era proved that the progress of civilization was an immutable law of history. Hegelian teleological faith in the Absolute Spirit of Freedom, materialist faith in scientific and technological advance, and political faith in liberal if not republican values were continually to be challenged, however, by human unwillingness to change, by the brutalities of class revolt, by the carnage of further revolution, and ultimately by the two world wars. The emerging model of the nineteenth-century historical novel, defined by the early novels of Walter Scott, arose concurrent with the onset of these volatile conditions, during the turbulent wake of the American and French Revolutions. The appeal of Scott's rendering of historical politics was accordingly multidimensional. Because his historical subjects had centered upon violent Jacobite, Puritan, or Covenanter uprisings and needed governmental responses to them (*Waverley, Old Mortality, Rob Roy, The Heart of Midlothian, Redgauntlet, Woodstock*), Scott's novels appealed to latent counterrevolutionary yearnings among and within his readers, as well as to the principle of the progressive stages of civilization.

Continuing revolution and continuing failure to reify the Rights of Man were to bring with them, for author and reader, a disturbing awareness of the destructive ironies of promoting revolution in the name of "progress." The hope for a good society and a better life lay in instituting the Rights of Man, but the restoration of order, the reemergence of necessary hierarchies of class and power, brought needed relief from revolutionary agitation and revolutionary violence. Nineteenth-century readers of the Waverley Novels were drawn toward such contradictory responses, not only by the novels themselves, but also by the failed hopes of revolutions continuing to transpire around them. Accordingly, reading historical fiction about revolution has long proven to be a discomfiting, if not a subversive activity. Yesterday's progressive assurances have not been realized, while yesterday's dire warnings have been confirmed in unexpected forms. From 1789 through 1917 (and perhaps still today), privileged people have been reluctant to consider that a revolution might be coming—until it has suddenly arrived.

This study will focus on some twenty-five historical novels, almost all of them canonical, in which civil war, revolution, or counterrevolution is central to the narrative. As Fredric Jameson has implied, all these novels arouse in us the response that they are somehow, at their deepest level, "about" the myriad dimensions of revolution. After 1776 and 1789, revolutionary fervor is associated with human rights and the rise of nationalism, but also with resentments of social class and economic inequality. Armed revolt against the perceived injustice of the old order, when successful, becomes inextricably tied to the prospect of a newly centralized national identity. But national themes are repeatedly presented within the implied universalist context demanded by "The Rights of Man" or, later, "The Rights of Labor." Just as Crane Brinton did when writing *The Anatomy of Revolution*, we still refer to "The French Revolution," "The American Revolution," and "The Russian Revolution," even though we recognize that nearly all Western revolutions after 1789 had international aspirations.

The chapter structure of my book is topical rather than chronological, a sequencing of issues and novelistic conventions rather than of authors. Studies of these individual novels abound; synthetic comparisons among them do not. Focusing on Edmund Burke, Thomas Paine, and Madame de Stael, my introduction, part historical overview and part theory, will explore opposed responses to the onset of revolution; these are the polemical texts Scott would have known in 1814. The chapters that follow will focus on themes, techniques, and tropes common to plotting and characterization in the novels chosen. Developing from the general to the specific, from metaphor and setting toward recurrent character types and narrative structures, my sequencing of chapters is designed to demonstrate differences among novelists who are adapting and altering Scott's tradition to suit new times, new perspectives, and the continuing revolutionary turmoil of their own eras. The novels chosen, from Scott to Marquez and beyond, form one tradition in which revolution is as an historical fact as well as a fictional subject.

Many twentieth-century readers accept the seeming premise that the historical novel portrays the past as past (ultimately following *Waverley*'s subtitle "'Tis Sixty Years Since"). A usually unstated assumption emerges that the historical novelist has sought to recreate the past in an objective, impartial, even detached manner. Whatever advantages this assumption may secure in suspending disbelief, it slights the pertinence of contemporary conditions to the portrayal of the past. Although historical novelists might wish to endorse past revolutionary aims, present circumstances repeatedly cloud and qualify the attempt. Amid sporadic violence by unemployed weavers and impoverished farmers, Scott tries to negotiate continuing resentment of the Act of Union between Scotland and England; Cooper, committed to America's experimental Republic, marries into the most prominent Loyalist ("Tory") family in New York; Dickens fears the ugliness of Chartist violence while approving Chartist Declarations of Right; Victor Hugo writes *Quatre-Vingt-Treize* in late-life political exile from Louis Napoleon's Second Empire; Anatole France writes under the shadow of the Dreyfus affair; Pasternak completes *Doctor Zhivago* under the imminent threat of Stalinist persecution. The troubled, ambivalent relation of past to present lends these novels a forceful sense of crisis.

These examples are signs of a continuing historical irresolvability. Despite a desire for certainty common among progressives and reactionaries alike, neither the promise nor the horror of the French Revolution was to end with Thermidor or even with Napoleon. As the upheavals of 1815, 1830, 1848, and 1870, together with the American Civil War, the Franco-Prussian War, and the rise of Marxism-Leninism collectively attest, an author's faith in progress and enlightenment was continually to be challenged. For some, the Terror had permanently disgraced republicanism. For others, the promise of liberal justice for an entire society was repeatedly being betrayed even as technological and scientific progress accelerated. Throughout the nineteenth century, the prospect of group action demanding political reform instinctually evoked fearful memories of guillotine or purge, along with hope. As a defining symbol of revolution, the guillotine simultaneously beheads the old order, while presaging the brutality of the new. The remembered road to leftist Terror from 1789 to 1793 therefore casts a deep shadow over the future within a genre ostensibly confined to a safely removed past.

As Perry Anderson and Fredric Jameson attest, comprehensive, searching criticism of the subgenre of historical fiction, written predominately by males about political and military conflict, began with Georg Lukacs's *The Historical Novel* (1937). In his first chapter, Lukacs argued that the historical novel arose during the aftermath of the French Revolution *because* European peoples had suddenly been compelled to acquire an acute sense of the passing of time amid the jolt of social change. By 1814, when *Waverley* was published, the seemingly fixed, isolated village life of farmers and artisans, dominated architecturally, economically, and politically by the village church and the local chateau or estate, had been fundamentally disrupted, perhaps gone forever. A new literary form was needed to demonstrate how the forces of history and politics were thought to impinge both upon representative men and upon today's "citizens." As developed by Scott, the historical novel placed an irresolute male protagonist amid a political crisis during which he wavers between the cultural appeal of an old regional aristocratic order and the political appeal of a new enlightened national order. The wavering fictional protagonist needed to be juxtaposed to a hero from history, an Hegelian "world-historical individual," who appears in a moment of crisis to embody the promise and/or the danger of social upheaval. Writer and reader become immersed in the uncertainty of being divided between two worlds, opposed in qualities, but seemingly equal in attraction and repulsion.[1]

Behind Lukacs's insights into Scott's "classical form" of historical fiction lie the premises of Lukacs's earlier text, *The Theory of the Novel* (1920). Searching for an Hegelian dialectic in literary history, Lukacs had argued that the differences between epic (a world ordered in values) and drama (a world in tragic conflict) had coalesced, for nineteenth-century readership, into the open-ended qualities of the novel. After the revolutionary era, the novel had become the genre of continuing uncertainty, "the epic of an age in which the extensive totality of life is no longer directly given," "the epic of a world that has been abandoned by God." Averse to the "via dolorosa of interiority" associated with then emerging high modernism, Lukacs in 1920 embraces a realism that, not yet Marxist, searches for the "totality" exemplified by the vast complexities of *War and Peace*.[2] Although Scott is scarcely mentioned in *The Theory of the Novel*, the Waverley Novels exemplify nearly all of the qualities by which Lukacs was defining the novel's significance and appeal. It is therefore consistent that, a generation later, the first chapter of *The Historical Novel* was to affirm Scott's precedence and centrality within a tradition claimed for realism. Scott's Scottish novels admirably suited Lukacs's already formed theory of realistic fiction. The open-endedness of the genre was perfectly suited to the conflicting responses nineteenth-century readers brought to the specter of revolution.

When Fredric Jameson made "The Case For George Lukacs" in Chapter three of *Marxism and Form* (1971), Jameson credited Lukacs with the realization that truly viable realism in fiction must avoid archetypal characters and presentist psychology in order to defend, diachronically, the processes of historical and social change: "Realism is dependent on the possibility of access to the forces of change in a given moment of history."[3] To conceive of characters in an historical novel as timeless archetypes from a distant past is to defeat the purpose of the genre. Balzac's La Comédie Humaine, not the Waverley Novels, serve as Jameson's standard for how a true realist's sense of character evolves amid changing social and economic conditions. Scott is not directly criticized, certainly not rejected, but neither is Scott's achievement foregrounded.

Jameson's *The Political Unconscious* (1981), one of the most influential critical works of the last half-century, presents a compelling Marxist overview of cultural history even though Jameson displaces Scott from the position Lukacs had accorded him. Jameson plausibly assumes that the lasting legacy of the French Revolution is, in material and ideological fact, not the Rights of Man nor any National Assembly, but the emergence of a bourgeois devotion to "freedom" of property rights that powered the Industrial Revolution in its early, entrepreneurial phase. The romanticism of Scott's era provided merely passive resistance to the forces of emerging capitalism. Consequently, the diverse kinds of revolutionary ends that Hegel and then Marx had once anticipated (the Absolute Spirit of Freedom, the rule of the working-class proletariat) have not yet—and may never—come to pass. Instead, the forces of economic exploitation, with the complicity of the ahistorical and individualistic perspective of literary high modernism, have left us in the "dis-associative moment of late monopoly or consumer or multinational capitalism."[4] As Jameson's title suggests, market commodification forces oppositional politics underground into the unconscious. From this perspective, recovery of a realist historical awareness becomes even more essential, but the novelists Jameson now chooses to exemplify it are Balzac, Stendhal, Flaubert, Gissing, and Conrad; they do not include Walter Scott.

The last chapter of Jameson's most recent exploration of these issues, *The Antinomies of Realism* (2013) is titled "The Historical Novel Today, or, Is It Still Possible?" His chapter title is, of course, a playful parody of many nineteenth-century fictional titles, including romance/novels by Scott and Cooper. Jameson's chapter develops an argument tentatively advanced in *The Political Unconscious* and earlier formulated in his often-reprinted essay "Postmodernism and Consumer Society" (1983). Because late monopoly capitalism thrives by obliterating a sense of history, the historical novel has devolved into a drugstore, supermarket, and airport kiosk commodity, especially after modernism has broken down traditional literary genres into the border-crossings characteristic of postmodernism. The great names of history have become "the detritus of the schoolbooks."[5] A diachronic world of cause and effect is being replaced by a synchronic world composed of simultaneous and disconnected images. Reaffirming Hegel via a negative, Jameson questions "How to have confidence in the presence and stability of any of the allegedly world-historical figures of the past when we have lost our own?"(260). When proclaimed revolutions are not enacted, they become evanescent images. To the extent that revolution was the implicit if not explicit subject of great historical novels, we must now confront the widespread "conviction that revolutions are always confiscated, when not already defeated" (261).

Jameson's hope for a radical resurgence of the realist tradition (now slightly redefined as Balzac, Stendhal, Tolstoy, Galdos, George Eliot, and Zola) remains intact, but where can the tradition established by Scott possibly figure within today's literary conditions? Jameson concludes that "The specialized sub-genre called the 'historical novel' has reached 'a kind of evolutionary dead end'" (264). This "evolutionary dead end" had in fact occurred long ago when *La Comédie Humaine* displaced the Waverley Novels. "Scott's own paradigm vanishes, giving way to Balzac, who writes, not historical novels, but contemporary novels which are profoundly historical" (264). As a result, "with Balzac's formal transformation, the historical novel in its earlier authenticity disappears" (274). At this moment, Jameson argues, the historical novel underwent a then unrecognized "extinction" (275).

For Jameson, the end of the Scott tradition needs to be confirmed in absolute terms: "vanishes," "disappears" and "extinction." For my purposes, however, it is crucial to remember that *The Antimonies of Realism* also contains an astute tribute to Scott. "Scott confirms our obscure suspicion that all genuinely historical novels must have a revolutionary moment as their occasion; a moment of radical change, which lifts their content out of the placid continuities of mere custom and of the picturesque daily life of this or that exotic moment of the past" (266). While disputing Jameson's unqualified dismissal of Scott's contemporaneity, I fully accept Jameson's premise that "genuinely historical" novels center upon a demonstrably valid "revolutionary moment." My selection of texts is based upon that premise. Conversely, to dwell upon the exoticism of bygone times, even though it ironically remains the key to *Ivanhoe*'s appeal, undermines the greatest strength of historical fiction.

Writing the history of the historical novel has faced a recurring problem in identifying masterpieces of the genre written after the mid-nineteenth century, particularly after the failed revolution of 1848 that had been so crucial to Lukacs. The difficulty of perceiving a continuance of Scott's tradition—as my concluding chapter will argue—ironically derives from the authority of Lukacs's work, as well as from the questionable displacement of Scott by Balzac. Critics and readers of *The Historical Novel* lose interest after Lukacs's first three chapters, being unwilling to follow Lukacs through his analysis of the little-known fictions of Conrad Ferdinand Meyer, Heinrich Mann, Leon Feuchtwanger, and other left-leaning realists, mostly German, whom Lukacs sought to position as weapons against Stalin and growing fascism. Jameson, as we have seen, then removes Scott's writings from centrality at the same time that he argues that the once valid form of the historical novel can no longer speak to the postmodernist sensibility of late monopoly capitalism.

There are additional reasons why Scott's revolution-centered form of the historical novel has continued to seem dead-ended. Richard Maxwell's recent monograph *The Historical Novel in Europe, 1650–1950* (2009) shows how the popularity of Scott conceived as a medieval romance revivalist (*Ivanhoe*, not *Waverley*, as the text in point) led to a literature of adventure, chivalry, sieges, and royal pretenders that would devolve, by century's end, into a massive subliterature Maxwell calls "Juvenile: children, play and history."[6] There is understandable critical and scholarly embarrassment here, especially amid the rise of feminist criticism. On the one hand, Scott's reputation has been tarnished by second-rate or juvenile literature for which he is not responsible. To discern Scott's art and complexity thus requires that his least worthy successors be overlooked.[7] On the other hand, Scott's writings, and Scott's historical paradigms continue to be respected, but defined as outmoded, even to the extent of suffering a long-ago "extinction." After *War and Peace*, there has been a seeming vacuum of literary achievement that has contributed markedly to denigration of the form. The true continuation of Scott's legacy needs now to be sought in new and worthy places.

TRANSFORMATIONS

The sense of a post Tolstoy-an vacuum has led to a slighting of the connections between later historical fictions and the paradigm established by Scott. Lukacs, Jameson, and Maxwell give short shrift to Flaubert's *Sentimental Education* (as opposed to *Salammbo),* to Hugo's *Quatre-Vingt Treize*, to Anatole France's *Les Dieux Ont Soif,* and to Zola's *La Debacle*, all of which deal with historical conflicts during French revolutions. These novels are cited, acknowledged, but finally set to the side as accomplished aberrations from the realist tradition the critic is pursuing, or from the escapist tradition of historical novels he is denouncing. Dickens's *A Tale of Two Cities*, virtually contemporaneous with *War and Peace,* is read as a transitional text, a sensational novel of lasting popularity that ultimately avoids the very historical issues it is raising. Later historical fictions like Pasternak's *Doctor Zhivago*, Lampedusa's *The Leopard*, Vidal's series of "Empire" novels, and Marquez's *The General In his Labyrinth*, novels in which revolution remain central, lie beyond the critic's time horizon. Insights into individual authors and texts abound but the controlling argument tends to be centrifugal, while the importance of Scott and the recurring focus of the historical novel upon revolution recede. Even Harry E. Shaw's fine, informative study *The Forms of Historical Fiction: Sir Walter Scott and His Successors* (1983), shows this same additive and separational argumentative structure.

   I maintain that there is an extended but clearly discernible tradition of the historical novel continuing between Walter Scott and Hilary Mantel, between Fenimore Cooper and Gore Vidal, between Alexander Pushkin and Boris Pasternak, between Stendhal and Anatole France. The tradition transcends the emerging nationalisms of the Napoleonic era (evident in my couplings) because it is based upon universal questions posed by the sudden awareness of historical time that Lukacs ascribed to the French Revolution and to the wide readership for Scott's novels. Formulations of the Rights of Man lent a universalist perspective to the very prospect of revolution. The flexibility of Scott's form in turn made the historical novel readily adaptable to emerging national cultures. The vital, enduring tradition of the historical novel must therefore be sought, not in writers deliberately imitating Scott, but in the *transformations* of the multiple conventions by which a "Waverley Novel" must be recognized. To substantiate this thesis, I propose to trace the development of the historical novel in a way similar to the method by which Le Bossu, Voltaire, C. M. Bowra, and C. Day Lewis defined the tradition of the epic—that is, through adaptations of conventions first established by Homer: proposition, invocation, council of chieftains, epic games, single combat, visit to the underworld, cultural prophecy, and so forth.

My chapter structure seeks to explore transformations of these conventions through two kinds of ordering. Within each chapter, novels will be treated in chronological order of their publication so as to trace the transformation of the particular convention that is the chapter's subject. The ordering of literary conventions among the chapters will proceed from the general to the specific. My introduction, part historical overview and part theory, seeks to convey what was at stake in the word "revolution" within early polemical assessments of the French Revolution known to Scott. The following chapters focus on techniques and tropes common to the historical novels I believe to be within Scott's legacy. My historical introduction is immediately followed by a chapter comparing the force of particular metaphors by which novelists sought to control the immense contradictions of historical forces within their revolutionary worlds.

After contrasting Scott's conceptions of the Puritan and "Glorious" Revolutions in England, concentrating on the rarely considered *Woodstock*, in chapter 2, I examine in chapter 3 the setting of many historical novels within variants of a contended "Neutral Ground," be it a military borderland, a cultural border-ground, or a city. In addition to being a place, the neutral ground functions as the objective correlative of the troubled inner "neutrality" of many a character caught in revolutionary indecision. Chapter 4 studies a developing pattern of characterization in which the central figure of the waverer is juxtaposed to a fanatic, whether a revolutionary or a counterrevolutionary. Chapters 6 and 7 examine two recurrent plot situations caused by the armed conflicts to which revolutionary agitation repeatedly gives rise: honor and dishonor in battle, and the justice of spying/traitor accusations in revolutionary courtrooms. Summary chapters follow on the growing appeal of the Old Order over time, and on the historically manipulative effects of the progressive marital ending. The ninth chapter suggests "New Directions" for Scott's legacy. Recent novels by Vidal, Marquez, and Mantel confront the same revolutionary issues through perspectives only partly postcolonial, and through literary techniques only partly postmodernist.

My conclusion returns to Lukacs's view of the pivotal 1848 revolution in France. To a greater or lesser degree, critics who decry the decline or extinction of the historical novel have been encouraged to take a wrong turn by accepting Lukacs's argument about bourgeois exploitation of a failed working class revolution. The crux of the issue is the recurring assumption that Flaubert's continuation of the historical novel tradition is to be found in *Salammbo* rather than in *Sentimental Education*. Lukacs had become convinced that, while writing *Salammbo*, third century BCE Carthage served Flaubert as a vehicle for an entertaining costume drama, set in a fully bygone era, but projecting present cultural and psychological issues back into the past. Like *Ivanhoe*, *Salammbo* seems to justify and to prompt the escapist directions many a late nineteenth-century writer of "historical novels" was to follow. I contend that *Sentimental Education* can and should be read as an informed historical novel confronting the Revolution of 1848 in Paris, just as Scott's novels of Stuart and Hanoverian Scotland must be read as historically informed novels of Jacobite and Covenanter counterrevolution.

Lukacs's insistence on *Salammbo* as a pivotal text of decline in the historical novel is itself paradoxical. Although Flaubert was no working class-sympathizer, and certainly no Marxist, his thoroughly ironic sense of the immediate outcome of the 1848 revolution, is in toto remarkably like the disillusionment of Marx's *The Eighteenth Brumaire of Louis Napoleon*. Had Lukacs considered *Sentimental Education* closely, rather than denouncing the world of *Salammbo*, he would have evaluated historical novels by Zola, Hugo, and Anatole France quite differently. Marx's insistence upon an heroic proletarian future eventually emerging from the wreckage of 1848, so unlike Flaubert's satire and/or melancholy, would surely give rise, Lukacs hoped, to a different kind of revolutionary historical novel—a kind that would never quite emerge. The revolutionary working-class perspective of masterful novels like Zola's *Germinal*, Gorky's *Mother*, or Steinbeck's *In Dubious Battle* are all based upon historical circumstances, and express strong revolutionary feelings, but they are presentist novels fundamentally different in setting, characterization, and class conflict from the "wavering" legacy established by Walter Scott. For those who believe that Balzac long ago displaced Scott, and for those who sense that the proletarian novel has reached a dead-end, there seems to be no continuous legacy for the Waverley Novels after the mid-nineteenth century. This book exists to challenge that assumption.

In the broadest sense, the continuation of Scott's legacy is sustained by the oldest and most familiar charge leveled against the historical novel itself, the charge of hybridity.[8] Whenever it was that the words "historical" and "novel" were first made into a compound term, the seeming contradiction of the combination has posed a lasting conundrum. Manzoni's "On the Historical Novel" (1850), begun in 1828 immediately after *I Promessi Sposi* was published, remains the first extensive consideration of the genre. Sharing with Ranke the belief that the aim of historical writing is to discover true, recoverable fact (*wie es eigentlich gewesen*), Manzoni attacks the historical novel as a genre that, despite Walter Scott's great accomplishment, futilely tries to mix historical fact with fictional invention. "In picking up a 'historical novel,'" Manzoni argues, "the reader knows well enough that he will find there *facta atque infecta,*—things that occurred and things that have been invented."[9] To mix history with fiction is therefore as "worthless" as the attempt to mix oil with water (78). "Joining together bits of copper and bits of tin does not make a bronze statue "(67).

Manzoni is well aware that the historical novel's claim upon "verisimilitude"—a convincing likeness of past actuality—had already been advanced in defense of the genre by Scott, Cooper, De Vigny, and John Wilson Croker, among others. But Manzoni will have none of such an argument: "The principal subject of the historical novel is completely the author's, completely poetic, because merely verisimilar" (125). When readers discover that history and invention simply do not mix, the historical novel as a genre must, Manzoni wrongly predicts, soon die out. The cliché that "the novels of Walter Scott were truer than history" will soon be exposed in all its falsity (126).[10]

In this regard it is important to remember that great early practitioners of the historical novel rarely, if ever, used the term "historical novel." Scott refuses to clearly differentiate the "romance" and "novel" elements of his fictions; he also, at other times, prefers to subtitle a novel as a "legend" or more simply as "a tale." Cooper's titles and prefaces show the same multiplicity. If *War and Peace* remains the greatest of all fictions dealing with revolutionary crises, to what genre does it exactly belong? While writing the book, Tolstoy referred to it, repeatedly, as "this work." It is "not a tale," "not a novel," "still less an historical chronicle." *War and Peace,* Tolstoy insists, does not quite fit into "the form of novel epic or story." What is its most accurate designation then? "*War and Peace* is what the author wished and was able to express in the form in which it is expressed."[11] True indeed, but not helpful for purposes of definition.

My point in connecting the evasive terminology of early practitioners to Manzoni's attack upon "the historical novel" as a named genre is not to demonstrate authors' confusion, but to defend their flexibility, their openness to the possibility of generic combinations that could promote the verisimilitude possible in combining fiction with history. Consider the genres and techniques that contribute to the composite of a Waverley novel: the eighteenth-century English novel, exemplified by Fielding; the national tale exemplified by Maria Edgeworth, the travels of a gentleman and his servant, sometimes resembling Cervantes, sometimes medieval romance; the gothic romance, without attestation of the supernatural; the epic's concern with warfare (civil, revolutionary, or international) and its meaning for national destiny; comedic inheritance of a family plot ending in marriage; picturesque descriptions of the Sublime and the Beautiful drawing upon the rapidly emerging tradition of landscape painting; plentiful use of dialogue and dialect attesting to the influence of Shakespeare; reliques of bardic Scottish poetry, sometimes written by Scott himself: a Fieldingesque third-person narrator who sometimes justifies historical license, but sometimes adds historical footnotes. The list is hardly exhaustive.

"The historical novel" most certainly *is* a hybrid ("loose, baggy monsters" was Henry James's famous phrase) but it is also a capacious form, capable of rendering a world entire, through literary forms of varied kinds and purposes. Whether an invention tarnishes or violates historical fact is not a determinative standard. If Bonnie Prince Charlie can interact with Edward Waverley in ways that enlist the reader's credibility, a compelling verisimilitude has been achieved. Lukacs and Jameson rightly required a convincing totality of the historical novel. Whether an historical novel needs be wholly "realistic" is another matter. The kind of historical Realism that Lukacs and Jameson sought in the historical novel was integral to Scott's model, but many other elements were also there to diversify and to sustain the tradition.

The capaciousness by which Scott's conventions could be transformed during later eras is implicit in theories of fiction advanced by recent influential critics who were not considering Scott as an exemplar. Bakhtin's emphasis on *heteroglossia* and *polyglossia* in the nineteenth-century novel justifies the ever-shifting copresence of conflicting styles, perspectives, and genres within one work. Many voices, many styles, many conventions, all existing in close proximity, resonate for the reader who finds himself or herself in an increasingly complex and relativistic world.[12] Similarly, Hayden White subverts the presumably clear distinction between historical fact and novelistic invention that Manzoni had taken for granted. Examining the same nineteenth-century historical narratives that the historical novelists had read (Ranke, Michelet, Tocqueville, Carlyle, Marx), White contends that the paradigmatic structure behind those narratives is essentially a variant of the literary forms studied by Northrop Frye in *The Anatomy of Criticism*. The major nineteenth-century historians, White contends, followed modes of emplotment deriving from romance, tragedy, comedy, and satire. These four "Modes of Emplotment" proceed through particular "Modes of Argument" to "Modes of Ideologies," be they anarchist, radical, conservative, or liberal.[13] If White's model of historiography is accepted, recovery of verifiable historical fact must always be shaped, if not subverted, by the historian's need to follow narrative paradigms deriving ultimately from literature. Carried to its logical ultimate, the possibility of any valid distinction between "history" and "the novel" would collapse. The Waverley Novels are, I contend, thoroughly amenable to the inclusive, flexible perspectives advanced by both Bakhtin and White. When Dickens, Hugo, France, Pasternak, and Lampedusa modified the conventions of historical fiction, their novels remained within the wide parameters set by the twin legacy of *War and Peace* and the Waverley Novels.

This study thus hopes to strike a balance, a synthesis if you will, between critical approaches long thought to be oppositional. It accepts the Marxian premise that people's responses to private and public issues are conditioned, if not determined, by underlying economic "modes of production" that determine social class and shape political and religious institutions. This Marxist premise is repeatedly affirmed by the Waverley Novels, however Toryish Scott's surface statements may seem, and however late-medieval the class structure of the Scottish novels may be.[14] Scott's characters are introduced into the narrative through sentences, often an entire paragraph, carefully situating them in terms of social class, economic condition, and religious heritage. Some characters prove to be so conditioned by cohesive societal forces that they need not worry over their decision when a question of revolutionary allegiance suddenly presents itself. Others—often those at the center of the narrative—will long waver and finally withdraw. But all are to be known by the societal conditions that have made them who they are. Those conditions do not forever define or circumscribe the individual, but the individual cannot be understood without them. Such is the great merit that constitutes the essence of Scott's legacy. We see every individual character's qualities and beliefs in the context of a whole society in crisis. As we admire, scorn, or pity them, we see beyond and beneath their words and actions to causal conditions of which they may not be fully aware. The emotional authority of the individual romantic eye, what Keats called the egotistical sublime, is thereby submerged within a wide, multifaceted context.

It is no wonder, then, that critics such as Lukacs and Jameson have been drawn to, and troubled by, the Waverley Novels and their relation to a changing "Realist" tradition, sometimes Marxist. Lukacs and Jameson have provided us the controlling insights into the significance of this relationship. But their approach brings with it two questionable assumptions. Marxist criticism anticipates a time of "totalization" when the forces allied against late monopoly capitalism, whether working-class proletarian or their late twentieth-century descendants, might lead the nightmare of history toward a new and better order. Great historical novels that do not share in this despairing hope, which would certainly include novels by Hugo, Zola, Anatole France, Lampedusa, Pasternak, and Vidal, are placed to the side because their counterrevolutionary fears seem stronger than their revolutionary hopes. To do so does not make these novels any less worthy as continuations of Scott's tradition. Scott had counterrevolutionary, even nostalgic yearnings at the same time that he held to progressive beliefs, at least for the United Kingdom. To assess the lasting quality of historical fiction, verisimilitude is a standard above and beyond the merits of any political creed.

I aim at sustained, recurring consideration of the novels chosen. Selective quotation in support of an apriori thesis or a developing argument has always been an unavoidable problem for literary critics, but especially so for critics committed to some form of literary theory, be it archetypal, deconstructionist, Marxist, New Historical, Postcolonial, or what have you. Quotations illustrating one's thesis, often in the form of summations filled with abstractions, are selected from a text and assumed to stand for the whole, while the rest is tacitly laid aside. This process is extremely effective for building a memorable controlling argument (vide Lukacs and Jameson), but it does so at the price of complexities and inconsistencies within the text itself. Among New Historicists, prolonged contextualizing can readily lose sight of the reading experience. The texture of the fictional narrative, to say nothing of its metaphoric language, is often lost.

The advantage of close reading is that it can retain a fuller experience of the entire text, at the twin risks of avoiding everything outside the words of the text and therefore seeming obvious. Despite suspect insistence on the crafted unity of a literary work, the New Criticism brought reader attention to the functions of a single word within a sentence or a line, of a single sentence within a paragraph or a stanza, and of a single incident within a developing plot. There is considerable value in remembering the function of the part within the whole. By examining ways in which the conventions of Scott's historical fictions have been transformed, I do not presume to have entirely avoided the problems of selective quotation and of obviousness. I do hope to minimize them. Through recurrent consideration and continuing quotation of a particular novel, I hope to convey its texture. My purpose in pursuing these methods is to demonstrate the evolving legacy of Scott's historical fiction through close study of the continuity of his fictional conventions.

To write of "texture" is to raise the problem of citing translations. I can manage French and German, but not Spanish, Italian, or Russian. Although it would obviously be best to quote novels and criticism only from the original languages, I cannot make such claims to mastery. It is also true, however, that certain translations—the Maude translation of *War and Peace*, the Baldick translation of *Sentimental Education*, and the Hayward and Harari translation of *Doctor Zhivago*, have been read and cited for so many decades that they have in effect, for many readers, become the texts themselves. There is no fully satisfactory solution to this problem for a person, like me, who does not control six languages. My unsatisfactory but necessary compromise is to use

English translations, trying not to place too much weight on the accuracy of any particular translated word or phrase.

Any selection of novels for comparative literary study is to some degree arbitrary. Why then will certain kinds of historical fiction concerning revolution not be included within the legacy I shall be considering? Four subgenres are relevant here: (1) novels, not based upon any actual historical event, in which a revolution is invented or imagined (Wharton's *The Valley of Decision*, Conrad's *Nostromo*); (2) novels that deal with revolutionary agitation but not revolution itself (Dickens's *Barnaby Rudge*, Dostoyevsky's *The Possessed*, Turgenev's *Fathers and Sons*, James's *The Princess Casamassima*, Conrad's *The Secret Agent*; (3) novels in which an important historical revolution serves primarily as a setting rather than a subject (Cooper's *The Pilot*, Thackeray's *The Virginians*, Malraux's *Man's Fate*); and (4) novels that are not written about the author's own country or culture (the novels by Wharton, Conrad, James, Cooper, Thackeray, and Malraux mentioned above).

Given the quality and canonical stature of most of these novels, their omission may be explained, but surely cannot be fully and convincingly justified. Nonetheless, I contend that novels of these overlapping kinds share qualities that set them apart from the Lukacsian "Realist" tradition I shall be studying and proposing to extend. Novels that concern an invented revolution, lacking a world-historical figure, offer little opportunity for the kind of legendary historical traditions whose familiarity have made them a part of the received historical record. Their authors are therefore drawn toward concerns apart from region, nation, and politics: timeless psychological conflicts or universal, cross-cultural change. Within the fictive country of Costaguana, the reader of *Nostromo* has been given a grand overview of the overwhelming force of Capitalism's growing "material interests" (the San Tome Silver Mine) over all kinds of political ideology, dictatorial or democratic.[15] And yet no single scene in *Nostromo* is more powerful than the suicide of the self-conscious progressive intellectual Martin Decoud, his pockets weighted with silver ingots, spiritually dead-ended and utterly alone amid the silent, boundless sea.

The same pattern occurs in *Man's Fate*. The details of the 1927 purge of the Comintern by the Kuomintang becomes less important, to both Malraux and his reader, than Ch'en's and Kyo's proto-Existentialist need to find significance and identity in a meaningless world by making a conscious choice to commit suicide. Similarly, Edith Wharton's Odo Vansecca, kingly Duke of the imagined Duchy of Pianura, rides away from his reactionary people's counterrevolution in a spiritual state so disconnected that only childhood memories of St. Francis retain even the possibility of meaning. Would-be revolutionaries who are embedded in a narrative without a concerted revolutionary uprising become separable studies of psychological types (Turgenev's Bazarov and James's Hyacinth Robinson).[16] Such interiority is characteristic of early twentieth-century modernism, to be sure, but it is also particularly characteristic of ambitious historical fictions that lack factual historical particularity. Novelists who write revolutionary historical novels about cultures other than their own risk disengagement and fragmentation; they sacrifice an impelling drive to express revolution's significance for a homeland. As the achievements of the historical fictions of expatriate writers like Conrad and James attest, though their emphases and goals are demonstrably different from Scott's model, they are certainly not inferior to it.

A last outsetting reminder about the origin of the term "historical novel." Richard Maxwell has demonstrated that the term "nouvelle historique" dates from as early as 1672, was long associated with Madame de Lafayette's *La Princesse de Cleves* (1678), and would lead to an eight volume *Collection of Historical Novels 1746–1747* by Nicolas Langlet du Fresnoy that was organized on the editorial principle: "to amuse the public I have chosen nothing but historical novels."[17] Recent scholarship by Ann Rigney, Susan Strehle, Katie Trumpener, Diana Wallace, and Nicola Watson has shown that women have written historical fictions, national tales, and dynastic historical romances that have taken many different forms. The focus and concern of this book is limited to those historical novels, widely read and admired, that have dealt with revolutionary crises that lead to civil or international war. Because of sharply divergent gender roles that prevailed during the nineteenth century, warfare and revolution were long assumed to be overwhelmingly male subjects. I include novels by women (Sarah Orne Jewett, Willa Cather, Margaret Mitchell, and Hilary Mantel) that are adaptable to, or clearly written within, the Scott tradition. By exploring Scott's particular legacy in the historical novel, I do not imply that there is no other.

***

I am indebted to the National Endowment for the Humanities for a fellowship that enabled me to write a first draft of this book during a year's leave from Middlebury College. The staffs at the Widener Library, at the New York Public Library, at the Boston Public Library, and at the Davis Library of Middlebury College have been patiently professional in the face of my requests, some of them passing strange. Colleagues and peers who have reviewed my project, read sections of the manuscript, or provided the kind of insights one needs to remember, include John Berninghausen, Lawrence Buell, Sergei Davydov, Stephen Donadio, Murray Dry, Wayne Franklin, Michael Katz, Ed Knox, Paul Monod, Charles Nunley, Nancy O'Connor, Jay Parini, Alison Stanger, and three who are no longer with us: George Dekker, Joel Porte, and Carol Rifelj. During four widely spaced years, courtesy of Stephen Donadio,

I have greatly benefited from teaching a Literary Studies course on the historical novel; in particular I have gained from the lively, forceful classroom comments of Kristina Brown, Casey Donoghue, Peter DeGoria, David Foote, Amy Francisco, Matthew Hale, and Ted Parker.

The editorial and production staff at Rowman and Littlefield have been admirably professional in their book-making, while remaining patient with my inquiries and digital failings. I am grateful to Jayanthi Chander, Nalini Jayaraman, Nick Johns and especially to Lindsey Porambo.

I wish to acknowledge the influence of the following books upon my thinking: Hannah Arendt, *On Revolution*; Crane Brinton, *The Anatomy of Revolution*; Victor Brombert, *The Intellectual Hero*; Nicola Chiaromonte, *The Paradox of History*; George Dekker, *The American Historical Romance*; Avrom Fleishman, *The English Historical Novel*; Francois Furet, *Interpreting the French Revolution*; E.J. Hobsbawm, *The Age of Revolution* and *Nations and Nationalism Since 1780*; Irving Howe, *Politics and the Novel*; Fredric Jameson, *The Forms of Marxism, The Political Unconscious, The Antinomies of Realism*; Paul Johnson: *The Birth of the Modern: World Society 1815–1830*; Georg Lukacs, *The Theory of the Novel* and *The Historical Novel*, Richard Maxwell, *The Historical Novel in Europe, 1650–1950*; Franco Moretti, *The Way of the World; The Bildungsroman in European Culture*; R.R. Palmer, *A History of The Modern World*; Simon Schama, *Citizens: A Chronicle of the French Revolution*; Harry Shaw, *The Forms of Historical Fiction*; Katie Trumpener: *Bardic Nationalism*. I have tried, often unsuccessfully, to restrict footnotes to citations of reference and citations of particular fact. Such compression must result in instances of neglecting scholarly indebtedness. These failings, like all others in this book, are unintentional but wholly mine.

The United States of America, anno 2018, is replete with societal conditions I have learned to associate with the onset of revolution: an immense national debt, ossified political institutions, entrenched office-holders, great and growing divergence of income among social classes, resentment of the transparent purchase of privilege, volatile public opinion, and legitimate fear of an extra-national "foreign" threat. All these conditions were present in France in 1789 and Russia in 1917, perhaps less so in England in 1640, in America in 1775 and in China during the period from 1911 to 1949. Nonetheless, my purpose is not to use literature as a template for possible revolution, however tempting it may be. I began this study before I had developed any sense of the totality of the conditions of revolution. I seek to compare great works of literature, not to indulge in thinly disguised prophecy.

The reading and research undertaken to write this book have been a continuing pleasure, an ongoing opportunity to learn. So should it be, given the quality and complexity of these novels, as well as the issues they raise.

John McWilliams
Middlebury, Vermont

NOTES

1. See Fredric Jameson, *Marxism and Form* (1971) and *The Political Unconscious* (1981). Perry Westbrook's informative recent overview of the historical novel titled "From Progress to Catastrophe" brings the history of the genre from Scott to a provocatively apocalyptic stopping point in the postmodern era: "Not the emergence of the nation, but the ravages of empire; not progress as emancipation, but impending or consummated catastrophe" ("From Progress to Catastrophe: the Historical Novel," *LRB*, 33 [2011], 24–28). On Hegel's "World-historical individuals," see his Introduction to *Lectures on the Philosophy of History*, translated by John Sibree and Ruben Alvarado (Aalten, The Netherlands: Wordbridge Publishing, 2011), pp. 26–27.

2. Georg Lukacs, *The Theory of the Novel*, translated by Anna Bostock (Cambridge, MA: M.I.T. Press, 1971), p.p. 56, 88, 92, 152.

3. Fredric Jameson, *Marxism and Form: Twentieth Century Dialectical Theories of Literature* (Princeton, NJ: Princeton University Press, 1971), p. 204.

4. Fredric Jameson, *The Political Unconscious: Narrative as a Socially Symbolic Act* (Ithaca, NY: Cornell University Press, 1981), p. 13.

5. Jameson, *The Antinomies of Realism* (London and New York: Verso, 2013), p. 288.

6. Richard Maxwell, *The Historical Novel in Europe, 1650–1950* (Cambridge and New York: Cambridge University Press, 2009). pp. 233–273.

7. Examples are two once popular historical romances about the French Revolution that are not included in this study: Baroness Orczy's *The Scarlet Pimpernel* (1905) and Rafael Sabatini's *Scaramouche* (1921). In such novels, revolution functions merely as a setting for adventure.

8. Sandra Bermann quotes P. Zagotti writing as early as 1820 in an article titled "Idee generali sul romanzo storico" that the genre is an "immoral, irrational, hybrid form, combining novel and history, false and true" (Bermann's Introduction to Alessandro Manzoni, *On The Historical Novel* [Lincoln and London: University of Nebraska Press, 1984]. p. 30, fn. 62). In a helpful survey, Jerome de Groot observes that Manzoni's "criticisms of the historical novel, in particular its innate falsehood, are still commonly deployed today, and might be said to be inextricably bound up in the form (Jerome de Groot, *The Historical Novel* [Routledge: London and New York, 2010], 31).

9. Manzoni, *On the Historical Novel*, p. 70.

10. It is probable that Manzoni, as he began his essay, read with indignation de Vigny's Preface to *Cinq-Mars* titled "Reflexions Sur La Verité Dans L'Art. " Vigny had written that "History is a novel of which the People are the author," that "the truth we ought to nourish is the truth of observation of human nature, and not the authenticity of fact," and that we must "Ask for a truth more beautiful than any true fact" (De Vigny, "Preface" to *Cinq-Mars* [Paris: Louis Conard, 1914], pp. ix, xii, translations mine). In the 1812 *Quarterly Review*, John Wilson Croker had written "That '*le vrai n'est pas toujours vraisemblable*' we do not deny, but we are prepared to insist that while the '*vrai*' is the highest recommendation of the historian of real life, the vraisemblable is the only legitimate province of the novelist who aims at approving

the understanding or teaching the heart" (quoted in Alexander Welsh, *The Hero of the Waverley Novels* (New Haven: Yale University Press, 1963), p. ix.

11. Leo Tolstoy, *War and Peace*, translated by Aylmer and Louise Maude, edited by George Gibian, 2nd edition (New York: W.W. Norton, 1996), pp. 1088–1092.

12. Bakhtin would insist that these elements are "heterogeneous stylistic unities" that "combine to form a structured artistic system." They are "those fundamental compositional unities with whose help heteroglossia can enter the novel." (M.L. Bakhtin, "Discourse in the Novel" in *The Dialogic Imagination*, translated by Caryl Emerson and Michael Holquist [Austin: University of Texas Press, 1981], pp. 262, 263. Whether Scott's generic combinations coalesce into as absolute a unity as Bakhtin assumes is unlikely but finally of secondary importance. *Heteroglossia* demands that the reader be alive to contrasting conventions and levels of language that are experienced almost simultaneously.

13. Hayden White, *Metahistory: the Historical Imagination in Nineteenth Century Europe* (Baltimore and London: Johns Hopkins University Press, 1973), pp. 29–31.

14. According to S.S. Prawer, Marx greatly admired Scott's *Old Mortality* (Prawer, *Karl Marx and World Reading* [New York: Oxford University Press, 1978], 396).

15. In at least five passages in *Nostromo*, Conrad returns to the phrase "material interests" (See *Nostromo: A Tale of the Seaboard*, edited by Jacques Berthoud and Mara Kalnins (Oxford and New York: Oxford University Press, 2009], pp. 139, 147, 271, 366, 374. In their "Introduction" Berthoud and Kalnins observe that *Nostromo* is "not a historical novel but a contemporary one, dealing with the displacement of post-colonial South American machismo culture by the North American version of it as virility of conquest"(xxi).

16. Irving Howe ascribed the missing sense of political totality in *The Princess Casamassima* to Henry James's individualistic temperament: "James showed himself to be brilliantly gifted at entering the behavior of political people, but he had no larger view of politics as a collective mode of action" (Irving Howe, *Politics and the Novel*, introduction by David Bromwich [Chicago: Ivan R. Dee, 2002, originally published 1957], 150). Howe does not take account of the effect upon James's novel of the lack of a revolutionary narrative drawn from known history.

17. Richard Maxwell, *The Historical Novel in Europe*, pp. 24, 27, 39, 40.

Introduction

Revolutions and Restorations

King Louis XVI: "Is it a revolt?"
Duc de la Rochefoucauld-Liancourt: "No, Sire, it is a revolution."

—Possibly anecdotal account of Louis XVI being informed of the fall
of the Bastille, July 14, 1789

"If the basis of popular government in time of peace is virtue, its basis
in time of revolution is virtue and terror—virtue, without which terror
is disastrous, and terror, without which virtue is powerless. Terror is
merely prompt, severe and inflexible justice. Terror is therefore an
emanation of virtue."

—Robespierre, Speech to the National Convention, February 5, 1794

To begin with an etymology: familiarity with three definitions of "revolution," and flexibility in their application, are essential to any understanding
of western cultural history since the Reformation. Throughout the sixteenth
and seventeenth centuries, and well into the eighteenth century, the word
"revolution" had not yet fully acquired its present primary meaning, which
is, according to the *OED*, "a complete overthrow of the established government in any country or state by those who were previously subject to it."[1]
Before the late eighteenth century, the word "Revolution" still retained
the restorative meaning of its Latin origin (*revolvo*, to turn back), a meaning that had been given mathematical confirmation by Copernicus (*De
Revolutionibus Orbium Coelestium*), who had mapped the ever-returning
movements of heavenly bodies and claimed them to be astronomical law,
changeless throughout time. Accordingly (as Walter Scott knew), many Puritans during the Cromwellian Interregnum believed that their revolutionary
Commonwealth would restore the purity of first-century Christian churches.

The long accepted Whig interpretation of England's 1688 "Glorious Revolution" maintained that Parliament's conferring of the throne upon William and Mary began a permanent *restoration* of England's legitimate protestant dynasty, the Tudors, against both the Puritan Commonwealth and the quasi-Catholic (and Scottish) Stuarts.[2] Prerevolutionary Boston's agitation against British rule was to be led by Samuel Adams, who insisted in newsprint and broadside that the Freemen of the Commonwealth of Massachusetts had to stand up now against the British in order to *restore* their legal rights as free-born British citizens. Clearly, political leaders could claim restorative purpose, while in fact enacting revolution.[3]

As late as 1770, to assert that the Interregnum, the Glorious Revolution, and New England's uprising were instances of "Revolution" required that a metaphor from scientific law lend authority to restorative political change. The Latin root and Copernican application of "revolution" still implied that political upheaval should return government to universal laws that were in origin both natural and divine, therefore valid and beneficial. The political and economic oppressions of the present, whether attributable to man's fallen nature or God's punishing will, were to be seen as encrustations and overlays that could be broken through, not by forging some new formulation of the "Rights of Man," but by returning to the practices of a time of greater integrity, purity, and honor. Here was an older definition of "Revolution" that Walter Scott, legally trained and historically informed as he was, fully understood and occasionally affirmed; he also knew, however, that this reversionary definition was rapidly becoming anachronistic.

The aftermath of the 1640 and 1688 revolutions, with which Scott was so concerned, had left hopes for a "restoration" of peace and order that were hard to substantiate. The Puritan Commonwealth had ended in the killing of the king, the sacking of churches, and the virtual dictatorship of Lord Protector Cromwell, before it gave way in 1660 to an entirely different kind of "Restoration." The Glorious Revolution had led to the bloody Jacobite "Rebellions" of 1715 and 1745, to continued fractious relations among England, Scotland, and Ireland (despite the Act of Union) and to the sense of venal patronage and over-worldly compromise associated with the word "Hanoverian." Even the American Revolution, which sought to avoid the internecine bloodshed associated with the British past, had its subsequent downside. Ten years after independence had been won on the battlefield, the hope for republican harmony dissolved into the bitter exchanges between opponents and supporters of the French Revolution, then into the formation of the Federalist and Republican parties, and ultimately into the vitriol of the 1800 election.

But it was the course of events in France that was primarily to change the very meaning of the word. After 1789, "Revolution" as "Restoration" no longer described felt reality. Enlightenment thinkers (Montesquieu, Rousseau,

Ferguson, Condorcet, Jefferson) had anticipated prospects for social progress, not cyclical return, in the passage of time. The *OED* cites uses after 1688 of the word "Revolution" meaning "complete overthrow" in writings by Evelyn (1688), Swift (1708), Bolingbroke (1726), Gibbon (1776), and Burke (1790). Political and cultural hopes were increasingly based upon stadialist theories of progressive societal stages, on abolition of institutions associated with "feudal" changelessness, on the prosperities of free trade, and on Deistic if not secular thinking, all of them associated with an emerging republican polity that would empower the reason of the Third Estate and thereby release human potential. If Revolution now meant creating the world anew ("The World Turned Upside Down" as the marching song declared), then initiating violence becomes justifiable. Throughout the nineteenth century, images of the French Revolution, whether in histories or historical novels, were to center upon panoramic scenes of justifiable protest turning into violent mobs: the Fall of the Bastille, not the resolution of the *Jeu de Paume*; the execution of Louis XVI, not the surrender of feudal privileges; the September Massacres, not the women's march on Versailles; the guillotine not *liberté, egalité* and *fraternité*. Justifying revolution had quickly become a double-edged sword.

Historical novels of revolution, following Scott, were to maintain a strongly national perspective, but the words of revolutionary overturn began in universalist, international thinking, first in America, then in France. The Virginia "Declaration of Rights" (June, 1776), The American "Declaration of Independence" (July, 1776), and the French "Declaration of the Rights of Man" (1789) all begin by justifying anticipated political change ("Revolution" in the old sense?) by declaring that the purpose of legitimate government is the protection of the timeless individual rights of "all men" to "life," "liberty," and either "property" (Virginia and France) or the "pursuit of happiness" (America). These rights are claimed to be incontrovertible and inherent in natural law, in the nature of experience, or in both; they are "certain inherent rights" (Virginia), "certain inalienable rights" (America), or "natural, inalienable and sacred rights" (France). Jefferson worked with George Mason's draft of the Virginia Declaration while writing the preamble to the Declaration of Independence. On July 11, 1789 in Paris, the Marquis de Lafayette, then a leader among the constitutional monarchists, submitted to Ambassador Jefferson the draft of the French "Declaration of The Rights of Man" for his suggestions.

Phrases from the Virginia Declaration can be found in the French Declaration and phrases from both the Virginia and French Declarations in the American Constitution and in the Bill of Rights. The exact lines of influence can never be determined, but the Virginia Declaration, based on Locke and the English "Bill of Rights" (1689), is clearly a source for the American Declaration of Independence, just as the American Declaration is for the French and both of them for the American Constitution and Bill of Rights. Whether or not the word "Man" was intended to exclude or to include women, all these documents are the result of collaborative thinking within the most universal terms its writers could conceive. The Copernican notion of unchanging natural and divine law is now being applied to claims upon individual liberty and collective equality that are presumed, especially in France, to inaugurate a new order in time. Sovereignty is to be disassociated from a sovereign monarch, in order to be newly associated with a sovereign people.

Differences between the American and French Declarations were to remain crucial. The sixth provision of the French Declaration begins with the sentence "Law is the expression of the general will." Robespierre would repeatedly cite Rousseau's concept of "the General Will"—and sometimes acknowledge Rousseau directly—in order to justify particular measures designed to defend the French Republic against enemies without and to purify it from enemies within.[4] However, neither the "Declaration of The Rights of Man," nor the history of the five years after 1789 suggests that the French revolutionaries, or the Constitution makers, ever thought through the ruinous inconsistency between a Republic designed to protect individual rights and a Republic determined to enact the "General Will" through statute law.

In the absence of a continuing plebiscite and of duly constituted institutions, who is it exactly that speaks for "the General Will"? Is it the National Assembly, the Legislative Assembly, the Constituent Assembly, the Paris Commune, the Jacobin Club, the Committee of Public Safety, or Maximilian Robespierre? Identifying Law as the expression of "The General Will" created an opening for demagoguery that was to lead inexorably to oppression of both individual and minority rights. By mid-1793, the remaining leaders of the Mountain, having expelled the Girondists, were prepared to pursue the General Will of the citizenry from its libertarian beginnings to its murderous end.[5] James Madison's thinking about the American Constitution, by contrast, centered around a separation and balancing rather than a concentration of power; his contributions to the *Federalist Papers*, written shortly before the French Revolution broke out, show his continual regard for the future preservation of minority and individual rights in a republic with a growing sphere of influence and a widening suffrage.

Historical novels were repeatedly to center upon trials involving a citizen's rights against detention during revolutionary times. The source of such narratives lies in revolutionary legislation itself. The seventh "Declaration of the Rights of Man" opens with a sentence that seems to belong with Articles 4–6 of the American Bill of Rights: "No man may be accused, arrested, or detained except in cases determined by law, and according to the forms prescribed thereby. Whoever seeks, expedites, executes, or has executed, arbitrary orders, must be punished." Considered in the context of the thousands of individuals in 1793 and 1794 who were jailed without warrant or charge, tried with minimal opportunity for defense, and summarily sentenced and executed, this provision created unforgettable irony. Until the twentieth century, Europeans would recall no legalized slaughter quite like it. How the last sentence of declaration seven ("Every citizen summoned or arrested in accordance with the law [i.e. 'the General Will'] must obey at once; he renders himself guilty by resistance") could be reconciled with declaration number nine ("Every man is presumed innocent until he has been declared guilty") baffles the mind.[6] The French "Declaration of the Rights of Man," like the never implemented French Constitution of 1793, is constructed as a succession of numbered points, not as an organic whole divided into consecutive articles with subdivisions, like the American Constitution. The American Constitution is a blueprint for workable republican government designed to minimize the dangers of usurpation of power by any group or interest; the French Constitution of 1793 reads like a Declaration of bullet points of republican virtue that could henceforth be realized through concentration of power.

As the Terror came to define the climax of French Revolution, so did the paradox of "Virtue" show how revolutionary political dreams became a nightmare. Robespierre's speech to the National Convention in December of 1793 justifying the rise of the Terror unshrinkingly separated the act of revolution from the likelihood of constitution making. Speaking on behalf of the Committee of Public Safety, Robespierre defends what he calls "revolutionary government," arguing that "revolutionary government" is fully justified, while trusting that "constitutional government" will follow from it. A lengthy quotation deserves parsing:

> The theory of revolutionary government is as new as the Revolution, which created it. There is no point looking for it in the books of political writers, who failed to foresee this Revolution, nor among the laws of tyrants, who, content to abuse their power, are little concerned to discover its legitimate foundations. Thus, for the aristocracy, this phrase is a mere subject of terror, or a term of abuse; for tyrants it is a scandal; and for many people, an enigma. We must explain it to all, so that we may rally good citizens, at least, behind those principles which govern the public interest.
>
> The purpose of government is to direct the moral and physical energies of the nation towards the goal for which it was established. The goal of constitutional government is to maintain the Republic; that of revolutionary government is to establish it. Revolution is war waged by liberty against its enemies; a constitution is the peaceful rule of victorious liberty. Revolutionary government must employ extraordinary activity precisely because it is at war.[7]

To understand how revolution begins time anew demands the complete disavowal of wisdom from the past. There can be no "restoration" whatever in

Robespierre's definition of revolution. "The theory of revolutionary government is as new as the Revolution," he claims. Henceforth a revolution, properly understood, is a "war waged by liberty against its enemies." France's
"enemies" are not named, nor are the methods of "extraordinary activity"
necessary to secure "revolutionary government." Whatever means will be
needed are justified by the crisis of a Republic struggling simultaneously to
maintain Virtue and Liberty even though its institutions and constitution have
yet to appear.[8]

As society begins anew, a progressive *Novus Ordo Saeclorum* (itself a
restoration through language) could thus be assumed to convey the will of
history. To Hegel in the mid-1820s, the sure prospect for post-revolutionary
Europe could be summarized in an apothegm: "World history is progress in
the consciousness of freedom." Absolute Spirit shows us that "God's will is
the idea of freedom."[9] Herbert Marcuse's summation of the Hegelian moment
was to be even more explicit: "Reason presupposes freedom" and "freedom
in turn presupposes reason."[10]

Although abstractions such as "Reason," "Freedom" and "Progress"
summon up the post-revolutionary zeitgeist, their historical power still
depended on specifically whom and what was thought to have defined the
French Revolution itself. Following Hayden White, Linda Orr and Ann
Rigney have shown that eight well-known histories of the French Revolution written in the 1840s and 1850s returned again and again to the same
cast of characters, the same sequence of plotted events, but with competing
interpretations.[11] After fifty years, no resolution as to which revolutionary
leader most convincingly personified the Revolution had emerged. It made
an immense difference whether Mirabeau or Condorcet, Danton or Robespierre, Desmoulin or Saint-Juste, served as the primary representatives
of reason, freedom, and progress. To choose the most contested example,
Danton was thought to embody both a saving humanity and sheer animal
desire, whereas his executioner Robespierre was thought to embody incorruptible purity and fanatic asceticism. Which of them best symbolized the
revolutionary spirit?

Similarly, was the fall of the Bastille, the Declaration of the Rights of Man,
the execution of the King, the creation of a secular Republic, the Terror or
the emergence of Napoleon the defining event of the revolution? To select
one person, one event was sure evidence of partiality; to select them all was
hopelessly self-contradictory; it made history a shapeless muddle. The problem of choice amid multiplicity has only grown in recent historical fiction.
By weighting Danton, Robespierre, and Desmoulin equally, without authorial
judgment, Hilary Mantel's *A Place of Greater Safety* (1992), to which we
shall return, compels her reader to confront this historiographical question
within a fictive world that is domestic as well as public.

The third definition of "revolution" is, of course, Marxist-Leninist, a compound term that should probably be spelled with a cautionary slash rather than the usual assimilative hyphen. Francois Furet has argued persuasively that twentieth-century Marxist historians' insistence on seeing the Bolshevik revolution as the fulfillment of the French Revolution (oppressed peasants aligned with hungry workers, Louis XVI with Nicolas II, Jacobin Clubs with Soviets, *Fraternité* with Comradeship etc.) is an historical illusion. In the historiography of twentieth-century Marxists, Furet argues, persistent celebration of the French Revolution has, by 1980, closed the "vicious circle of that commemorative historiography" by which "the Bolsheviks were given Jacobean ancestors, and the Jacobins were made to anticipate the communists."[12] Furet's argument reveals a fissure important to this study. None of the historical novelists with whom we will be concerned, no matter how sympathetic to economic injustice, was prepared to assimilate 1789 with 1848 or 1917 in so direct and commendatory a fashion.

The fissure, however, counters our expectations of genre. The essence of the revolution, to Francois Furet, is to be found not in popular revolt of the people against oppressive monarchical or capitalist powers, but in the vacating of supportive institutions during the *Ancien Regime*, in the new power obtained through individual public discourse, and in the growing centralization of government that continues throughout the entire revolutionary era (46–61). Furet's view, professedly indebted to Tocqueville, privileges continuities in institutional culture, and changes in political culture, over the familiar narrative history of revolutionary confrontations. In its essence, however, the historical novel must be committed to the visualization of human conflict over time. Such was Scott's practice, which was to influence Michelet's dramatic narratives and those of his contemporaries. It was a mode that could have been used to promote Marxist revolutionary causes within historical fiction, were it not that Scott's values and the social structure of Scotland in 1700 did not lend themselves to Marxist presentation.

Karl Marx held a different view of the way causes cohere than the view Scott had made prevalent in historical fiction. In the experiences of Scott's characters, the Puritan Commonwealth, the Glorious Revolution, and the American and French Revolutions seem to have suddenly arisen, to have simply and suddenly "happened," because of some combination of causes, many of them undetected at the time. After 1848, however, a working-class revolution against economic oppression was to be continually anticipated by Marx and Engels, then unrelentingly planned by Lenin. The sense of inevitability associated with an Hegelian future of Freedom and Reason was channeled first into the Socialist hopes of 1848, then into the goals of the Commune of 1871 and finally into the long-planned Communist agitation and militant subversion of 1917. Surely the multiplicity of interpretations that the French

Revolution had accrued by the 1840s led Marx to develop, in the *Manuscripts of 1844* as well as in the *Communist Manifesto*, the need for one synthetic analysis of the causes of social oppression, an analysis that could anchor the revolution sure to follow.

Because Marx and Engels assumed history was driven by economic antagonisms based on social class, they saw Liberty, Equality, and Fraternity as paper political ideals, legalisms that weakened aristocracy but have economically benefited only the bourgeois, while leaving the industrial and agricultural working classes without Freedom, Equality, or any sense of Fraternity beyond themselves. Nationalism, they believed, was becoming a new pseudo-religion by which the bourgeois cover up growing class antagonisms. The terms of reality have shifted. Tyranny defined as seigniorial rights, titled privilege, and ecclesiastical power are now anachronisms. Political appeal to the *Patrie* must, in a shrinking world, give way to an economic appeal to the *International*. Tyranny is redefined as the "estrangement" and "alienation" of labor caused by new technologies enabling manufactured goods to gain "surplus value" for capitalist owners. A wage is not truly a contract between people; it is bought labor and sold time. Reforms enacted by legislatures, changes of dynastic regime, and the making of constitutions might support but can never cause the needed revolution. The goal of revolution transcends 1789; the method remains uncertain. Marx calls for nothing less than "a practical movement, a revolution" that will cause not only the "dissolution of all classes" but "the alteration of man on a mass scale."[13]

Karl Marx greatly valued public discussion, public speeches, wide publication of individual writings, and freedom of discussion, all in the service of economic freedom. Lenin's view of revolutionary process could not have been more different. Marx had needed to wait for support from the working class before he could plan the revolution; Lenin knew that his patience in exile had to be limited. In *State and Revolution* (1917), Lenin approvingly quotes a late life statement by Engels advocating the need to force a revolution: "Revolution is the act whereby one part of the population imposes its will upon the other part by means of rifles, bayonets, and cannons, i.e. extremely authoritarian means."[14] Revolution conceived as political overturn that would guarantee the dignity of individual natural rights now seems as anachronistic as "restoration" had seemed in 1793.

Among Lenin's favorite words of commendation, first emphasized in "What Is To Be Done?" (1902), then in his articles on the 1871 Paris Commune, and finally in *State and Revolution,* are "agitation," "secrecy," "training," "propaganda," and "professional revolutionary." Special contempt is accorded to "liberals" whose public revolutionary displays are "spontaneous," "amateur," and therefore self-defeating. As a member of the "revolutionary socialist intelligentsia," Lenin believed that, because the proletariat by itself could attain nothing more than "trade union consciousness," members of the working class must be kept out of Bolshevik power circles.[15] Lenin fastened upon one of the few passages in which Marx had explicitly advocated "smashing" the State, then repeated the word five times in order to present the "smashing" of the state as Marx's essential and continuing purpose.[16]

THE STRUCTURE OF REVOLUTION

Few subjects can be more challenging than the comparative study of revolutions. In recent decades, none has attained more deserved acclaim than Theda Skocpol's *States & Social Revolutions: A Comparative Analysis of France, Russia & China* (1979). Her work, like Furet's, belongs within a broadly sociological framework that leads back to Tocqueville. Skocpol deemphasizes political thought and changes in polity, in order to emphasize how institutional change does or does not respond to pressures of social class.[17] As in Tocqueville's *The Ancien Regime and the French Revolution* (1856), Skocpol's arguments are arresting, but they do not apply readily to the narrative structure of historical fiction. More pertinent to the three definitions of "revolution" are two synthetic studies that were to remain broadly influential throughout the late twentieth century: Crane Brinton's *The Anatomy of Revolution* (1938) and Hannah Arendt's *On Revolution* (1963).

The two works have much in common beyond their selective focus upon the American, French, and Russian revolutions—to which Brinton had added the Puritan Revolution of 1640. Both authors are open to Marxist assumptions about social class and political economy, but neither has any tolerance for Marxist-Leninism or the totalitarian outcome of proletarian revolution. Both contend that major western revolutions arose during times of incompetent dithering by dynastic monarchies that led reformers and intelligentsia to demand needed change. Both authors see civil or international war as an essential cause for the growth of a revolutionary mentality. After compromise fails to establish a constitutional monarchy, power is increasingly concentrated within small committees of leftist extremists. The greatly increased power of the central, federated state becomes revolution's only sure outcome. As revolutionaries gain power and exercise governance, their commitment to serve the sovereign people leads to diminished concern for guaranteeing individual rights.[18]

Neither Brinton nor Arendt chooses to consider the constructive outcomes—widening of the franchise, lessening of legal privilege, improved civil service, disestablishment of churches—that revolutions had often achieved. Instead, both authors seek to dispel their readers' naiveté about the nature of revolution itself; they seek to issue a warning about the growth of totalitarian government, whether Fascist or Communist, whether German, Russian, or Chinese. To them, defensible revolution could follow the course of French Revolution only up to the rise of the Terror. The American Revolution, with its end in constitution making, offered the preferable model. Theirs is a libertarian view of revolution shaped by the pre- and postwar contexts of World War II.

Nonetheless, different aims lead them in different directions. Brinton focuses on substantiating a single paradigm of the consecutive stages of revolution:

> In all our revolutions there is a tendency for power to go from Right to Center to Left, from the conservatives of the old regime to the moderates to the radicals to the extremists. As power moves along this line, it gets more and more concentrated, more and more narrows its base in the country and among the people, since at each important crisis the defeated group has to drop out of politics.[19]

After a crisis of Terror, a period of Thermidor must ensue, not only because of the remembered atrocities of Terror, but because human nature cannot long sustain a crisis mentality that demands group commitment. Revolutionary politics will therefore reverse direction, moving from Left back to Right, ending in some measurable changes, but certainly not the creation of a new world, even in Russia (209, 259). No revolution could ever fulfill the *OED* definition of a "revolution" as a "complete overturn."

To Brinton, unlike Arendt, the economic causes of revolution are central. More than the rage of hungry masses is needed. Revolutionary economic deprivation grows from empty monarchical treasuries, burdensome tax policies leveled on all classes, and the expenses of wartime. Changes in revolutionary polity (from monarchy to constitutional monarchy, to republic, to empire, and thence centralization) reflect underlying changes in the temper of the people. Constitutions, Bills of Rights, and statute laws emerge from the political attitudes of a demanding populace.

Hannah Arendt seeks to uncover history-altering differences among revolutions, rather than devising a single paradigm that unites them. To her, the redemptive value of the American Revolution depends upon the popular ratification of a Constitution based upon clear separation of legislative, executive, and judicial powers, then amended by a Bill of Rights guaranteeing protection of individual rights against government. The cumulative errors made after 1792 in France, some of them reenacted in Russia, were based upon confusions of "public liberty" with "civic liberty," a Republic of Virtue with a Republic of Laws, and nationalism with culture.

To Arendt, "happiness" is a much misunderstood revolutionary aim; Jefferson rightly considered happiness a right for the individual to pursue, not a policy for the General Will to decree.[20] Arendt therefore insists upon a clear distinction between rebellion and revolution: "The end of rebellion is liberation, while the end of revolution is the *foundation* of freedom" (133, italics mine). Arendt's repeated approval of writings by John Adams, who revered contract and detested the outcome of the French Revolution, are fully consistent with her memorable claims that the word "democracy" was not in use in France until 1794 and that, of the fourteen constitutions written by French legislatures between 1789 and 1875, none was ever ratified (112, 137).

Behind Arendt's attacks on inchoate notions of the "General Will" and "the Virtue of the People" lie her memories of totalitarian appeals to the *Deutsches Volk* and the Supreme Soviet. The grindings of economic injustice, important as they are, are less revolutionary than the demagogue's will to dictatorship on behalf of self, party, or nation. As Madison had predicted, any republican polity must control the problem of majority faction. Because constitution making is "the noblest of revolutionary deeds," the failure of Robespierre to construct protective governmental institutions led to political apocalypse: "what eventually set the world on fire was precisely a combination of these two, of national revolutions or revolutionary nationalism, of nationalism speaking the language of revolution, or of revolutions rousing the masses with nationalist slogans" (149–150). Revolutions that promote nationalism will prove the enemy of individual liberty, whether they are labeled "fascist" or not.

To Crane Brinton, Arendt's selection among causes and her inflammatory language led her to distort if not falsify their common subject matter. In the biographical appendix to his 1965 edition of *The Anatomy of Revolution*, Brinton glossed his entry on Arendt's *On Revolution* with the following judgment: "Emotional, intellectual, full of existentialist despair, poles apart from the approach attempted in this book" (291). In fact, the two poles were not as far apart as Brinton believed. Many of Brinton's and Arendt's insights are parallel. But the power of Arendt's text, like Crane Brinton's angry dismissal of it, attests to the importance of determining whether the commendatory connotations of "revolution" can be justifiably extended to embrace policies of national unity and forced economic equality that interfere with individual liberty.

FIRST PROPHECIES

Although the disjunctions and overheated rhetoric common to 1840s histories of the French Revolution has been traced to the political instabilities of the fifty intervening years, the same compulsion to excess was present within first responders. Linda Orr has shown how the Republic that had executed its king was later impelled, during times of bourgeois monarchy, to pen narratives that were "headless" in literary form and volatile in historical judgment.[21] Similar qualities of "headlessness" may be found, however, in two famous texts known to Scott: Burke's *Reflections on the Revolution in France* (1790) and Paine's rejoinder *The Rights of Man* (1792), both written before Louis XVI was executed. The anger Burke vents against the National Assembly, and the contempt Paine expresses in his dismissal of Burke, precede headlessness. They derive from disagreement over the very meaning of "revolution." Both authors recognized that different meanings of the word posed different paradigms for the future of political society. A semantic difference became a predictive gulf between them.

Reflections on the Revolution in France begins with fifteen closely reasoned pages establishing a clear distinction between the Glorious Revolution of 1688 and the French Revolution of 1789. Thereafter Burke launches into 200 pages of often-brilliant rant that shifts from topic to topic without chapter divisions, without section separations, without logical sequence of subject and often without restraint of diction or shift in tone. The underlying impetus for Burke's fear and rage is the inability of English supporters of the French Revolution to understand what a justifiable revolution is. The French Revolution will infect England if the directives contained in the word "revolution" are not properly understood.

By detailed reference to the 1689 *Declaration of Right* and the 1701 *Act of Settlement*, Burke argues that the Glorious Revolution had, by acts of parliamentary legislation, maintained the principle of hereditary monarchical succession, first through William and Mary, and later through Sophia of Hanover, both of them ultimately of Stuart lineage.[22] When difficult choices of royal legitimacy had to be made, Parliament had established its power to confer executive power on a monarch, but not the power to create a new polity or to pick whomever it chose as king. Arguing for a Whig principle prevalent since the 1701 Act of Settlement, Burke traced the Rights of Englishmen to Magna Charta, not to any formulation of natural right, let alone to any "Declaration of the Rights of Man" suddenly discovered by "speculists" (58). "The Revolution was made to preserve our *antient* indisputable laws and liberties, and that *antient* constitution of government which is our only security for law and liberty" (31). Now, in 1790, the restorative model of revolution must be clearly reaffirmed, but with a proviso that grants Parliament the right to legislate changes that preserve the merits of the unwritten British constitution and the Common Law. Society is a living contract between generations past, present, and future; it can grow only from within its base (96).

The French concept of revolution, as Burke summarizes it, threatens individual liberties that a just revolution would preserve. It creates a Republic based on today's speculations codified into a paper Declaration of the

Rights of Man. When the unelected French National Assembly doubles the representation of the Third Estate into a number equal to the first and second Estates combined, then decides to vote as one body rather than three, it abrogates separation of powers, centralizing the power of legislation into just one Estate. New taxes levied to relieve growing government debt constitute "the distinctive mark of a boundless despotism" (109); it is nothing less than retrospective taxation without representation. Arguing that enforced secularization is a form of intolerance, Burke maintains that seizing church lands in order to fill empty governmental coffers will now recur because "revolutions are favourable to confiscation" (156). When Burke angrily argues, "to make a revolution is to subvert the antient state of our country," he is clearly caught between an older definition of revolution that is rapidly losing traction, and a new one that he fears and abhors.

Amid Burke's questionable facts, inflammatory adjectives, and absurd overstatements, we find acute, memorable prophecies of the post-revolutionary future. Burke predicts widespread confiscation of personal property, the continued devaluation of the *Assignats*, rising prices for bread, and a demand for constrictive price controls. The National Legislature will degenerate into an arena for verbal posturing because it lacks any stipulated procedures for passing legislation. The stagey swearing of oaths, whether on the Tennis Court or in the National Assembly, is a telling sign of the disappearance of any inner bond of "fealty" to the needed ligatures of society. A new kind of public political theatre will emerge, based upon demagogic speeches, *lanterne* and coffee house politics, leading to an ever-fracturing sequence of competing cabals and committees.[23]

To gain needed authority, Burke predicts, extremism on behalf of equality will become *de rigeur*: "moderation will be stigmatized as the virtue of cowards" (275). Instead of empowering "the people," the French revolution will overturn power among social classes:

> The whole of the power obtained by this revolution will settle in the towns among the burghers and the monied directors who lead them. The landed gentleman, the yeoman and the peasant have, none of them, habits, or inclinations, or experience, which can lead them to any share in this the sole source of power and influence now left in France (195).

Although Burke and Marx are not names we readily link with one another, both writers perceived the emergence of bourgeois power through French revolutionary rhetoric, and saw in the new moneyed class a force for increased economic inequality.

Burke predicts that the new Republic, if it survives, will be held together by only three forces: (1) increasing taxation to fill the treasury; (2) the rapidly growing power of the city of Paris; and (3) the power of a national army, raised by conscription, to support the wars of the revolutionary Republic against foreign enemies on all sides (191). The probable end of all the agitation, posturing, and scheming will be the emergence of a "popular leader . . . active in propagating doctrines, and establishing powers" who will himself determine the meaning of "liberties" in the absence of the monarch (247). To borrow Marx's title, Burke was predicting the eighteenth Brumaire of France's first Napoleon.

Burke's insights derive from his view of what a true "revolution" should have been. He had forthrightly supported the American Revolution primarily on the grounds that the colonists were defending their long established liberties (the word "liberties" connoting powers as well as "freedoms") as British citizens. In the final paragraph of his *Reflections*, Burke describes himself as one who "does not wish to belye the tenour of his life"; "almost the whole of [his] public exertion has been a struggle for the liberty of others" (249). The author's support of the American Revolution and his attack upon the French Revolution were, Burke contends, of a piece. It was the declared purpose and anticipated course of revolution that had shifted ominously beneath him, and made his contrasting responses to the two revolutions seem contradictory even though they were consistent.

To deny that Burke believed in "natural rights" is to caricature his position. "Natural rights" not only exist for Burke; they provide, as the revolutionaries contend, a standard of "abstract perfection" that needs always to be remembered. The folly of the new model of "Revolution" arises when men succumb to the belief that it could ever be possible fully to constitute "natural rights" within any system of human government:

> Government is not made in virtue of natural rights, which may and do exist in total independence of it; and exist in much greater clearness, and in a much greater degree of abstract perfection: but their abstract perfection is their practical defect. By having a right to every thing they want everything. Government is a contrivance of human wisdom to provide for human *wants*. (60)

Government must always remain a flawed "contrivance," and will never be the shining mirror of man's natural rights. Human "wants" will never be satisfied, no matter how man's "natural rights" may be defined in paper declarations. "Their abstract perfection," Burke would remind all readers, "is their practical defect." Here is the moderate realism that later readers, wary of revolution and its Napoleonic consequences, would find in the novels of Walter Scott.

The ecstatic, progressive predictions in Thomas Paine's *The Rights of Man* (1791, 1792) are every bit as plausible, and as historically verifiable, as

Burke's dire warnings. Paine argues that the uncertain nature of a hereditary monarchy, combined with the unequal economics of late medieval class privilege, have made civil war a destructive constant of the old order. Because monarchical dynasties will always be tied to national wars, only international republicanism can bring the prospect of peace. To rename peasants and aristocrats as "citizens," and to grant them legal citizenship status, is to attach a people's loyalty to a *patria* where equality of legal right and the full benefits of civilization will develop. In all republics there will be ongoing need for a graduated income tax, which Paine twice calls a "progressive tax" designed to support widows and widowers, the aged, and the poor.[24] Income taxes should be used to break down primogeniture and to provide what we now call "vouchers" for worthy, poor parents to better their children's education. The visible growth of international commerce will, if tariffs remain low, provide the best guarantee of peace among republican nation states. "From what we can foresee, all Europe may form but one great republic" (445). This last hope was to continue through Napoleon's Grand Empire, to the League of Nations, the United Nations, the Common Market, and the European Union.[25] Walter Scott was to publicly support some, but not all, of these measures.

Paine's way of grandly introducing the "Declaration of the Rights of Man" is to immediately precede italicized quotation of the first three principles ("Men are born, and always continue free and equal") with a refutation of Burke's notion of revolution:

> What were formerly called revolutions, were little more than a change of persons, or an alteration of local circumstances. They rose and fell like things of course, and had nothing to their existence or their fate that could influence beyond the spot that produced them. But what we now see in the world, from the revolutions of American and France, is a renovation of the natural order of things, a system of principles as universal as truth and the existence of man (383).

The fallacy of the old view of "revolution" is revealed to be precisely what Burke believed to be its merit: a return to the stable principles of mixed government. For Paine, so static a "revolution" could only confine progressive forces within one limited "spot" in time.

The very meaning of "revolution" therefore needs to be changed. Paine argues that, because the "Declaration of the Rights of Man" has attracted universal attention, his age is witnessing "a scene so new, and so transcendently unequalled by any thing in the European world, that the name of a revolution is diminutive of its character, and it rises into a regeneration of man" (353). "Regeneration" will move mankind forward into a new order, not backward. With no hint of his sometime scorn for Biblical authority, Paine interprets

Genesis 1–3 as God's endowing Man with Rights of Liberty and Equality that mankind was long to betray. Today's new republican order will regenerate mankind after millennia in which man has remained fallen, sunk in monarchy and aristocracy. From such politicizing of the term "regeneration," it is but a short step to Paine's influential conclusion to the entire work: "The present age will hereafter merit to be called the Age of Reason, and the present generation will appear to the future as the Adam of a new world" (505). The doubled temporal direction of Paine's thought is telling: as revolution creates a new world, man will be restored to his lost Adamic identity.

My claim for the validity of Burke's and Paine's opposed set of predictions is admittedly selective, though true, I believe, to their general arguments. The French Revolution was to prove so complex and diverse in its effects that both sets of prophecies remain plausible. By selecting one's evidence, while postulating time limits that fit one's desired outcome, both views become equally valid. Nonetheless, a similarity of "headless" rhetoric binds them. Because the revolution is conceived as the overwhelming crisis of western history, both authors are drawn toward absolute statement, inflammatory adjectives, repetition, an eddying of argument. Warnings against ever-shifting conspiracies fill both works, as they were to do throughout the revolution itself. Written at the height of gathering crisis, neither author has the time or the patience for qualification.

Burke argues through sarcasm, denunciation, and scene painting, but mostly through dark metaphors, many of them highly imaginative, some of them silly. Paine argues through high-minded abstractions and journalistic directness, relieved by anecdote and occasional statistics. Both write into and through their subject at white heat, but without a clear successive outline, trusting to the power of single sentences and paragraphs to persuade the reader. Such rhetoric becomes self-sustaining and exclusionary. Burke will grant no merit to the recent redefinition of revolution, nor to the activities of French revolutionaries, nor to Rousseau. Paine will grant no merit to the older model of revolution, nor to inherited institutions, nor to his former friend and associate Edmund Burke. Their only shared purpose is to write effective polemic at a time of world crisis, a purpose for which reasoned qualification would be counterproductive.

AFTERSHOCK

By the time Walter Scott began to publish the Waverley Novels, during the 100 Days and then after Waterloo, Burke's and Paine's opposed judgments on the revolution had been forever complicated by the figure of Napoleon Bonaparte, libertarian and emperor, reformer and opportunist, the symbol of how revolutions centralize the growth of governmental authority in a dictatorial figure (Cromwell, Stalin, Mao). A Jacobin sympathizer in 1792, Napoleon had subdued royalist uprisings in the south of France, won military victories for the Directorate, and become empowered as First Consul thanks to the blessing of Sieyes. After the coup d'etat of Eighteenth Brumaire (1799), Napoleon devised a written constitution for a Republic and submitted it to a popular referendum; his Constitution received 3 million votes and nearly unanimous voter approval. Between 1800 and 1803, he centralized French administration, and abolished the Provinces as legal entities by reconfiguring France as 130 *Departements* led by Prefects responsible directly to national government. Exemptions from taxes, notably from the Taille, were eliminated. In 1803, the Napoleonic Code enacted one legal system for all of France. The several codes abolished the Three Estates, abolished legal privilege, abolished hereditary offices, abolished manors and guilds, and reorganized the French Civil Service by approving only salaried positions appointed according to talent. The Napoleonic Codes established legal equality throughout France in matters of criminal procedure, trial rights, commercial law, torts, contracts, and liability to conscription. By means of the Concordat, Napoleon recognized the Catholic Church as "the church of France," while supporting the legalizing of religious toleration.

All of these measures are outgrowths of revolutionary principles that had been widely advocated during the five years after Louis XVI had reluctantly convened the Three Estates. In these varied ways, Napoleon represented the fulfillment of revolutionary promise after the interim years of Terror and Thermidor. Moreover, these same reforms, deriving from the twin principles of meritocracy and legal equality, created lasting procedures, institutions, and administrative offices, most of which would endure through the failed constitutions, failed republics, and failed empires of nineteenth-century France.

But, in achieving these reforms, Napoleon had pursued compromising, cynical policies that had proven temporarily effective, but permanently sullied his reputation. As Consul, he both deported Jacobins and executed royalists (the Duke of Enghein), thereby making dramatic gestures of defending his "Republic" against its enemies to the left and to the right. He welcomed émigrés, royalists, Jacobins, constitutional monarchists, police spies from the years of the Terror (Fouché) and political trimmers like Talleyrand (whom Napoleon called "a pile of shit in a silk stocking"[26]) back into France and into the government whenever their services were advantageous.

After promoting a written constitution for the Republic in 1799, Napoleon made a new Constitution in 1804 so that he could crown himself as emperor of the French in the presence of the Pope. The new constitution flatly declared, with scant regard for revolutionary ideals, that "the government of the republic is confided to an emperor."[27] In 1804 he began to award hereditary titles of nobility to those whose loyalty or services he especially sought to enlist. Most important, Napoleon remained careful not to allow the creation of a legislature that might empower popularly chosen candidates through an extensive suffrage. Candidates for the Legislative Assembly were chosen from a predetermined list of "Notables"; a Notable would then be voted into the legislature by a national electorate not exceeding about 40,000, but he would have the power only to approve legislation, not to initiate it. Consequently, any "republican" basis for a Napoleonic legislature had little in common with the degree of popular empowerment already constituted in the United States House of Representatives and in the British House of Commons.

Doubts about Napoleon's republican credentials seemed secondary subtleties when placed beside Napoleon's admired, fearsome image as a military genius and implacable pursuer of power. As the conquering Emperor, he inspired admiration, sometimes reverence, for instituting codes of progressive reform among backward-looking peoples. He also inspired resentment, sometimes loathing, for taxing and conscripting the local populace, for placing puppet rulers in charge of conquered nations, and for subverting local institutions in the name of international uniformity. The national glory won by the Grande Armeé compromised his claim to advance international republicanism, especially among peoples whose countries he had overrun.

Adding to the associations linked with the name "Napoleon" were memorable remarks of Napoleon Bonaparte the man. Beside numerous words of generosity, loyalty, and honor, which even Tolstoy was to grant him, are to be set remarks like the following; "No society can exist without inequality of wealth, and inequality of wealth is not possible without religion"; "A throne is just a plank of wood, upholstered in velvet. One actually governs with boots and spurs"; "Look at my self-proclaimed 'virtuous republicans!' Why, all I have to do is hang gold braid on their clothes and they are mine"; "If I belong to a political party, why then I am for that party; if I belong to an army, then I am for my army. If I belong to a political state, why then I am for my political state. If I were black, I would be for the blacks. But being white, I am for the whites. Being powerful, I am for power. That's the only truth about me. The opposite you may tell to the schoolchildren."[28]

Even if only half of these statements are verifiable, and if all were sharpened in the retelling, we are still faced with an age symbolized in a man of many faces. Napoleon represented, to the reader of 1815, the contemporary embodiment of what the French Revolution had created. But what was it? How could one possibly assess the entirety of what "Napoleon Bonaparte" had been made to represent? How to weigh the hundreds of thousands of dead bodies, and the disappearance of long-known local worlds, against the progress of reformed political institutions, legal equality, and technological advance?

By the end of Madame de Stael's *Considerations on the Principal Events of the French Revolution* (1818), Napoleon so dominates her text that he seems to define the revolution. Of de Stael's 760 pages, 230 are devoted to Napoleon's policies, tactics, and character, but very few pages to his battlefields. Madame de Stael struggles to maintain a Burkean contrast between the practical regard for inherited liberties evidenced during England's 1688 Revolution and the unreasoning pursuit of republican virtue and national glory that increasingly defined the revolution in France. Her Burkean hopes for France gradually dissolve. Napoleon Bonaparte has destroyed the promise that Revolutionary France might evolve into a constitutional monarchy guaranteeing individual rights, the rule of civilian law, and a widened suffrage.

Madame de Stael struggles to be fair. She had met Napoleon more than once, conversed with him, and observed him carefully. She does not dismiss Napoleon's progressive policy declarations as hypocrisy designed merely to arouse support. She regards him rather as a force of egoistic will so strong that it corrupts first his moral self, then his talents, then his nation. "For him, nothing exists but himself; all other creatures are ciphers. The force of his will consists in the impossibility of disturbing the calculations of his egoism."[29] De Stael begins and ends her *Considerations* by affirming a presumably universal law soon to be crucial to Hegel: history demonstrates the progress of Reason under the aegis of Liberty. De Stael's narrative, however, leaves us wondering exactly how, given the wreckage of Europe in 1818 and the difficulties of the Bourbon Restoration, Liberty and Reason will ever emerge into any kind of lasting harmony.

By 1820, the option of selecting only the good or the bad of Napoleon's revolutionary legacy had become intellectually indefensible. The prospect of republican peace or dictatorial tyranny or violent anarchy seemed equally remote, equally simplistic.[30] The sure judgments of Burke or Paine, compelling though they might be emotionally, no longer resonated for the exhausted, confused European world whose readers were eagerly buying copies of *Waverley*, *Old Mortality*, and *The Heart of Mid-Lothian*.[31] Scott's popularity must in part be ascribed to the complexity with which, while recreating the Scottish Wars before and after 1688, Scott had juxtaposed the old with the new, the privileged with the persecuted, and the honorable with the dishonorable. The Waverley Novels uncovered both merit and shame within all parties, while showing that revolution is no sudden irruption; it always has a long foreground.

TORY PROGRESSIVE

The magnum opus of Scott's last years is not a Waverley novel, nor even the collected Waverley Novels, but his *Life of Napoleon Buonaparte, Emperor of the French* (1827), well over a million words, variously published in seven, five, three and nine volume sets. The *Life of Buonaparte* is prefaced by a seventeen-chapter "Preliminary View of the French Revolution," virtually a volume in itself, which comprises almost one quarter of the immense work. In assessing Revolutionary France, Scott's tone and vantage point, as one might expect, maintain Burke's sense of political outrage, but without the luxury of satire, tempered by consideration for his wife's French heritage and the centuries of Scottish-French alliance. Burke's *Reflections on the French Revolution*, Scott claims, has "had the most striking effect on the public mind of any work in our time."[32] Scott criticizes only the "exaggerated colours" of Burke's descriptions whenever Burke demonstrates how Bourbon "despotism" was precipitously transformed into the "unembarrassed license" of 1793 (I, 110).

Scott reaffirms Burke's view that, due to the lack of legislative procedure, the French Revolution had to devolve into scenes of overwrought political gesture and/or mob rule. He accepts Burke's conviction that the transformation of the Three Estates into the National Assembly was inevitable due to the growing power of middle-class merchants and newly wealthy professionals, especially lawyers. Like Burke and Madame de Stael before him, Scott faults the revolutionaries, even the constitutional monarchists, for forsaking their civic responsibilities, while Assignats were plunging in value and country chateaux were burning: "What were the National Assembly doing at this dreadful crisis? They were discussing the abstract doctrine of the rights of man, instead of exacting from the subject the respect due to his social duties" (I, 76).

The acuity of Burke's predictive insight leads Scott to exclaim, "no political prophet ever viewed futurity with a surer ken" (I, 110). Scott also anticipates arguments Tocqueville was later to emphasize in *The Ancien Regime and the French Revolution*. "Centralization" may not be the word Scott uses, but Tocqueville's concept is everywhere. As the French nobility became increasingly dependent on the monarchy, respect and cooperation between the country nobleman, his bailiff, and his peasants collapse (I, 27). The disarray of tax policies under the Ancien Regime was to continue long after 1789 because "the privilege of avoiding or refusing to pay taxes [became] the most unequivocal and not the least pleasing part, of the Frenchman's newly-acquired freedom" (I, 91). The draining of money and talent from the provinces to Paris persists through the restoration of the monarchy in 1815. Equality of right turns into a demand for equality of condition, leading Scott to predict a leveling downward in terms very like those Tocqueville was to describe in *Democracy in America* and in *The Ancien Regime*: "Any practical attempt to remedy the inequality of rank in civilized society by forcible measures may indeed degrade the upper classes," Scott insists, "but cannot improve those beneath them" (I, 89).

What is truly distinctive about Scott's disillusioned perspective on the French Revolution, perhaps on any revolution, is his concern for the attitudes and duties of the rural upper class, whether titled or not. As a prominent Scottish landowner, committed to the well-being of local farmers and artisans, Walter Scott persistently distinguishes, in a way neither Burke nor de Stael nor Tocqueville does, between the "nobility" and the "gentry." In spite of revolutionary turmoil, a landed gentleman remains a community leader responsible by honor of social class to his community as long as he retains wealth and standing. To Scott, there was and is a major distinction between the *Haute Noblesse* at court, who are nothing more than courtiers, and the *Noblesse Compagnarde* who remain in the provinces, loyal to their local populace, but increasingly resentful as centralization and revolutionary agitation deprive them of power (I, 26).

The word "nobility," Scott believes, less and less connotes the gentry who live quietly, honorably, and productively on their estates; instead "nobility" has become associated with the glittery pretense of court life, with noble titles (often newly bought), and with the fashionable life of the metropolis, be it Paris or London. Like Madame de Stael, Scott is fully aware of the problem posed for France by Napoleon's recently ennobled military officers and entrepreneurs (Marx's "bourgeois"). Such "noblemen" have forsaken their obligation to maintain the bond of community among social classes whose differences in wealth, education, and merit are in fact ineradicable: "The noble had neglected and flung from him the most precious jewel in his coronet—the love and respect of the country-gentleman, the farmer and the peasant" (I, 28). After 1789, and continuing into the post-Napoleonic world, the titled nobility increasingly resemble a brightly gilded hilt with its sword-blade gone, its power lost to willing self-corruption (I, 28).

The pertinence of Scott's observation about the *Noblesse Compagnarde* to the point of view in his historical novels is of paramount importance. To what social class do almost all the protagonists of the Scottish novels (Edward Waverley, Henry Morton, Frank Osbaldistone, Reuben Butler, Edgar Ravenswood etc.) belong? They are either members of, or related to, the lesser rural gentry or nobility, often with connections to the professional and mercantile classes. But they do not belong in London, often not in Edinburgh, nor are they quite at home in a farmer's cottage, a counting house, or a lawyer's office. Inheriting a goodly modicum of land or possessions, they are curiously dispossessed young men vacillating inbetween worlds. Although their sense of their social place in eighteenth-century Scotland has clearly been eroding, they project an empathetic point of view for the nineteenth-century reader. In 1815, Scott's reader was likely to be as privileged, educated, and troubled about his or her insecure position in the post-revolutionary world as Scott's protagonists had been in 1665 or 1745. Scott's young men retain within their ordinary selves an importance greater than they or their society can presently recognize.[33]

In the later volumes of the *Life*, Scott would render Napoleon through revealingly contradictory judgments: admiration for his generalship, commendation for his courage, patriotism, and administrative efficiency; concern for his selling of noble title and advocacy of an appointed meritocracy; contempt for his vanity, egomania, and grasping after dictatorial powers. Nonetheless, Napoleon is infinitely preferable to Danton ("neither good by nature, nor by principle nor political calculation"), to Marat ("a madman raised into consequence only by circumstance"), and to Robespierre ("a cold, creeping, calculating hypocrite, whose malignity resembled that of a paltry and second-rate fiend") (I, 242).

Scott's view of the course of revolutionary change retains much of the common ground between Burke and Madame de Stael. While denouncing the atrocities of regicide and Terror, Scott honors the libertarian goals of constitutional monarchists, then formulates a general principle for assessing the worth and danger of revolution:

> In the proper sense, equality of rights, and equality of laws, a constitution which extends like protection to the lowest and highest, are essential to the existence and to the enjoyment of freedom. But to erect a leveling system designed to place the whole mass of the people on the same footing as to habits, manners, tastes and sentiments, is a gross and ridiculous contradiction of the necessary progress of society (I, 88).

To substantiate the first of these propositions, Scott praises political benefits enacted by the French National Assembly. Many of them recall Thomas Paine: trial by jury, freedom of the press, religious toleration, the granting of pardons, and abolition of political privileges, especially the *lettres de cachet*. However, true progress is advanced by maintaining economic and cultural class distinctions—a proposition that would eventually prove difficult to assimilate to the Marxist cast of Lukacs's literary realism.

Whenever the demand for equality of legal right derives from prior commitment to individual liberties, Scott believes that fundamental political change becomes justifiable. Revolution can therefore be defensible on grounds other than Copernican restoration of harmonious motion. Revolution to advance "equality of laws" and "the enjoyment of freedom" is a valid precondition of the "necessary progress of society." Understandably, Scott turns aside from the insoluble question of the degree to which armed violence against one's own people is defensible in pursuit of liberty and equality. The ultimate danger of revolutionary ideology is not the near certainty of bloodshed, but the emerging notion that a "leveling system" will create a mass culture in which everyone's ideas, tastes, merits, and social standing are held to be equal.

The prospect of equality of individual condition is therefore judged to be *anti-progressive* as well as unobtainable. Financial, technological, and educational progress will result in the increasing, not decreasing, of differences among the social classes. To Scott, as to Adam Ferguson, this fact must be bluntly declared as a single-sentence universal law: "As society advances, the differences of ranks advances with it" (89). Whether the emerging polity be a republic or a constitutional monarchy, differences among social classes will increase as the status of all classes is raised. Such a moderate position is best labeled, in the terms of the 1820s, as that of a "Tory Progressive." Scott does not condone "revolution" in Burke's or Paine's restrictive senses, nor does he like Madame de Stael's worry that Napoleon has killed progressive change. He accepts elements of all three viewpoints, filtered through an 1820s awareness that libertarian revolution repeatedly ends in a reverse sequence of autocracy followed by restoration.

NOTES

1. *The Oxford English Dictionary* (Oxford: Oxford University Press, 1971), p. 617. A careful study of the shifting referents and meanings of the word "revolution" between 1500 and 1850 is needed.

2. Steve Pincus has recently challenged the validity of this argument by claiming it to be a highly selective "Establishment Whig" claim that has dominated British thinking about 1688 from the age of Walpole, through Burke and Macaulay to Trevelyan and beyond, even to the tercentenary. See Steve Pincus, *1688: The First Modern Revolution* (New Haven: Yale University Press, 2009), 3–29.

3. Bernard Bailyn concluded "the primary goal of the American Revolution, which transformed American life and introduced a new era in human history, was not the overthrow or even the alteration of the existing social order but the preservation of political liberty threatened by the apparent corruption of the constitution" (*The Ideological Origins of the American Revolution* [Cambridge, MA: Harvard University Press, 1967] , p. 19). Under most conditions, "preservation" provides a more hopeful, less volatile motive for revolution action than "restoration." The Committees of Correspondence in 1770s Massachusetts were composed of determined but reluctant revolutionaries. See "Boston Revolt and Puritan Restoration: 1760–1775," chapter seven of John McWilliams, *New England's Crises and Cultural Memory* (Cambridge: Cambridge University Press, 2004).

4. The revolutionary opening sentence of Book One, Chapter One of Rousseau's *The Social Contract* (1762) implies that Rousseau's idea of freedom is primarily collective, not individualistic: "Man was born free and everywhere he is in chains." The opening sentence of Book II, Chapter One confirms it: "The first and most important consequence of the principles established above is that the general will alone can direct the forces of the State according to the object of its founding, which is the common good" (Jean-Jacques Rousseau, *The Social Contract and the First and Second Discourses*, ed. Susan Dunn [New Haven: Yale University Press, 2002], 156, 170).

5. The French Constitution of 1793, never implemented, varies the phrasing only slightly: "The law is the free and solemn expression of the general will." See *The French Revolution: Introductory Documents*, ed. D.I. Wright (St. Lucia: University of Queensland Press, 1974), 173.

6. "Declaration of the Rights of Man," in *The French Revolution: Introductory Documents*, 58–61.

7. Robespierre, "Rapport sur les Principes du Gouvernement Revolutionnaire," December 25, 1793 in *The French Revolution: Introductory Documents*, translation D.I, Wright. p. 199.

8. Robespierre's passage begs the vexing question of the differences, or lack of them, between the terms "liberalism" and "republicanism" during the era from 1770 to 1830. Through study of Adam Smith, Adam Ferguson, Thomas Paine, James Madison, Germaine de Stael, and Benjamin Constant, Andreas Kalyvas and Ira Katznelson contend that liberalism originated in eighteenth-century republicanism: "Political liberalism burst from the shell of a republican chrysalis" (Kalyvas and Katznelson, *Liberal Beginnings: Making a Republic for the Moderns* [Cambridge: Cambridge University Press, 2008], p. 5). My sense is that a clear distinction between "republicanism" and "liberalism" did not emerge until John Stuart Mill's *On Liberty* (1859) and that overlap between the two terms would continue long after Mill's time, at least until "democracy" replaced "republicanism" in common parlance.

9. G.W.F. Hegel, *Lectures on the Philosophy of History*, translation by John Sibree and Ruben Alvarado (wwwwordbridge.net, print, 2011), pp. 17, 18.

10. Herbert Marcuse, *Reason and Revolution: Hegel and the Rise of Social Theory* (1954), second edition (New York: Humanities Press, 1968), p. 9.

11. Linda Orr, *Headless History: 19th Century French Historiography of the Revolution* (Ithaca: Cornell University Press, 1990); Ann Rigney, *The Rhetoric of Historical Representation: Three Narrative Histories of the French Revolution* (Cambridge: Cambridge University Press, 1990). With regard to multiplicity of literary form, Orr concludes, "The Romantic project seeks to dissolve autobiography and history, subject and object, form and content, text and society, history and daily life, fact and *fantasme*, theory and story, and then sort them out again" (6). Rigney cites Scott as "the original catalyst and model for the historians' emphasis on vivid narration" (4). Such loosening of historiographical boundaries followed from Scott's own mingling of history and fiction.

12. Francois Furet, *Interpreting the French Revolution*, translated by Elborg Forster (Cambridge: Cambridge University Press, 1981), pp. 10, 6. Originally published as *Penser La Révolution Francaise* by Gallimard in 1978.

13. Marx and Engels, *The German Ideology* (1845) in *The Marx-Engels Reader*, edited by Robert C. Tucker, (New York and London: W.W. Norton and Co.), 2nd edition, p. 193.

14. Engels, *Die Neue Zeit* (1913) quoted by Lenin in *The State and Revolution* (New York and London; Penguin Books, 1992), p. 57.

15. Lenin, *What Is to Be Done?*, Lenin Internet Archive, pp. 17–19.

16. See Lenin's writings and speeches on the Paris Commune in Karl Marx and V.I. Lenin, *Civil War in France* (New York: International Publishers, 1988), pp. 92, 94, 106, 126, 128.

17. Social revolutions and political revolutions are, in Skocpol's model, separable entities: "Social revolutions are rapid, basic transformations of a society's state and class structures. . . . Political revolutions transform state structures but not social structures and they are not necessarily accomplished through class conflict" (Theda Skocpol, *States & Social Revolutions: A Comparative Analysis of France, Russia & China* [Cambridge: Cambridge University Press, 1979], p. 4). The distinction Skocpol makes here would not have occurred to Scott, Cooper, Tolstoy, Hugo, and Pasternak—or at least not in the same way.

18. In the English speaking world, the famous—and timely—fictional expression of the horror of totalitarian centralization is, of course, George Orwell's *1984*, published in 1949.

19. Crane Brinton, *The Anatomy of Revolution* (1938) (New York: Random House, 1965), p. 123.

20. Hannah Arendt, *On Revolution*, introduction by Jonathan Schell (New York and London: Penguin Books, 2006), pp. 65, 106, 124–126, 149–150.

21. "The king was at the imaginary head, and like the body of Christ, all society participated in him. When the king's head fell, that society was literally left headless. Power that stood at the top, clear and identifiable, dissolved in a shape with neither center nor official hierarchy" (Orr, *Headless History*, p. 15). In Orr's view, the volatile confusions of becoming headless, emerging in 1792, remain latent during the regime of Louis Philippe, and then permeate the histories of the Revolution published during the 1840s (145–146).

22. Edmund Burke, *Reflections on the Revolution in France 1790*, edited by L.G. Mitchell (Oxford and New York: Oxford University Press, 1993), p. 3.

23. On this point Furet's argument closely resembles Burke's. Furet was to write: "Language was substituted for power, for it was the sole guarantee that power would belong only to the people, that is, to nobody" (Furet, *Interpreting the Revolution*, p. 48).

24. Edmund Burke and Thomas Paine, *Reflections on the Revolution in France and The Rights of Man* (Garden City, NY: Doubleday, 1973), 491.

25. Paine's faith that prosperity and harmony flow from free trade and equality of political right clearly assumes that commerce will continue to be conducted by contractual agreements between small tradesmen of the kind he had known in Philadelphia and had encountered in Adam Smith's *The Wealth of Nations*. Unlike Burke, Paine did not anticipate the power that banks and manufacturing interests would wield as the industrial revolution accelerated. On Paine's years in Philadelphia see Eric Foner, *Tom Paine and Revolutionary America* (Oxford: Oxford University Press, 1976).

26. Quoted in Simon Schama, *Citizens: A Chronicle of the French Revolution* (New York: Random House, 1989), 678.

27. R.R. Palmer, *A History of the Modern World*, 2nd edition (New York: Alfred A. Knopf, 1960), 375.

28. Biographical facts about Napoleon and quotations presumably spoken by Napoleon are derived from Robert Asprey, *The Reign of Napoleon Bonaparte* (New York: Basic Books, 2001); Paul Johnson, *Napoleon, A Life* (New York: Penguin, 2002); Alan Schom, *Napoleon Bonaparte* (New York: HarperCollins, 1997).

29. Germaine De Stael, *Considerations on the Principal Events of the French Revolution*, edited with an introduction by Aurelian Craiutu (Indianapolis: Liberty Fund, Inc., 2008), p. 409.

30. Irving Howe cogently described immediate post-Napoleonic Europe as "a time when the monarchies tried, with a conspicuous lack of conviction, to restore what was forever gone and the republicans, exhausted by the fury of their own regime, lacked the strength to claim their historical privilege" (Howe, *Politics and the Novel*, introduction by David Bromwitch [Chicago: Irvin R. Dee, 2002], p. 27).

31. Franco Moretti observed: "without Napoleon literary history would have been entirely different, for we would not have had that dynamic ambitious and ambiguous hero who dominates an entire century. His restless ambiguity makes him the natural representative of an age. . . . Everything divides in two, each value is opposed by one of equal importance" (Moretti, *The Way of the World: The Bildungsroman in European Culture*, translated by Albert Sbragia, new edition [London and New York: Verso, 2000], p. 76).

32. Walter Scott, *The Life of Napoleon Buonaparte, Emperor of the French, with a Preliminary View of the French Revolution*, 3 volumes, (Philadelphia: Carey, Lea & Carey, 1827) I, 110.

33. Ina Ferris has shown how "the Waverley novels opened up the novel to the male gender as both writing and reading, establishing novel writing as a literary activity and legitimating novel reading as a manly practice (Ferris, *The Achievement of Literary Authority: Gender, History and the Waverley Novels* [Ithaca: Cornell University Press, 1991], p. 80). Alexander Welsh's important monograph, *The Hero of the Waverley Novels* (1963) describes Scott's protagonists as passive and prudent to the verge of being unaware or uninterested in politics; the Waverley hero seems to care for gentlemanly propriety and the stability of inherited property above all else. Welsh's approach minimizes the impact of the tumultuous historical and political worlds within which Scott's protagonists act. My approach will emphasize that impact. Walter Scott wrote in an immediately post-revolutionary world about revolutionary times.

Chapter 1

Metaphor and the Control of History

To have a command of metaphor is the mark of genius; to make good
metaphors implies an eye for resemblance.

—Aristotle, *Poetics*, ca. 330 BCE

If we would speak of things as they are, we must allow that all the art
of rhetoric, besides order and clearness, all the artificial and figurative
application of words eloquence hath invented, are for nothing else but
to insinuate wrong ideas, move the passions, and thereby mislead the
judgment; and so indeed are perfect cheats.

—John Locke, *An Essay Concerning Human Understanding*, 1690

In the post-Napoleonic western world, how does one make sense of the
contradictory outcomes of recent history?—revolution and restoration;
progress and slaughter; libertarian aristocrats and royalist peasants; legal
equality and persistent privilege; the hope for a peaceful republic and the
fact of civil war. While writing an historical novel, one can order the confusing multiplicity through direct statement, through control of fictional
plot, through shifts of setting, through falsifying history, or by clinging to
history. Direct statement is likely to sacrifice fiction to essay. Rendering full
historical complexity tends to multiply fictional family plots to the verge of
incoherence. Marriage bells tolling for hero and heroine at the novel's end
cannot, by themselves, convince us that the revolutionary world has been
restored to order. Distorting the historical record, whether by commission
or omission, is effective only if undetected. Slavish adherence to historical
fact, on the other hand, destroys the *vraisemblance* upon which great historical fiction depends.

1

At important narrative moments, historical novelists turned to metaphor as the most effective, perhaps the most desperate, means of controlling the contradictions and ambiguities, fictional and historical, that spread out before their imagination. Figurative language, celebrated since Aristotle as a "mark of genius" in poetry and drama, would seem to be less suited to the hybrid nature of the historical novel. Aristotle had explicitly preferred metaphors that establish likeness through reasoned comparison; in the era of Coleridge and Hegel, however, metaphor became more commonly associated with the power of the imagination, even though the essence of metaphor—"the apparent likeness of things essentially different" in Coleridge's phrase—remained constant.[1] How much and what kind of metaphor was appropriate to the writing of historical fiction? The vehicle of an effective metaphor could imply without proving that there is an underlying shape to the welter of factual events, but dwelling upon a seemingly disconnected metaphor could undermine the novel's historicism.

Denis Donoghue's *Metaphor* emphasizes both the desire for transformation immanent in metaphor and the limitations upon its realization. "Metaphor, more than simile or metonymy, expresses one's desire to be free, and to replace the given world by an imagined world of one's devising."[2] Consequently, Donoghue argues, "the essential character of metaphor is prophetic" (51). The prophetic quality of metaphor in turn suggests transformation: "In extreme cases, the change is revolutionary; it issues in a possible world, proclaimed by the audacity of the metaphor" (91). Ultimately, therefore, "the best metaphors are revolutionary, not merely descriptive—although descriptions too may be revelations" (51). Nonetheless, metaphors can appeal only from the imagination of the author to the imagination of the reader: "Metaphors offer to change the world by changing one's sense of it" (51), but the offering of such promise is contingent upon the fact that by themselves "Metaphors cannot establish anything" (64). We should always be aware that the similarity revealed by metaphor is not equivalence, even within the greater affinity claimed by use of simile.

Donoghue's emphasis on prophetic, revelatory metaphor is best adapted to lyric poetry, particularly the romantic poetry of Blake, Shelley, Keats, Goethe, or Hugo. Historical prose, especially the historical novel, requires of metaphor an additional and different function, fleetingly mentioned by Donoghue when he notes that metaphors can also be "helpful in organizing experience" (64). This chapter will argue that, to Scott and the historical novelists who follow, especially Tolstoy, metaphors are necessary to give shape to the complexity and contradictions of the author's historical sense. As the novelist describes a landscape or street scene, the rendering of a physical object provides a metaphor for the revolutionary narrative as a whole. The object, itself insensate, becomes animated as metaphor, sometimes personified.

Re-invoked later in the text, it can become so elaborated as to resemble a conceit. Although the metaphor cannot erase the memory of contravening events, it embodies the author's uncovering of a force that permeates the revolutionary world. This kind of metaphor serves to organize and synthesize disparate experience, historical and fictional. It should not surprise us that many of these metaphors, like the revolutions whose course they symbolize, are metaphors of motion through time. Such metaphors perhaps may be, as Locke contended, "perfect cheats" but the resemblances they reveal can also be experienced, as Aristotle contended, as "the mark of genius."

The jolting awareness of change through historical time, of which Georg Lukacs wrote, appears in the opening chapter ("View of the French Revolution") of Scott's *Life of Napoleon Buonaparte*. Scott's first sentence addresses the ironies of historical memory: "When we look back on past events, however important," it is crucial to recall "the fears, hopes, doubts and difficulties" they aroused, even though they have ended in "an outcome quite different from whatever was anticipated."[3] The unexpected reversals of history are best conveyed by conceiving of time, not as a gently flowing river, but as a torrent, a deluge: "When the rush of the inundation was before our eyes, and in our ears, we were scarce able to remember the state of things before its rage commenced, and when, subsequently, the deluge has subsided within the natural limits of the stream, it is still more difficult to recollect with precision the terrors it inspired when at its height" (17). We are compelled to recollect time as a river flooding into "rage" and "terrors" that subside but do not disappear. Time should no longer be conceived as a gentle stream placidly flowing on amid almost unchanging surroundings. Revolution creates countercurrents, then cataracts, in the river of time. Because our memory seeks to repress or minimize past crises, it becomes the duty of Napoleon's biographer—or the author of the Waverley novels—to revivify the confusions of the deluge.

The river of time progressing unexpectedly over a cataract was to become a preoccupation in the artistry of the next generation. Consider the hundreds of poems and paintings of Niagara Falls, Thomas Cole's ambitious four-stage allegory, *The Voyage of Life* (1842) and Thomas Carlyle's "Shooting Niagara—and After?" (1867). Among them is Victor Hugo's "The French Revolution" (1844), a rendering of the river of history, which begins by defining all revolutions as "formidable liquidations of history" and "elemental creations of laws" that first "unleash electric freedom," then "lay low tyranny throughout the universe" and finally "cause to issue from gigantic demolition the radiant future of the human race."[4] Words like "liquidations, "electric," and "gigantic demolition" are the diction of what Umberto Eco calls Victor Hugo's "sublime excessiveness."[5] Excessive sublimity is necessary, however, because Hugo's metaphor must itself do the work of history. Under a cloudless sky, men embark on the river of time and "abandon themselves gaily to the current of the stream, with no idea and little concern whither they are going." The "hoarse deep sound" first heard faintly then louder ahead does not dispel the joys of today's journeying. Hugo then complicates the cliché. The current becomes "swift and furious" seeming to turn backward upon itself until, when men perceive they are headed toward a gulf, they suddenly understand that "what they took for a river was a people" and that they had been "plowing through souls, violent, bruised, full of hate and fury." The *Ancien Regime*, like the Revolution to come, devours its own children. As the people go over the precipice, "all founders, a whole society, with its laws, its manners, its religion, its beliefs, its arts, its past, its history—foundering like a fisherman's bark."

Civilization's terrifying descent over the cataract outdoes "mere catastrophe; it is chaos. It is darkness, horror, tumult, foam, an eternal and lamentable groaning." But the groaning proves not to be "eternal." The falling waters are gathered and redirected by an undefined "God." Cloud gives way to rainbow; "all has foundered, nothing is lost"; "all is engulfed, nothing is dead." Were you to live one hundred years longer you would "behold the river larger, behold the people greater." In after ages, future generations will pause to retrace the steps of time, "bow their heads, and dream upon this fall of a society and of a monarchy, upon this mighty cataract of civilization that we call the French Revolution" (144–148). The river sweeps the contrarieties of time and society into one stream whose end is a democratic re-visioning of God's covenantal rainbow. Not for a moment does Victor Hugo doubt that worldwide progress will emerge from revolutionary cataclysm. Although in 1844 the times may still seem to be "chaos," Hugo's metaphor is confidently prophetic; he does not need to cite historical fact, any more than he needs to qualify superlatives. His metaphor directs the course of history.

More than any historical novelist we shall consider, Dickens conveys his meaning through metaphor rather than historical reference. Nearly every chapter of *A Tale of Two Cities* contains an elaborate metaphor of the kind defined in this chapter: Woodman Fate and Farmer Death, the mist on Shooter's Hill, "blood" written in wine on a wall in Faubourg St. Antoine, the Gorgon's Head, "The Golden Thread," knitting the names of the condemned, coming storm, rising sea, the Bastille, spreading fire, "Echoing Footsteps," "Drawn to the Loadstone Rock," plague, fever, the grindstone, and, of course, the guillotine. All these metaphors energize and animate the individuals to whom they refer and the two cities in which they exist. Metaphors of special importance are highlighted in chapter titles (those in quotation marks above).[6] Woodman Fate, echoing footsteps, and rising sea are repeatedly invoked in order to convey an overwhelming sense of inevitability and fatality that steadily darkens until the final chapter. Charles Darnay cannot resist the magnetic attraction of the loadstone rock that is revolutionary France. Flood, fire, plague, and fever—natural but perverse forces all—must gather to destructive crisis. Neither Dr. Manette, Monseigneur, Darnay, Lucie, nor Madame Defarge can do anything to stay, or even to alter, the gathering power of these metaphoric forces. Individuals can oppress or murder other individuals, they can help those they love to grieve and to endure, but no secure retreat from the forces impelling revolution exists. The footsteps of necessity echo ominously even within the Soho retreat of the Manette family. Throughout the novel, forces of metaphor rather than facts of the past do the work of history.

I select only one of Dickens's metaphors for extended consideration. Lynn Hunt has shown how, especially after 1791, ritual entertainments and ceremonial pageants spread rapidly within French political culture, provoking revolutionary agitation.[7] Here is Dickens's rendition of the notorious revolutionary dance called the carmagnole:

> There could not be fewer than five hundred people, and they were dancing like five thousand demons. There was no other music than their own singing. They danced to the popular Revolution song, keeping a ferocious time that was like a gnashing of teeth in unison. Men and women danced together, women danced together, men danced together, as hazard had brought them together. At first, they were a mere storm of coarse red caps and coarse woolen rags; but, as they filled the place, and stopped to dance about Lucie, some ghastly apparition of a dance-figure gone raving mad arose among them. They advanced, retreated, struck at one another's hands, clutched at one another's heads, spun round alone, caught one another and spun round in pairs, until many of them dropped. While those were down, the rest linked hand in hand, and all spun round together; then the ring broke, and in separate rings of two and four they turned and turned until they all stopped at once, began again, struck, clutched, and tore, and then reversed the spin, and all spun round another way. Suddenly they stopped again, paused, struck out the time afresh, formed into lines the width of the public way, and, with their heads low down and their hands high up, swooped screaming off. No fight could have been half so terrible as this dance. It was so emphatically a fallen devilry—a healthy pastime changed into a means of angering the blood, bewildering the senses, and steeling the heart. (288–289)

Dickens's grotesquerie resides in the occasion as well as the body movements; the dancers are celebrating the execution as well as the release of prisoners from the guillotine. Thus, it is the absolutist kill-or-liberate process of revolutionary justice itself, as symbolized in the guillotine, which arouses the insane devotion of the crowd: Robespierre's "Virtue" and "Terror" combined.

Words are being sung without music because the thrill of the carmagnole lies in intra- and intersexual dancing as well as in "keeping a ferocious time." The force of the dance resides in the horrific combination of spasmodic gestures within a pattern of relentless regularity, reinforced by the jerky staccato rhythms of Dickens's monosyllabic verbs. Immense energy is being expended for no purpose other than to reverse upon itself and to prepare for more of the same. The dancers are revealed to have become raptors who "with their heads low down, and their hands high up, swooped screaming off." Dickens does not need to insist so blatantly upon the scene's "devilry" or to inform his reader, at passage's end, that the emotions driving the car-magnole are "types of the disjointed time." The controlled, mad violence of revolution, the spasms of its contradiction, are implicit in the disjointed rhythms of the dance and the prose that renders it.

The younger Tolstoy, like Aristotle, preferred metaphors based upon rea-soned justification, rather than those that risk imaginary excess. Much as he admired Dickens, the Tolstoy who wrote *War and Peace* could not convince himself that the power of Dickens's "golden thread"—Lucie Manette's "faithful service of the heart" (100)—could ever be fully sufficient to regen-erate others, even within one's domestic circle, let alone within one's com-munity, fellow soldiers, or countrymen. In some passages, Tolstoy seems to long for one controlling moral law, for some overarching explanation amid the contradictory multiplicities of the Napoleonic era. But in other passages, Tolstoy relishes immersing his reader in contradictions as a way of subverting not only mono-causal and progressive views of history, but the very possibil-ity that there might be any adequate explanation for the ways of the world. Scott had implied the ambiguities of history by amassing its many contraries; Tolstoy uses metaphor to address those contrarieties explicitly.

As Napoleon's army prepares for the Battle of Austerlitz, Tolstoy consid-ers whether there is any pattern or meaning to the sequence of events. He develops a lengthy epic simile even though he dismisses the epic as an out-moded literary form. Historical events occur, Tolstoy claims, like the work-ings of a tower clock:

> One wheel slowly moved, another was set in motion, and a third, and wheels began to revolve faster and faster, levers and cogwheels to work, chimes to play, figures to pop out, and the hands to advance with regular motion as a result of all that activity.
>
> Just as in the mechanism of a clock, so in the mechanism of the military machine, an impulse once given leads to the final result; and just as indifferently quiescent till the moment when motion is transmitted to them are the parts of the mechanism which the impulse has not yet reached. Wheels creak on their axles as the cogs engage one another and the revolving pulleys whirr with the rapidity of their movement, but a neighboring wheel is as quiet and motionless as though it were prepared to remain so for a hundred years, but the moment comes when the lever catches it and obeying the impulse that wheel begins to creak and joins in the common motion the result and aim of which are beyond its ken.

Just as in a clock, the result of the complicated motion of innumerable wheels and pulleys is merely a slow and regular movement of the hands which show the time, so the result of all the complicated human activities of 160,000 Russians and French—all their passions, desires, remorse, humiliations, sufferings, outbursts of pride, fear, and enthusiasm—was only the loss of the battle of Austerlitz, the so-called battle of the three Emperors—that is to say, a slow movement of the hand on the dial of human history.[8]

By simile's end, free will is denied to everyone, including Napoleon who is never said to have given any order to begin forming battle lines. There is no prime mover, no eighteenth-century clockmaker-God, for either the clock itself or for the Battle of Austerlitz; on "impulse" a clock lever turns and waiting military officers deploy. Highly individualized soldiers, Russian and French, whom we have seen exercising a modicum of free will, now function as cogs driven by an unseen mechanism. As the clock hands move, the figures on the clock "pop out" for their moment in time, but as quickly recede.

Tolstoy contradicts himself in assessing the rate of time. He entertains, but does not fully accept what Henry Adams was to call "The Law of Acceleration." At first we are told, "wheels revolve faster and faster," but later "the result is a slow and regular movement of the hands." The inconsistency has its perhaps intentional point. Time is by universal agreement measured by the artifice of regular intervals on a clock face, but time is experienced, especially during the Napoleonic era, as acceleration. And what will this particular passage of time eventually signify? The clock hands and troop movements of 1805, the epoch-making Battle of Austerlitz, will add up, in the end, merely to one slow movement of the hand on "the dial of human history," perhaps no more than a second of historical time.

Tolstoy's Second Epilogue explores the multicultural conundrum of fate and free will. If Tolstoy offers any firm conclusion, it is that free will exists only for limited decisions that affect the individual. As soon as an individual is regarded as an integral part of any group, the individual's ability to act becomes necessarily limited, his or her free will constrained. The wider one's perspective upon society and upon historical time, the less free will one can claim to exert. If so, then a metaphor generated by the smallest and most ordinary of objects could reveal the interworkings of fate and free will. Seeking conclusion through metaphor rather than abstract argument, Tolstoy devises an ironic variant of Isaac Newton's apple:

When an apple has ripened and falls, why does it fall? Because of its attraction to the earth, because its stalk withers, because it is dried by the sun, because it grows heavier, because the wind shakes it, or because the boy standing below wants to eat it?

Nothing is the cause. All this is only the coincidence of conditions in which all
vital organic and elemental events occur. (538)

Causes of even the smallest incident are so multifarious that "nothing is the
cause." Speculation about "the cause" of any and all events as complex as the
fall of a single apple is therefore ultimately unresolvable. Barred from proof
of causation, we can understand only "the coincidence of conditions," some
of which might be morally determined.

If one considers the metaphors of the tower clock and the apple together,
one can logically conclude that, though we might know how events occur,
we can never know why. Although one hesitates to assert that there can be
any reliably true assertion about the entirety of *War and Peace*, perhaps this
conclusion is as defensible as any. But it is a conclusion that none of Tolstoy's great predecessors in the writing of historical fiction—Scott, Cooper,
Pushkin, Dickens—would have been prepared to accept as valid. Scott would
never have been willing to conclude "Nothing is the cause," no matter how
fully he might have assented to the willed complexity with which Tolstoy
rendered historical forces.

As Marx, Lukacs, and Jameson all attest, the world of 1850 was no longer
the world of 1814. Just as *War and Peace* adapted the conventions of Scott's
form to a much wider historical canvas, so Tolstoy wrote with sweeping, self-
contradictory authority about relativistic universals. Deterministic assumptions about human conditioning were becoming hard to ignore: in biology,
organic evolution increasingly supplanted taxonomies of timeless species; in
political thought, the recognized importance of economic forces increasingly
supplanted the proclaimed justice of contractual agreements. In the historical novel, Victor Hugo embodies these shifts. His youthful belief that God's
covenantal rainbow assured civilization's progress after the cataclysm of
revolution was proving hard to sustain.

After supporting Louis Napoleon as successor to Louis Philippe in an 1847
speech before the House of Peers, Hugo's apartment was invaded and he was
temporarily apprehended. As a member of the Académie Francaise and the
National Assembly, Hugo was as distressed by the total breakdown of law
and order into street barricades, as he was by the impoverished living conditions of the working class of Paris. However, Hugo's hope that the second
Emperor Napoleon might lessen class resentments while advancing freedom
of speech and universal suffrage did not long survive. When Louis Napoleon
ordered the National Assembly to be occupied by troops, then dismissed his
entire cabinet, Hugo denounced him. By 1852 Hugo was forced into hiding,
and thence into exile, neither of which silenced his opposition.

After eighteen years of exile in the Channel Islands, this pattern of hope,
disappointment, revolt, and exile was to be essentially repeated. Returning

to Paris at the outset of the Third Republic, Hugo tried to arouse French resistance against the encircling Prussian Army. He also strove to support the quasi-socialist aims of the Commune, which he called "an admirable thing stupidly compromised by five or six deplorable ringleaders."[9] Like Karl Marx, Hugo denounced the impending bloody suppression of the Commune by Thiers's "Party of Order," only to be exiled again, this time from Belgium. Calling for amnesty, Hugo returned to Paris, where he encountered a virtual police state, prompting him to leave France once again, returning for two years to Guernsey (1872–1874). *Notre Dame De Paris* and *Les Miserables* were now a decade or more behind him, there were not many years ahead, and his novel on the French Revolution had not yet been written.

To convey a heightened sense of determinism, Hugo's *1793* contrasts static visual symbols with flexible animated metaphors. The crises of Hugo's narrative develop around two symbolic structures, one representing the *Ancien Regime*, the other the Revolution. Royalist insurrectionary forces in the Vendeé defend a massive medieval tower, La Tourgue, against Republican battalions sent from Paris to pacify the region. The Republican forces carry with them a guillotine, which they assemble to dispense justice. At the end of an extended siege, the Marquis de Lantenac, who owns La Tourgue, and his grandnephew Gauvin, who commands the Republican battalions, both embrace execution on the guillotine rather than sacrifice either their beliefs or the honor of their word.

Hugo finds much to denounce, little to praise, in the kinds of social justice that the tower and the guillotine represent. In the last chapter, the two structures are juxtaposed as equally inhuman creations:

> Between the two wooden beams was a square basket. The monster was painted red. The whole was made of wood except the triangle—that was iron. One would have known the thing must have been constructed by man, it was so ugly and evil-looking; at the same time it was so formidable that it might have been reared there by evil genii. This shapeless thing was the guillotine.
>
> In front of it, a few paces off, another monster rose out of the ravine. La Tourgue—a monster of stone rising up to hold companionship with the monster of wood. . . . In La Tourgue were condensed fifteen hundred years (The Middle Age), vassalage, servitude, feudality; in the guillotine one year—'93; and these twelve months made a counterpoise to those fifteen centuries.[10]

Although Hugo ascribes the word "heroic" to the valor and the integrity of both the Marquis de Lantenac and Gauvin, the opposed times they represent are not worthy of their self-sacrifice. No human civilization can evolve from either structure. Cimourdain, the lapsed priest turned Republican judge, whose idealism seems modeled on Robespierre, shoots himself only after he mercilessly condemns his beloved former student Gauvin to death. At novel's end, the reader can only assume that commitment to the monstrous structures built by civilization cannot promote individual human virtue.

The tower and the guillotine are blatant symbols that stand motionless in temporal opposition but underlying similarity to one another. The extended metaphor Hugo introduces at the beginning of the novel provides a more searching and original paradigm for revolution—apparently any revolution—as nature's law of seemingly aimless destruction carried out by man's machines. Embarking from England for Brittany in an armed corvette in order to further the counterrevolution, the Marquis de Lantenac observes a twenty-four-pound cannon, loose of all its moorings, destroying everything in its path as his ship lurches back and forth in the waves:

> A gun that breaks through its moorings becomes suddenly some indescribable supernatural beast. It is a machine which transforms itself into a monster. This mass turns upon its wheels, has the rapid movements of a billiard-ball; rolls with the rolling, pitches with the pitching; goes, comes, pauses, seems to meditate; resumes its course, rushes along the ship from end to end like an arrow, circles about, springs aside, evades, rears, breaks, kills, exterminates. It is a battering ram which assaults a wall at its own caprice. Moreover, the battering ram is metal, the wall wood. It is the entrance of matter into liberty. One might say that this eternal slave avenges itself. It seems as if the power of evil hidden in what we call inanimate objects finds a vent and bursts suddenly out. It has an air of having lost patience, of seeking some fierce obscure retribution; nothing more inexorable than this rage of the inanimate. (27)

Revolution and war are here inseparable; the gun that is meant to defend you, destroys you. As humans become machines, machines become human. The motions of the cannon are as jerky, violent, insane, and seemingly random as the motions of Dickens's carmagnole. The essence of Terror is neither guillotine nor tower; it is the surreal process by which man creates machines for revolution, or for counterrevolution. Such machines unmoor evil itself. The motion of the cannon, unlike the tower or even the guillotine, leaves man helpless; the sailors are indeed witnessing "the entrance of matter into liberty."

Unlike Tolstoy, Hugo identifies the prime mover behind the accelerating wreckage and death. It is the inexorable surge of the sea, an implacable natural force determining every movement of man's seemingly complicit weaponry: "the horrible cannon flings itself about, advances, recoils, strikes to the right, strikes to the left, flees, passes, disconcerts, ambushes, breaks down obstacles, crushes men like flies" (28). The monstrous cannon is eventually stilled, but Hugo provides little consolation, certainly nothing suggesting peace or promise. The surging sea does not recede. With Lantenac's assistance, a gunner inserts an iron bar between the spokes of one of the cannon's wheels, bringing it finally to a halt. Because the gunner's negligence was responsible for the cannon's unmooring, Lantenac promptly orders the gunner to be shot—a decision in which human justice maintains cannon justice. Peace and promise, rainbow's end, are evidently to be achieved only in some kind of afterlife. Cimourdain's suicide after condemning Gauvin to the guillotine implies that human justice, be it military, revolutionary, or a combination of both, must be transcended. The novel's last lines, describing the simultaneous deaths of the two republicans Cimourdain and Gauvin, imply that, although revolution provides no earthly redemption, honorable self-sacrifice earns true sanctity elsewhere. "And those two souls, united still in that tragic death, soared away together, the shadow of the one mingled with the radiance of the other" (390). Hugo, however, offers no conjecture about the destination to which the two true souls are soaring. If heaven is the effective metaphor for the kind of justice that will transcend 1793, Hugo is unwilling to reify its existence.

Like Hugo's *1793,* Anatole France's *The Gods Will Have Blood* (1912) is a late life novel by a public intellectual who had supported practicable measures many liberals had been advocating since the 1789 Revolution: universal adult suffrage, universal free education, and expanding the rights of labor. The existence of Hugo's *1793* is, however, never acknowledged in Anatole France's text; his silence about Hugo's novel acknowledges distance and implies criticism. Noble, self-sacrificial deaths are as conspicuously absent in *The Gods Will Have Blood* as are the acts of physical heroism so prevalent in *1793.* Practicable progressive measures are of little concern to Anatole France's revolutionaries; for them the honor of suicide is not even a consideration. Instead, Anatole France's novel, initially titled *Evariste Gamelin,* is a masterful study of a young revolutionary's descent into fanaticism during the later months of 1793. The irresistible twin forces of sexual desire and the thrill of judicial sentencing subvert Evariste's adolescent sensitivity to human suffering and his youthful faith in liberty and equality. By easy, unforeseen stages, Gamelin's republican idealism, proclaimed as virtue, leads him to bribery, false witness, political assassination, and sadomasochistic lust.[11]

As Evariste descends from boyhood compassion, to youthful republican idealism, to adulation of Marat and Robespierre, and finally into a need to kill the Republic's enemies anywhere, his embrace of Terror is rendered through seemingly incongruous metaphors drawn from the worlds of painting and artisanry. As an art student in 1789, Gamelin has learned to scorn the presumably outmoded paintings of Watteau, Boucher, and Fragonard; he associates all three, simplistically, with the corrupt wealth of a weak, feminized aristocracy. Conversely, his enthusiasm for the paintings of Jacques Louis David derives from his yearning to be seen making masculine gestures of heroic virtue that are both Roman and Republican. In the meanwhile, Citizen Jean

Blaise, owner of a print shop who knows the realities of the art market, warns Evariste that images that readily sell now have titles like "The Undressed Nun"; David's print designs for the Republic's Fetes will soon become scrap paper drawn over by other art students once the revolution collapses.

Evariste's ambitions as a creative artist are focused on two contrasting paintings. *The Tyrant Pursued to Hades by the Furies* is his bid for revolutionary fame, an immense canvas portraying a tyrant of the *Ancien Regime* driven into hell, a canvas that he has neither the money nor the inner resources to complete. His second canvas, also based on neoclassic reference, is its authentic, intimate opposite:

> There was far more of genius and originality in a canvas of smaller dimensions, also unfinished, which hung in the best-lit corner of the studio. It was of Orestes, whom his sister Electra was holding in her arms on his bed of pain. The girl was putting back with a moving tenderness the matted hair that hung over her brother's eyes. The head of the hero was tragic and fine and in it was a marked resemblance to the painter's [Gamelin's] own face.[12]

By novel's end, the words "tragic and fine" accumulate multiple ironies. As a magistrate passing judgments for the Paris Commune, Evariste's face becomes distorted with the painful pleasures of sentencing the presumed enemies of the Republic to death. The painting serves as a metaphor for judicial process: Electra and Orestes provide the mythic parallels that will reveal it. The Electra of Evariste's life, his sister Julie, will spit on him with hatred, calling him "Cain" and a "Monster" because he has sentenced her émigré lover to death as a *ci-devant* aristocrat (216). On three occasions we see Evariste held in a woman's arms on his "bed of pain," but he is not held there by his sister. Evariste and his lover Elodie, the art shop owner's daughter, derive sexual pleasure from savage intercourse that becomes increasingly bloody as Evariste's political sentencings become ever more compulsive. Sexual perversion and political terror merge. The Tyrant pursued by the Furies proves not to be, as Evariste had anticipated, a nobleman of the *Ancien Regime*, but Evariste himself, who never understands what he has wrought in his two paintings.

Aware that his creative paintings are unsalable, Evariste's need for money to support himself and his mother leads him to design packs of playing cards that will, like the new revolutionary calendar, alter the way days are counted and sums reckoned. Evariste describes the virtues of his project:

> Our playing-cards are a disgraceful contrast to the new order. The very names of king and knave offend patriots' ears. I've planned and designed a pack of new Revolutionary playing-cards in which kings, queens and knaves are replaced by Liberties, Equalities and Fraternities. The aces are called Laws. When a player makes his call he says Liberty of clubs, Equality of spades, Fraternity of diamonds (51).

The new revolutionary cards may all be named, but what are the rules of the game? All we know, metaphorically, is that Laws (Aces) will trump Liberty (Kings), Liberty (Kings) will trump Equality (Queens), and Equality (Queens) will trump Fraternity (Jacks-Knaves-Fraternities). The new card pack does not eliminate the underlying and controlling principles of hierarchy and capture. Equality is subject to Liberty just as Queens are to Kings; Evariste submits to Elodie's sexuality, just as Jacks and Knaves submit to Queens. Blaise informs Evariste that three other proposals for revolutionary playing cards have already failed commercially. Almost a year before Thermidor, Blaise rightly senses that "nobody cares a damn anymore about the Revolution; everybody's sick to death with the sound of the word" (52).

Evariste's playing cards reverse the usual function of metaphor; instead of inanimate objects becoming alive, revolutionary ideals become inanimate cards. As metaphors, the cards in Evariste's pack are the opposite of Brotteaux's hand-carved marionettes, just as Brotteaux, an aged, kindly, disillusioned aristocrat, serves as the foil to Evariste himself. Convinced that revolutionary politics is folly, Brotteaux judges life according to the pursuit of pleasure (including acts of kindness) and the avoidance of pain (including acts of injustice). Brotteaux survives by fashioning sets of marionettes and selling them to shop owners and street peddlers. His marionettes are his pointed but silent dramatization of the insane and absurd revolutionary world he sees about him. The revolutionaries themselves cannot decode that world. Marat, Robespierre, and Evariste Gamelin, convinced of their own free will and the importance of their actions, cannot read the meaning of the street play that Brotteaux's marionettes perform before them.

Although Anatole France repeatedly describes the making of the marionettes, their faces remain unseen. There is nothing of the *roman a clef* here, no guessing as to whom the historical models for Ace Laws and King Liberty might be. Instead, all revolutionaries—perhaps all of mankind—are to be seen as puppets manipulated by unseen forces, possibly by a God or at least by sardonic artist-creators like Brotteaux and Anatole France. Understanding and self-control come through historical perspective, through Brotteaux's reading of his beloved Lucretius, but not through today's puppet revolutionaries, nor today's trumped cards.

Shortly after Gamelin acquires the power of passing sentence upon enemies of the Republic, Brotteaux reveals that his trade has become politically dangerous: "A member of the Committee of Safety of the Section inspected my shop yesterday, and when he saw our dancing dolls he declared they were anti-revolutionary. . . He said our little dolls insidiously mocked at the National representatives. In particular, you had caricatured Couthon, Saint-Just and Robespierre and he seized the lot" (138). Brotteaux denies that he has had any specific persons in mind. Knowing that the Republic's functionaries believe traditional popular entertainments to be contemptible, he craftily replies that the government surely will recognize that his "masks and "faces" are but figures from *Commedia del Arte*, merely "these Harlequins, these Scaramouches, these Colins and Colinettes and Zerlinas" (138). In fact, the dancing dolls ironically are "anti-revolutionary"; theirs is an unchanging world of timeless charm, and timeless folly. Brotteaux is particularly fond of fashioning the doll Scaramouche because Scaramouche reminds him of arrogant lawyers dressed in black who strut about giving longwinded speeches.

Among many mechanistic metaphors conveying the accelerating journey toward modernity, none was as important as the railroad. Walt Whitman, Leo Tolstoy, Emile Zola, Frank Norris, André Gide, and Henry Adams among writers; Turner, Monet, De Chirico, and Magritte among painters; W.H. Jackson and Alfred Stieglitz among photographers; Currier and Ives in popular print culture, all testified to the railroad's centrality. In the main, the railroad was seen as a nearly irresistible deterministic force bringing to the twentieth century speed, connectivity and energy, movement for all, ease and wealth for some, labor and poverty for many. Renderings of the railroad are simultaneously foreboding and celebratory; as Thoreau predicted, the railroad may run you over, but it also releases possibility. Among the legendary events of the onset of the Russian Revolution in 1917 were: the stopping of Tsar Nicholas's army-inspection train and the imprisoning of the royal family; Lenin's secret arrival in St, Petersburg via sealed, armored train from Switzerland; the Bolsheviks' seizure of Moscow's railroad stations before the forced disbanding of Kerensky's Constituent Assembly. The railroad was rightly perceived to be the fulcrum of power.

Except for the months of Yurii Zhivago's forced service in the Forest Brotherhood, and his few months of retreat with Lara to the rural peace of Varykino, the railroad remains a constant presence in his life. As a ten-year-old boy, Yurii hears the "plaintive hooting of engines" while brooding over his mother's death.[13] The narrative of *Doctor Zhivago* begins when Yurii's penniless, dissolute father throws himself to death from an express train. Pasternak precedes his short account of the killings of Bloody Sunday 1905 with a long account of the Moscow railroad strike in which wages, job security, sabotage, and corrupt contracting were bitterly contested. On Yurii Zhivago's way to and fro the Austrian Front in 1914, and again when he departs for Yuriatin, he describes the confusing disorder of track-sides and stations where conscripts, volunteers, officers, officials, peasants, merchants, and entire families wait, seemingly endlessly, to discover whether and when they might board a train. Commissar Komarovsky's psychosexual power over Lara continues until novel's end, when his special train arrives ominously at Varykino, waiting for him on a siding until Komarovsky can take Lara half unwillingly to Vladivostok, away from Zhivago forever. Zhivago suffers his fatal heart attack while waiting in a stifling, broken-down Moscow trolley car, a demeaning end for a man of great ability and high humanitarian values. The novel's longest single description of railroads is of locomotives that no longer work. As inflation soars, the economy flounders, and the civil war begins, Zhivago looks out over the train yards near Yuriatin:

> At the end of the tracks there was a large graveyard for old engines. Locomotives without tenders, with smokestacks shaped like the tops of knee boots or like beakers, stood smokestack to smokestack amid piles of scrap.
> The engine graveyard below and the human graveyard above, the crumpled iron on the tracks and the rusty iron of the roofs and shop signs of the suburb, composed a single picture of neglect and age under the white sky scalded by the early morning heat. (247)

Pasternak here visualizes a human graveyard beyond a graveyard of locomotive engines. Together they "comprised a single picture." The great hope of progress Zhivago had momentarily associated with the Bolsheviks ("the revolution broke out willy-nilly, like a sigh suppressed too long. Everyone was revived, reborn, changed, transformed" [146]) has turned into "a single picture of neglect and age." As a metaphor of the mechanical motion that underlies history, Pasternak's railroad highlights breakdown and dysfunction, not the implacable continuance immanent in Hugo's cataract, Dickens's carmagnole, and Tolstoy's clock.

The failed promise of the revolutionary engine intensifies the rapidity with which Bolshevik Communism falls into civil war. Vivid descriptions of the beauty of meadows, forests, and rivers alternate with images of run-down tenements and graveyard devastation, suggesting that the revolution is being fueled and betrayed by class envy (not classlessness) and by divisive politicians of every stripe, especially by politicians in CHEKA, the Forest Brotherhood, and the Communist Party. The horror of the Civil War is therefore at the forefront of the novel rather than Lenin, Kerensky, or the latest party policy sent from Moscow. While Yurii Zhivago, always on the periphery of historical events, trudges across central Russia, trying to avoid Reds, Whites, and Greens during the Civil War, the metaphoric meaning of the railroad seems everywhere before him. He passes abandoned train after abandoned train, buried in snowdrifts and empty of fuel, now serving "as strongholds for armed bands of highwaymen or as hideouts for escaping criminals or political fugitives" (378).

As Zhivago returns by train from the western front to Moscow in 1917, he recalls how "three years of changes, moves, uncertainties, upheavals; the war, the revolution; scenes of destruction, scenes of death, shelling, blown up bridges, fires, ruins—all this turned suddenly into a huge empty meaningless space" (174). His past disappears into a void, leading him to hope that a new reality awaits: "the first real event since the long interruption was this trip in the fast-moving train, the fact that he was approaching his home, which was intact, which still existed" (174). Although he momentarily associates the train with restoration of home and family, his experiences with Bolsheviks and the Forest Brotherhood soon persuade him that the revolutionaries believe otherwise: "It turns out that those who inspired the revolution aren't at home in anything except change and turmoil, they aren't happy with anything that's on less than a world scale. For them transitional periods, worlds in the making, are an end in themselves" (296–297). Revolution has no final station; it is fueled by nonexistent ideals formulated in abstractions never reified in people or things tangible. The only recourse for revolutionaries is therefore to drive engines to their wreckage.

Throughout the novel, Pasternak maintains a counterpoint between the two admirable, flawed men who love Lara: Yurii Zhivago and Pasha Antipov. Although Antipov is a "non-Party man," distrustful of all bureaucracy (250), his commitment to the Marxist critique of capitalism is absolute, even though the end of proletarian revolution remains unclear to him. Antipov first discovers that he must abandon his unsatisfactory marriage to Lara, join the Russian army, and then the Russian revolution, when he sits at night on an overturned boat, gazing at the stars. A "harsh darting light" suddenly inspires what he believes to be an epiphany: "An army train, puffing clouds of yellow, flame-shot smoke into the sky, rolled over the grade crossing going westward. . . . [Antipov] smiled, got up, and went to bed. He had found a way out of his dilemma" (108). Bent on following the moving light, Antipov is oblivious to the fact that his commitment to a new life will bind him to the iron rails of revolution.

When Antipov again enters Zhivago's life, Antipov has become a public figure under the name Strelnikov ("the Shooter"), also nicknamed Razstrelnikov ("the Executioner") (250). Although Strelnikov is a member of neither the Red army nor the Bolshevik party, he commands an express train that travels the rails at will, shelling and razing any town that opposes Bolshevik control (250). When Zhivago, who had left the Russian army as it was disintegrating, is apprehended by Strelnikov, Strelnikov sees Zhivago as a "deserter" and a sentimentalist, at a time when "sympathizers and loyal doctors" have become especially suspect. Zhivago in turn concludes, "this man [Strelnikov] was entirely a manifestation of the will" (248). Unaware that Strelnikov is Lara's husband, Zhivago turns his recent encounter with Strelnikov into a metaphor for the nature of a revolutionary. Zhivago tells Lara: "He [Strelnikov] is a doomed man. I believe that he'll come to a bad end. He will atone for the evil he has done. Revolutionaries who take the law into their own hands are horrifying not because they are criminals, but because they are like machines that have got out of control, like runaway trains" (296). The train metaphor, now a simile, does double duty: always within the rails of Bolshevik ideology, Strelnikov's train is nonetheless "out of control."

Strelnikov's express train, the derelict locomotive engines, and the abandoned conscript trains are three seeming opposites that come to the same destructive end. Train journeys are either off schedule or without schedule. Long slow trains are brought to frequent halt by a range of causes natural, mechanical, and political. In scenes that eerily prefigure World War II, Russians of various classes and occupations are herded together into boxcars, guarded by soldiers whose most important duty is to keep the deeply resentful labor conscripts under the tightest possible control. The railroad captures and encapsulates Pasternak's view of twentieth-century Russian history: a revolutionary journey into nowhere, at once tedious, deadly, and directionless.

THE RELEASE OF METAPHOR

Cataract, carmagnole, clock, apple, loose cannon, playing cards, puppets, and railroad, not one of these metaphors for revolution allows controlling power to individual free will. Except for the cataract, all imply that progress is an illusion lost to the forces of chance, mechanization, and directionless energy. To have selected them for unwilling emphasis is to release counter-progressive assumptions about the course of history.

The importance of these metaphors is not that they are effective in their context (they certainly are) but that they are not representative of the entirety of the novels in which they are imbedded. Dickens, Tolstoy, and Hugo develop their metaphors in one passage only; their novels struggle toward, and arrive at, final affirmations, as befits Scott's legacy. Anatole France and Pasternak elaborate their metaphors into virtual conceits, but neither author risks concluding generalizations about the future. The larger narrative scheme of the novels, in almost every instance, reflects the authors' intent to convey a balanced view of the prospects for social and political progress. The dark, deterministic nature of the metaphors thus suggests that the metaphors were suddenly conceived at moments when the author's pen was driven by a need to release suppressed doubts and fears. In some of the passages, those by Dickens and Hugo particularly, the need for release seems so strong that the rendering of the metaphor becomes a sardonic act of disgorgement. The power of such metaphoric expression is, in all likelihood, a reflection of the authors' awareness that longstanding hopes of republican revolution have not been fulfilled in the world around them, while conditions of Terror have periodically recurred.

If we assume that historical novelists develop such metaphors as a release from verisimilitude, we may presume that, using Denis Donoghue's terms, the metaphors serve the purpose of imaginative "revelation," however temporary. For the nineteenth-century historical novelist, there is a grid of responsibility that wills the emergence of progress, but there is also an underlying distrust that subverts any enlightened end to time's journey. Because Scott initiates the paradox, the literary conventions that form his legacy lead the reader to mistrust historical clichés in which the *Ancien Regime*, followed by revolutionary liberty, followed by republican politics, together demonstrate the progressive advance of civilization. Scott's legacy, I contend, is defined by a political moderation based upon such mistrust.

A note on the metaphor that provides the epigraph for this book: We cannot now know whether Simon Bolivar's legendary deathbed words, highlighted in Marquez's *The General in His Labyrinth*, truly were "those who serve revolution plough the sea." We do know that these words appear verbatim in one of Bolivar's last letters in which he is striving to convey the meaning of his life.[14] As rendered in English, "ploughing the sea" subsumes the dead nautical metaphor "ploughing the waves" but turns it into a superb image of futility. To plough a field enables one to harvest within boundaries and visible markers. To plough the sea is to progress nowhere within a world lacking limit or definition. No wonder Bolivar's metaphor has proven memorable; it exactly suits the underside of nineteenth- and twentieth-century expectations.

NOTES

1. Samuel Taylor Coleridge, *The Friend*, ed. Barbara E. Brooke (Princeton: Princeton University Press, 1969, II, 280). Coleridge's familiar distinction between the Primary and Secondary Imagination in the *Biographia Literaria* illuminates the difference between metaphor's function as imaginative recreation and its function in revealing congruent qualities. In our time, Paul Ricoeur's *The Rule of Metaphor* has emphasized the imaginative power of metaphor in philosophic terms. Ricoeur argues that metaphor creates a "new predicative meaning which emerges from the collapse of the literal meaning" ("The Metaphorical Process as Cognition, Imagination and Feeling" in *On Metaphor*, ed. Sheldon Sacks [Chicago: University of Chicago, 1978], p. 144).

2. Denis Donoghue, *Metaphor* (Cambridge: Harvard University Press, 2014), p. 86.

3. Walter Scott, *The Life of Napoleon Buonaparte, Emperor of the French with a Preliminary View of the French Revolution* (Philadelphia: Carey, Lea & Carey, 1827), I, 17.

4. Victor Hugo, "The French Revolution" (1844) in *Victor Hugo's Intellectual Autobiography: Postscriptum de Ma Vie, Being Late Uncollected Works*, translated by

Lorenzo O'Rourke (New York: Haskell House, 1971), 222–229. Originally published 1907.

5. Umberto Eco, "Excess and History in Hugo's *Ninety-Three*" in *The Novel: Forms and Themes*, ed. Franco Moretti (Princeton: Princeton University Press, 2006) II, 274.

6. Charles Dickens, *A Tale of Two Cities*, edited with an introduction by Richard Maxwell (New York: Penguin Books, 2003), 3–4.

7. Lynn Hunt, *Politics, Culture and Class in the French Revolution* (Berkeley: University of California Press, 1984).

8. Leo Tolstoy, *War and Peace*, The Maude Translation, 2nd edition, (New York: W.W. Norton & Co, 1966), 223–224.

9. Graham Robb, *Victor Hugo* (New York: W.W. Norton & Co., 1997), 465.

10. Victor Hugo, *Quatrevingt-treize (Ninety Three)*, translated by Frank Lee Benedict, Introduction by Graham Robb, 2nd edition (New York: Carroll & Graf, 1998), 384.

11. Harry Shaw acknowledges that Anatole France "gives some sense of the larger historical processes at work during the period," then immediately counters "but he depicts public life and historical process only to show their unimportance" (*The Forms of Historical Fiction: Sir Walter Scott and His Successors*, 103). I do not share Shaw's dismissive judgment. Revolutionary values remain important in Anatole France's novel even though they are betrayed during the Terror. Liberty and Equality are being lost amid the corrosive rationalizations of animal desire.

12. Anatole France, *The Gods Will Have Blood (Les Dieux Ont Soif)*, translated with an Introduction by Frederick Davies (New York: Penguin Books, 2004), 36.

13. Boris Pasternak, *Doctor Zhivago*, translated by Max Hayward and Manya Harari, Introduction by John Bailey (New York: Pantheon Books, 1991), 4.

14. Simon Bolivar, letter to General Juan José Flores, November 9, 1830 in *El Libertador: Writings of Simon Bolivar*, translated by Frederick Fornoff, edited by David Bushnell (Oxford: Oxford University Press, 2003), p. 146.

Chapter 2

Scott

The Totality of History

"The only writer since the restoration of the Bourbons who has enjoyed a really popular success is Sir Walter Scott."

—Stendhal, "Scott's Appeal to the French Public," *New Monthly Magazine* (1825)

"In ten years time, the reputation of the Scottish novelist will have declined by half."

—Stendhal, "Walter Scott and La Princesse de Cleves," *Le National* (1830)

"Sir Walter Scott, as all the world knows, was the inventor of the historical romance. . . . The effect of *Waverley* was like the sun bursting through the clouds or like the invention of gunpowder or steam. . . . Certain it is that the historical romance is more popular, and embraces a much wider circle of readers, than either *The Iliad* or the *Paradise Lost*."

—Archibald Alison, "The Historical Romance," *Blackwoods Magazine* (1845)

Archibald Alison's tribute shows that Stendhal's dismissal of Scott's continuing popularity had been decidedly premature. In fact, the Waverley Novels were to retain their resonance, edition after edition, translation after translation, surviving bowdlerization into adolescent fiction, and the ridicule of William Hazlitt and Mark Twain, until the very end of the century. The onset of modernism, however, caused a steep decline in Scott's reputation. The modernist demand for concision and implied meaning, modernist predilection for psychological interiority, and modernist distrust of narrative omniscience were to transform the Waverley Novels from a shelf of beloved books into an anachronism blocking the growth of twentieth-century literary art.[1]

Only eight years after Henry James famously described the historical novels of Thackeray, Dumas, and Tolstoy as "loose baggy monsters, with . . . queer elements of the accidental and the arbitrary,"[2] Joyce published *A Portrait of the Artist as a Young Man* (1916), which would for at least the next fifty years be read and taught as the prototype of the modernist novel that had finally blown away Victorian moralistic prolixity. Now that the modernist era is behind us, we may reverse the viewpoint and inquire what Walter Scott might have thought of Joyce's *Portrait*. The Waverley Novels show Scott to have been, like Joyce, well aware of the dangers of parochial nationalism, the folly of a disintegrating family's pride, and the divisive absolutes of institutional religion. But Stephen Dedalus's concluding dismissal of nation, family, and religion would surely have led Scott to wonder whether Stephen had achieved any degree of true maturity, or had only regressed further into adolescent rebellion. Were "silence, exile and cunning" sufficiently constructive inner responses to the corrupting complexities of the twentieth century?[3] How exactly was Stephen Dedalus—or James Joyce—to "forge in the smithy of my soul the uncreated conscience of my race" merely by expatriating from Ireland to Paris or Trieste? (276). Was the prospect of becoming "the artist" enough to fulfill the lifetime responsibilities of man and author? Vivid though Stephen's memories of family life and education might be, was there not something self-indulgent, indeed prolix, about the way Stephen's singular perspective is privileged by Joyce's new narrative techniques?

PROTOTYPE: A MOSAIC

Scott had pursued entirely different aims. As Walter Bagehot observed, Scott's greatness lies in his ability to render the totality of an historical age without resorting to any single historical thesis or any moral dogma.[4] At their best, Scott's novels seem to unfold into the next open page, enabling the narrator to entertain diverse judgments for the sake of the widest possible historical totality. No character's viewpoint is privileged; villains are as rare as heroes. Characters are both self-determined and historically conditioned. No character is self-sufficient; none can convincingly place the blame for his or her failings on society's institutions. An individual's qualities are measured in a wide historical and social context, not according to any personal moral or aesthetic system. Expatriation, as the lives of Flora MacIvor, Henry Morton, Effie Deans, and Markham Everard all attest, proves a dead-end unless it is temporary. The influences of family, class, religion, and nation are not escapable; they shape one's continuing identity.

Consequently, a Waverley novel is a mosaic, its adjacent pieces often jux-taposed, but convincing and memorable when viewed as a whole and from a temporal distance. The immediacy of effect achieved by Joyce or Faulkner is alien to it. Scott achieves in narrative fiction what later narrative histori-ans, influenced by Scott, would attempt through comprehensive research: to render the essence of an era, at a time when the pieces of the past can serve to clarify past and present simultaneously.[5] Unfortunately, too many readers, attuned to twentieth-century fictional technique (prose in the Hemingway tradition), are prone to give up on a Scott novel, before the filling in of the mosaic becomes discernible.

Neither in Scott's prefaces nor his occasional essays did he define or defend his particular kind of fiction. Any hypothetical distinction between "The Historical Romance" and "The Historical Novel," a distinction that would become a lasting twentieth-century scholarly concern, did not interest him, in part because in Scott's era the two terms were used interchangeably.[6] We must turn to his fictions themselves, especially to Scott's early master-pieces, for guides to his deeper intent. In an early chapter of *Waverley*, Scott considers, in a half-facetious, Fielding-esque manner, whether his readers, especially his women readers, may not be disconcerted, even repelled, by the seeming intrusion of history into fiction:

> I beg pardon, once and for all, of those readers who take up novels merely for amusement, for plaguing them so long with old-fashioned politics, and Whig and Tory, and Hanoverians and Jacobites. The truth is, I cannot promise them that this story shall be intelligible, not to say probable, without it. My plan requires that I should explain the motives on which its action proceeded; and these motives necessarily arose from the feelings, prejudices, and parties of the times. I do not invite my fair readers, whose sex and impatience give them the greatest right to complain of these circumstances, into a flying chariot drawn by hippogriffs, or moved by enchantment. Mine is an humble English post-chaise, drawn upon four wheels, and keeping his Majesty's highway.[7]

A prototype for Scott's historical novel is being established here. During any time of crisis (in *Waverley*, the '45 Jacobite rebellion), no rendering of men's motives and actions could be either "intelligible" or "probable," without due consideration of the "feelings, prejudices, and parties of the times." From a flying chariot, one sees nothing; from a slow-moving post chaise, one can see both the parts and the entirety of the landscape. The politics to be detailed may now seem "old fashioned," but their consequences have proven to be as long-lasting and as vital as the terms "Whig and Tory"—that is, not "old fashioned" at all.

To extend and oversimplify only slightly, Scott is here outlining a literary form in which the fictional narrative, built upon romance conventions involv-ing the dangers of warfare and the complications of courtship, is imbedded in an historical context centered upon political revolution. The romance (marital property settlements) affects the outcome of history; the political history affects, if not determines, the course of the romance. To make his new kind of hybrid intelligible, Scott's fair reader must understand the "Whig and Tory" aspects of the narrative; the male reader must understand that, even in a crisis, there is a complex daily world beyond war, politics, and money.[8] To understand Scott as an historical realist is, therefore, necessary to any full understanding of his achievement.[9]

Near the end of *Waverley*, Scott offers a very different metaphor for the pace of his narrative:

> I must remind my reader of the progress of a stone rolled down hill by an idle truant boy; . . . it moves at first slowly, avoiding by inflection every obstacle of the least importance; but when it has attained its full impulse, and draws near the conclusion of its career, it smokes and thunders down, taking a rood at every spring, clearing hedge and ditch like a Yorkshire huntsman, and becoming most furiously rapid in its course when it is nearest to being consigned to rest for ever. Even such is the course of a narrative like that which you are perusing. (480)

Although the sense of gathering historical forces intensifies as we read Scott's best novels, the unity and acceleration he sought proved difficult to attain. As Scott acknowledged in his prefaces, the connective details between history and fiction too often expanded before him, sometimes requiring an overhasty tying up of loose threads.

The underlying problem lay in the accumulating totality of the historical context itself. The pieces of the mosaic sometimes expanded beyond coherence and beyond control, much like the contradictions in the history they were recreating. Too often Scott would then try to make marital endings somehow validate a progressive future. But when the ending comes coherently together, when fiction and history coalesce, whether in "progress," compromise or decline, as in the endings of *Waverley, Rob Roy, The Bride of Lammermoor, The Heart of Mid-lothian and Woodstock*, the reader of the 1820s knew he or she was being taken on a new and impressive kind of journey.

The narrative frame of *Old Mortality* provides insight into Scott's response to the charge of antiquarianism often used to discredit his historicism as window dressing. Beyond serving as a *memento mori* (nearly all the major characters die by novel's end), Scott's title serves as a justification for what the historical novelist does. Robert Paterson, legendized as "Old Mortality," has devoted his life to cleaning and repairing the neglected tombstones of the "Whig Martyrs," the Covenanters who had been tortured, or died in battle, at the hands of the Royalists during the Killing Times of 1679. Like the novel named for him, Old Mortality restores to visibility the tombstones of history. He pursues his restorative craft with unflagging belief that a better understanding of history, if not moral benefit, will derive from making the

Covenanters' tombstones visible. His trade thus conveys a silent rebuke to all who would forget the past in order to live in a presumably better future. There is dignity, death, and perhaps futility in Old Mortality's restoration of the past, but there is nothing quaint about it.[10]

A neglected quotation from Scott's reviews demonstrates the seriousness of his intent to write fictions that clean the tombstones of history. In an 1826 review of John Galt's *The Omen*, Scott seems to subsume his own novels, together with those of Galt and James Hogg, within one general statement:

> Historical novels may operate advantageously on the mind of two classes of readers; first, upon those whose attention to history is awakened by the fictitious narrative, and whom curiosity stimulates to study, for the purpose of winnowing the wheat from the chaff, the true from the fabulous. Secondly, those who are too idle to read, save for the purpose of amusement, may in these works acquire some acquaintance with history, which, however inaccurate, is better than none.[11]

By separating "the true from the fabulous," the historical novel redeems the novel as a genre from the old charge of providing mere entertainment. Romance and history work together to provide the "amusement" the reading public needs, but the lasting significance of the historical novelist's created world is ultimately historical.[12]

Seeking in a different way to set "amusement" aside, Coleridge fastened upon a political and historical explanation of Scott's fame. The Waverley Novels show us why the western world must long continue to view the French Revolution as the watershed of history:

> The essential wisdom of his [Scott's] subject lies in this,—that the contest between the loyalists and their opponents can never be *obsolete*, for it is the contest between the two great moving principles of social humanity; religious adherence to the past and the ancient, the desire and the admiration of perma- nence, on the one hand; and the passion for increase of knowledge, for truth, as the offspring of reason—in short the mighty instincts of *progression* and *free agency* on the other. In all subjects of deep and lasting interest, you will detect a struggle between two opposites, two polar forces, both of which are alike nec- essary to our human well-being, and necessary each to the continued existence of the other.[13]

Coleridge's claim for Scott is, in the most general sense, accurate. Scott often thought in terms of these two polar forces, identifying them with the Old Order and the New. Moreover, Coleridge's Hegelian sentences substantiate Georg Lukacs's claim that the French Revolution had created, for western man, a new awareness of the passing of time. But as a guide to the ways in which Scott renders the particular historical moment of crisis in any of the Scottish Waverley Novels, Coleridge's tidy dualism proves misleading.

In Scott's novels concerned with revolutionary change, conflicts are never simple, never fully clear, and never the same. During revolutionary times, values are muddled and perceived identities are redrawn, causing allegiances to shift, even though underlying character remains unchanged. Coleridge's formulation would lead us to assume that one group of forces is clearly identifiable with the past (Scottish Jacobites, Catholics, Highlanders, and royalists) and the other clearly identifiable with the present (English Hanoverians, Protestants, Lowlanders, merchants, lawyers). Scott's understanding is, as we shall see, never so binary or one-dimensional; if it were, Scott would simply be rehearsing misleading historical clichés.

From the outset, Scott challenges our expectation of such clichés. In *Waverley*, Fergus MacIvor enters the novel as a leading Jacobite and Highland chief fiercely loyal to his clan, but Fergus proves to also be an international courtier bent upon gaining money and title through politics, especially in London once Bonnie Prince Charlie's counterrevolution seems successful. Colonel Talbot, the Englishman who rescues Waverley, serves the Hanoverian army and monarchy with an honorable sense of principle, but he also surreptitiously aids the presumably traitorous Waverley in order to save Waverley's life and recover his property. To complicate the ironies even further, Talbot is consumed by absurdly anachronistic prejudices against Scots. Does Fergus MacIvor represent Coleridge's "religious adherence to the past" and does Talbot represent Coleridge's "mighty instincts of progression and free agency?" Both British history and individual lives, Scott knew, are far more complicated.

The complicating of cliché continues in *Old Mortality*. If we identify Claverhouse and the Royalists with the Old Order, we slight the fact that they are in fact victorious during the Killing Times. The Royalists, not the Covenanters, claim to support religious tolerance. Conversely, if the Covenanters represent a protestant future that embraces rights for the common man, why are they united only by their pledge to restore the intolerant Puritan-Presbyterian "Solemn League and Covenant" of 1643, and why are they so decisively the novel's losers?

During the 1820s, Scott's breadth of perspective would be absorbed into historical novels by Cooper, Balzac, and Pushkin. For their readers, contemporary references updating the Old and the New would have readily suggested themselves. To be sure, Puritans and Stuarts, Hanoverians and Jacobites, were hardly the same as Jacobins and Royalists, Legitimists and Bonapartists, Decembrists and Czarists, yet readers of western nations could find in the complexities and contradictions of seventeenth- and eighteenth-century Scotland a compelling mirror of their own uncertainties, confusions, and political reversals.

To pursue Bagehot's insight: how does a Waverley novel avoid a controlling "thesis" of history and the moral "dogma" that almost inevitably accompanies it? Consider first the arc of Scott's narratives. A deep-seated political and social conflict builds toward an historical crisis, whether it takes the form of a rebellion, a civil war, a revolution, or a counterrevolution. The reader feels that an underlying conflict between the Old Order and the New Order is at stake even though he or she rapidly becomes unsure whether that binary division is as clear as many of its participants would like to believe. The opposed historical forces, usually more than two, as well as the fictional characters who represent them, are given fair play in the narrator's descriptions. Each has virtues and vices, assets and liabilities, admirable and reprehensible qualities, which are not always the opposite of the other.

The setting for the conflict, to borrow a term from the subtitle of Cooper's *The Spy*, is a variant of the "neutral ground," a geopolitical no-man's-land caught between the opposing forces. Whenever large-scale military conflict occurs, the neutral ground consists of an area between two armies, fought over by both and possessed by neither, as in Cooper's Westchester County and Lake George, in Pushkin's Ural and Volga River regions, and in Walter Scott's Lowlands. Control of a castle (Scott's Stirling Castle) or a fort (Cooper's Fort William Henry, Pushkin's Fort Tatischev) or a prison (Scott's Edinburgh Tollbooth, the Bastille of collective memory) proves crucial to the plot, serving as a symbol of the brutality and loss that accompany victory. Such buildings function very like a Bakhtinian chronotype, a symbolic entity, not unlike Eliot's "objective correlative," in which "temporal and spatial determinations are inseparable from one another, and always colored by emotions and values."[14]

The Lowlands of Scotland, particularly the treacherous border region along the Highland Line, deepen the reader's awareness of the complexities of rebellion and revolution. Divisions cultural as well as political, complicating any allegiance, are to be found everywhere: divisions between England and Scotland, London and Edinburgh, Highland and Lowland, mountain pass and fertile plain, Anglican and Puritan, Anglo-Catholic and Covenanter, Jacobite and Hanoverian, royalist and parliamentarian, army and army, clan and clan, nobleman and peasant, cateran and cattle drover, among others. Differences of language (English, Scots, Gaelic) are continuing evidence of the difficulty of human communication, for Scott's reader as well as his characters. Rebellions divide families; lines of loyalty crisscross within them while inner character traits change but slowly. To sort it out requires 500 pages for one revolutionary conflict and multiple novels to comprehend the period from 1640 to 1790. To fully resolve all cross conflicts within one historical point of view, one thesis, is impossible. Despite Scott's work on his magnum edition, the kind of controlled comprehensive overview Balzac was to seek for his fictions in *La Comedie Humaine*, and Faulkner for his Yoknapatawpha novels, is not a possibility for the Waverley Novels.

The neutral ground is itself a metaphor. The geographical borderlands make visible a person's uncertainties of mind and conflicts of heart. Edward Waverley, Henry Morton, Frank Osbaldistone, Edgar Ravenswood, and Markham Everard all grow to manhood mediating contrasting beliefs deriving from family heritage and personal experience. Their difficulties in arriving at decision make them appear neutral or weak to their contemporaries, vulnerable to suspicion from both sides. The central figure of a prototypical Scott novel is therefore a waverer ("Waverley") between what appear to be the Old and the New; he is attracted to both, sometimes repulsed by both, but totally committed or totally opposed to neither.

Educated and privileged, often a member of the gentry or the lesser nobility, the waverer is immersed in cultural and political conflicts few of which he has thought through in advance. Edward Waverley, Henry Morton, Frank Osbaldistone, Edgar Ravenswood, Reuben Butler, Cooper's Lionel Lincoln, Cooper's Duncan Heyward, and Pushkin's Pyotr Grinyov all conform to the type, and most of them quite closely. Important women protagonists—Balzac's Marie de Verneuil, Scott's Jeanie Deans, Pushkin's captain's daughter—share many of these same qualities although, given the gender assumptions of the era, women's primary role is to save others, rather than decide matters of allegiance.

None of these protagonists stands for, or speaks for, the common man. Scott was not writing for the masses. Edgar Johnson has tellingly observed "the guinea and a half or two guineas for which Scott's novels sold . . . rendered them a luxury out of reach for all except a very small segment of the population."[15] Instead Scott's protagonists represent ways in which the privileged reader of 1820, aware of recent revolutions and restorations, might imagine his or her participation in revolutionary conflict. ("How would I act in such a conflict? Would I see it as a rebellion, a restoration or a revolution?") We see the emerging conflict through the protagonist's eyes even though his perceptions are controlled by an omniscient narrator. Precursors of the narrative "center of consciousness" advanced by Henry James, such protagonists are a testament to the political confusion of the immediate post-Napoleonic era.[16]

The counterpart of the protagonist may be called "the Historical Hero." For many a reader, a novel was thought to be "historical" because, about two thirds of the way through, the reader directly encounters Bonnie Prince Charlie, Grahame of Claverhouse, Rob Roy, the Marquis of Montrose, George Washington, the Marquis de Montcalm, Oliver Cromwell, the Duke of Argyle (and later Queen Caroline), Pugachev (and later Queen Catherine the Great)—to say nothing of *Ivanhoe*'s Richard the Lion Hearted. Some of these historical figures are first introduced in disguise, or under an alias, during the early part of the narrative. They usually make their true appearance at a moment of crisis, not necessarily in revolutionary history, but during a moment of decision in the fictional protagonist's life. The defining quality of Scott's historical heroes, especially Bonnie Prince Charlie, Grahame of Claverhouse, and Oliver Cromwell, is a deep need to believe that their qualities and position of leadership are based upon moral principle and political rectitude.

The historical hero provides the wavering protagonist an influential glimpse into a Hegelian "world historical individual," but their meeting does not by itself resolve conflicts of value. Among the historical heroes recreated by the first generation of historical novelists, almost all of them would prove to be, despite their arresting and admirable qualities, leaders on the losing side of history. George Washington of Cooper's *The Spy*—a testament to Cooper's faith in New World republicanism—is the great exception to the pattern; *Waverley*'s pretentious Bonnie Prince Charlie is the prototype. The historical hero thus represents attractive forces that the protagonist and the contemporary reader will ultimately need to temper if not discard. Tolstoy's characterization of Napoleon Bonaparte was, of course, to be the *ne plus ultra* of this effective emplotment practice. Perhaps the desire to visualize leaders on the losing side of history suggests that post-Napoleonic readers, as early as Scott's time, were as skeptical of progress as they were of heroism.

In the Waverley Novels, age is not necessarily associated with the Old Order, nor youth with the New. Following Shakespearean precedent, comic characters are often drawn from the servant and peasant classes and identifiable by dialect. The bond between the protagonist and his personal servant bends, but never breaks. To Scott, the relation of servant to master remained beneficial to both, whatever political reversals may occur. The height of selfless loyalty is usually shown by men and women who are not in authority and not of the higher classes: Evan Dhu, Old Mortality, Frederick Vernon, Douce Davie Deans, and Jeanie Deans. The same general pattern would resurface in Cooper's Harvey Birch, Cooper's Hawkeye, Balzac's Galope Chopine, and Pushkin's Marya Mironov. For their loyalty, usually to a losing cause, these figures often pay dearly with their money, their property, and/or their life.

Family relations, centered upon women, are not structured in a way likely to lead the wavering protagonist toward lasting revolutionary commitment. Elderly, single women whose identity derives from an inherited estate attest to the precariousness of even the most prominent families caught in the midst of civil conflict. So, however, do the wives of peasants and artisans, forced into desperate shifts to save whatever they can. Mothers as well as fathers are conspicuously absent. Just as the male protagonist is so often a virtual orphan, so the contrasted images of the marriageable young woman, the Fair Lady and the Dark Lady, face their precarious worlds with little or no parental guidance. However committed they may be to the right or wrong of the historical crisis, their underlying attachments remain local and familial. Confrontational dialogue about revolutionary times, sometimes resembling set speeches, alternates with the wary politesse characteristic of the nobility, gentry, and propertied classes. Not all Dark Ladies are sensual, intellectual, and exotic: not all Fair Ladies are domestic, loving, and conventional. But what remains true, among the first generation of historical novelists, is that the protagonist marries the fair lady at novel's end.[17]

Surely this doggedly repeated convention served as political and social reassurance in an especially unsure time. The marriage of the wavering protagonist and the fair lady tempers the shadowed memory of lingering historical hostilities, of opportunistic politics, and of fields of dead bodies. Scott was not merely rewriting the ending of Shakespearean comedy. The reader of 1825, as well as Scott himself, needed to believe that the restoration of the family to loving stability would somehow palliate his or her experience of the chaos and failed promise of the Revolutionary and Napoleonic eras. The desire for return to social stability, to a brighter future, and to some form of Legitimism coexist uneasily within the marital ending that Scott's readers came to anticipate.

SCOTT IN HIS OWN TIME

Thousands of visitors to Scott's grand late-life estate, Abbotsford, acquire an image of him reinforced by his late-life honorific title as Sir Walter Scott. Readers of *Ivanhoe* are likely to think of Abbotsford as fashionable medieval revival architecture of the nineteenth century. Readers of the Scottish novels are surprised to encounter Scott's historical possessions, among them a claymore of the '45, Archbishop Sharpe's grate, the keys of the Edinburgh Tolbooth, military relics of Culloden and Waterloo, Rob Roy's dirk, gun, and broadsword, a sword given by Charles I to the Marquis of Montrose, a set of Napoleon's pistols, and a clock belonging to Marie Antoinette. It is difficult not to regard such possessions as relics and trophies. Abbotsford seems to have been built to sustain a life of pastoral retreat in which the owner could luxuriate in lordly antiquarianism isolated from contemporary reality. "Revolution" in any sense of the word seems to belong to the closed past.[18]

Katie Trumpener's *Bardic Nationalism* suggests an alternative way of evaluating the significance of the life Scott was building as laird of Abbotsford. By 1815, the union of Scotland and Ireland within the United Kingdom, together with the rise of the British Empire, were leading to contradictory feelings of political as opposed to cultural nationalism. The desire to associate political and economic progress with the growth of the United Kingdom and the rise of the Empire was countered by the desire to preserve and to treasure remnants of the fast disappearing cultural past. Antiquarianism was therefore not merely nostalgia; it was also an act of historical protest on the part of a former nation and a surviving culture. Assurance of progress conflicted with what Trumpener calls "historical mourning."[19]

Scott's praise for the Act of Union while treasuring Rob Roy's dirk attests that he deeply shared both kinds of response. He sought a progressive national future together with regional cultural traditions—not a combination easy to achieve. The "Scottish Common Sense" philosophy in which he had been educated believed in a Stadialist view of history in which change proceeds through consecutive stages of civilization. Time flows from one stage into another (barbaric to agricultural to commercial etc.). The past was not a bygone era, nor was the future separate from the present, either for Scotland or for England. Restorative revolution had occurred periodically throughout the stages. Revolution as cataclysmic overturn, however, did not fit the Stadialist model of organic change. When time allegedly began anew just across the English Channel, revolution suddenly acquired new urgency. How would a young lawyer raised during the Scottish Enlightenment respond?

No one had been more important in forming Scott's outlook on history and politics than the revered Adam Ferguson, Professor at Edinburgh University, and father of Scott's dear friend of the same name. Ferguson's most important work, *An Essay on the History of Civil Society* (1767), published in no less than seven editions before 1814, accepted the reality of continuing change, but questioned the premise that change was progress. The advances of each stage were achieved at corresponding loss. How, Ferguson wondered, could "progress" be a law of history if the heights of human civilization remained the Greek city-state and the Roman Republic?

The recent growth of commerce, the rise of a propertied merchant class, and the beginnings of industrialization all portend the next change, signaled by individual drive for wealth and power obtained through new technological and industrial advances. Ferguson accepted these developments, then beginning in Scotland, as facts of the future. During the 1760s, however, the rise of the fervor to create a revolutionary Republic based upon the Rights of Man was not within his ken. The word "revolution" scarcely ever occurs in Ferguson's *Essay*; when it does, it is used in its regressive sense. Change is inexorable but rarely occurs through violent overturn: "Mankind, when they degenerate, and tend to their ruin, as well as when they improve, and gain real advantages, frequently proceed by slow and almost insensible steps."[20]

Walter Scott shared Ferguson's skepticism of progress based upon individualism, industrialization, the drive for money, and the control of monarchical urban courts. Like Ferguson, Scott believed that, at any stage of civilization, men both degenerate and improve, decline and progress. Strength and stability will emerge from an empowered merchant class, but the drive for money will corrode the spirit of community. Ferguson divides "the dispositions of men" into "two principle classes: the selfish and the social." He values the social, arguing that it inclines mankind "to live with our fellow creatures and to do them good," to develop "the passions of the sexes, the affections of parents and children, . . . above all that habit of the soul by which we consider ourselves as but a part of some beloved community . . . whose general welfare is to us the supreme object of zeal, and the great rule of our conduct" (53–59).

To attain these ends, Ferguson values above all what he calls "probity," a virtue that combines "candour, friendship, generosity and public spirit" to which, in other passages, he adds the "Common Sense" virtues of prudence, toleration, temperance, and fortitude (35–43). Scott was always to affirm Ferguson's skepticism of individuality and his concern for the well-being of the greater community. Theirs is a shared Enlightenment skepticism.

Scott could not however, like Ferguson, slight the prospect of revolutionary overturn. During a student debate held by the Speculative Society in 1793, Scott defended the "Inviolability of the Person of the Monarch" only six months after Louis the XVI was guillotined—and surely with Charles I in mind.[21] By 1794, England and Scotland were preparing for a French invasion; admirers of Thomas Paine, including weavers in Dundee, erected Liberty Trees in sympathy with American and French revolutionary ideals. One year later, Napoleon's armies were invading the Netherlands. In 1796 Scott was elected quartermaster and secretary of an eighty-man volunteer regiment of cavalry, the Edinburgh Light Dragoons. He was experiencing the French Revolution less as a voicing of new ideas of social justice than as an invasion of Great Britain.

Fears of French invasion and British revolution lasted twenty years. When Napoleon invaded Russia in 1812, British trade with Europe and America was dwindling, British mills in Manchester and Glasgow were closing, and food prices were rising yet again. Angry crowds of hungry, displaced textile workers in northern England smashed the new frame looms, destroyed threshing machines, and turned village market days into forced reselling of crops at auction prices. Scott wrote Robert Southey "You are quite right in apprehending a Jacquerie; the country is mined below our feet."[22] While writing *Waverley*, Scott followed the course of Napoleon's Russian campaign with intense interest. After learning of Napoleon's devastating retreat from Moscow, Scott celebrated "the downfall of the most accursed and relentless military despotism that ever wasted the blood and curbed the faculties of a civilized people."[23] Who could less resemble this characterization of Napoleon Bonaparte than uncertain, impressionable Edward Waverley? The contrast surely strengthened Scott's nationalistic feeling for the entirety of Great Britain, not Scotland or England alone.

In 1816 the British economic crisis deepened further. Food prices fell and then rose abruptly, while the wages of English and Scottish handloom weavers fell by perhaps 40 percent, leading to widespread rural and urban unemployment. "Bread or Blood" was a rallying cry for the desperate and dispossessed. In 1818, Scott published *Rob Roy*, which contains Baillie Jarvie's memorable account of how, during the early eighteenth century, the Highlands were suffering 50 percent unemployment, many displaced Scottish tenants were resorting to "thigging and sorning" (begging and robbing), and many a laird was compelled to seek large loans from Glasgow merchants in order to support his family and his tenants.[24]

The worst year was 1819, infamous because of the so-called "Peterloo Massacre" in Manchester, a gathering of some 80,000 protestors who, calling for universal male suffrage and annual election of the House of Commons, were fired upon by royal soldiers, resulting in eleven dead and about four hundred wounded. Revolutionaries who planned to assassinate the British cabinet (the Cato Street Conspiracy) were caught and hanged. The Duke of Wellington, whom Scott greatly admired, could only hope "that the world will escape from the general revolution with which we all seem to be threatened."[25]

Scott's apprehensions never became so dire or so universal. While arguing that the shooting of the Peterloo protestors was justifiable crowd control, he regretted the killing and recognized the desperation of worker conditions. He argued publicly for a national income tax to relieve workers' conditions and educate the poor. He supported the local poor by providing them labor at Abbotsford. Scott was, however, caught in an untenable contradiction of political belief. Revolution, which he had first experienced as a French invasion, he now experienced as an uprising of workers and the poor. Either kind of forced revolution was unacceptable. "Liberty" and "equality" were now besmirched abstractions and "fraternity" was increasingly defined in mass national terms (*La Patrie*) rather than one's local community or region. Scott was suspicious that politicians advocating progressive legal change were more likely to be demagogues than gentlemen with their constituents' interest at heart. He opposed the Reform Bill of 1830, not because he approved of rotten boroughs or disapproved of expanding the suffrage, but because he believed the politicians elected from Manchester or Birmingham would betray their electors to serve their own interests. Such an argument was probably too subtle to be understood, or too self-assured to be accepted, in a public forum. When Scott spoke against the Reform Bill, Jedburgh laborers shouted their ultimate insult at him: "Burke Sir Walter."

These biographical facts show that, throughout the time he was writing the Waverley Novels, but especially while he was writing the Scottish novels (1814–1820), Scott was fully aware of the possibility of a revolution of organized industrial workers, and its tenuous connection to French revolutionary aims. But Scott never allows the possibility of worker revolution to enter into the Waverley Novels themselves. He had no interest in tracing the historical causes of the industrial workers' agitation that he saw around him. One may account for the absence by asserting that all the Scottish Waverley Novels, even *Guy Mannering* and *Redgauntlet*, take place before worker agitation fully arose. Such a claim would be a rationalization that avoids the issue. The more likely reason is that Scott's model for the historical novel cannot readily assimilate worker agitation as a revolutionary subject. The gentlemanly wavering protagonist cannot credibly tend a loom or shovel coal. A worker is unlikely ever to meet a world historical hero. Worker warfare is not waged on battlefields and workers do not advance their cause through verbal exchanges with aristocratic legislators. The proprieties of conversation among Scott's genteel characters have no place in worker dwellings. If the bond between servant and master bends but does not break, what future is there for equality of condition, or even for full equality of legal right? Scott may have favored a higher income tax to relieve economic distress, but the endings of his novels never suggest that the happily married couple should be prepared for property realignment. The question then arises. Could the kind of revolution anticipated by Marxist critics of the historical novel ever possibly have emerged from the model Walter Scott had so successfully established?

"NEITHER WHIG NOR TORY": SCOTT AND SEVENTEENTH-CENTURY "REVOLUTION"

For Scott as for Crane Brinton, modern revolutions begin with the first overturn of the Stuarts. Therefore, 1640 is the point of origin in thinking about revolution. As Blair Worden has shown, the period of the Civil Wars, Commonwealth, and Protectorate has been sequentially titled "The Great Rebellion," "The Interregnum," "The Puritan Revolution," and "The English Revolution," depending on the shifting concerns of the age.[26] Although these terms seem interchangeable, there are consequences in choosing among them. Those who would deny that a revolution had occurred must confront the fact that, between 1650 and 1660, the King, the Monarchy, the House of Lords, the Royal Prerogative Courts, and the established Anglican Church, had all been abolished, replaced with a polity titled a Commonwealth, a polity that only a very few advanced thinkers called a republic. To many alive during that decade, these changes (the world turned upside down as the 1640s ballad proclaimed[27]), must have looked like a "Revolution" in the *later* sense of the word—a violent overturn for progressive ends.

Conversely, those convinced that "Revolution" is indeed the appropriate term must confront the fact that King, Monarchy, Lords, and established church were all to return in 1660. The reign of Charles II, a "revolution" according to the word's older meaning, has ever since and by general consent been called the "Restoration." Because revolutions since 1789 have been assumed to be willed affairs, we identify and write about "revolutionary leaders." After seven years of civil wars, however, there is no evidence that anyone before 1649, even among the Levellers, had written in any depth about the future of England's "Republic" or "Commonwealth." There had been shrill protests, angry denunciation, calls for reform, and violence aplenty throughout the civil wars, but not a revolution as a planned and willed overturn. Battles were fought over the *prerogatives* of king versus parliament, prelacy versus presbytery, but not for the express purpose of creating a new order. As J.G.A. Pocock, Lawrence Stone, and Christopher Hill have all agreed, whatever their differences, "Nobody then, willed the English Revolution; it happened."[28]

Not until 1819, after Scott had published eight Waverley novels, did he write directly about the civil wars, the Commonwealth, and the Protectorate. Long after the Glorious Revolution and the Act of Settlement, the era of the Civil Wars and "Puritan Revolution" was to remain a period of British history that Englishmen and Scots of moderate persuasion, whether Whig or Tory, preferred not to recall. Thought to be the political descendants of Roundheads, Whigs bore the guilt of regicide and therefore preferred to date revolutionary triumph from the peaceful accessions of William and Mary and the Hanoverians. Thought to be the political descendants of Cavaliers loyal to king and church, Tories knew they had twice been dramatic losers in the history of the monarchy. Parliament and Whig grandees were the leaders of a rapidly growing mercantile and agricultural economy. Many Tories preferred not to be associated with the agitation behind recurring Jacobite "conspiracies." Silence about the "Interregnum," ready praise for the Glorious Revolution among Whigs, and acceptance of it among most Tories, proved to be the wiser course.[29]

Scott advanced an historical overview about the 1649 revolution only late in his career and only when it became necessary, in *Tales of A Grandfather* (1828), which surveys seventeenth-century Scottish history in its entirety. The period from 1640 to 1669 is summarized as a period of Whig "excess" and the period from the Restoration until 1688 as a period of Tory "excess." The achievements of 1688 are then said to have resolved the conflict by an almost Hegelian synthesis:

Such was this memorable Revolution which . . . decided the fate of a great kingdom without bloodshed, and in which, perhaps for the only time in history, the heads of the discordant factions of a great empire laid aside their mutual suspicion and animosity. . . . To the memory of this Convention or Parliament

[the Convention that offered William the throne and passed the Bill of Rights]
the Brittanic kingdoms owe the inestimable blessing of a constitution fixed on
the decided and defined principles of civil and religious liberty.[30]

Scott's wording here is precise. He uses the capitalized word "Revolution"
for one of very few times in the entire work. A "great empire" has emerged
from 1688, but that great empire is "the Brittanic kingdoms" not just England.
The word "constitution" subsumes both the unwritten constitution of England, and Parliament's 1689 document the "Bill of Rights." "Civil and Religious Liberty" are the purpose of this "memorable Revolution," not equality
or fraternity. Only the phrase "perhaps for the only time in history" strikes a
discordant though deeply patriotic note.

Scott's dividing of the seventeenth century into periods of Whig and Tory
excess prevents the reader of 1828 from regarding history as a closed book.
Scott cites mid-seventeenth century origins for the terms "Whig" and "Tory,"
but anachronistic insistence upon applying them to the entire century enables
him to connect the revolutionary past to the reader's present:

> A man who considers that, in the general view of the Constitution, the monar-
> chical power is in danger of being undermined by the popular branches, and who
> therefore supports the Crown in ordinary cases of dispute, is a Tory; while one
> who conceives the power of the Crown to be more likely to encroach upon the
> liberties of the people, throws his weight and influence into the popular scale,
> and is called a Whig.[31]

To balance the interests and values of Whig and Tory, Scott continues, is
"the sure mode of preventing aggression, either on the rights of the Crown
or the privileges of the people." Whig and Tory should be like taut ship's
ropes straining against each other in order to keep the ship of state on course.
Scott's is a politics of moderation amid conflict; a moderation that can sustain
a progressive people through revolutionary crises, be they in 1649, 1689, or
after 1828. Such a balance, Scott implies, had been conspicuously missing in
France from 1789 to 1815.[32]

When Scott chose to write a novel about the battles of Montrose during the
first Civil War (1644–1645), he well knew he was writing about a defeated
royalist rebellion that would soon lead to the execution of Charles the I,
thence to the Stuart restoration of 1660, and finally to the origin of Jacobite
rebellion during the immediate aftermath of the Glorious Revolution of
1688.[33] However, *A Legend of the Wars of Montrose* resists the easy kinds of
predictive irony that the long historical view encourages. The reader is placed
in the immediate, confusing historical moment, just before Cromwell's rise,
when there are not yet recognized groups of Levellers, protestant Independents, or diehard Stuart loyalists by which historical forces could be aligned.

Scott's overview of the bewildering situation in which rebellion/restora-
tion/revolution arises requires careful attention to sort out its historical complexities. In 1644, the island of Britain consists of two separate nations ruled
by one King, each with its own peerage and Parliament (in Scotland temporarily resummoned as the "Convention of Estates"). There are two opposed
Scottish armies. The Covenanter army, supporting the English Parliament and
led by David Leslie, is opposed by the royalist army led by Montrose, which
has recently been granted full governing powers by King Charles I.

Montrose's royalist army contains, in addition to loyalist Anglicans and
Catholics of the northeast Highlands, many Lowlanders and royalist Presbyterians. Leslie's army, duly commissioned by Scotland's Convention of
Estates, contains, in addition to Covenanters and western Scots, both Highlanders and Lowlanders, many supporters of the English Parliament who
have not signed the Solemn League and Covenant. There are significant
numbers of Englishmen in both Scottish armies. Two thousand Irish troops
fight with Montrose under the command of Colkitto, a Scot disinherited from
a MacDonald sept. Significant numbers of mercenaries had been bought by
both armies. At his tedious but likeable best, the mercenary is represented
in the novel by Dugald Dalgetty. As an historical fact, however, the narrator
states that all mercenaries introduce a "calculating and selfish character" into
the military, a "degeneracy" by which Scotland has been "contaminated with
a more than usual share."[34]

The makeup of Scotland's two armies will affect history but is only a part
of what the individual must bring to a decision of allegiance. Family, faith,
money, and daily life along the Highland line are shaped by the volatile,
slowly deteriorating clan system. The Marquis of Montrose, now a royalist general, had formerly signed the National Covenant. His hereditary clan
enemy, the Marquis of Argyle, who raises large numbers of Scots for the
Parliamentary army, is craftily politic in claiming to maintain allegiance to
the king. After Montrose's forces surprise and defeat Argyle at Inverlochy,
Argyle's poorer clansmen, resenting their laird, join Montrose. When Montrose's soldiers begin to live off the land, however, farmers whose lands
have been pillaged join Argyle. Scott's narrative follows Montrose's successive triumphs, but the novel's last page reminds the reader that Montrose's
"brief and glorious career" ended in his disastrous defeat by Leslie's army
at Philiphaugh (181). Scott probably thought it unnecessary to mention one
of the legendary moments of Scottish history: Argyle declined to witness the
beheading, drawing, and quartering of Montrose in Edinburgh in 1650, but is
said to have secretly rejoiced at Montrose's demise.[35]

Scott repeatedly shows us that, in the historical moment, it is local motive
and temporary circumstance, not religious faith or political belief, which
determines men's actions. Unsure whether to march south to attack London,

or march east to attack Argyle, Montrose decides that the prospect of crushing "the rival of his own house and the chief support of the Presbyterians . . . was a picture too flattering to feudal vengeance to be easily relinquished" (130). Sir Duncan Campbell, as shrewd and honest a nobleman as the novel affords, exclaims "What signifies it . . . to the Highland Chiefs whether King or Parliament got uppermost?" (71). Sir Duncan's own service to Argyle ironically confirms his point: "he was supposed rather to have joined the Covenanters out of devotion to his chief than real respect for the cause either of liberty or of Presbytery" (241).

How then, in the Scottish Waverley Novels, did seventeenth-century revolution arise? The answer provided by *A Legend of The Wars of Montrose* is implied but clear. Events that would end in the Glorious Revolution began in confused civil wars fought primarily for temporary personal advantage and shifting clan loyalties. During the early 1640s in Scotland, Parliament and King, prelacy, and presbytery, posed secondary distant issues, often claimed merely for purposes of rationalization. No one could possibly sort out all the compromising crosscurrents and contradictions caused by loyalties of family, sept, clan, religion, church, local government, national government, and monarchical government. The countryside was still half in the stage Adam Ferguson would have called barbarism. No character in *A Legend of the Wars of Montrose* foresees anything remotely like a republic or a French revolution; no loyalist knows he is fighting for an eventual restoration. In a larger sense, no character in the novel can possibly know what he or she is doing. The so-called Puritan Revolution does not occur, nor is it mentioned, within Scott's narrative. As the Marquis of Montrose wins battles for his king, only the reader knows that Charles I will soon be executed and a Commonwealth will emerge. A subtle dramatic irony prevails in the differing degrees of historical awareness possessed by author, reader, and historical characters.

Scott's second and last novel about the Puritan Revolution was to be far more ambitious and comprehensive. John Buchan long ago observed, quite correctly, that Scott's still neglected *Woodstock* (1826), his second novel about the Civil Wars and Puritan Revolution, "ranks high among the novels for the architecture of its plot." Buchan claimed *Woodstock* to be "almost the best written of the novels" despite Scott's trying personal circumstances: bankruptcy, his beloved wife's death, his own aging, and the economic condition of Great Britain.[36] Nowhere is Buchan's tribute to the "wise and mellow philosophy" of *Woodstock* more in evidence than in Scott's generalization about the likely outcome of all revolutions: "In revolutions, stern and high principles are often obliged to give way to the current of existing circumstances; and in many a case, where wars have been waged for points of metaphysical right, they have been at last gladly terminated, upon the mere hope of obtaining general tranquility."[37] The implications here are certainly mellow and arguably wise. Revolutions are immediately and inevitably linked to waging war. Revolutionary aims and motivations, especially those based on claims of "metaphysical right," exhaust themselves as battle deaths accumulate, leading to eventual recognition of diminished revolutionary achievement.

Woodstock describes the immediate aftermath of Cromwell's major victory at the Battle of Worcester (September 3, 1651), the climactic end of the first Civil War, in which Parliament and the New Model Army overwhelmed royalist military forces, and transformed a monarchy into a commonwealth. Oliver Cromwell is at the zenith of his power. Charles II, King of Scotland but not King of England, appears as a disguised page on the run from Cromwell's soldiers. The fictional narrative, confined to two months, takes place on a sequestered royalist nobleman's estate near Oxford (recently Charles the First's center of operations), with one visit to Windsor Castle (now held by Cromwell), and a final chapter set in London in 1660 as the Stuart Restoration begins. Nothing is as a visitor in 1689, or a reader in 1826, would have expected.

The recent changes Scott describes in England in 1651 accord with the historical changes Christopher Hill summarized in *The Century of Revolution 1603–1714* (1961) and in *God's Englishman: Oliver Cromwell and the English Revolution* (1970). The Divine Right of Kings, a claim vital to James I and the House of Stuart, is assumed to be fully discredited as a principle of monarchy. "No Bishop, No King" has ironically passed from a royalist and churchly warning into a present day reality. Bishops are excluded from the House of Lords, which is about to be vacated. Royal prerogatives for the control of appointments and for special monarchical courts have been successfully challenged. Parliament has gained control, not only of taxation, but of the right of property. It is proceeding to confiscate royalist land holdings; among them is Woodstock, the Lee family estate, one of the King's lodges and hunting preserves.

Although power is being concentrated within the property-holding gentry and merchants in the House of Commons, the suffrage is not being markedly widened, despite the demands of the more radical factions (the Levellers, Scott's fictional Bletson). Amid the clamor of many factions, and the threats of royalists, the need for a strong military presence based on merit has become increasingly apparent (Cromwell's New Model Army, the historical Major General Thomas Harrison). The Rump Parliament suspects Cromwell as much as Cromwell suspects the Rump Parliament. True power resides in Parliament's select "Council of State" within which Cromwell, as commanding General of the New Model Army, retains the strongest influence. Governing voices that claim to stand for religious toleration, or for a Presbytery, or for the established Church of England combined with religious toleration, are rarely in a position to practice what they preach (Cromwell, Bletson, Everard, Reverend Holdenough).

The pertinence of these changes to 1689 and 1789, and even to the Jacobite rebellions between them, would have been immediately apparent to Scott's readers. No one then or now can plausibly deny that the Puritan Revolution, the Glorious Revolution, and the French Revolution shifted power within England and France toward national legislatures and away from monarchy and royally appointed officials. Control by men of property over the power of taxation, with only a slight expansion of the suffrage, is common to the revolutions of 1640, 1688, 1776, and 1789. Desire for some form of a Republic (limited in England in 1640 and in 1688) becomes a public issue in America and France. A widely recruited national army is essential to the success of all four revolutions.

Woodstock shows us that such generalizations are never evident during the moment history is lived. No one except the fictional Commissioner Bletson has any interest in theorizing about the political future; a sometime acquaintance of James Harrington, Bletson is allotted two pages, then dismissed as a superstitious coward whose cautiously avowed atheism gains no traction. Insofar as there is any revolutionary motive among the Parliamentarians and the New Model Army, it is the desire to somehow bring about the Kingdom of God on earth. "Repent for the Kingdom of Heaven is at hand" (*Matthew 4:17*, Christ's first preaching in the New Testament). Cromwell repeatedly but not consistently declares that he is only the "instrument" of God in bringing about the reign of Virtue. Thomas Harrison, a dedicated Fifth Monarchy Man, retains considerable, but not determinative, influence upon Cromwell. As in the Book of *Revelation*, the political makeup of the earthly Apocalypse remains beyond man's ken. However, as Scott shows from his first chapter onward, if a revolution is occurring in England, it is an inchoate religious revolution that looks backward in order to look forward.

Although the dominant will of Oliver Cromwell prefigures Napoleon, whose *Life* Scott was then writing, Cromwell's career also presages events important during British counterrevolutions. William, Mary, Anne, and then the Hanoverians were to do to Jacobite nonjurors very much what Cromwell's Commonwealth has done to Laudians: disempower and periodically execute them. When Scott describes the Scottish royalist army marching south in 1651 to be defeated by Cromwell at the Battle of Worcester, anyone who has read *Waverley* will recall Scott's vivid description of the Jacobite army marching south to Derby in 1745 in futile hope of capturing London and toppling the Hanoverian regime. Scott quotes Cromwell's legendary claim that his victory at Worcester had been the sign of God's "great and crowning mercy" upon him (95). Scott's reader would surely have noted the similarity of Cromwell's self-glorification to Napoleon's crowning himself emperor of

France in the presence of the pope. What does it mean, we wonder, when a *crowning* is the sign of completed revolution?

In the end, Scott will not allow his reader to forget that Puritan Revolution was to be followed by Stuart Restoration. Throughout the narrative, Charles II is granted equal fictional space to his foil, Oliver Cromwell. Power may be passing permanently toward Parliament, but the monarchy, the House of Lords, and the powers of the bishops were all, like the Bourbons in 1815, to return. The regicides of 1649, including Thomas Harrison, were to be hanged, drawn and quartered, or harried to Puritan New England. Four years after quasi-regal burial in Westminster Abbey, Lord Protector Cromwell's body was to be exhumed and publicly hanged, its trunk thrown into a pit, and its head fixed on a pike outside Westminster Hall, where it was to remain for the next twenty-four years. To adapt Verignaud's metaphor, the Puritan Revolution may not have eaten its own children, but its Protector was to be devoured by the *Ancien Regime* he had displaced.

Although neither Charles II nor James II may have referred directly to the "Divine Right of Kings," they often spoke and acted as if they were still entitled to it. Under the Commonwealth and Protectorate, many Presbyterians and Independents did not favor religious toleration, but Oliver Cromwell did. In 1673, however, the passing of the Test Act legalized religious discrimination in civil life. When James II issued the Declaration of Indulgence in 1687, one of his purposes was to further the influence of Catholic appointees, a practice that Parliamentarians during the 1640s had detested, feared, and effectively prevented. Thus does history undo history.

From what political viewpoint, then, can the reader of *Woodstock* convincingly view history? Which revolutionary overturn sets the values by which the merits of church-state relations and the limits of military authority, as well as Scott's characters, should be understood? Should the Puritan Revolution be judged by the standards of 1653, 1660, 1689, 1707, 1745, 1815, or 1826? Given the historical totality with which Scott renders the Cromwellian world, was it possible for him or his reader not to judge Charles II as an imprudent loser very like Bonnie Prince Charlie of *Waverley*? Knowing that Oliver Cromwell rarely lost a battle, and that his service as Lord Protector ended in his dissolving the Rump Parliament and in his ruling of England through Major Generals in fifteen Military Districts, was it possible for Scott or his reader not to see Cromwell, at least intermittently, through the guise of Napoleon Bonaparte? The historical perspective from which *Woodstock* was written had to remain irresolvably complex if not openly contradictory.

Without obtruding historical parallels, Scott presents 1651 as a watershed year that prefigures France in 1793. *Woodstock*'s readers would have been reminded of France's recently executed monarch, of the split between Girondists and Montagnards, of emergency conditions claimed by the

Committee of Public Safety, of a disempowered nobility, and of the need for a controlling force that resides only in the army. The situational counterpart to Oliver Cromwell is Robespierre; Cromwell's counterpart in character, however, is Napoleon.

The loyalty of the influential Royalists and influential Cromwellians is maintained at the price of their reason, prudence, and self-control. The two symbiotic historical figures introduced midway through the narrative, Cromwell and Charles II, prove to have opposite virtues and failings. Surrounding them is a swirl of historical splinter groups whose intermingled political and religious principles are impossible to sort out. At various points in the narrative, Scott mentions Anabaptists, Antinomians, Brownists, Diggers, Familists, Fifth Monarchy Men, Grindlestonians, Levellers, Muggletonians, Nullifidians, Pelagians, Prelatists, Quakers, Ranters, Remonstrants, and Resolutioners—to say nothing of the Presbyterians and Independents with whom these sectarians intermittently ally themselves.

Scott cares little for the particular politics of such groups, and even less for the particulars of their theology. His concern is to demonstrate that the emerging principle of religious tolerance pays a price in divisive faction, just as forced doctrinal unanimity pays a price in spiritual conscience. To remember the civil wars as a clash of clearly defined principles is a simplistic falsity of human memory. Surrounded by the confusions and dangers of the present, facing an open future, Markham Everard, a Presbyterian Colonel, and Alice Lee, a royalist nobleman's daughter, must find their way to marriage, to a worthy allegiance and to beliefs that might endure.

Scott's prominent royalist characters bring no benefit to England's future beyond devotion to the vacant Stuart monarchy and to aristocratic custom. The aged Sir Henry Lee, keeper of the King's Park and Lodge at Woodstock, anticipates confiscation of his family estate, pending its sequester, by three Parliament-appointed commissioners. As intransigent, choleric, and helpless as King Lear, upon whom he is clearly modeled, Sir Henry Lee defies all Puritans, Parliamentarians, and their Commissioners. If need be, Sir Henry is prepared to defend Woodstock with only his own sword. He denounces his beloved nephew Markham Everard because Everard serves reluctantly in Cromwell's army. Sir Henry then virtually disowns his beloved daughter Alice (Cordelia) because she tries to defend Markham from false accusation of treason. As a representative royalist, Sir Henry Lee is contrasted to Markham's childhood friend, Roger Wildrake, whose significance is indicated by the novel's subtitle "the Cavalier." True to the cavalier stereotype and to his surname, Captain Wildrake is brave, witty, impulsive, and charming; he is also persistently drunk and rarely able to control his tongue. However honorable and likeable Lee and Wildrake may be, neither of them is capable of planning a better future for country, king, or family. A sentimental nostalgia for the Old Order is hard to detect anywhere in *Woodstock*.

Scott's two historical adversaries never meet. Opposites in character, Charles II and Cromwell represent flawed causes, even though both men are partially redeemed by acts of personal generosity. Disguised as a Scottish page, Charles II seems always the imposter, alternating between gestures of aristocratic grace and crude mockery of the Scottish people who, unlike the English, have crowned him their king. His concern for England's political future is limited to his own restoration as monarch. Charles's only purposeful activity, while a fugitive in Sir Henry Lee's household, is to try to seduce Sir Henry's daughter Alice, to whom he proposes what is, in effect, a morganatic marriage. Scott's summary of Charles's character ("a good-humored but hardhearted voluptuary") is more forgiving than the historical Cromwell's dismissal of Charles ("Give him a shoulder of mutton and a whore, that's all he cares for") but the two judgments are similar in kind.[38] Alice Lee knows that Charles II does not possess the qualities needed in a constitutional monarch: "chivalrous courage . . . love of his people . . . political prudence . . . moral virtues and religious faith . . . temperate, wise and frugal . . . a worthy gentleman" and "the best father" (267–268). There is no monarch or "protector" of such qualities anywhere on the novel's horizon.

To Scott, Cromwell personifies historical forces that will be needed long after 1651. Cromwell's genius in inspiring and leading an army in battle is his one constant merit. Off the battlefield, it is impossible to determine whether Cromwell is driven by love of England, love of "liberty," personal ambition, belief in toleration, a puritan desire to restore the principles of the early Christian church, or a providential mission to institute God's Kingdom. Cromwell speaks favorably and convincingly of them all at diverse moments. Leaders, however, are especially prone to compromise their own positions, a quality Scott also detected in Napoleon. Cromwell defends personal property rights, even as he confiscates royalist holdings. He defends landed gentry, merchants, and yeomen, as long as they do not subscribe to Levellers' principles of wide extension of the suffrage and communal ownership of land.[39] Napoleon was to advance himself through similar compromises.

The keys to Scott's characterization of Oliver Cromwell are Cromwell's obfuscation of language and his guilt in approving regicide. Whenever Cromwell gives a military order, his words are direct, clear, and commanding. Whenever he is unsure of another's motives, however, Cromwell is "wont to invest his meaning, or that which seemed to be his meaning, in such a mist of words, surrounding it with so many exclusions and exceptions, and fortifying it with such a labyrinth of parentheses, that though one of the most shrewd men in England, he was, perhaps, the most unintelligible speaker that ever perplexed an audience" (85). Scott knew that medical doctors had on at least two occasions diagnosed Oliver Cromwell to be afflicted with melancholia. Because Scott believed Cromwell was unwilling to admit to his own inner troubles, those troubles surface abruptly and dramatically whenever he is surprised into a surge of guilt. "Agitated by inward and indescribable feelings" upon seeing a portrait of Charles I, Cromwell fearfully laments that the "melancholy features" of the dead king will forever survive through Van Dyke's art to remind future generations of Charles the First's "woful tale" (98).

Not unexpectedly, Cromwell immediately rationalizes his approval of regicide ("It was a stern necessity—it was an awful deed"), and then accounts for his complicity in Charles's execution by concluding, "the oppressed consciences, the injured liberties of England, were the banner that I followed" (98). The scene is later repeated when Cromwell contemplates killing Charles II while leading a troop raid upon Woodstock. This time Cromwell is overheard muttering the words "hard necessity" before he breaks down "into a flood of tears" at the recognition that "I am called Parricide, Blood-thirsty Usurper, already, for shedding the blood of one man, that the plague might be stayed" (403, 404). Regicide, we know, had remained a crucial issue to Scott because of the execution of Louis the XVI—an epoch-making regicide Scott was then condemning in his "Preliminary Essay on the French Revolution."

Cromwell's defining qualities prove to be closely interrelated. His obscurity of language when discussing ideas and motives reflects his inability to think through his political beliefs in advance of required action. Brilliance, courage, Puritanism, patriotism, a will to dominate and belief in "liberty" carry him to leadership in the Commonwealth, and later to become Lord Protector, but they are not enough. Scott's Cromwell repeatedly claims that his continuing success is proof that he must be enacting God's Providential will. From Scott's perspective, it is ever thus with men of greatness (Napoleon) who lack the prudence and self-insight to discern at what point devotion to principle ends and self-aggrandizement begins. Scott's Cromwell is one of his most memorable and complex creations, judged by both literary and historical standards.

Just as the partial redemption Charles II earns by releasing Alice Lee is tainted by self-interest, so is Oliver Cromwell's integrity first elevated but then undermined by novel's end. Charles II escapes as a fugitive to Flanders, while Cromwell's troops capture all those who have aided him. Cromwell orders the prisoners to be executed, then changes his mind after a few hours of solitary rest. By freeing Markham Everard, Reverend Holdenough, Reverend Rochecliffe, Sir Henry Lee, and even Colonel Albert Lee (Sir Henry's son and the prime agent in Charles II's escape), Cromwell makes possible a restorative if not progressive ending. Without Cromwell's intervention, Woodstock would never have been restored nor would the marriage of Markham and Alice have occurred.

Because Cromwell has a humane instinct to forgive, he promptly represses his own severities. He does not remember that, in a moment of rage, he had ordered all prisoners executed: "What execution, what Malignants?" (440) he confusedly asks Captain Pearson, his aide-de-camp. Tactical calculations also motivate him. To execute his prisoners, Cromwell says, would make "all those of their classes cry sacrilege, and alienate them from us for ever" (440). Freeing Reverend Holdenough and Markham Everard should prove an effective tactic: "I must gain the Presbyterian interest over to us if I can" (441). Human motivation, in Scott's best work, is rarely transparent, never simple and never mono-causal.

Markham Everard, like Waverley, is a gentleman of good will caught between opposing powers, but he is much less the waverer. Older and more experienced than Waverley, free from any romantic appreciation of Stuart aristocracy, Everard has joined the New Model Army because he believes that Cromwell, and Cromwell alone, can bring peace and order out of the Parliamentary and religious quarreling he sees around him. A moderate Presbyterian committed to toleration and therefore indignant at Laudian persecution, Everard tells Sir Henry Lee "I have drawn my sword neither hastily, nor without due consideration, for a people whose rights have been trampled on, and whose consciences have been oppressed" (51).

Nonetheless, Everard respects the integrity and loyalty fostered by the institutions of monarchy and church. After publicly disapproving of the execution of Charles I, Everard has reconciled himself to a Commonwealth in which power is shared by the Parliament and a strong executive. Everard is, however, not a republican, certainly not a Leveller. He thinks, as Cromwell does, in terms of practical expedients rather than ideal polities. Everard's practicality leads him to fear that the great advantages of a monarchy with limited powers might well be lost in Cromwell's Commonwealth. Loyalty to honor and family will, he trusts, eventually prove more powerful than any political allegiance. In all these ways, Markham Everard speaks for the balanced values Walter Scott would have cherished had he been living in 1651. The telling consequence is that Everard, like Scott, can find no faction, no party, to which he can give unqualified allegiance.

Everard's Presbyterian faith and service as a Colonel in the New Model Army prove grievously offensive to Sir Henry Lee. Conversely, Everard's disapproval of the Commissioners' confiscation of Woodstock, and his refusal to betray Charles II's hiding place, prove so grievously offensive to Cromwell that Cromwell arrests him. Under suspicion by both royalists and parliamentarians, Everard is required, as a Colonel, to read letters sent to the New Model Army by royalists who would betray their monarch, as well as letters sent by self-interested Puritans who seek to bribe Cromwell. As he reads such letters, Everard thinks to himself:

Gracious Providence, where is this to end! We have sacrificed the peace of our families, the warmest wishes of our young hearts, to right the country in which we were born, and to free her from oppression; yet it appears, that every step we have made towards liberty, has but brought us in view of new and more terrific perils, as he who travels in a mountainous region, is by every step which elevates him higher, placed in a situation of more imminent hazard (68).

During revolutionary times, reason and liberty may elevate a patriot to honorable conduct, but ascending moral heights will expose him to the ever-greater danger of venal political realities. Scott repeatedly wrote that revolutionary crises bring out the best and worst qualities of mankind; no convincing account of revolution recognizes one without the other.

Everard's wary, prudential view of a republican future of divided powers proves to be incapacitating in ways that challenge the accommodating resolutions of Scott's earlier novels. The royalist cause turns out not to be "ruined" (103). Scott's last chapter emphasizes the irony of Major General George Monk's New Model Army welcoming Charles II back to London in 1660 amid a tumult of popular joy. Monk's placing Charles II on the throne is the historical counterpart to Cromwell's reversing the confiscation of the Lee estate, thereby enabling Markham and Alice to marry. The Puritans, not the Royalists, have assured the Restoration.

Such an ending challenges Scott's former assumptions about the forward movement of history. Within Scott's fictional plot, as in Interregnum history, contrarieties have led to near exhaustion followed by welcome reversion (the relaxations of Thermidor). Sir Henry Lee, now approaching senility, dies in ecstasy after being embraced by England's restored Stuart monarch. His daughter Alice and her husband Markham, having spent the past six or seven years in wary retirement from all service to Commonwealth or Protectorate, stand at the edge of the celebrating crowd. As the royal procession moves past them, Charles II, politic to the end, approaches Markham and exclaims, "Colonel Everard, we shall see you, I trust, at Whitehall" (454). Everard replies neither with word nor gesture. Rather than publicly decline service to his king, Everard chooses the honor of silence. He chooses marginality because he knows too much.

As the cheering of the crowd dies away, Scott's reader cannot help but recall the eventual fate of the Stuart Restoration now being so happily celebrated. Memory of the future flight of James II, the Act of Settlement, and two Jacobite attempts at counterrevolution expose the excess of the joy in 1660; revolution and restoration amount in fact to an emptying out, a void of constructive political possibilities, a resolution but not a solution. No party possesses truth. Although Scott wrote no novel directly about 1688, he repeatedly stated that the greatness of the Glorious Revolution lay in its realistic, pragmatic compromises. As the narrator of *Woodstock* bluntly forewarns his readers, "Our political convictions will please neither Whig not Tory."[40]

FORKING PATH

The case against Scott was first made *in extenso* by William Hazlitt's essay "Sir Walter Scott" in *The Spirit of the Age* (1825). Hazlitt sustains a witty, distorted attack on Scott's politics, Scott's prose style, Scott's literary form, and Scott's deference to monarchical "legitimacy" both English and French. Hazlitt assumes that any romancer of the past must ipso facto be a spokesman for retrograde Tory politics. For Scott to have written at such dreary length without coming to conclusion shows the unwillingness of Scott and his adoring public to engage present realities: "Sir Walter Scott is undoubtedly the most popular writer of the age, the 'lord of the ascendant' for the time being. He is just half of what the human intellect is capable of being: if you take the universe, and divide it into two parts, he knows all that it *has been*; all that it *is to be* is nothing to him."[41] The true Walter Scott, Hazlitt claims, is "a prophesier of things past" whose "speculative understanding is empty, flaccid, poor and dead" (99). If Scott were to describe the Millennium he would "lay the scene in Scotland five hundred years ago" and then belabor his reader with "facts and worm-eaten parchments to support his drooping style" (99–100).

The Waverley Novels would be merely harmless, Hazlitt contends, were it not that "through some odd process of servile logic," Scott "administers charms and philters to our love of legitimacy, making us conceive a horror of all reform" (113). Scott's trick "in restoring the claims of the Stuarts by the courtesy of romance" is to thereby enable "the House of Brunswick and the Bourbons" to be "more firmly seated" (111). By appearing to condemn counterrevolution, Scott supports today's illegitimate "Legitimacies." The hidden effect of Scott's fiction is therefore to promote "loyalty founded on would-be treason; he props the actual throne by the shadow of rebellion" (111).

Behind these allegations lie Hazlitt's public stance as the embattled liberal exposing the reactionary Tory, and Hazlitt's adulation of Napoleon as the defender of the common man. Ignoring the contradictions Scott found in the totality of history, Hazlitt reduces Scott to the monarchical novelist whom complacent readers in Regency England and Restoration France wish to revere. Behind the façade of the knighted Sir Walter, there is only a time-server hiding out in the past in order not to challenge the oppressions maintained by post-Napoleonic Legitimacy.

Struggling against Hazlitt's kind of distorted half-truths, the contemporary novelists most immediately affected by Scott needed to establish difference even as they showed their indebtedness. In reviewing Lockhart's *Life of Scott*,

Cooper was to reargue the issue of Scott's presumably "Tory" values in a manner more judicious than Hazlitt. As an advocate of New World republicanism, Cooper criticized Scott's constitutional monarchism without accusing Scott of truckling to legitimacy. Pushkin took a different political tack from Hazlitt but nonetheless challenged Scott's wearying length and seeming pointlessness. Although Pushkin conceded "the chief beauty of Walter Scott's novels lies in the fact that we are shown times long gone . . . in a contemporary, down-to-earth perspective," Pushkin issued his own challenge: "Wait and see, once I've got my act together, I will take that Walter Scott to task."[42] While following Scott's conventions in plot and characterization, Pushkin did in fact "take that Walter Scott to task" by reducing the customary 400-page length of a Waverley novel into a 100-page novella in which every paragraph counts. Stendhal, as we have seen, wrongly predicted that Scott's reputation would undergo a 50 percent decline by 1840. The protagonists of Stendhal's *The Red and the Black* (1830) and *The Charterhouse of Parma* (1839), caught up in the political conflicts of post-Napoleonic Europe, do not waver between the Old and the New, nor dwell on family heritage and family honor. Julien Sorel and Fabrizio del Dongo worry far less about what they ought to do, than how they are going to succeed. Their self-interested ambitions indicate a need to deflect their age's anxiety about continuing revolution and counterrevolution.[43] Their tacit political amorality is not of Scott's world.

The immense change in Balzac's fiction from *Les Chouans* (1829) to *Pere Goriot* (1834) shows the emergence of a very different kind of historical fiction. As Balzac was assembling *La Comedie Humaine* in 1843, he wrote Madame Hanska that *Les Chouans* had been "full of Cooper and Walter Scott, with in addition a passion and *verve* due to neither of them."[44] In 1829, however, Balzac's indebtedness had been far more evident than his reservations. From *Waverley* had come the Old Order and the New, the historical context of a counterrevolution (Scotland in the '45, Brittany in 1800), the need for a supporting invasion from royalist forces, the elegant noble leader of a losing cause (Bonnie Prince Charlie, the Gars), and an admirable manly officer who prevails among the victors (Hanoverian Colonel Talbot, Napoleonic Commandant Hulot). From both Scott and Cooper came the setting of the contested neutral ground, controlled randomly by bands of marauders, and unwelcome regiments of national armies. From Cooper's *The Spy*, came the plot patterns of spying and disguise, and the reminders that gold coin motivates almost all parties. From *The Last of the Mohicans* came the original title for the novel (*Le Dernier Chouan*), a central massacre (at the chateau de la Vivatierre, as at Fort William Henry) and the characterization of Marche a Terre, whose stealthy brutalities are modeled on Cooper's Magua. Four separate passages liken Brittany's savage Chouans to the Hurons and Mohicans of Cooper's vast forests. In awkward anticipation of metafiction, Balzac recognizes that his reader is more likely to understand the Chouans through Cooper's novel, than through prior historical knowledge.

Although Balzac took an extended trip to Fougeres to familiarize himself with Brittany, he was by 1828 fully engaged in the daily realities of succeeding in Restoration Paris, a world of fragile peace, dominated by an aristocracy half old and half new, a world where sexual passion was glorified, infidelity fashionable, and where money had become the increasingly admitted measure of all things. As titled family names moved up and down, in and out, of society, the show of wealth seemed ever necessary to cloak the accumulation of debt. Here was to be Balzac's world, not the semicivilized provincial world of Brittany in 1800, but the urban world of the nineteenth century. It has long been a post-Jamesian cliché, a half-truth, to contend that *La Comedie Humaine* marks the emergence of the contemporary realistic novel that, later developed by Flaubert, would dominate late-nineteenth-century fiction. The realistic legacy of Scott's historical novel is the other half of that truth. Balzac had no intention to disparage or supplant Scott. He regarded *La Comedie Humaine* as a massive *historical* study, derivative from Scott, that would, by its contemporary settings, interconnected volumes, and greater attention to sexual passion, bring the Waverley Novels into the near present.

Balzac's 1843 Preface, to *La Comedie Humaine*, written as he was gathering thirteen volumes for publication as a single comprehensive work, mentions only one author beside himself in any detail: Walter Scott. Claiming to have been disgusted by "the dry and sapless dictionaries of facts which are called history," Balzac says he had "turned to the works of Walter Scott . . . who had just then placed the imprint of his wondrous method upon a species of composition hitherto unjustly rated as secondary."[45] The "wondrous method" of Scott, Balzac rightly observes, resides in his ability to bring all facets of literature and life together into a totality, a holistic rendering of a civilization: "He brought together drama, dialogue, portraiture, description, scenery, the supernatural with the natural—two elements of his epoch; and side by side with poesy and majesty he placed the familiarities of the humblest speech" (ix). Here is criticism among peers that is of the highest order.

Balzac's Preface shows that Scott was both the great model and the great blocking force for continued development of the realist novel. Balzac is careful not to attack Scott, as Hazlitt had done, as an antiquarian living in a retrograde past. Instead, Balzac stakes out the present as the proper ground for today's historical novelist: "Society as it exists in France was therefore to be the historian; I was to be its secretary" he famously announces (x). By making his own claim upon the *historical* value of describing contemporary life, Balzac honored Scott, separated himself from him, and developed a new kind of historical fiction no longer directly concerned with revolution as political and military overthrow.

Chapter 2

Stendhal and Balzac established a different kind of historical realism that would develop side by side with Scott's tradition of the revolutionary historical novel for well over a century. The divergence must be understood, not as the simple adverse reaction of "realism" to "romanticism," or of "present" to "past," but as a branching into an alternative tradition. The remainder of this book will refocus its attention on the conventions of Scott's model of the historical novel and their development. Whether the conventions of Scott's paradigm could ever have convincingly served the Marxist expectations for historical realism is a vexed question. I shall argue that Scott's kind of historical novel was finally incapable of persuasively assimilating a Marxist realist perspective.

NOTES

1. A few prominent examples: E.M. Forster, "I do not care for him [Scott] and find it difficult to understand his continued reputation. . . . He is seen to have a trivial mind and a heavy style. He cannot construct. He has neither artistic detachment nor passion" (*Aspects of the Novel*, 1927): Virginia Woolf, "There are some writers who have entirely ceased to influence others, whose fame is for that reason both serene and cloudless, who are enjoyed or neglected rather than criticized and read. Among them is Scott" ("Sir Walter Scott," 1940); Dorothy Van Ghent, "incoherent structure equates with an incoherent world view; essentially valueless for us, no matter how attractive certain single elements of the book may be" (*The English Novel: Form and Function*, 1953); F.R. Leavis, dismissing Scott in a footnote, "Scott was primarily a kind of inspired folklorist. . . . The heroics of the historical novels can no longer command respect" (*The Great Tradition*, 1948). Scott's academic rehabilitation began with David Daiches's cogent article "Scott's Achievement as a Novelist" (1951) but as late as 1983 Harry E. Shaw could correctly declare, "The Waverley Novels remain the least-appreciated and least-read body of major fiction in English" (*The Forms of Historical Fiction*, 1983). For an overview of Scott's literary reputation see Richard Waswo, "Scott and the Really Great Tradition" in *Critical Essays on Sir Walter Scott; The Waverley Novels*, ed. Harry E. Shaw (New York: G .K. Hall, 1996), pp. 70–80.
2. Henry James, Preface to *The Tragic Muse* in *The Art of the Novel*, foreword by R.W.B. Lewis, Introduction by R.P. Blackmur (Boston: Northeastern University Press, 1984), p. 84. It is often forgotten that James wrote the famous phrase "loose baggy monsters" in the form of a question: "What do such large loose baggy monsters, with their queer elements of the accidental and the arbitrary, artistically mean?" Thirty years earlier, James's view of Scott, in his essay on Nassau Senior (*North American Review*, 1864) had been much more complimentary.
3. James Joyce, *A Portrait of the Artist as a Young Man*, ed. Seamus Deane (New York: Penguin Group, 1992), p. 269.
4. By 1858, Bagehot was in a position to offer an insightful overview of the Waverley Novels: "Sir Walter had no thesis to maintain. . . . He [Scott] could

understand (with a few exceptions) any considerable movement of life and action, and could always describe with easy freshness everything which he did understand; but he was not obliged by the stress of fanaticism to maintain a dogma concerning them" (Bagehot, "Sir Walter Scott," *National Review* (1858) in *The Critical Heritage: Sir Walter Scott*, ed. John O. Hayden, 2nd edition [London: Routledge, 1995], p. 397).

5. For Scott's influence on 19th century historicism, see the informative studies of Scott's "hybridity" by Ann Rigney, *The Rhetoric of Historical Representation: Three Narrative Histories of the French Revolution* (Cambridge: Cambridge University Press, 1990) and *Imperfect Histories: The Elusive Past and the Legacy of Romantic Historicism* (Ithaca and London: Cornell University Press, 2001). Rigney's studies expand upon Hayden White's insight that nineteenth-century historicism develops from broadly shared literary forms.

6. In his *Encyclopedia Brittanica* article on Romance, Scott defined a romance as "a fictitious narrative in prose or verse; the interest of which turns upon marvelous and uncommon incidents" and a novel as "a fictitious narrative, differing from the Romance, because events are accommodated to the ordinary train of human events and the modern state of society." The two genres are obviously not mutually exclusive; they form a spectrum ("An Essay on Romance" in *Miscellaneous Prose Works* [Edinburgh: Cadell and Co., 1827], VI, 155, 156).

7. Sir Walter Scott, *Waverley; or, 'Tis Sixty Years Since*, ed. Andrew Hook (New York: Penguin Books, 1985), p. 63.

8. Ian Duncan argues persuasively that Scott was influenced by David Hume's skeptical, realist sense of the dailyness of life as lived (*Scott's Shadow: the Novel in Romantic Edinburgh* [Princeton: Princeton University Press, 2007], pp. 29, 119, 137). I believe Hume's balanced *History of England* had a similarly great effect on Scott's view of the issues of monarchical legitimacy during the seventeenth and early eighteenth centuries.

9. It could perhaps be demonstrated that critics most dismissive of Scott have fastened upon the awkwardness of his romance but neglected his historical insight. While providing a new emphasis on revolution, I will follow the "realist" tradition of interpreting Scott's novels that originated in Lukacs and has been maintained, in differing non-Marxist ways, by David Daiches, Avrom Fleishman, Harry E. Shaw, David Brown, and Jane Millgate.

10. The contentious issue of whether Scott had slandered the Covenanters, an issue debated at length in *Old Mortality*'s first reviews, might have been tempered by considering the function of Robert Paterson, who gives the novel its title, but never appears in Scott's narrative. See Ina Ferris, *The Achievement of Literary Authority: Gender, History and the Waverley Novels* (Ithaca: Cornell University Press, 1991), pp. 140–194.

11. Scott, review essay on John Galt's *The Omen* in Joan Williams, ed., *Sir Walter Scott on Novelists and Fiction*, (London: Routledge and Kegan Paul, 1968), p. 299. Originally published in Ballantyne's Novelist's Library, 1826.

12. The view Scott expresses here illustrates the distinction Katie Trumpener has drawn between Maria Edgeworth's comparatively atemporal national tale, seeking to preserve Scottish or Irish culture, and Scott's historical novel, concentrating on

political conflict and cultural change (Trumpener, *Bardic Nationalism* [Princeton: Princeton University Press, 1997], pp. 130–133). Trumpener argues convincingly that the historical novel (mostly written by men) grew out of the national tale (mostly written by women). Scott's continued admiration for, and friendship with, Maria Edgeworth thus becomes all the more revealing.

13. Samuel Taylor Coleridge, letter to Thomas Allsop, April 8, 1820 quoted in *Walter Scott: the Critical Heritage*, ed. John O. Hayden (London and New York: Routledge, 1995) p. 180.

14. M.M. Bakhtin, *The Dialogic Imagination*, edited by Michael Holquist, translated by Caryl Emerson and Michael Holquist, (Austin: University of Texas Press, 1981), p. 243.

15. Edgar Johnson, *Sir Walter Scott: The Great Unknown* (New York: The Macmillan Co., 1970), I, xxiii.

16. Alexander Welsh captures the wavering temperament and social class of the Waverley protagonist with admirable clarity. Welsh does not, however, often consider the importance of the political context in which the wavering protagonist is enmeshed. Welsh emphasizes instead the gentlemanly qualities that compel the protagonist to act with honor, but to withdraw as quickly as possible back into propertied genteel status. My reading of the causes and import of the protagonists' wavering is quite different. See Alexander Welsh, *The Hero of the Waverley Novels* (New Haven: Yale University Press, 1963).

17. In the last chapter, the reader is told that Edward Waverley marries Rose Bradwardine (*Waverley*), Henry Morton marries Elizabeth Bellenden (*Old Mortality*), Frank Osbaldistone marries Diana Vernon (*Rob Roy*), Reuben Butler marries Jeanie Deans (*The Heart of Mid-lothian*); Markham Everard marries Alice Lee (*Woodstock*). Among Scott's immediate successors, the pattern continues: Peyton Dunwoodie marries Frances Wharton (*The Spy*), Duncan Heyward marries Alice Munro (*The Last of the Mohicans*); Piotr Grinyov marries Marya Mironov (*The Captain's Daughter*). Only Balzac's *Les Chouans* forms an exception—an exception that surely contributed to Balzac's turning toward a different kind of novel.

18. Biographical and historical information in this section is drawn from the following sources: John E. Archer, *Social Unrest and Popular Protest in England 1780–1940* (Cambridge and New York: Cambridge University Press, 2000); James Chandler, *England in 1819: The Politics of Literary Culture* (Chicago: University of Chicago Press, 1998); Ian Duncan, *Scott's Shadow: The Novel in Romantic Edinburgh* (Princeton: Princeton University Press, 2007); Arthur Herman, *How the Scots Invented the Modern World* (New York: Broadway Books, 2001); Christopher Hill, *The Century of Revolution 1603–1714* (London: Thomas Nelson and Sons, 1966); Edgar Johnson, *Sir Walter Scott: The Great Unknown*, 2 vols. (New York: Macmillan, 1970); Bruce Lenman, *The Jacobite Risings in Britain, 1689–1746* (Aberdeen: Scottish Cultural Press, 1995); J.D. Mackie, *A History of Scotland* (London; Penguin Books, 1991); Graham McMaster, *Scott and Society* (Cambridge: Cambridge University Press, 1981); Stuart Semmel, *Napoleon and the British* (New Haven: Yale University Press, 2004); John Sutherland, *The Life of Walter Scott: A Critical Biography* (Oxford: Blackwell, 1995).

19. Katie Trumpener, *Bardic Nationalism* (Princeton: Princeton University Press, 1997), p. 27.

20. Adam Ferguson, *An Essay on the History of Civil Society*, ed. Fania Oz-Salzberger (Cambridge and New York: Cambridge University Press, 1995), p. 257. On Ferguson's political thought in the context of classical republicanism see Kalyvas and Katznelson *Liberal Beginnings: Making a Republic for the Moderns*, pp. 51–87 and Duncan Forbes, "The Rationalism of Sir Walter Scott" in *Critical Essays on Sir Walter Scott*, ed, Harry E, Shaw, pp, 183–197. See also Forbes's introduction to his edition of Ferguson's *Essay on the History of Civil Society* (Edinburgh: Edinburgh University Press, 1966) pp. xii–xli.

21. While awaiting execution, Louis the XVI had reputedly been absorbed in details of the execution of Charles I.

22. Edgar Johnson, *Sir Walter Scott: The Great Unknown*, I, 394.

23. Ibid., I, 437.

24. Walter Scott, *Rob Roy*, ed. Ian Duncan (Oxford and New York: Oxford University Press, 1998), p. 301.

25. Wellington's quotation is from R.R. Palmer, *A History of the Modern World*, 2nd edition (New York: Alfred A. Knopf, 1960), p. 447. John Prebble argues that Scott's efforts as pageant master of King George IV's visit to Edinburgh in 1822 were motivated by Scott's desire to control worker protests by providing a patriotic distraction (*The King's Jaunt*, pp. 9–21). The traditional explanation has been that Scott's service to the King was an outgrowth of his nationalism and his support of the 1707 Act of Union. Ian Duncan and Katie Trumpener complicate Scott's motivation in yet another way. The King's visit also served as an occasion for advancing Scottish cultural nationalism by reenacting old customs.

26. Blair Worden, *The English Civil Wars 1640–1660* (London: Orion House, 2009), pp. 1–3.

27. Joseph Frank, *The Levellers* (New York: Russell and Russell, 1969), p. 118 and bibliography. First published 1955 by Harvard University Press.

28. Christopher Hill, "A Bourgeois Revolution," in *Three British Revolutions: 1641, 1668, 1776*, ed. J.G.A. Pocock (Princeton: Princeton University Press, 1980), p. 134. Christopher Hill insists that 1640–1660 should be called a "Revolution" not because revolution was intended but because of the upheaval's later effects on the economy and on social class. Lawrence Stone is more circumspect, arguing that the key descriptor of the era should be "instability" and that the one undeniable change was to discredit the Stuart notion of the Divine Right of Kings (see Stone "The Results of the English Revolutions of the 17th Century," ibid, pp. 23–109).

29. Jonathan Swift characteristically refused to be silent. Gulliver summarizes seventeenth-century British history as "only an heap of conspiracies, rebellions, murders, massacres, revolutions, banishments, the very worst effects that avarice, faction, hypocrisy, perfidiousness, cruelty, rage, madness, hatred, envy, lust, malice and ambition could produce" (*Gulliver's Travels*, [1726] in *Gulliver's Travels and Other Writings*, ed. Louis Landa [Cambridge: Houghton Mifflin Company, 1960] p. 106).

30. Scott, *Tales of a Grandfather* (Boston: Sanborn, Carter and Bazin, 1855), Second Series, Volume II, pp. 76, 77, 105. The *Tales* were written for descendant

generations, not for adolescent grandsons. Their length and complexity of syntax preclude them from the category of children's literature. Edgar Johnson's biography of Scott shows that *Tales of a Grandfather* was extremely popular, attracting readers of all ages.

31. Scott, *Tales of a Grandfather*, Series 2, volume 2, p. 76.

32. Ian Duncan observes that "Scott—writing in the shadow of the event [the French Revolution]—sought to contain revolution's apocalyptic potential, to fold it back into 'the continuum of history' in part by displacing it into the past, and in part by investing it with the tropes of fiction: the Humean medium of the conventional, the customary, the everyday" (*Scott's Shadow*, p. 136). "Contain" is the right word to convey Scott's intent. Scott's literary problem in writing an historically specific novel, however, still remained: by what means and at what historical moment should one combine fiction and history so as to render the containment of revolution convincing?

33. Scott initially had given the novel the more accurate title, *A Legend of the Wars of Montrose*. Unlike Scott's earlier characterization of royalist and Jacobite leaders (Claverhouse and Charles Edward Stuart), John Grahame, Marquis of Montrose is much more important for the historical movement he represents than for his inner character.

34. Scott, *A Legend of the Wars of Montrose,* ed. J.H. Alexander (Edinburgh and New York: Edinburgh University Press and Columbia University Press, 1995), pp. 157, 158.

35. A close reading of Bruce Lenman's *The Jacobite Risings in Britain 1689–1746* repeatedly demonstrates the bewildering variety of economic interests, social classes, political groups, regional loyalties, religious affiliations and nationalities that made up the ever-shifting components of the "Jacobite" risings from the time of "Royalist" Montrose through the "Pretender" Charles Edward Stuart. As Lenman's historical specifics multiply, generalizations about Jacoobitism become increasingly suspect, even for one single uprising. See Lenman, *The Jacobite Risings in Britain 1689–1746* (Aberdeen: Scottish Cultural Press, 1995), especially p. 283.

36. John Buchan, *Sir Walter Scott* (London: Cassell, 1987), pp. 300–302.

37. Sir Walter Scott, *Woodstock or The Cavalier* (Boston: IndyPublish.com, 2011), p. 70.

38. Scott, *Woodstock,* p. 264; Christopher Hill, *God's Englishman: Oliver Cromwell and the English Revolution* (New York: The Dial Press, 1970), p. 179.

39. Maurice Ashley argues that "Oliver Cromwell had not in fact made up his mind when he dissolved the Long Parliament what form of government he intended to put in its place" (*Cromwell's Generals* [New York: St. Martin's Press, 1955], p. 106). Scott's characterization of Cromwell and of Commissioners Harrison and Desborough accords with Ashley's portrayals of them.

40. *Woodstock* p. 127. Six years later, Christian Isobel Johnstone echoed Scott's political self-description in her essay "The Political Tendency of Sir Walter Scott's Writing" (1832): "The tendency of all his [Scott's] writings has been to enlighten and expand the minds of men, by enlarging their affections; by making them *neither Whig nor Tory*, but something infinitely better than both" (quoted by Ian Duncan, *Scott's Shadow*, p. 304, italics mine).

41. William Hazlitt, "Sir Walter Scott," in *The Spirit of the Age*, 4th edition (London: George Bell and Sons, 1886), p. 99.

42. Mark Altschuller, "The Rise and Fall of Walter Scott's Popularity in Russia" in Murray Pittock, ed., *The Reception of Sir Walter Scott in Europe* (London: Continuum, 2006), pp. 216, 217.

43. I here develop ideas expressed in Franco Moretti's *The Way of the World: the Bildungsroman in European Culture* (London: Verso, 1987) especially chapter 2.

44. Honoré de Balzac, letter to Madame Hanska, 1843 quoted in Marion Ayton Crawford's introduction to *The Chouans* (New York: Penguin, 1986), p. 24.

45. Honoré de Balzac, *La Comedie Humaine*, translated by Katharine Prescott Wormeley (New York: Atheneum Society, 1885), I, viii.

Chapter 3

Transforming the Neutral Ground

A recurrent concern about literary setting is the distinction between space and place. Following Gaston Bachelard, Yi-Fu-Tuan, and others, we have recognized that a space does not evolve into a place until it is invested with human feelings and meaning. We use the terms "setting" and "scene" when we conceive of an action transpiring within or in front of an environment that has been given meaning, symbolic, psychological, or historical, as in the cognate term "dramatic setting."[1] As Roger Sale has demonstrated, attention shifted during the romantic era from symbolic setting to the particular environment, with the result that "place has a larger role than ever before in shaping lives."[2] Nowhere is this shift from generic backdrop to affective environment more in evidence than in the Scottish Waverley Novels, which Sale does not consider.

Scott's practice was to choose a particular geopolitical setting that had the advantages both of historical accuracy and openness to the psychology of revolutionary danger. In the subtitle to *The Spy*, Cooper was to give this kind of setting a local habitation and a name: "A Tale of the Neutral Ground." Historically, "the Neutral Ground" had been the term commonly applied to Westchester County, New York, throughout the American Revolution. When choosing to emphasize the "neutral ground," however, Cooper also knew that *Waverley, Old Mortality, Rob Roy, A Legend of Montrose*, and *The Bride of Lammermoor* had developed many complex facets of the neutral ground before him. Those complexities, both in the Waverley Novels and in historical novels to follow, deserve more sustained consideration than they have yet received.

To set an historical novel in a neutral ground simultaneously releases the dangers and opportunities of the unknown. The reader initially experiences the neutral ground as a geopolitical area—contested by forces of the Old Order and the New, but possessed by neither. Until the end of the fictional

narrative, the neutral ground will be riven by shifting military and political
partisans; few parts of it are ever "neutral" in allegiance or political belief.
Power shifts continually, leaving the future open until the novel's resolution.
The setting thus becomes a metaphor for a revolutionary world.

For characters who pass through the neutral ground, the wearing of a mask,
adopting a pseudonym, shifting allegiance, and changing one's identity are
often necessary, even though they know that the harsh judgments of hindsight
await. The one Scott character whose name and inner identity do not shift is
the wavering protagonist who is continuously pressured to resolve his beliefs
and his allegiance. He might prefer to be neutral, but changing circumstances
make neutrality suspect from both sides. Whether he claims allegiance to history's eventual victors or losers, he discovers that their values and conduct are
less than wholly admirable. He may shift allegiance, or he may endure rebellion and revolution without public commitment, but in the end he withdraws
to the peace of restored property and the marital life of the landed gentry,
whatever the new political order may be. The protagonist's own heart lends a
psychological dimension to the neutral ground, doubling the military conflict
visible within the setting.[3]

The neutral ground is thus a "space" that has recently become a borderless
"place" invested with the fears and ambitions of many partisans. The foreground narrative of many Waverley Novels pictures a young man of precious
little military or political experience travelling north into disputed territory
near the Highland line (Waverley, Frank Osbaldistone, Darsie Latimer). With
or without a servant, he travels across meadows, crosses hilltops, and stops in
town taverns, but most often he is seen riding along narrow pathways through
hillside glens. He crosses rocky streams, dense woods, clearings with cottage
farms, occasional cataracts or chasms. Such descriptions are probably faithful
to the topography of early eighteenth-century Scotland, but they are also an
objective correlative for the protagonist's mental state. He cannot know or
see what may be around the next bend in the path. Mists are frequent, danger
likely, and uncertainty constant. He travels through a country reinforcing the
anxious confusion of his mind.

Until *The Heart of Mid-Lothian* (1818) first brought the historical novel to
the city of Edinburgh, *Waverley* had defined Scott's neutral ground as a border
country without borders. Scott assumes that his reader will at the outset accept
a simplistic commonplace: the Highland culture to the north, based upon the
clan system, tenant agriculture, the French alliance, tolerance of Catholicism,
and loyalty to the Stuart monarchy, opposes the dominant English culture to
the south, based upon mercantile estates, deeded property, Protestantism, and
loyalty to the Hanoverian kings, whom the Jacobites regard as present-day
usurpers. There are, however, as Scott repeatedly shows, Jacobites in England
as well as the southern Lowlands; there are Hanoverians in the Highlands

as well as the northern Lowlands. There are staunch Anglicans and staunch Protestants in both the Jacobite and the Hanoverian armies.

For Scott, the Lowlands near the Highland line are the focal point of conflicting groups and conflicting values. But the forces that shape individual allegiance are never simple binary dualities, such as "reason" versus "passion," "ecstasy" versus "despair," or today's clichés of "heredity" versus "environment" and "nature" versus "nurture." Individuals attempt to sort out the ever-varied influences of ancestry, education, social class, temperament, youthful experiences, friendships, love, economic pressure, military circumstance, and political principle. Single forces may be readily identifiable, but their shifting combinations affect individuals in different, plausible ways. Therein lies Scott's persuasiveness; he gives his reader a complex world entire.

In *Waverley*, as the 1745 Jacobite counterrevolution gathers momentum, the baffling quality of the neutral ground becomes increasingly evident. Communications over the disputed mountainous terrain are so undependable that Edward Waverley does not know that Prince Charles Edward Stuart has landed at Moidart, even though Fergus's Jacobite clansmen are training for battle beneath his eyes. In a region dominated by Jacobite troops, British Major Melville, serving as Justice of the Peace, seeks unsuccessfully to arrest Waverley under a British Law passed in Edinburgh shortly *after* the seemingly suspended 1707 Act of Union. In such a situation, with whom does jurisdiction reside? Stirling Castle is held by the Hanoverians, but nearby Doune Castle is held by the Jacobites. The Jacobites control Holyrood Palace and the streets of Edinburgh, but not Edinburgh Castle. Characters who can speak more than one language (English, Lowland Scots, or Gaelic) can hide their meaning and hence their identity with comparative ease.

The treachery of the neutral ground is first evident in the powers wielded by the Caterans and by Donald Bean Lane. Fergus MacIvor, Highland Jacobite laird though he is, secretly employs Highland cattle thieves in order to exact protection tribute from Lowlanders, especially from Lowland Jacobite gentry now weaponless because of the Disarming Act that followed the failed 1715 rebellion. While publically insisting that James III is the only rightful king of Great Britain, *de jure* though not *de facto*, Fergus continues to steal the cattle of fellow Jacobites who will not pay him blackmail for protection. Donald Bean Lane—a scurrilous liar, thief, and killer—serves as Fergus's chief operative. By changing his identity and his language, Bean Lane successfully suborns Waverley's Hanoverian regiment, a regiment made of Englishmen recruited by Waverley from the vicinity of his ancestral estate, but now stationed in Edinburgh. Due to Bean Lane's treachery, Waverley is cashiered as an officer in the Hanoverian army. Sure that he has been publicly dishonored but oblivious to the consequences of his own wavering, Waverley deserts the English army and joins the Jacobite cause. His former regiment, deceived and in disarray, is cut to pieces by the Jacobites at the Battle of Preston Pans.

How does Scott render the significance of Donald Bean Lean topographically? Waverley's very first sight of the Highlands is of "a blue outline in the horizon" that gradually swells into "huge gigantic masses, which frowned defiance over the more level country that lay beneath them."[4] Helpless to find his own way or to understand looming Highland defiance, Waverley is led by Evan Dhu up through Bailly-Brough pass at sunset along a "path that winded up a chasm between two tremendous rocks," following "a foaming stream" between an "inaccessible" mountain on one side and "a shroud of copsewood on the other" (135). The middle course is the only way through, but Waverley knows neither how to negotiate it, nor where it leads. One magnificent eagle is visible but it is surrounded by "a thousand birds of prey, hawks, kites, carrion-crows, and ravens disturbed from their lodgings" (135). Wading through a bog at nightfall, Waverley is entranced by the glow of an expanding red ball at the horizon. The red ball is not the sunset, however, but the refracted light of Donald Bean Lane's campfires "kindled in the jaws of a lofty cavern" (140). Waverley prepares to meet "a stern, gigantic, ferocious figure, such as Salvator would have chosen to be the central object of a group of banditii" (141), but Donald Bean Lane proves to be disappointingly thin and short, with "small, pale features," "rather a diminutive and insignificant figure" (141).

Waverley's predisposition toward romance leads him to misunderstand almost everything he sees. A carrion crow if ever there were one, Donald Bean Lane is nothing like a banditti by Salvator Rosa, but he nonetheless embodies, for the remainder of the novel, the hellish, self-interested behavior released by the conditions of neutral ground. He is anything but "a diminutive and insignificant figure." What is so remarkable in Scott's imagining of this scene, a kind of initiation *manqué*, is that there is no obtrusive literary symbolizing; environmental details appropriate to the romantic sublime suggest to the reader brutal realities that Waverley cannot see.[5]

Donald Bean Lane and the Caterans force the reader to confront the hidden forces that grow in times of civil war. The vacuum of power within the neutral ground enables crafty opportunists and lawless predators to rise. We meet a sequence of middle-aged men, of middling success and of varied social class, who view the mayhem of revolutionary conflict as their ticket up to wealth and power. These men are usually law-honest and nonviolent but always ready to bend moral and political principle to fit the opportunity of the moment. Among them are Scott's Andrew Fairservice (*Rob Roy*), Cooper's Colonel Wellmere (*The Spy*), Pushkin's Shvabrin (*The Captain's Daughter*), Tolstoy's Vasili Kuragin (*War and Peace*), Zola's Delaherche (*La Débacle*),

Lampedusa's Tancredi (*The Leopard*), and Vidal's Alexander Hamilton (*Burr*). Astute and self-reliant, these opportunists are to be distinguished from revolution's lawless, lower class marauders who seek the safety of bullying in groups.

Claiming semi-military authority, the marauders bribe, rob, burn, and kill with surprising ease, disappearing as suddenly and swiftly as they appear. The conditions of the neutral ground shield them all: Scott's Caterans, Cooper's Cow-Boys and Skinners (*The Spy*), Balzac's Chouans, Pugachev's Cossacks ("The Captain's Daughter"), Zola's *franc-tireurs* (*La Débacle*), the Greens, and the Forest Brotherhood of the Russian Civil War (Pasternak's *Doctor Zhivago*). Novelists, critics, and readers have been reluctant to accord the opportunist and the predator the significance they deserve. In the context of world-changing issues of the Old Order and the New, the opportunists and the predators seem to be lowlifes from society's nether regions who are of secondary importance. But they are always there, appearing in sudden bold relief, subsiding, and then reappearing. The lawless predators are usually put down as revolutionary violence subsides, but the crafty opportunists persevere, gathering resources with which they will enter the post-revolutionary era. Their presence seems an inevitability of revolutionary conditions; Napoleon Bonaparte can be regarded as their epitome.

A central building, usually an estate house, serves as the focal point, the Bakhtinian chronotype where the paradoxes of the neutral ground meet. Tully-Veolan reflects the Jacobite character of its owner, Baron Cosmo Bradwardine. Proudly displaying its crumbling heraldic stone bears, Tully-Veolan has not changed, and will not change, despite its evident decay. The building, like its owner, stands for an honest reverence for tradition, but is more than a little ridiculous in the futile ways its traditions are maintained. The reader is introduced to Tully-Veolan as Waverley rides through the adjoining hamlet of the same name. The "straggling village" of Tully-Veolan is little more than "a straggling kind of unpaved street" lined with mud and thatch houses, at whose doors "old men, bent as much by toil as years," their eyes "bleared with age and smoke," gaze vacantly outward, aroused only by "the incessant yelping of a score of idle, useless curs" (74, 75). These villagers are not the idle hangers-on they appear to be; they are tenants and local tradesmen whose livelihood is tied to Baron Bradwardine's lands. Waverley notes the odd visual proximity of the estate and the village, but he does not understand the economic tie between them. Instead, once Waverley has entered the tree-lined avenue of the Bradwardine estate, Waverley becomes "so much pleased with the placid ideas of rest and seclusion excited by this confined and quiet scene, that he *forgot* the misery and dirt of the hamlet he had left behind him" (77, italics mine). These are revolutionary conditions that Scott's protagonist (and perhaps his readers) would prefer not to see.

Scott's awareness of tenant poverty does not lead him to condemn Baron Bradwardine as a hard-hearted aristocrat in the way Dickens was later to blame Marquis St. Evrémonde. Where Dickens fastens upon the cruelty of the aristocratic heart, Scott gives us historical context. Bradwardine and his daughter Rose are in a particularly trying situation:

> Tully-Veolan having become a very unpleasant, and even dangerous place of residence for an unprotected young lady, on account of its vicinity to the Highlands, and also to one or two large villages which, from aversion as much to the Caterans as zeal for presbytery, had declared themselves on the side of Government [the Hanoverians], and formed irregular bodies of partisans who had frequent skirmishes with the mountaineers, and sometimes attacked the houses of the Jacobite gentry in the braes, or frontier between the mountain and plain. (304)

The vulnerability of the Bradwardines leaves them more compromised, more helpless, than the cruel authority exercised over the peasantry by the Evrémondes. During the course of Scott's narrative we hear of English troops, Jacobite troops, Caterans, and bands of pro-Government guerillas all enforcing, momentarily, their notions of justice in the neutral ground. We do not hear of any police presence seeking to enforce the laws of Scotland or Great Britain.

Commentary on the novel's opening scenes has concentrated, not on Waverley's initial encounter with Donald Bean Lean, but on the scene in which Waverley feels impelled to join the Jacobites after he hears Flora MacIvor singing a Scottish battle song in Gaelic. All the components of textbook "romanticism" are here: the attraction of an ancient preindustrial culture, minstrelsy, solitude in the mountain, a waterfall in the glen, a sensual woman (later called "the Dark Lady") who symbolizes an unearthly beauty—together creating an exotic experience that releases wonder bordering on ecstasy.[6] The scene also, however, has hidden political causes and political consequences. Because Flora's loyalty to the Stuarts is unalloyed, Waverley associates the purity of this transcendent moment, out of time and space, with the presumed purity of Flora's Jacobite cause. He unconsciously wishes to efface images of today's Scotland, as symbolized by the village and estate of Tully-Veolan, and replace them with romantic images of Highland culture tinged by French connections.

Waverley experiences Scotland as a sequence of discrete experiences in borderless places: Tully-Veolan, Bean Lane's cave, Flora's glen, Fergus's hall at Glennaquoich, and the gathering of Fergus's clansmen. Like his desultory education in Froissart and chivalric romance, Scotland's neutral ground provides immediate sensory appeal but no means of thinking through problematic issues. Waverley seems never to have confronted the import of the Glorious Revolution, nor the question of Stuart right to the British throne. As biographers have noted, Waverley's education recalls Scott's own, but that fact alone cannot explain the readiness with which Scott's readers identified with Waverley as a likeable representative of the privileged and educated classes. If Waverley's initial indifference to political realities is to be regarded as an educational anomaly, why should this identification have occurred? The explanation may lie in a human tendency deeper than Waverley's readings in Froissart would suggest. How many people have ever thought through questions of political legitimacy at the moment when a revolution or counterrevolution occurs?[7]

The pressures of complex, changing circumstances prompt Waverley first to accept a Captaincy in a Hanoverian Regimen, then to declare fealty to Bonnie Prince Charlie, then to fight with the Jacobite army, then to quit the Jacobite army (in effect deserting), then to reacquire honor and status as the scion of Waverley-Honour, and finally to possess a restored Tully-Veolan through his marriage to Rose Bradwardine. Until his marriage, none of these compulsive decisions results from a clear and comprehensive view of his situation. The conditions of the neutral ground as well as his own temperament do not allow it. His restoration and marriage are a handy way for Scott to suggest the eventual reconciliation of Jacobites and Hanoverians after bitter memories of the Battle of Culloden Moor. Would that all participants in the '45 had been so fortunate!

Only once during the ever-shifting conditions of Waverley's experiences does he reflect on the underlying merit of the Jacobite cause. Lingering as a visitor at the MacIvor's Highland estate, smitten by the glamorous courage of Fergus and the romantic loyalty of Flora, Waverley pauses to reflect upon what he half fears he is about to do:

> He felt inexpressible repugnance at the idea of being accessory to the plague of civil war. Whatever were the original rights of the Stuarts, calm reflection told him, that, omitting the question how far James the Second could forfeit those of his posterity, he had, according to the united voice of the whole nation, justly forfeited his own. Since that period, four monarchs had reigned in peace and glory over Britain, sustaining and exalting the character of the nation abroad, and its liberties at home. Reason asked, was it worthwhile to disturb a government so long settled and established, and to plunge a kingdom into all the miseries of civil war, for the purpose of replacing on the throne the descendants of a monarch by whom it had been willfully forfeited?[8]

Because Waverley's final question is clearly rhetorical, (the answer is "no"), the passage as a whole seems a rare instance in which we hear the voice of Scott speaking through Waverley, rather than the viewpoint of Waverley himself. Waverley has heretofore shown no concern for the monarchical rights of James III or Charles Edward Stuart, let alone of Charles I or James II. Accordingly, the perspective of "reason" that governs this one passage will have little if any effect on Waverley's future feelings, thoughts, or conduct. Although Scott assumes the Whig view that James II had "willfully forfeited" the crown in 1688, Waverley has formed no position at all on the controversy of dynastic succession. His time of emotional commitment and military service to the Jacobite cause is still ahead of him, not behind him.[9]

With little understanding of political history, Waverley tries to discern the path that will salvage his honor, his family's honor, and the well-being of those dear to him. If there is any clear single path to those ends, he cannot find it. Nor does his mind allow him to consider how changed institutions might reshape power toward the end of political justice. Through Talbot's political and financial interventions, Waverley will be restored to honor, wealth, gentry status, and a fulfilling marriage, but his happy survival is as much due to circumstance and to chance, as to merit. For apolitical citizenry, is it not ever thus?

Until the Rebellion of '45 is nearly over, Waverley would like to believe that Fergus and Flora MacIvor, Bonnie Prince Charlie, Evan Dhu, and their Jacobite adherents are romantic revolutionaries bent on restoration. Major Melville and Colonel Talbot, stolid figures of middle-aged common sense, regard Jacobites as counterrevolutionaries rebelling against lawful king and lawful government on behalf of a reactionary culture. Accordingly, Waverley initially resents Melville and Talbot even though they provide him sensible advice and bring about his escape from Hanoverian reprisals. The judgments of Waverley's unwelcome mentors are ultimately confirmed by Waverley's growing perception that the Jacobite Rebellion is more of a civil war than a restoration.

Scott challenges expectation by selecting as his novel's major historical battle the Jacobite victory at Preston Pans. Its military alignments foreshadow Napoleonic warfare by ironically intimating Jacobite defeat. As the victorious Jacobite army marches toward London under the banner *Tandem Triumphans*, Waverley surveys the uneven line of separable clan forces, each headed by a laird and a few well-armed gentlemen, but followed by an array of gillies, peasants, tenants, and finally "bandits," many armed only with a scythe, a stake, or "a gun without a lock" (324). With few cavalry and one piece of artillery, riven by interclan jealousies, these men will nonetheless, for the moment, best a well-trained and fully equipped Hanoverian army unified under one commander. Clan warfare has, however, no chance against a modern national army armed with artillery. For Scott's readers, the future success of Napoleonic methods of warfare is there to see.

Neutrality proves to be a major cause of Jacobite failure. Bonnie Prince Charlie had expected men of Stuart sympathies in the north of England to join his army, but very few did. The Jacobite army marches through northern English towns from which wealthy men have fled. Those who remain, the poor and the ignorant, stand on the side of the road, "stared and listened, heartless, stupefied, and dull," gazing "with astonishment, mixed with horror and aversion, at the wild appearance, unknown language, and singular garb of the Scottish clans" (390). Despite the Act of Union, in which Walter Scott firmly believed, the English and Scottish peoples are not truly one people, and certainly not one culture. For the sake of self-preservation, the ground of the southern Lowlands and northern England is outwardly neutral, but inwardly hostile to the prospect of Jacobite counterrevolution, even if it can be justified as restoration.[10] While participants, including Waverley, turn aside from civil war, irreconcilables remain north and south. Scott's "Postscript," with its assurance that, by 1814, "the gradual influx of wealth, and extension of commerce, have since united to render the present people of Scotland a class of beings as different from their grandfathers as the existing English are from those of Queen Elizabeth's time" (492) rings a bit hollow in its assumption that cultural uniformity will prevail in the post-Napoleonic world. To be a part of Great Britain has never been the same as being English, as political feelings in today's Scotland have repeatedly shown.

"THE LAW OF THE STRONGEST"

Cooper's resentment at being dubbed "the American Scott" argues a need to adopt yet transform the literary conventions that had defined the Waverley Novels. The need would never be more pressing than during the writing of his first historical novel, *The Spy* (1821), a tale that confronts revolution in the neutral ground as explicitly as can be imagined. The similarities between the civil wars despoiling the Hudson Highlands and the Scottish Highlands suggest Cooper's implicit, admiring challenge to Scott. *The Spy* opens in September of 1780. For three years the British army has been occupying New York City and Manhattan Island, while George Washington's army has remained along the Hudson in northern Westchester County guarding against British advances along the New York—Montreal waterway. The farmlands between the two armies have been reduced to a wasteland invaded and plundered by British "Regular" troops, by American "Continental" Troops, and by their allied paramilitary guerilla bands, the Cow-Boys and the Skinners. Farmers are unwilling to seed crops that would almost surely be confiscated. Civil authority, as in the Lowlands of *Waverley*, is markedly ineffective. But the cultural and linguistic complexities that characterize Scott's border country are much diminished. The changing combinations of self-divided allegiance (royalist vs. parliamentarian, clan vs. country, Celt vs. Englishman,

Anglican vs. Presbyterian, nobility vs. peasant etc.) so apparent in *A Legend of the Wars of Montrose* and in *Waverley*, do not recur. Cooper's natural ground is alternatively controlled by the four differentiated military groups. Not only does America have a less diverse cultural history than Scotland; an epoch-making, successful republican revolution, not a failed counterrevolution, must emerge from the American conflict.

Accordingly, Cooper needs to resolve the anarchy of the neutral ground more definitively than Scott. At the beginning of *The Spy*, the reader is encouraged to identify the waverer with the landowning neutral, Mr. Wharton, but after the foreground action moves away from Mr. Wharton's estate, the figure of Harvey Birch more and more dominates the novel, replacing the waverer with an unequivocal spy-patriot of common class origin. Cooper's first paragraph opens with a sense of place recalling Scott ("a solitary traveller was seen pursuing his way through one of the numerous little valleys of West-Chester . . . in a thick mist"), but shadowy, stormy pathways will gradually lift until the neutral ground is finally replaced, in Cooper's last chapter, by a resplendent new nation.[11] Observing a golden and explicitly *western* sunset, Mr. Harper (George Washington) is made to remark "how grand! How awfully sublime!—may such a quiet speedily await the struggle in which my country is engaged, and such a glorious evening follow the day of her adversity" (50). Considered in its entire trajectory, Cooper's narrative is shaped by his determination to show how the progress of civilization must inevitably advance in an open land where the dead hand of the past has little force, where republican political feelings are heightened by the stresses of natural survival, and where a despised commoner can become an unacknowledged national savior.

Cooper's will to affirm revolutionary republicanism is, however, almost entirely the narrator's overlay. The foreground of the novel, the action that transpires within the neutral ground, is rendered with a ferocity so memorable that republican progress seems merely an idea, however powerful. Thirty-four of Cooper's thirty-five chapters take place within the neutral ground, often at darkening sunset, in a barren cleaning, or on a deserted roadway. At novel's end, we do not see Westchester's neutral ground transformed into America the Beautiful—or the Sublime. Instead all Cooper's characters vacate the neutral ground, while transformation occurs elsewhere. Until the close, the true power operative within the neutral ground is defined by one of the American justices presiding over British Captain Henry Wharton's trial: "Its name, as a neutral ground, is unauthorized by law; it is an appellation that originates with the condition of the country. But wherever an army goes, it carries its rights along, and the first is, the ability to protect itself" (302). The thuggish leader of the Skinners sums up the same notion of controlling power in fewer, simpler words: "The law of the neutral ground is the law of the strongest" (180).

The novel's second paragraph summarizes the ways by which conditions of the neutral ground affect human behavior within it:

> The county of West-Chester, after the British had obtained possession of the island of New York, became common ground, in which both parties continued to act for the remainder of the war of the revolution. A large proportion of its inhabitants, either restrained by their attachments, or influenced by their fears, affected a neutrality they did not feel. The lower towns were, of course, more particularly under the dominion of the crown, while the upper, finding a security from the vicinity of the continental troops, were bold in asserting their revolutionary opinions, and their right to govern themselves. Great numbers, however, wore masks, which even to this day have not been thrown aside; and many an individual has gone down to the tomb, stigmatized as a foe to the rights of his countrymen, while in secret, he has been the useful agent of the leaders of the revolution; and on the other hand, could the hidden repositories of divers flaming Patriots have been opened to the light of day, royal protections would have been discovered concealed under piles of British gold. (10)

Cooper's narrative confirms these observations in every detail. A man's political principles are shaped by his need to identify today's proximate power. There is neither place nor leisure here for the prolonged romantic uncertainties of a Waverley. Instead, the chief "waverer" of *The Spy*, the rapidly aging Mr. Wharton, is motivated not by search for an honorable solution, but by fears for his politically divided family and his considerable possessions. Affecting a neutrality he does not feel, Mr. Wharton's decency has rendered him passive even unto "imbecility" (22).[12] Nearly every male character figuratively or literally wears a mask whenever he encounters others; men, unlike women, cannot act as they are or speak as they believe. Reputation has little to do with merit or real allegiance. The truest of American revolutionary patriots is reviled as a British spy (Harvey Birch); the publically revered patriot has recently been bought by British gold (Benedict Arnold).

In his last preface to *The Spy*, Cooper was to specify that he had chosen "Patriotism" for his theme (6). The epigraph to the novel, famous lines from Scott's "Lay of the Last Minstrel," confirms Cooper's intent: "Breathes there a man with soul so dead, /Who never to himself hath said, /This is my own, my native land!" (1). Scott's lines are printed as a statement, not a question.[13] Although Cooper's wife, Susan Augusta De Lancey, belonged to the most prominent Loyalist family remaining in New York, Cooper was determined that his novel would, ultimately, vindicate the American Revolution. He believed that American progress depended on fashioning a republic in which educated gentlemen would be elected either because of, or in spite of, legal rights of equal opportunity. He sought to affirm the potential nobility of the most lowly (Harvey Birch) as well as the most exalted (George Washington).

But Cooper was determined to do so without vilifying the British or the "Tories," especially the De Lancey family, who had included among its members the leader of the infamous Cow-Boys. More generally, Cooper sought to promote patriotism while fully rendering the grim conditions of the neutral ground within which revolution had been achieved. How to do so, when human behavior in the neutral ground demonstrated scant respect for man's right to life, liberty, and the pursuit of happiness?

Inconclusive battles between uniformed Regulars and Continentals occur after surprise attacks, but are conducted without cruelty or massacre, in accord with lingering eighteenth-century notions of military honor. The sudden violence inflicted by both the Cow-Boys and Skinners is bestial, sadistic, and usually unprovoked. The significant difference between the two vigilante groups is that the Cow-Boys are hardly ever seen, whereas the Skinners control Cooper's narrative. The Skinners rob Harvey Birch of his gold, burn Harvey's house, deliver him up to the American Army, shoot a defenseless woman (Isabella Singleton), plunder the Wharton estate, and burn their home, forcing the family to leave the neutral ground for the comparative safety of Virginia. In part, Cooper may intend the contrast between Cow-Boys and Skinners to rehabilitate the De Lanceys' reputation. But his motivation is surely more than familial; he did not need to emphasize American thuggery so persistently. The Skinners embody Cooper's increasingly angry acknowledgment, for which he would later pay dearly in public opinion, that one consequence of revolutionary republicanism is the release of violent, criminal, mob impulses, especially among the lower classes. By contrast, the Porteous riots in Scott's *Heart of Mid-Lothian* seem conducted with controlled dignity.

The conditions of the neutral ground dictate that the only way to control the Skinners is not by law, but by their own methods. Upper class officers like British Captain Henry Wharton and American Major Peyton Dunwoodie are too gentlemanly to inflict lasting punishment, but Captain Lawton, a physically imposing Virginian, is not. Only Lawton has the courage to denounce the Skinners as "more than savages; men who, under the guise of patriotism, prowl through the community, with a thirst for plunder that is unsatiable and a love of cruelty that mocks the ingenuity of the Indian" (289). Lawton understands that the Skinners represent republican demagoguery in the making: "Fellows whose mouths are filled with liberty and equality, and whose hearts are overflowing with cupidity and gall" (289). Lawton and his troopers ambush the Skinners in an orchard, strip them, tie them to apple trees, cut the branches into whips, and then administer "the law of Moses—forty save one" (211). Lawton orders that no whip-stroke shall be counted until twelve practice strokes make every trooper's aim accurate. One kind of "Patriot" sadistically subdues another. To the reader's uneasy satisfaction, Lawton enforces the Skinner creed ("the law of the neutral ground is the law of the strongest") upon the Skinners themselves.

Repeated images of the gallows undermine hope for deliberative legal procedure. Captain Henry Wharton, then Harvey Birch, then Frances Wharton, and finally the Skinner chieftain all shudder with terror as they unexpectedly brush up against a hastily constructed gallows. They have good reason. Hanging in the neutral ground is an impulsive decision linking immediate expediency to social class. In 1780, gentlemen captives condemned to die were by law to be granted the dignity of being shot, but commoners and gentlemanly officers caught as spies were summarily hanged. In his role as double agent for the Americans, commoner Harvey Birch has been haunted by the gallows since the onset of the war. Captain Edward Wharton, found guilty of spying by George Washington's specially appointed military court, knows that Washington has very recently hanged British Major John André, a gentleman spy like himself.

The end of the 1780 fictional narrative brings these motifs effectively together. The leader of the Skinners, scurrilous to the end, observes that the British Regulars are now defeating the Continentals. He therefore offers to pay Harvey Birch, whom he believes to be a British spy, protection money for safe passage through the British lines. A moment too late to practice yet another turn of deception, the leader of the Skinners is apprehended by a band of Cow-Boys. His claim to be a recent convert to His Majesty's cause, his desperate pleas of "Down with the Congress," "Hurrah for the King," avail him nothing. In full view of the glorious Hudson, he is slowly and methodically hanged to the satisfaction of all except Harvey Birch, who identifies with the Skinner's death agony, even though Harvey has been the targeted victim of Skinner atrocity:

> Birch continued gazing on this scene with a kind of infatuation. At its close he placed his hands to his ears, and rushed towards the highway. Still the cries for mercy rang through his brain, and it was many weeks before his memory ceased to dwell on the horrid event. The Cow-Boys rode steadily on their route, as if nothing had occurred; and the body was left swinging in the wind, until chance directed the footsteps of some straggler to the place. (384)

Through the power of such passages, we conclude that the Cow-Boys, not Washington's troops, are to exact retributive justice against the Skinners. For Fenimore Cooper, raised to share Federalist revulsion at the French Revolution, the kind of terror aroused by the gallows in 1780 seems to prefigure the terror aroused by the guillotine in 1793. Harvey Birch is experiencing an early version of the revolutionary nightmare that would seem to have no end.

The ever-accumulating brutalities of the neutral ground allow for no convincing resolution from within. At the end of the novel, Cooper simply removes all remaining members of the Wharton family except Henry Wharton to Virginia. Before doing so, he devises the only scene in which admirable characters come together without disguise, free of the danger of imminent arrest, and able to speak freely. Throughout the narrative, Cooper has endowed Harvey Birch with Rob Roy's mastery of local terrain, Rob Roy's mysterious identity, and Rob Roy's almost supernatural ability to appear and disappear as needed.[14] Cooper arranges for Mr. Harper, Harvey Birch, and Frances Wharton, three admirable patriots, to separately climb, at night, to Harvey Birch's hidden hut high atop a mountain. There, momentarily removed from danger, true identities can be acknowledged. The disguises Harvey has needed to maintain false identities can be openly displayed. Mr. Harper can be disclosed to be George Washington. Washington can declare that his sense of honor has led him to secretly enable Henry Wharton to escape American execution as a British spy. Only in Harvey Birch's hut can the godlike Washington give Frances his paternal blessing as spiritual Father of his country. "God has denied to me children, young lady," Washington tells her: "But you are my child. All who dwell in this broad land are my children, and my care; and take the blessing of one who hopes yet to meet you in happier days" (362). The childless leader of the revolution thus acquires the *kingly* benignity to become the Father of his republican people.

The neutral ground is abandoned in Cooper's last chapter, an epilogue in which the cleansing sublimity of Niagara Falls and a victory in the War of 1812 are invoked for triple purpose: to vindicate the American Revolution, to show the survival of the republic, and to elegize Harvey Birch's selfless devotion to the Patriot cause, for which he has given everything he has—family, gold, reputation—except his own inner integrity. The last words of the novel narrow the reader's horizon from Niagara Falls to the body of Harvey Birch, "the SPY OF THE NEUTRAL GROUND, who dies as he had lived, devoted to his country, and a martyr to her liberties" (407). A male hero of such low social origin and absolute commitment to a progressive cause does not belong at the center of a Waverley novel. Scott's custom is to ascribe the virtue of absolute, personal allegiance either to a subordinate male retainer (Evan Dhu) or to a woman (Jeanie Deans). When revolutionary violence ends, Scott's genteel protagonists consolidate property through marriage; Harvey Birch's integrity, by contrast, is measured by the totality of his lonely sacrifice. To the youthful Cooper, new world republicanism could lift the common man beyond the old-world temporizing Scott believed necessary to maintaining social continuity.

George Washington's handwritten note is the only object Harvey treasures as he dies on the battlefield. It resolves one problem at the price of revealing another. George Washington and Harvey Birch, heroes from the highest and the lowest of American social classes, emerge as symbiotic, childless patriarchs of the new nation (399). The despised, distrusted Yankee peddler, who spits on Mr. Wharton's andirons, and the unfailingly genteel Mr. Harper are revealed to have been wholly one in their patriotic republicanism and fully equal in moral stature. Cooper thereby implies an equivalence of cultural value that Scott would surely have questioned.

Why, however, has it never been possible for Harvey Birch's relationship to George Washington to be revealed during the thirty years since the revolution has ended? Washington's explanation of the need for secrecy ("you already know the lives that would be sacrificed, should your real character be revealed" [399]) was no longer valid after peace was declared in 1783. Cooper clearly felt it necessary to protect George Washington's spotless purity of reputation as America's revolutionary patriot. Throughout the novel, Washington has been using Harvey Birch as a spy. Cooper's reader had been informed, at the end of the first chapter, that "The convenience, and perhaps the necessities, of the leaders of the American arms, in the neighbourhood of New York, had induced them to employ certain subordinate agents of extremely irregular habits, in executing their lesser plans of annoying the enemy" (20). Here is a cautiously worded but clear admission that convenience and necessity required "the leaders of the American arms" (who else but George Washington?) not only to tolerate but to "employ" the Skinners? The taint of such a connection, however, ran counter to the revolutionary hagiography expected during the American 1820s.[15] The Father of the country may have needed to employ Skinners as well as spies, but the connections need not be directly addressed. The detailed workings of George Washington's New York spy ring have at long last been disclosed in Alexander Rose's *Washington's Spies* (2006). In history, the conditions of the neutral ground have evidently retained a longer reach than Fenimore Cooper had been prepared to admit in fiction.

The neutral ground portrayed by Scott and Cooper is a rural farm region, distant from a small city, interspersed with forts, and devastated by military forces during a revolutionary crisis. Variants of this sense of revolutionary place recur in historical novels soon to follow: in *The Last of the Mohicans* (Fort William Henry on Lake George), in *The Chouans* (Brittany's hardscrabble countryside), and in *The Captain's Daughter* (forts amid steppes along the Volga). The title of Dickens's *A Tale of Two Cities* signifies an important mid-century transition soon to be developed in Flaubert's *Sentimental Education*. Revolution now centers in cities. As the rhetoric of Dickens' famous opening paragraph indicates, London and Paris are both opposite and the same. Although oppressive living conditions for common men prevail in both places, Dickens consistently contrasts the desperate starvation of the

Faubourg Saint Antoine with the tolerated criminality of London and the British court system. Dickens's portrayal of French rural life is limited to picturing vast, declining feudal estates being burned and overrun by angry peasants, without any evidence of a middle class. Rural life in England, by contrast, is never depicted at all. Fog and mist arise on the Rochester road leading toward Paris, not in glen or meadow; London streets, not lowland paths, lead confusedly nowhere. Only within the Manettes' domestic retreat in Soho, a suburban pastoral enclave, do the best of familial values survive, threatened though they are by the footsteps of urban revolution.

A sense of a revolutionary place is not as important to Dickens as it had been to Scott and to Cooper. We do not feel the pressure of immediate surroundings to the same degree. For Dickens, hatreds of social class antedate and determine the cruel privilege of Monseigneur's salon and the breadlessness of Paris streets. Dickens's plot allows the French revolution to come to an end, not through imposition of civil force, nor the exhaustion of the Terror, but through the self-sacrificial humanity of Sydney Carton, the very British decency of Miss Pross and Mr. Jarvis Lorry, and the financial stability afforded by Tellson's Bank. Despite the sporadic violence of contemporary Chartist agitation, Dickens wishes to believe that individual human benevolence (especially English benevolence exercised through law and finance) can and will overcome revolutionary class envy. Here are urban dangers and urban remedies.

Zola combines the two kinds of neutral ground while separating them. Although most of *La Débacle* (1892), the capstone novel of the Rougon-Macquart series, takes place in rural Alsace and Lorraine, Zola ends his narrative with failed revolution in Paris. In his letters, Zola described the subject of *La Débacle*—the Franco-Prussian War and the Commune of 1870–1871—through dire superlatives: "the collapse of a dynasty," "the crumbling of an era," the "abomination of civil war," and a "frightful catastrophe."[16] Applying Verignaud's metaphor, Zola refers to his novel's subject as "that fratricidal conflict, that wretched nation completing the work of destruction by devouring its own children!"[17] To assume that the force of Zola's title *La Débacle* could be adequately conveyed by such a mild English equivalent as "the debacle" (or even "the downfall") is extremely misleading. Perhaps the best title of all would be the phrase Zola discovers near novel's end: "a catastrophe without a name" (399). In the twenty-first century, the title we now give to Zola's wartime subject risks further belittling in historical memory. Within the contexts of World Wars I and II, histories that continue to minimize the total national defeat, brutal civil war, and failed revolution that France suffered in 1870 and 1871 by applying to them the familiar phrase "Franco-Prussian War" reduce *débacle* to a merely local warm-up for twentieth-century carnage.

For Zola and liberal minded readers in 1892, the events of 1870–1871 were a national "catastrophe" turning into yet another promising, failed revolution. The lowest estimate of the number of Parisian Communards shot or otherwise massacred by French troops (not by the Prussians) during the Bloody Week of May 22, 1871 was 17,000, more than those executed, also by Frenchmen, under the Terror of 1793. To Karl Marx, Vladimir Lenin, and Leon Trotsky, the Commune was the first, albeit brief, triumph of socialist/communist revolution. To Emile Zola, however, the word *débacle* signified the corruption of the regime of Louis Napoleon, the necessary end of Bonapartism, and the demise of the Second Empire. In literary terms, Zola conceived of *La Débacle* as the apocalyptic finale to his Rougon-Macquart series; it was to be its central novel, twice as long as any of its predecessors. When it also proved to be his bestselling single novel, Zola was elated, remarking "the success of *La Débacle* surpasses all my hopes."[18]

The wavering of Zola's protagonist derives from an unstable, headstrong spirit rather than political indecision. Maurice Levasseur joins the revolt of the Paris Commune after a year of enduring the incompetence, futility, and repeated defeat of the French armies. Of genteel origin like Scott's protagonists, Maurice has been raised to revere Napoleon Bonaparte as a godly revolutionary; now, however, Maurice finds himself surrounded by rebellious soldiers who will not rebel. In Paris, he is not surprised to discover that the Commune's elections have put into power, not a government of committed revolutionaries, but a "strange mixture of moderates, revolutionists, and socialists of every sect and shade" (397–398), among whom there is no unanimity, and no ability to enact whatever legal reforms they manage to pass. No hopeful Marxist horizon emerges. From Maurice's perspective, which Zola does not challenge, the cause of the Communards' revolt must be traced, not to socialist or communist tracts, but to the humiliation of the French army and the dispirited condition of the French people under the Second Empire.

Although most of the novel takes place on the Franco-German border, the conditions under which we experience war in the countryside and later in Paris are remarkably similar. The artillery of the highly disciplined Prussian army, controlling all hillsides, encircles entire French armies that have retreated first to Sedan and later to Metz. Despite the battle bravery of some French units, the French are reduced by their own disunity, by starvation, by disease and by despair to surrender separate armies of 80,000 and 40,000 men. The Prussian strategy succeeds for the crucial third time during the siege of Paris, as Von Moltke's and Bismarck's troops encircle the city, waiting for the newly recruited French army to overthrow the Commune. Zola describes the French army invading Paris from Versailles, destroying the barricades, and killing all defenders, street by street, from west to east. The *débacle* is not a "Franco-Prussian War"; it is Frenchmen against Frenchmen, countryside against city, a republic declared by an urban uprising that is then put down by a national government of suspect legitimacy. Among officers and enlisted men, discipline and self-control break down. Some join the Commune, believing in its virtue; some join the Versailles army believing in its patriotism. After the wasted Emperor Louis Napoleon surrenders and is imprisoned by the Prussians, the provisional French government under Adolphe Thiers submits to Prussian bidding and conquers its own revolutionary people. Throughout the novel, the Prussians outthink and outmaneuver the French, then wait for the French to defeat themselves. Zola's view of revolutionary "progress" makes Scott's seem ambivalent and Cooper's innocent.

Why catastrophe follows them so unrelentingly continues to torment the soldiers of the 106th Regiment of the Line, whose misfortunes Zola follows throughout the narrative. The regiment is a cross section of the French nation: a staunch Colonel and an equally staunch Lieutenant both committed to the barely remembered grandeur of Napoleon Bonaparte's France, a Sergeant who doggedly does their bidding, a Corporal who honorably fights for French soil, and a group of privates (a kind of chorus) who are opportunists, or pietists, or skulkers, or stolid to the verge of stupidity. Seeking to dominate them all is a scurrilous agitator and sometime socialist named Chouteau, who advances himself by a combination of intellectual pretense and disparagement of anyone in authority. As an example of how human refuse rises through revolution, Chouteau is a darkened version of Bletson in Scott's *Woodstock*.

At various points in the narrative, members of the regiment affix blame for the gathering catastrophe. No one defends Emperor Louis Napoleon, who has none of his uncle's strength of character. The lower ranks complain about the Second Empire's display of luxury, its condoning of the purchase of office and title, and its vainglorious blunders in foreign policy, but they summon only enough will to desert, not to protest. Silently or openly, all members of the regiment agree that French generals they never see are both incompetent and cowardly, as indeed the historical generals, whom Zola characterizes by name, seem to have been.

Committed to rendering the deterministic power of natural forces, Zola regards the terrain of war as an essential cause of military behavior. The conditions of the terrain, in the streets as well as on the field, are as important to Zola as they had been secondary to Dickens. The first two parts of Zola's novel, leading toward Paris and the rise of the Commune, take place along the borders of Germany, France, and Belgium. The terrain in Alsace and Lorraine proves to be yet another variant of the neutral ground. The populace speaks at least two languages, with dialectical variants, leaving many French soldiers virtually wordless. National borders are not defined. Farmers hoard food. Communications are cut. The French army has no maps of Alsace or

Lorraine, because they are convinced that the only map they might need would point their way to Berlin. There are so many cross paths, hillsides, rivers, farm fields, and villages that the French become lost in every sense of the word. In other surroundings, effective order might have been preserved, but conditions in Alsace and Lorraine make the disintegration of French army units an inevitability.

The group able to function most effectively under these conditions is the paramilitary force known as the *franc-tireurs*, natives who know the languages and the terrain, and are employed to convey needed information to French officers:

> Their professed purpose was to wage a sort of guerilla warfare, lying in ambush behind hedges, harassing the enemy, picking off his sentinels, holding the woods, from which not a Prussian was to emerge alive; while the truth of the matter was that they had made themselves the terror of the peasantry, whom they failed utterly to protect and whose fields they devastated. Every ne-er-do-well who hated the restraints of the regular service made haste to join their ranks, well pleased with the chance that exempted him from discipline and enabled him to lead the life of a tramp, tippling in pothouses and sleeping by the roadside at his own sweet will. (93)

Change the proper nouns and every word of this passage is applicable to the Skinners and Cow-Boys of *The Spy*. The rise of such guerilla bands is a sure outcome of civil war, just as growth in the power of the central state is a sure outcome of revolution, for worse or for better. But there is a difference. Cooper could not refrain from the pleasure of describing the hanging of the Skinner leader. For Cooper, justice will prevail, even though vigilante force is sometimes necessary to achieve it. After the French surrender at Sedan, Zola provides detailed descriptions of how Sambuc, leader of the *franc-tireurs*, slits the throat of a Prussian spy, bags his body, throws it into the Meuse, and escapes punishment entirely. The *franc-tireurs*, unlike the Skinners, slide away to practice their guile another day.

In topographical detail, Zola's neutral ground recalls both Cooper and Scott. The novel's first paragraph describes a disordered regimental march based on false rumors of Prussian troop movements, that takes place under "the fitful light of the overcast August day, beneath the lowering sky that was filled with heavy drifting clouds" and "purplish mists that lay on the horizon" (27). The forests along the roadsides recall *The Last of the Mohicans*: "the only signs of vegetation were the everlasting pine woods with their dark verdure" (57). As the French troops finally straggle into Sedan "the darkness settled down on them, denser and denser, the chill mists rose from the stream and enshrouded everything in a dank, noisome fog" (134). For weeks, the French soldiers have known only that they are marching unto exhaustion, without direction into a borderless world northeast toward Germany. Such obscurities end, however, in total entrapment in Sedan, where an 80,000-man French army is blocked in a valley of the Meuse, relentlessly shelled, massacred, and then imprisoned on the Iges Peninsula, from which there is no exit except through total surrender. The fog lifts revealing a *débacle* in every sense of the word. Panoramic hilltop descriptions of the valley's beauty alternate with repeated images of the "black swarm" of the encircling Prussian artillery (142).

At novel's end, the *débacle* shifts from Alsace to Paris, but internecine conditions of the neutral ground continue, as does Prussian encirclement. Brave talk, bribery, robbery, starvation, high prices, emigration, desertion, sacrifice, exemplary punishments, and lawlessness prevail on the city's streets. We hear of the agreements struck at Versailles between Thiers' government and the Prussians, but we do not see them. Nor is Zola interested in detailing the revolutionary politics of the Communards. In his view the Commune arose, not because of revolutionary political theory, liberal or Marxist, but because Parisians were determined somehow to salvage national honor in spite of the Prussian invasion and the many Frenchmen who had betrayed them from within.

The Parisians and refugees who unite to form the revolutionary Commune feel bound by national precedent. They must lay claim to past glories they cannot equal or reenact past failings they cannot avoid. The French armies cite memories of 1793 to gather support for the cause. While proclaiming "On to Berlin," the French armies sing the Marseillaise (9), but forget to procure maps of Alsace. As the Prussians march toward Paris, the ever impulsive Maurice has a "vision of what was to be: the empire overturned and swept away amid a howl of universal execration, the republic proclaimed with an outburst of patriotic fervor, while the legend of '92 would incite men to emulate the glorious past, and, flocking to the standards, drive from the country's soil the hated foreigner with armies of brave volunteers" (199). After the Prussian army encircles Paris, the French fly two flags, the tricolor of 1793 and the red flag of 1848; leaders of both the Garde Nationale and the Commune give rousing speeches at the Place de la Bastille. Zola renders the building of barricades in the streets as both a military strategy and a tribute to the republicans of 1848. As conditions in Paris worsen, there arises "a fierce longing of the extremists to place themselves in control in order that they might save France by the methods of '92'" (386). In all these ways, the nation bent on progress looks backward for salvation. Although the guillotine is burned to crowd applause, the Committee of Public Safety is reinstated with wary approval. Zola makes no attempt to determine whether such symbolism was driven by faith in the republic or cynical use of propaganda; the symbolism was simply, under the circumstances, a psychological necessity if the defense of Paris were to continue.

Nothing in Zola's novel contradicts the following historical facts. The establishing of the Commune confirmed the end of the Second Empire. It declared a republic, and armed itself in defense of France. It passed legislation widening the suffrage, disestablishing the Catholic church and secularizing education. In theory it supported socialism: "the right of each one of us to share (to the extent of his individual contribution) in the collective fruit of labor which is the basis of social wealth."[19] But the term Zola most frequently uses to describe activists on behalf of the Commune is "insurgents" not "revolutionaries." To Georg Lukacs's dismay, Zola minimizes the importance of alternative political beliefs because he sees the creation of the Commune as an act of desperation following defeat and capitulation. The Commune comes into existence because of a civil war based less on republicanism or socialism, than on inner divisions within city and countryside. Zola's Communards have as much contempt for Thiers, the National Assembly, and the French army at Versailles as they do for the Prussians.

Because reforms have had no time to be enacted, Zola does not claim to know whether the Commune could have turned urban revolt into revolutionary achievement. The rapidity with which the populace of France capitulates and then attacks the Commune signifies more than widespread fear of the few committed socialists in the Commune, be they followers of Proudhon or of Marx. It suggests an underlying weariness with the revolution itself, a weariness traceable back through the remembered experiences of 1848, 1830, and the Thermidorean reactions of 1815 and 1794. Familiar patterns recur: highminded words do not mesh with street realities; barricades are overrun and torn down; individual rights disappear; reprisal becomes bestial for civilians and soldiers alike.

The closing chapters of *La Débacle* describe the demise of the Commune in graphic detail, culminating in the infamous massacre of the last armed holdouts backed up against the *Mur des Fédérés* in Pere Lachaise Cemetery. The controlling mood darkens and Zola's imagery reddens, as failed revolution turns toward apocalypse. The artillery of the Versailles army (again, not the Prussian army) sets fire to Paris buildings. Once the Versailles infantry gains control of the streets, they set fire to Communard buildings. The Communards in turn set fire to the barricades as they are overrun. As despair increases, the Communards set fire to the Tuilleries, the Legion of Honor, the Council of State, and the d'Orsay Barracks. To Maurice, recently enlisted among the Communard defenders, the burnings of revered national sites provide a last cleansing ecstasy: "let the whole city go up in flame; let its people be cleansed in the fiery purification!" (403).

The sky reddens to all horizons. In the last thirty pages, Zola (an author not known for understatement) repeats the word "flame" at least twenty-five times, "fire" twenty-five times, and "burning" thirty times.

"Conflagration" serves as the controlling abstraction (twelve repetitions), but verbal color requires borrowings from epics: "smoldering funeral pyre," "sea of flame," "blood-red sky." In the novel's last pages, the simple decent Corporal Jean Macquart, who is barely literate and has no political beliefs whatsoever, survives to begin the rebuilding of a new, still indiscernible France.[20] It is as if French revolution itself has finally, perhaps blessedly, expired in the city's flames. Images of the consummation of all things coalesce: a twilight of the Gods, a purgative fire, the red horse, red dragon, red lake, and red city of *Revelation* (another kind of revolutionary text). Such imagery would be ascribed to the modern "unreal city" described as endlessly "burning" in the third part ("The Fire Sermon") of T.S. Eliot's *The Wasteland*.

Lukacs viewed Zola as a "liberal positivist" whose quasi-scientific notion of *Le Roman Expérimental* was only a dodge to make literary realism accord with lingering bourgeois values. Although Zola had courageously opposed the evils of capitalism, he was "far too naïve a liberal all his life, far too ardent a believer in bourgeois *progress*." After the suppressed revolutionary promise of 1848, a truly courageous literary realist would have engaged the spectacle of life from working class socialist premises, rather than linking realism, as Zola had done, to the Balzacian role of spectator historian. Such a double accommodation, Lukacs concludes, shows that "Zola's fate is one of the literary tragedies of the nineteenth century."[21] The narrowing focus of the demands Lukacs made on the historical novel after 1848 is evident here. The purgative apocalyptic ending of *La Debacle*, based upon disillusionment with mankind's political behavior, liberal or socialist, either sinks Zola's novel beneath Lukacs's critical demands, or lifts his novel beyond them.

In twentieth-century historical novels, changes of power occur in cities, even if the novels are set in the eighteenth century. Anatole France's *Les Dieux Ont Soif* (1912) and Hilary Mantel's *A Place of Greater Safety* (1992) take their reader outside revolutionary Paris for, respectively, one chapter and a few brief passages. Howard Fast gives us *Citizen Tom Paine* in Philadelphia and in Paris, summarizing Paine's experiences in England only from a distance. Pasternak's *Doctor Zhivago* and Lampedusa's *The Leopard* balance city against countryside, but the revolutions they describe are inconceivable without the street fighting in Moscow and Palermo. America is defined in Gore Vidal's seven volume *Novels of Empire* by Washington, New York, and Los Angeles. In the view of twentieth-century authors, agitation for revolution arises less from agricultural discontent and "feudal" class divisions, than from the unjust power of liquid assets and the expanded role of the media, primarily newspapers and periodicals.

AMERICA'S CROMWELL?

The Washington D.C. of Gore Vidal's *Lincoln* (1984) is an urban neutral ground that barely escapes open street warfare. As the novel begins, six states have seceded, leaving Washington a culturally southern city, nominally the capitol of a "Union" that in fact consists only of the North and the internally divided "border states." In the first scene, President-elect Lincoln, accompanied by detective Pinkerton armed with brass knuckles and a derringer, has arrived incognito in Washington in order to avoid assassination by pro-Confederate "plug-uglies" while passing through Baltimore.[22] The nation's capital is a ten square mile parallelogram surrounded by slave states, its rail lines and outer roads threatened, sometimes controlled, by pro-Southern insurgents.

Like the dome of the Capitol, everything in the city seems half-finished, a place where "nothing works" (22). Depending on the season, the streets are filled with frozen mud or choking dust; the stink of the canal, Potomac Fever, and the danger of typhoid, syphilis, and small pox are daily realities. Conversations take place in makeshift conference rooms, in hotels, boarding houses, barrooms, oyster houses, theatres, and whore houses, but not in family homes. Runaway slaves and confederate army deserters walk the streets in uneasy freedom. Because pro-Southern sentiments are acceptable, there is little need to affect neutrality. "Dixie" is openly sung in barrooms and false ID's are readily purchasable. Lincoln concludes that Washington is "a truly sickly place" (294); Ulysses Grant is even more blunt: "I hate this city. Worse than Sodom and Gomorrah" (520).

Vidal's fictional plot, centering around nineteen-year-old David Herold, describes the conspiratorial activities of a ring of confederate spies that acquire Union military secrets through prostitutes, well-connected "Secessionist Ladies," tradesmen serving the White House, and the merchants of Central Market. "Night-riders" carry Union military memoranda along the roads to Richmond. An organization calling itself the "National Volunteers" is in reality composed of confederate informers and would-be assassins. After the Army of the Potomac is finally assembled, minimal law and order is maintained in the city, but due only to the presence of Union soldiers. Jubal Early's confederate cavalry remain a threat to Washington as late as 1865. As a character in the novel, the city is second only to Abraham Lincoln himself. Vidal's rendering of a squalid, sinister Washington seems motivated by a desire to upend every monumental association a visitor of 1984 might have had touring Washington D.C. as the nation's capital. In the midst of its city streets, the treacherous and obscure lowlifes of the Lowlands, Westchester Country, and Alsace emerge only slightly reconfigured. The plug-uglies, David Herold's barroom cronies, and Vidal's "National Volunteers" are hard to distinguish from Scott's caterans, Cooper's Skinners, or Zola's *franc-tireurs*.

By seeking to preserve the Union through any military means, while assenting to the continuation of slavery wherever it has been legal, Lincoln can be plausibly regarded as either a revolutionary or a counterrevolutionary. To Alexander Stephens, and to Mary Todd Lincoln's secessionist family, Lincoln's opposition to the extension of slavery is a quasi-abolitionist violation of both a Constitutional right and the Compromise of 1850. They regard his unionist policy as revolutionary. To immediate abolitionists, to Radical Republicans, and even to Secretary of the Treasury Salmon P. Chase, Lincoln's refusal to abolish slavery in the border states seems timidly retrograde, a willingness to allow a pre-republican America to fester and to flourish. Politicians define their opponents by alleging similarities to figures of the French Revolution. From the unionist perspective, the Radical Republicans who oppose Lincoln deserve to be repeatedly disparaged as "Jacobins." General McClellan's theatrical posings earn him the contemptuous nickname of "Little Napoleon" (recalling Victor Hugo's *Napoleon Le Petit*?) as well as a nickname of opposite connotations "the Great American Tortoise" (341).

Vidal's Lincoln sees himself as neither revolutionary nor counterrevolutionary. In the midst of civil war, while battlefield killings impel the citizenry toward the extremes of immediate abolition (the Radical Republicans) or accomodationist peace (the Copperheads), Lincoln knows that the success of his unionist policy, during and after the war, depends upon a proper regard for securing the borderlands where the war will be fought. Maryland, West Virginia, Kentucky, and Missouri—the Border States—occupy a great deal of Lincoln's attention during cabinet policy discussions. Lincoln recognizes that, if the Emancipation Proclamation were to free slaves within the border states, the reaction of border state slaveholders might well cost the North the victory. To refrain from punishing slaveholders, especially those from free states that have remained within the Union, will be essential to any practicable policy for Reconstruction. The city of Washington, within which Lincoln is virtually confined, epitomizes the contradictory qualities of all these kinds of porous borders. Similarly, the Union, considered as a whole, replicates the dangers of the city. In these ways, the daily experiences of living in Washington D.C. unconsciously shape Lincoln's wisest policies.

The treacheries of Washington are reproduced within the Union government. The three most powerful figures of Lincoln's cabinet—William Seward, Solomon P. Chase, and Edward Stanton—all distrust one another personally and politically, in part because they have ambitions to supplant Lincoln, in part because they are prepared to tell lies whenever necessary. All three however, are able, intelligent, and devoted to the Union. Other cabinet members, such as Simon Cameron, are fundamentally corrupt; still others, such as Gideon Welles, are unimaginative or absurd. Congress, in its turn, reflects the self-serving divisions within the cabinet. The continued posturing and regrouping among Congress's Radical Republicans, Unionist Republicans, Peace Democrats, and Unionist Democrats depend on their fluctuating perceptions of battle success. Those abolitionist senators whom many of Vidal's readers might be predisposed to admire, Thomas Fessenden of Maine and Charles Sumner of Massachusetts, have their own self-interested motives, of which Abraham Lincoln is quite aware.

The narrative structure of Vidal's novel alternates between Washington's streets and governmental offices. Although shadowy venality and self-serving permeate them both, Vidal never explicitly acknowledges the similarity, leaving the reader to conclude that the time and the place are one. Such subtlety justifies Harold Bloom's claim that *Lincoln* shows Vidal to have become "a masterly historical novelist, now wholly matured, who has found his truest subject, which is our national history during precisely those years when our political and military histories were as one, one thing and one thing only: the unwavering will of Abraham Lincoln to keep the states united."[23] Vidal's Lincoln is ultimately alone in exercising power for national benefit. The "Divine Providence" Lincoln periodically invokes is his own inner will writ large.

Lincoln's methods for dealing with a world of treachery combine unfailing shrewdness, a calculated sense of humor, and constant regard for the long view. Seemingly listless and awkward, Lincoln listens attentively, his eyes nearly closed, while his cabinet or family members debate policy. He knows how to play the ambitions of one cabinet member against another to his own advantage. He is adept at both casuistry and false modesty. Whenever it is not time to offer his opinion, or to make a decision, Lincoln plays neutral by feigning a nap or resorting to his fund of Illinois frontier stories. As he remarks to his secretary John Hay, "When there is so much you *cannot* say, it's always a good idea to have a story ready. I do it now from habit. . . . In my predicament, it is a good thing to know all sorts of stories because the truth of the whole matter is now almost unsayable; and so cruel" (386).[24]

Whether the creation of the Confederate States of America was a revolutionary or counterrevolutionary act, Lincoln refuses to recognize the legal existence of the Confederacy either in public or in private conference. He craftily maintains the legal fiction that the Union has never been dissolved; instead, he remarks that ill-defined "elements" needing to be crushed have temporarily led the populace of several of our states astray. But Lincoln's pursuit of military victory, Vidal emphasizes, compels him to adopt one unconstitutional means after another. He calls up the militia, establishes a draft and *proclaims* emancipation, all without Congressional approval. When needed, Lincoln suspends habeas corpus, suspends trial by jury, shuts down newspapers, and orders the seizure of telegrams. On his own initiative, he requisitions money from the Treasury and then orders Secretary Chase to print paper money upon demand. He informs the Maryland legislature that he will arrest all its members if they vote to secede. When the constitutionality of Lincoln's measures is challenged, it is discovered that there is no copy of the US Constitution in the White House. Lincoln remains unabashed. The nights and days of Vidal's Lincoln are made miserable by many different matters, national and familial, but worry over the constitutionality of his means of preserving the Union does not appear to be one of them.

Civil war and revolution arise from a public demand for some form of "Liberty," but the context in which liberty is disputed, symbolized in the neutral ground, invites repression and authoritarian control. Secretary of State William Seward, who had mistakenly judged Lincoln to be a crude bumbler, has by 1864 discovered a different kind of leader:

> For nearly three years, a thousand voices, including his own, had called for a Cromwell, a dictator, a despot; and in all that time, no one had suspected that there had been, from the beginning, a single-minded dictator in the White House, a Lord Protector of the Union by whose will alone the war had been prosecuted. For the first time, Seward understood the nature of Lincoln's political genius. He had been able to make himself absolute dictator without ever letting anyone suspect that he was anything more than a joking, timid backwoods lawyer given to fits of humility in the presence of all the strutting military and political peacocks that flocked about him. (459)

At this moment, Seward is made to perceive truths that Vidal wishes to advance. Challenging American mythology, Vidal grants that the South had held a plausible view of a state's "Liberty." During the 1850s Stephen Douglas's advocacy of "popular sovereignty" had held equal plausibility. Neither liberty, equality, nor fraternity with the slave was ever President Lincoln's controlling purpose. The counterrevolutionary value of preserving the Union led Lincoln to prosecute the war by any necessary *dictatorial* means.

Accordingly, Lincoln can still be regarded as the savior of the nation, not because of any Christ-like martyrdom, and certainly not because "Abraham Lincoln freed the slaves." Lincoln was rather America's Cromwell, a Lord Protector who should continue to arouse uneasy admiration for his much needed strengths.[25] To his great credit, Vidal had completed the extensive research necessary to make his heretical characterization plausible. Lincoln's political aims, like his character, are wholly admirable; his means are regrettable but necessary. If Lincoln is to be seen as America's Cromwell, Lincoln emerges as a more wholly admirable leader than the Cromwell of Scott's *Woodstock*. Gore Vidal's political desiderata unfold at the point where the extreme Right and extreme Left meet.

Readers of *Waverley, The Spy, La Débacle,* and *Lincoln* know from the outset that the Jacobites, the British, the French, and the Confederates will eventually be overwhelmingly defeated. To choose the neutral ground as the space/place in which to portray civil war and revolution therefore has, among advantages already discussed, the additional benefit of an illusory openness. As the protagonist(s) travel along directionless paths or shadowy city streets into mists of trouble, their environs suggest that the historical outcome of revolutionary struggle might be as indiscernible to the reader as to the protagonist. This effect is not limited to the suspension of disbelief that enables the reader to gauge the protagonist's responses against a known historical outcome. Obscurities of place also suggest that what the reader assumes to be historical fact was at the time a venture with many possible outcomes leading toward destinations no one could foresee. Historical determinism is thereby affirmed and confounded simultaneously. An historical novel true to the written and legendary evidence must seem, on its surface, to be the most predetermined of narratives. But, at its best, the historical novel counters this expectation by creating a neutral ground in which there are many roads into an unknown political future, a place in which human allegiances are unsure, often self-divided, and sometimes cagily neutral.

NOTES

1. The following studies of literary setting have proven particularly helpful to me: Gaston Bachelard, *The Poetics of Space* translated by Maria Jolas (Boston: Beacon Press, 1994); George Dekker; *The Fictions of Romantic Tourism: Radcliffe, Scott and Mary Shelley* (Stanford: Stanford University Press, 2005); Roger Sale, *Closer to Home: Writers and Places in England, 1780–1830* (Cambridge; Harvard University Press, 1986); Gillian Tindall, *Countries of the Mind: The Meaning of Place to Writers* (Boston: Northeastern University Press, 1991); Leonard Lutwack, *The Role of Place in Literature* (Syracuse, NY: Syracuse University Press, 1984). Consideration of Romantic aesthetics of landscape and setting, in painting and in literature, begins with the dialogue between Burke's *A Philosophical Inquiry into the Origin of Our Ideas of the Sublime and the Beautiful* (1757) and William Gilpin's *Observations Relative Chiefly to Picturesque Beauty* (1786). None of these terms were used, nor can they be used, with the precise consistency that this opening paragraph implies.

2. Roger Sale, *Closer to Home,* p. 1.

3. Both George Dekker and James Wallace have pointed out that Scott's definition of the term "Neutral Ground" in the prefatory materials to *Ivanhoe* had referred, not primarily to a No-Man's land, but to common cultural ground. See George Dekker, *James Fenimore Cooper: The American Scott* (New York: Barnes and Noble, 1967, p. 33) and James D. Wallace *Early Cooper and His Audience* (New York: Columbia University Press, 1986, p. 90). Scott's phrasing is "that extensive neutral ground, the

large portion, that is, of manners and sentiments which are common to us and our ancestors." Here "neutral ground" suggests the human heart unchanging through time. But Scott may also be signaling, as he does elsewhere in the preface to *Ivanhoe*, a change in the direction of the Waverley Novels. The neutral ground as geopolitical place would henceforth be less important than the neutral ground as a measure of the cultural continuities of time. My belief is that Scott's later novels sacrificed their specificity of revolutionary history because of the shift.

4. Sir Walter Scott, *Waverley, or 'Tis Sixty Years Since*, edited with an introduction by Andrew Hook (New York: Penguin Books, 1972), p. 73.

5. Here and elsewhere, I am indebted to Jane Millgate's insight "Romance is not in competition with historical truth in *Waverley*; it is the medium through which that truth is expressed" (*Walter Scott: The Making of the Novelist*, p. 40). The connotations of the terms "romance" and "realism" draw us toward misleading abstract opposites.

6. Summing up previous interpretations, George Dekker has analyzed the scene as a "Tourist Transport," a set piece built upon Waverley's predilection for sublime and picturesque aesthetic experience, revealing his feminine as well as masculine sensitivities (*The Fictions of Romantic Tourism*, pp. 126–141).

7. Chapters 1–6, completed in 1805, maintain a light satiric tone reminiscent of Fielding, but chapter seven, describing Waverley and his soldiers arriving in Dundee, refers ominously to Waverley's "wavering and unsettled habit of mind which is most averse to study and riveted attention" (73). Scott resumed work on the manuscript in 1813. The eight intervening years had witnessed Napoleon's rise to his highest point of power. Distant threats were no longer to be treated lightly; wavering young men need be prepared.

8. *Waverley*, p. 222. As the histories of England by David Hume and Lord Macaulay both attest, a major issue separating Whigs from Tories, Hanoverians from Jacobites, had been whether James II had "abdicated" the throne in 1688 or had fled from England in hope of later restoration. James II had reputedly thrown the Great Seal into the Thames. The 1689 Bill of Right states unequivocally that James II had "abdicated" leaving the throne "vacant." In this passage Scott three times uses the word "forfeit," a term even stronger than "abdicate."

9. During the uneasy peace of 1814, the pertinence of *Waverley*'s rendering of the "miseries of civil war" to the threat of invasion or revolution was not lost on British readers. An anonymous reviewer contended that Scott's novel should elicit a thankful prayer: "May the peace, which our exertions in the cause of all that is great and good have purchased and secured to the world around us, descend 'twice blessed' upon our native land. If the history of those bloody days, which is embodied in this tale, shall by an early and awful warning inspire the nation with a jealous vigilance against the very first symptoms of their recurrence, we shall consider that not even the light pages of fiction have trifled in vain" (review of *Waverley*, *British Critic*, 1814 in John Hayden, *Scott: The Critical Heritage* [London: Routledge, 1970], pp. 68–69).

10. Scott's portrayal of the ironic consequences of the victory of Preston Pans is historical verisimilitude at its best. Carlyle, who wished to reduce Scott's stature, nonetheless acknowledged: "These Historical Novels have taught all men this truth: . . . that the bygone ages of this world were actually filled by living men, not by protocols, state-papers, controversies and abstractions . . . History will henceforth have to

take thought of it" (Carlyle, "Sir Walter Scott" (1838), in *Critical and Miscellaneous Essays* [London: Chapman and Hall, 1888] iv, 177).

11. James Fenimore Cooper, *The Spy: A Tale of the Neutral Ground,* introduction and notes by Wayne Franklin (New York: Penguin Books, 1997), p. 9.

12. *The Spy,* p. 22. Wayne Franklin footnotes "imbecility" as synonymous with "weakness" (22). The startling effect of the word "imbecility" may also reflect Cooper's belief that Mr. Wharton's way of maintaining his neutrality is, in the context of its time and place, a sign of senility or mental imbalance. "Imbecility" can thus be read as another means of distinguishing *The Spy* from the Waverley Novels. As George Dekker observed "weak, corrupt, vacillating Scott's wavering heroes may be at their worst, but they are never, like Mr. Wharton, contemptible" (*James Fenimore Cooper: The American Scott* [New York: Barnes & Noble, 1967], p. 33).

13. Cooper's intent that *The Spy* be read in the context of Scott's writings is indicated not only by the epigraph to the novel, but the epigraphs to the separate chapters. Eleven epigraphs are from Shakespeare and six from Scott's poems; no other writer is accorded more than three.

14. The difference between Scott's Rob Roy and Cooper's Harvey Birch is as telling as the similarity. During the climactic battle of the 1715 rebellion, the battle of Sherrifmuir, Rob Roy stood motionless within the Jacobite lines, unwilling to fight for either side. To Scott, Rob Roy is an uneducated man of heroic prowess, strong personal loyalties, local financial interests, and no interest in political principle. By Scott's time, thanks in part to Daniel Defoe, Rob Roy had become an heroic legend, a Robin Hood of the Highlands. Scott chooses to emphasize the limitations of the historical man. Unlike Scott, Cooper was intent upon creating in Harvey Birch a legendary figure for explicit patriotic purpose.

15. Remarking on American expectations for literary patriotism after the War of 1812, Wayne Franklin argues that *The Spy* not only asserts American cultural independence, but *enacts* it (*James Fenimore Cooper: the Early Years* (New Haven: Yale University Press, 2007), pp. 277–278. See also, in this connection, John P. McWilliams Jr., *Political Justice in a Republic: James Fenimore Cooper's America* (Berkeley: University of California Press, 1972, pp. 32–64). Transforming Scott's literary conventions—in this instance redefining the waverer—was an essential part of Cooper's literary nationalism.

16. "Ce n'est pas la guerre seulement, c'est l'ecroulement d'une dynastie, c'est l'effondrement d'une époque" (William J. Berg and Laurey K. Martin, *Emile Zola Revisited* (New York: Twayne-Macmillan, 1992), pp. 180–181; Elliott M. Grant: *Emile Zola* (New York: Twayne Publishers, 1966), pp. 88, 154. Zola's dire terms are not exaggerations; see John Merriman, *Massacre: The Life and Death of the Paris Commune* (New York: Basic Books, 2014).

17. Emile Zola, *The Downfall (La Débacle),* translated by E.P. Robbins (New York: Mondial, 2008), p. 397.

18. Elliott M. Grant, *Emile Zola,* p. 162.

19. See Rupert Christiansen, *Paris Babylon: The Story of the Paris Commune* (New York: Viking, 1995), p. 295.

20. Zola's last work describing Paris as a revolutionary city, *Paris* (1898), argues that the truly revolutionary force of the future will be scientific not political. See

Priscilla Parkhurst Ferguson, *Paris as Revolution: Writing the Nineteenth Century City* (Berkeley: University of California Press, 1994), pp. 205–212.

21. Georg Lukacs, "The Zola Centenary" (1949) in *Studies in European Realism* (London: Hillway Publishing Co., 1950) reprinted in *Critical Essays on Emile Zola*, ed. David Baguley (Boston: G.K. Hall, 1986), pp. 84, 86, 89.

22. Gore Vidal, *Lincoln: A Novel* (New York: Random House, 1984), p. 15.

23. Harold Bloom, "The Central Man: On Gore Vidal's *Lincoln*" *New York Review of Books*, July 19, 1984, pp. 5–8, reprinted in *Gore Vidal: Writers Against the Grain*, ed. Jay Parini (New York: Columbia University Press, 1992), pp. 221–229.

24. Vidal's view of the risky but effective way Lincoln appointed and then controlled his cabinet is remarkably similar to Doris Kearns Goodwin's *Team of Rivals* (2005). Their renderings of historical contexts and of Lincoln's tactics are much the same. Vidal's characterization of Lincoln, as admiring as Goodwin's, is considerably darker in its appraisal of Lincoln's options and of Lincoln's instinctive suspicion.

25. In his essay "The Second American Revolution" (1981), Vidal sharply questioned increasing presidential assumption of war-making powers, yet concluded that "Lincoln proved to be a satisfactory dictator; and the Union was preserved" (*The Selected Essays of Gore Vidal*, ed. Jay Parini [New York: Doubleday, 2008], p. 388). Vidal did not rest easy with his seeming admiration for Lincoln's dictatorial methods. While researching Lincoln's life during 1979–1980, Vidal remarked: "Generally I don't care for dictators"; "Lincoln is our Bismarck, and that's how I plan to show him" (Fred Kaplan, *Gore Vidal: A Biography* [New York: Doubleday, 1999], p. 737). Vidal would give the very last words of *Lincoln* to perceptive, youthful John Hay: "It will be interesting to see how Herr Bismarck ends his career" (657). By 1867, Hay has become convinced that Lincoln had done a "great and terrible thing . . . by giving so bloody and absolute a rebirth to his nation" (657).

Chapter 4

Waverer and Fanatic

The credibility of historical novels portraying revolution depends, to a degree still unrecognized, on maintaining a balance between waverer and fanatic. The mind of the wavering protagonist, who shapes the viewpoint of the reader, fastens upon politically committed characters, fictive or historical, who expand in significance until they are revealed to be fanatics. The fanatic can be a royalist or a republican, a Legitimist or a Communard, a reactionary or a utopian. As the narrative develops, the encounters between waverer and fanatic must be kept intermittent but intense, leaving unresolved questions behind them.

If the historical forces that the fanatic represents lose *all* power at novel's end, the novel's progressive resolution is likely to seem simplistic (a vulnerability of the Scott model). If the fanatic dominates at novel's end, however, the outcome is likely to seem overdetermined and needlessly despairing. The changing feelings Waverley expresses toward Flora and Fergus MacIvor are, for Scott, the prototype of the waverer/fanatic relationship. The changing feelings Tolstoy's Pierre Bezuhov expresses toward Napoleon are its apogee. Given the frequency of the contrast, we may infer that the credibility of an historical novel's revolutionary conflict cannot be separated from the credibility of the symbiotic relationship between waverer and fanatic.

This chapter will pursue the once accepted, recently disparaged critical approach called "character criticism." The two-century-old assumption that characters imitate people in "real" life (Samuel Johnson to A.C. Bradley to E.M. Forster) has been vigorously challenged by post-Structuralist and deconstructionist critics who question whether word corresponds to thing. As early as 1974, Helene Cixous argued "So long as we do not put aside 'character' and everything it implies in terms of illusion and complicity with classical reasoning and the appropriating economy that such reasoning supports, we will remain locked up in the treadmill of reproduction."[1] Terry Eagleton argued that the prevalence of "identity" and "character" as staples of literary analysis reinforces western cultural values of individual identity and freedom upon which capitalism depends.[2] Martin Price proclaimed, "Character, then, is an invention, and it is with that I wish to start."[3] Baruch Hochman promptly demurred: "I have been pained because the substance of literature is dissipated if we pretend that characters have nothing to do with people."[4] But by 1988, Jonathan Arac wrote, "character may be understood as one possible effect of language under certain historical and social conditions."[5] Whether the concept of "character" can ever be abandoned may be doubted but the question raised by deconstructionist theory remains: what exactly is the connection between inter-referential word-signs within a novel and the characteristics of the human beings novelists sought to portray?

My concern with this perhaps unanswerable question is, and should be, limited to characterization in the pre-Modernist historical novel dealing with revolution. Unless the author's intentions are thought to be irrelevant to their writings, it is absurd to claim that Scott's Cromwell, Scott's Bonnie Prince Charlie, Scott's Claverhouse, Pushkin's Pugachev, Tolstoy's Napoleon, or Tolstoy's Kutuzov, can be separated from the historical beings whose names they bear. Without these world-historical figures, the words describing their fictional characterizations could not exist. Similarly, were we to remove the historical narrative of the English Civil Wars, the '45 Jacobite rebellion, Pugachev's rebellion, and the Napoleonic Wars from their respective novels, what would be left?

It is not surprising therefore, that attacks on characterization grew alongside the privileging of Nabokov, Pynchon, and the *Nouveau Roman*, while slighting the development of the historical novel. This is not to say, however, that we should assume that fictive characters and their historical models are synonymous. To a degree, it is helpful to apply Forster's contrast of round and flat characters to the waverer and the fanatic. However, historical persons are rarely as "flat" as novelists make them, nor are waverers quite as "round." The structuring of the novel imposes limits and presents opportunities. Therefore I prefer to analyze the relationship of waverer to fanatic while accepting the compromise terms that Scott, Cooper, Manzoni, and De Vigny all favored: "vraisemblance," "verisimilitude." Make your characters, historical or fictional, seem as if they had existed. Do not knowingly falsify history, but feel free to invent details—including spoken words—in such a way as to make fiction and history hard to separate.

MORAL SCRUPLES AND THE CIVIC COST OF REVOLUTION

Upon first encountering the MacIvors, Waverley would like to believe they are romantic figures, admirably apolitical. In truth, Flora's upbringing in a

Benedictine convent and in the Old Pretender's court intensifies her Jacobite loyalty by sheltering her from the compromising realities of Scottish politics. Although Fergus openly risks his life on behalf of the Stuarts, his loyalty is sullied by his recourse to shady means for self-centered ends. By introducing brother and sister as near twins with similar first names, Scott complicates the motivation of the revolutionary: "her [Flora's] loyalty, as it exceeded her brother's in fanaticism, excelled it also in purity."[6] Purity and fanaticism are here advanced as complementary and not opposing qualities; Waverley cannot fathom their paradoxical conjunction. From Scott's viewpoint, no political cause can be commendable for its purity, but an individual's commitment to it could be. Purity, loyalty and fanaticism form a single continuum not a triangulation of opposites. As Scott well knew, to have been "incorruptible" during the outbreak of a revolution can quickly change into fanaticism as well as corruption.

Waverley's "wavering and unsettled habit of mind" (73) renders him unable to perceive the connections among these three feelings. He is caught up in the '45 without any grounded, historical context by which allegiance could be determined. He gradually becomes aware of the deviousness and cruelty of Fergus's tactics, but the purity of Flora's fanaticism, inseparable from her sexual and cultural appeal, is beyond his understanding. After the Jacobite army has collapsed in retreat, Waverley is dumbfounded by the opposite ways in which Fergus and Flora meet the collapse of the Jacobite cause. Unafraid and self-collected, the worldly Fergus dies the death of a defiant hero, his severed head fixed as a warning trophy on the Carlisle castle gate facing Scotland. Flora's "purity" shrivels into pallor, weakness, and near insanity as she immures herself in a French convent. Both outcomes are unexpected, but both are in character. Fanatical purity can be spiritually broken in ways that opportunism can rise above, even in defeat.

Even more directly than in *Waverley*, the plot of *Old Mortality*, often regarded as Scott's best historical novel, is constructed around the symbiotic relationship between wavering protagonist and political fanatic. Scott portrays the Covenanters' rebellion during the "Killing Time" of 1679 as the climactic outcome of the Independent/Presbyterian thrust for religious self-determination so powerful during the Cromwellian Civil Wars. The arming of the Covenanters also foreshadows protestant/parliamentary supremacy over the Stuart monarchy during the Glorious Revolution of 1688. Like Waverley, Henry Morton joins a rebellion that might have become a revolution, then defects from it in order to salvage his sense of honor and the future of those he loves. Even though Morton, unlike Waverley, has formed his own values and beliefs from the outset, he wavers in commitment because neither the Covenanters nor the royalists prove to be consistent in their goals or just in their methods.[7] Without any sure sense of inner values, Waverley is driven by changing circumstance. Although Morton is in the midst of a massive rebellion, he willingly adheres to no group because he will not discard reasoned and just scruples.

As polar determinants of Henry Morton's future, Scott pits one historic fanatic against another. Morton, son of a Covenanter, has been raised to believe in moderate values Scott finds admirable within their seventeenth-century context: liberty of religious conscience for all Protestants, one king for two nations, a "free" Scottish Parliament, distrust of royal absolutism, the supremacy of civil over military law. In temperament, however, Morton is no stock Puritan; he is "unsullied by fanatic zeal."[8] His predilection to favor the Covenanters' cause is made more complex by the troubling presence of his father's associate John Balfour of Burleigh. To Burleigh, the Solemn League and Covenant of 1643 has acquired the authority of a biblical covenant for which he is prepared to die. Charles II's willingness to swear to the Solemn League and Covenant to gain the throne, his later violation of his oath, and his oppression of select protestant preachers while "indulging" others, have cumulatively convinced Balfour that Charles II is an opportunist, a traitor, and an infidel, as well as an adulterer. What obligation does Henry Morton have to honor his father's religious politics, when defensible Covenanter principles are expressed in such vengeful, absolute terms?

A brave leader, shrewd military strategist, and coldblooded murderer of the Anglican Archbishop of Scotland, Burleigh believes that armed resistance to Charles II and the royalists will lead to progress: a new king (or a republic), a Presbyterian establishment (or liberty of conscience), and a reformed nation (or two nations). Whether Balfour's principles amount to a call for revolution in the old or the new sense of the term is left to the reader. Burleigh defines his unfixed aims as "the reformation both of church and state, the rebuilding of the decayed sanctuary, the gathering of the dispersed saints, and the destruction of the man of sin" (229). These values sound like restoration, a turning backward to true Reformation by dethroning the "man of sin" recently "restored" to power in the person of Charles II.

If fanaticism is defined as absolute personal commitment, it is unclear whether Burleigh is a fanatic on behalf of reformed religion or political change. Scott knew how difficult it was, throughout the seventeenth century, to separate the two. What remains clear to Henry Morton, as to Scott's reader, is that Burleigh is less fanatical than the demagogic ministers among the Scottish Covenanters (Mucklewrath, MacBriar, and Kettledrummle) who blindly apply Old Testament scripture to gathering civil war in order to justify both regicide and a protestant establishment.[9]

As revolutionaries, the Covenanters do not agree on any purpose or any tactic. After the Covenanters' initial victory at Drumclog, but before their debacle at Bothwell Bridge, the leaders convene to decide future policy:

Some proposed they should march to Glasgow, some to Hamilton, some to Edinburgh, some to London. Some were for sending a deputation of their number to London to convert Charles II to a sense of the error of his ways; and others, less charitable, proposed either to call a new successor to the crown, or to declare Scotland a free republic. A free parliament of the nation, and a free assembly of the Kirk, were the objects of the more sensible and moderate of the party. (206)

As Henry Morton listens to the demagoguery, he understands that, whenever revolutionary adherents are so self-divided, it is wise policy to listen and to compromise. Burleigh draws the opposite, cynical conclusion: in the midst of civil war or revolution, the power of the word "free" lies in its release of immediate energies that worried, precise definition of the word "freedom" would only dissipate. Fight first and argue later is his perhaps practical but unaccepted counsel. Scott thereby raises a vexing question of the timing of revolutionary action: at what point does forced unanimity of revolutionary purpose become necessary?

Because of the honor of family allegiance, Henry Morton and Burleigh save each other's lives. Burleigh's graphic descriptions of royalist persecution persuade Henry Morton to join the Covenanters' quest for presumed "freedom," even though Morton strongly disapproves of Covenanters' methods, especially those of the Cameronian absolutists (234, 235). Because Burleigh must lead an army of rebellion, he has no time for Morton's scruples. Like Napoleon, Burleigh is not to be contravened. As Burleigh inspires his adherents, Scott describes his "stern and harsh features, in which ferocity was rendered more solemn and dignified by a wild cast of tragic enthusiasm. His brow was that of one in whom some strong o'ermastering principle has overwhelmed all other passions and feelings, like the swell of a high springtide" (72). Such Byronic diction suggests the intensity and the transience of revolutionary "tragic enthusiasm." Every high springtide will recede; even revolutions follow seasonal law.

Claverhouse enters *Old Mortality* as Burleigh's equally Byronic counterpart, a leader of physical courage, aristocratic manners, and dark good looks outspokenly committed to royalist defense of Stuart legitimacy (144). Scott immediately undermines admiration for Claverhouse, however, by describing his merits as "perverted" by the circumstances of civil war:

Profound in politics, and embued, of course, with that disregard for individual rights which its intrigues usually generate, this leader [Claverhouse] was cool and collected in danger, fierce and ardent in pursuing success, careless of facing death himself, and ruthless in inflicting it upon others. Such are the characters formed in times of civil discord, when the highest qualities, perverted by party spirit, and inflamed by habitual opposition, are too often combined with vices and excesses which deprive them at once of their merit and of their luster.[10] (144)

The reader's admiration for Claverhouse is here contained within terms of moral criticism ("disregard," "perverted," "vices," "merit"). What emerges is a dark political pessimism rarely associated with Walter Scott. Scott's fear is that civil war breeds a fanaticism that destroys the potential good of revolution. Word for word, these sentences could have been written to describe, not only Scott's Napoleon, but John Balfour of Burleigh, who is Claverhouse's opposite in appearance, religion, and politics. The fanatic temperament rising to power on both sides renders any reasonable compromise highly unlikely.

Claverhouse will not treat with Covenanters, whom he unequivocally describes as "rebels" and "fanatics" (185, 225). Unlike Morton (or Scott), Claverhouse believes that, even in everyday life, military authority must supersede civil authority. He and his dragoons terrify the citizenry by brutally punishing all acts they deem to be rebellion, including outdoor preaching. In his person, however, Claverhouse remains engaging, even likeable. Readers are led to admire him against their will. He is unfailingly courteous to civilians below him as long as they do not oppose the government. Claverhouse spares Henry Morton's life not only because of family associations but because he admires Morton's courage in criticizing royalists as well as Covenanters.

Claverhouse knows himself in ways Balfour does not. Riding beside Claverhouse as his captive, Morton drops a "hint" that Claverhouse and Burley might be surprisingly similar in character:

> "You are right," said Claverhouse, with a smile; "you are very right—we are both fanatics; but there is some distinction between the fanaticism of honour and that of dark and sullen superstition."
>
> "Yet you both shed blood without mercy or remorse," said Morton, who could not suppress his feelings.
>
> "Surely," said Claverhouse, with the same composure; "but of what kind?— There is a difference, I trust, between the blood of learned and reverend prelates and scholars, of gallant soldiers and noble gentlemen, and the red puddle that stagnates in the veins of psalm-singing mechanics, crack-brained demagogues, and sullen boors." (355–56)

Here is a psychological complexity possible for the novelist but unlikely for combatants during the moment of historical crisis. Claverhouse is allowed to know that, during civil war, enemy leaders of equal ability are both likely to turn fanatic. He is prepared to acknowledge that his own fanaticism is based less on loyalty to his monarch, or on reservations about Puritan "superstition," than on instinctual class distinctions between "noble gentlemen" and "sullen boors." To Scott, class-consciousness is always latent in revolutionary conflict, no matter how genuinely one may believe in political and religious principle. Such insights were surely a major source of Lukacs's admiration for Scott's epoch-defining achievement.

The comparative stature of Burleigh and Claverhouse shifts and finally coalesces in surprising ways. After the Covenanters' defeat at Bothwell Bridge, Balfour's fanaticism shades into lunacy. Without avengers to lead, he becomes a refugee in a cave, declaiming into the silence with sword raised and bible in hand. Claverhouse by contrast dies an honored martyr to the Scots' victory at Killecrankie for which he is primarily responsible. Yet amid the ever-shifting fortunes of their last years, both men became closet Jaco-bites. By so doing, Burleigh violates his religious principles, and Claverhouse his loyalty to the reigning monarch. Before Burleigh dies, ironically at the hands of a Dutch protestant mercenary, Burleigh even offers to join Claver-house's troops, whom he wrongly believes to have inherited the Covenanters' mantle of biblical avengers. Both of the novel's fanatics thus become the eventual losers, their absolutism preventing them from accommodating until it is far too late.

Henry Morton tries to stay detached from both kinds of fanaticism, but he is drawn first into, then out of, the Covenanter rebellion by the force of personalities stronger than his own. Amid the madness of the Killing Time, Morton's judicious moderation earns him little but misunderstanding and depression: "I am weary of seeing nothing but violence and fury around me—now assuming the mask of lawful authority, now taking that of religious zeal. I am sick of my country—of myself—of my dependent situation—of my repressed feelings" (78). From the outset, Morton has shown no trace of Waverley's naive enthusiasm. Seeing no prospect of an honorable commit-ment to either side, Morton longs to immigrate to the Low Countries.

Morton remains in a "dependent situation" until novel's end. He agrees to assume a command within the Covenanters' army primarily because of fam-ily circumstance and Burleigh's force of persuasion. Anticipating the disaster at Bothwell Bridge, Morton futilely tries to parley an honorable peace with the royalist army. After the Covenanters are defeated, Morton has no choice but to accept Claverhouse's offer of safe passage to the Low Countries where Morton will remain *hors de combat* for ten years until the "Glorious Revolu-tion" of 1688 has been achieved. *Old Mortality* invokes future revolutionary compromise, but does not validate it in descriptive detail. In the Scottish novels, Scott was never to do so.

While Claverhouse gains personal stature at Burleigh's expense, Protes-tants and Parliament gain control of public life. Although Morton reacquires status and respectability by marrying his beloved Edith Bellenden, Scott's ending is curiously lacking in celebration.[11] Accordingly, the final pages of *Old Mortality* have seemed to many readers to be forced, hasty, and incomplete. The charge is true in narrative detail, but there is an additional consideration. Scott's ending reflects his conviction that a life lived according to judicious moral scruples is likely, under revolutionary circumstances, to become remarkably ineffectual. During the Killing Time, fanatics long overpower both waverers and men in the middle. Those who adhere to scruples of moral conduct may become sidelined for life, no matter how real their merit. Scott's last novel of recent British revolutionary history, *Woodstock*, was to develop this dispiriting possibility further. Despite their acumen, experience, and cultural patriotism, Markham Everard and Henry Morton choose to live their later years on the farthest political margin.

PUGACHEV'S REBELLION AND THE WAVERLEY PROTOTYPE

Pushkin's characterization of a revolutionary fanatic was firmly based in biographical fact before Pushkin fictionalized him. *A History of Pugachev* (1834), still cited as a reliable historical source, quotes extensively from available documents, avoids grand conclusions and refrains from speculating about Pugachev's motives.[12] Careful research and precise writing produce a coherent, credible account of a growing civil war that, by comparison to the class complexity of the English and French revolutions, can best be described as a peasant rebellion. Along the Ural River, an illiterate Cossack and escaped convict named Emilian Pugachev, claiming to be Tsar Peter III (dead in 1762), gathered Cossacks, Bashkirs, and Kalmyks in order to drive out the military and civilian authority of the centralizing Russian government in Moscow. Claiming to provide "liberty and freedom" from serfdom, from all taxes and from conscription, Pugachev also promised his followers land ownership, bread, money, salt, rifles, and gunpowder. Within the terms of British history familiar to Scott, Pugachev could be seen as a Leveller or a Digger turned violent, an anarchic populist who sought revolution by monarchical imposture.

Pugachev's strategy, remarkably successful for fifteen months, was to besiege a governmental fort, demand its surrender, kill all soldiers who resisted, enlist those who willingly surrendered, and then move on to the next fort. While gathering Russian defectors, he kept his forces moving quickly over known terrain. Recruits were always leaving, but more were usually joining. His army, totaling at times twenty thousand men, besieged Orenburg for six months, burned Kazan, seized manufactories and distilleries throughout the region, and threatened to march on Moscow. Before Pugachev was captured, caged, sent to Moscow, tried, quartered, and beheaded, the forces of his rebellion had killed about 1,600 local nobility and town officials. Empress Catherine II referred to Pugachev's "army" as "a rabble of miscreants who have at their head a deceiver as brazen as he is ignorant."[13] Unlike the Old and New "Pretenders" of the Jacobite era, Pugachev had no plausible *de jure* claim to counterrevolutionary authority; he was an imposter, no matter how powerful his cause.

The historical details of *The Captain's Daughter* reaffirm the grid of documentary fact Pushkin had uncovered while writing *A History of Pugachev*.[14] Both works describe a rebellion that could be termed a revolution only according to the word's regressive meaning. Although the historical Pugachev cared little for religious belief, his forces carried the Cossack flag with the cross of the Schismatics (Old Believers) in its middle. Pugachev sought and enjoyed power, not as a republican, but as an alternative autocrat. In the 1770s, he challenged abuses with no consideration for the rights of man, or any new political order. As would-be Tsar, Pugachev holds court among his followers, dispenses patronage (offices, coins, and concubines), and passes criminal judgments at will.

Any favorable view of Pugachev and his followers could therefore be based only upon pre-Enlightenment values. Pugachev resisted centralization and progressive change in order to take murderous revenge against real Russian oppressions, including torture and mutilation as well as serfdom. The insurgents sought to preserve what they regarded as traditional religion and agricultural custom against modernizing encroachment. In practice, however, "liberty" seems to have meant little more than the license to confiscate, bully, burn, rape, and kill; it has no connection to proto-republicanism or proto-socialism. Accordingly, in *The Captain's Daughter* (1836), Pushkin was to use the word "enlightenment" only once, in a judgment looking back at 1773 from the vantage point of the early nineteenth century.[15] As experienced by Piotr Grinyov in 1773, the world of the Urals remained oblivious to Enlightenment values of which Pushkin was keenly aware. As revolutionaries in the Age of Revolution, Pugachev and his followers are even less civilized than Balzac's Chouans and far less admirable than Cooper's Indians.

As we have seen, Pushkin was determined, as he began to plan historical fiction, to "take that Walter Scott to task." Pushkin's stated ideal of good prose—"precision and brevity"[16]—indicates that his short sentences and scarcity of adjectives would convey his literary challenge to Scott's prolixity. But Pushkin's view of Scott's fiction was simultaneously admiring. Not only did Pushkin acknowledge that Scott was the major novelist of the post-Napoleonic world, an author whose "chief beauty lies in the fact that we are shown times long gone . . . in a contemporary, down-to-earth perspective."[17] Pushkin admired French historians who, because of Scott's influence, had shown that legend, treated as legend, was an important part of the historical record.[18] So the legends of Pugachev became important evidence of his times, just as legends of Montrose and Claverhouse had recently been woven into the history of the British Civil Wars. The inclusion of legendary evidence greatly strengthens verisimilitude.

The Captain's Daughter seamlessly refashions biography within the conventions of the Waverley novels. Piotr serves as the waverer, Pugachev as the fanatic. The novella begins as Piotr Grinyov, seventeen-year-old only son of a country gentleman of moderate wealth, is told by his father that he is to enlist as a mid-level officer in the Tsar's army. Educated in a desultory way by a tutor, indifferent to politics, Piotr is sent away from the family estate to mature in the provinces through a presumably safe military experience in his monarch's service. He is oblivious to the rebellion he is about to encounter, but emotionally ready for excitement, even romance. Piotr's situation is, in sum, exactly the same as Edward Waverley's. Like Waverley, he will accompany an ill-organized, ill-equipped army of rebellion, eventually withdraw from it, and then, after the rebellion is brutally suppressed, marry contentedly and resume the quiet life of the country gentry.

Without directly mentioning Scott, Pushkin has devised an analogue—half an admiring variant, half a parody—to Scott's model of historical fiction. The flat desolation of the steppes has little in common with the topography of Walter Scott's Highlands except their essence—borderless danger. Pushkin's neutral ground is less a cultural composite than a cultural void. Piotr is astonished to find that the "fortress" he has been sent to defend is nothing more than a badly-gated village: "I looked from side to side, expecting to see menacing battlements, towers, and a rampart, but saw nothing except a village surrounded by a log fence" (22). Pugachev is regarded as "the Pretender" just as Charles Stuart had been "the Young Pretender," but Pugachev's coarse peasant brutalities prove to be the opposite of Bonnie Prince Charlie's febrile grace.[19] Piotr's groom Savelyich, like Scott's Evan Dhu, offers to die in place of his condemned master, but Savelyich is spared from having to prove it by being released by Pugachev. How quickly noble self-sacrifice turns into farce! Marya Ivanovna Mironov, the Captain's daughter with whom Piotr falls in love, has the tender decency and courageous common sense of Waverley's Rose Bradwardine, but Marya has none of Rose's political awareness. Piotr meets no rebellious aristocratic dark lady like Flora MacIvor, whose character is unimaginable amid the steppes of Central Asia.

These changes toward what was later to be called "realism" are perfectly suited to Pushkin's restrained, concise sentences. But it is difficult to determine whether the changes are meant to parody Scott, to acknowledge Russian cultural limitations, or both, depending on context. To cite just one such ambiguity, Piotr refers to the brutal pretension of Pugachev's "court" trials as a "terrible comedy."[20] At what point in his life could Piotr have conceived of this complex, oxymoronic phrase? From the beginning, Piotr is penning his memoir as an older man, thereby altering Scott's customary limited-omniscient point of view.[21] Piotr's political and social attitudes have not fundamentally changed; the past he remembers has rather become clarified for him. He now sees a "terrible comedy" in events he once surely saw as terror *or* comedy. When recounting his experiences during Pugachev's rebellion, the older Piotr often remarks upon his youthful naiveté. When judging the rebellion from the time of writing his memoir, Piotr writes as a loyal Russian gentleman who exclaims, near novel's end, "God save us from seeing a Russian revolt, senseless and merciless" (113). *Caveat Lector.* Such a one-sided summary outburst, however understandable, is not true to the revolutionary experiences Piotr has already recorded for us.

Pugachev's rebellion was indeed terrifying and brutal, but it was neither "senseless" nor "merciless." Piotr provides more than a few details of Russian cruelty and oppression toward the Cossacks, whose cultural identity and practices are being suppressed, very like the Highlanders after 1745. Through the responses of young Piotr, Pushkin altered his earlier characterization of Pugachev in the *History* in order to make Pugachev far more complex than a mere imposter, reactionary, or thug. Pugachev is fanatic in his quest for power, but also has moments of gratitude, affection, good sense, and surprising mercy.[22] He rightly predicts that his illiteracy will make him vulnerable to followers who will turn against him. Pugachev spares Piotr's life after the rebels conquer Fort Belogorsky (the historical Fort Tatischev). Pugachev even saves the Captain's daughter first from death, later from rape. As Piotr's unforgettable nightmare implies, Pugachev looms as Piotr's unacknowledged father-substitute, an oddly priest-like figure who, unlike Piotr's blood father, offers to bless his son, even though, as a "black bearded peasant," he seems to be filling the room with "dead bodies" and "pools of blood."[23] In Piotr's mind, filial atonement and sacrilegious atrocity horrifyingly merge into the incomprehensible, double face of the revolutionary fanatic.

Similarly, the elder Piotr recalls his youthful responses to Pugachev's rebellion as a protracted state of emotional confusion. After the "terrible peasant" of his dream offers to bless him, Piotr recalls that "terror and confusion possessed me"—and he conveniently woke up (15). After the fall of Fort Belogorsky, when Pugachev pardons Piotr, then orders him to kneel down before "our father" for a blessing, Piotr is unsure whether to rejoice or feel humiliated; he recalls only "my feelings were too confused" (64). As Pugachev orders the execution of Commandant Mironov and his wife, who have publicly called Pugachev a "thief" and "imposter," Piotr stands immobilized, "confused by the terrible impressions of the day" (66). When Pugachev urges Piotr to join the rebellion, Piotr does not know whether to be amused or terrified; he remembers only "I was confused" (73). When Pugachev proposes to hang the villainous Shvabrin, Piotr is plunged into "confusion" because he feels both regret and joy (94). The word has become Piotr's litany:

tragi-comedies may have their rules, but "terrible comedy" provokes ongoing "confusion."

Piotr remembers his last sight of Pugachev before execution as if his shameful response had deserved confessional:

> I cannot express what I felt on parting from this terrible man, a monster of evil to all but me. Why not confess the truth? At that moment I was drawn to him by warm sympathy. I longed to tear him away from the criminals whose leader he was and to save his head before it was too late. (106)

Piotr is endeavoring to separate his personal response ("warm sympathy") from the historical situation ("a monster of evil to all but me") so as to discredit his conflicting emotions as youthful naiveté. He acknowledges the intensity of contrary emotions that the fanatic arouses, while safely confining it to the past. "I cannot express what I felt" writes Piotr. Waverley had felt similar confusion over the death of Fergus. To Henry Morton, Claverhouse is both his savior and his enemy. Fanatics may lose, but the memory of them lingers on, half against the will.

The elder Piotr's horrified repudiation of the rebellion keeps his written memory of Pugachev's mercies under control. Piotr condemns the peasant revolt in unqualified terms:

> There was no lawful authority anywhere. The landowners were hiding in the forests. Bands of brigands were ransacking the country. The chiefs of separate detachments arbitrarily meted out punishments and granted pardons; the vast region where the conflagration had raged was in a terrible state. (113)

To dwell upon past historical atrocities is the older Piotr's way of avoiding the darker question of the fanatic's inscrutability. Piotr's "warm sympathy" for Pugachev can never be allowed to overcome his feeling that Pugachev's generosity is impulsive, but his cruelty instinctive. Similarly, Piotr's liking for the Mironovs never overcomes his unadmitted condescension toward them as good people of a lower social class. Progress for Piotr evidently does not entail changes in the social order. Except for the abolition of torture by Tsar Alexander in 1801, the elder Piotr mentions no evidence of Russia's cultural progress after the suppression of peasant revolution.

These several sorts of confusion render Piotr even more incapable of acting than Waverley. Pugachev's rebellion is put down by others; the people whom Piotr loves are rescued by others.[24] At the beginning of the narrative, Piotr is a privileged young man as callow as he is ignorant. He pretends manhood by getting drunk, by losing at billiards, by contracting a large gambling debt, and by provoking a needless duel over love poetry. He tries to display authority by bullying his groom and condescending to provincials. By the end of the rebellion, Piotr has lost much of his ignorance, but he remains callow and passive, a mere observer who has muddled through, thanks to a pleasant exterior, good will, good fortune, and the help of others. At memoir's end, we see no evidence that Piotr has attained the sensible good citizenship Scott ascribes to Waverley.

Initially similar in character, Waverley and Piotr also differ in their willingness to engage in the chaos of rebellion. Waverley promises fealty to the Young Pretender; Piotr refuses to join pretender Pugachev's forces. Waverley engages in the battles of Preston Pans and Clifton; he defends a disarmed Hanoverian officer about to be murdered. Piotr, however, does remarkably little to defend Fort Belogorsky except to rush out and be captured. After Waverley becomes disillusioned with the Jacobites, he seeks to extricate himself by journeying to London to right his reputation. Piotr is saved from conviction and exile to Siberia only because his beloved Marya journeys to St. Petersburg to plead his case to Catherine the Great.[25]

Pushkin separates morality from politics to a degree Scott would have found dangerous, if not reprehensible. Waverley continues to presume that, Jacobite or Hanoverian, there is a morally right choice and it is his duty to pursue it, even if he can never quite find it. Although Henry Morton is wary of any personal claim to integrity, he too searches to discover a middle path of political right and human decency. The few decisions Piotr ever makes are based upon different kinds of motive. Piotr's one life-changing decision, whether or not to accept Pugachev's appeal to join the rebellion, plunges him into understandable hesitancy. Pugachev importunes him twice but Piotr deflects both appeals. The third time, Pugachev offers Piotr the opportunity to be his Field Marshal and a Prince, then forces the issue: "what do you say?" "No," I answered firmly. "I am a gentleman by birth; I swore allegiance to the empress; I cannot serve you" (73).

Piotr's appeal to class allegiance is more than a momentary rationalization. Whether Piotr is grasping at certainty or not, his persistent references to social class—peasant or gentry—control his sense of revolutionary motivation. Henceforth, Pugachev will address Piotr, half seriously and half jeeringly, as "your honor." Three times Piotr will justify his withdrawal by claiming to have acted as "an officer and a gentleman." As Pugachev and Piotr drive silently together in a carriage, Pugachev asks Piotr for his thoughts, to which Piotr curtly replies: "How can I help thinking! I am an officer and a gentleman; only yesterday I was fighting against you and today I am driving beside you and the happiness of my whole life depends upon you" (98). To be an officer and a gentleman evidently gives Piotr sufficient right not directly to answer a peasant like Pugachev. At his trial for treason, Piotr responds indignantly to questions of where and why he joined Pugachev's rebellion by claiming that "as an officer and a gentleman I could not possibly have entered Pugachov's service or have carried out any commissions of his" (116–117). Scott's concern for his protagonist's multiplicity of motive narrows into Pushkin's insistence that gentlemanly allegiance will, in a revolutionary crisis, prove decisive, especially if it is a rationalization.

For Piotr, considerations of social class will continue to take precedence over issues of social justice. Introducing the sixth chapter of his memoir, which he titles "Pugachev's Rebellion," the elder Piotr accounts for the rise of the rebellion in stadialist terms far more judgmental than those of Adam Ferguson:

> This vast and wealthy province was inhabited by a number of half-savage peoples who had but recently acknowledged the authority of the Russian sovereigns. Unused to the law and habits of civilized life, cruel and reckless, they constantly rebelled, and the Government had to watch over them unremittingly to keep them in submission. (47)

Once again, the elder Piotr allows sweeping historical judgments to simplify and assuage troubling personal memories. Adjectives like "half-savage" and "civilized" firmly separate the rebel from the gentleman. According to the broadest geocultural categories of the 1820s, Pushkin's rebellious Cossacks are to Muscovites, as Scott's rebellious Highlanders are to the English, as Cooper's forest Indians are to the whites, and as Balzac's rebellious Chouans are to the Parisians. But it is crucial to remember that for Pushkin, unlike the other three novelists, judgments passed in accord with the discourse of savagery and civilization usually emanate from an imagined character rather than from the author.

DARNAY AND MADAME DEFARGE: "THE SANGUINE MIRAGE OF DOING GOOD"

Charles Darnay, the protagonist though hardly the hero of *A Tale of Two Cities*, is yet another "young gentleman," "well-grown and well-looking," caught between cultures, faced with vexing ambiguities and dangerous choices.[26] He is introduced as his own double. In France, his public identity is to be Marquis St. Evrémonde, young heir to a vast crumbling estate, but in England he is Charles Darnay, earning a reclusive living as a language teacher—half a liberal aristocrat, half a wage-earning professional. Looking as if he were Sydney Carton's twin, Darnay also figures as Carton's alter ego, the prepossessing gentleman whom the drunken Carton would like to be, affianced to the woman Carton loves. Suspected as a republican in England, then suspected as an aristocrat in France, Darnay first undergoes a trial for treason in England, then a double trial as an émigré and an aristocrat in Paris. The grime and crime of London, the corruption of English judicial practices are no less visible than the poverty of St. Antoine and the luxuries of the Parisian aristocracy.[27]

High-minded helplessness is the key to Dickens's waverer; his good-willed hesitancy deprives him of free will. Darnay can neither fully withdraw from, nor fully engage in, the French Revolution. Seeking to free himself from the curse of aristocratic privilege, symbolized by his sadistic uncle, Darnay renounces his title and his estate. In France he feels "bound to a system that is frightful to me, responsible for it, but powerless in it" (129). In England, however, he feels guilt at abandoning responsibility for his French inheritance, his family name, his servants, and his peasants. Although Darnay had formerly hoped to free his estate "slowly . . . from the weight that drags it down" (130), he has retreated to a life of middle-class domestic bliss in which he is responsible only to those he loves. As the footsteps of revolution invade the peace of his Soho garden, he discovers that his "renunciation of his social place had been hurried and incomplete" and that he must return "to stay bloodshed and assert the claims of mercy and humanity" (251, 252).

An aristocrat who has renounced both privilege and reform, an admirer of George Washington but no revolutionary, Charles Darnay would like to remain apolitical.[28] Thoroughly likeable, he perceives the outer world through the "shadowy conceptions of a gentle mind" (264). Darnay returns to France in 1792 without understanding the conditions of revolutionary Paris and without considering how he might redress the injustices of the *Ancien regime* on the Evrémonde estate. To "stay bloodshed" and extend "mercy" and "humanity" are, for him, aims sufficiently specific. Goodwill shall surely earn its due reward. Among the many waverers facing revolution in historical novels, Darnay is the most oblivious to revolutionary forces, with perhaps the least reason to be so.

As a participant in civic life, Darnay's honesty and good-willed innocence earn him less than nothing. His steward Gabelle, whom he has returned to France to save, is freed by vengeful revolutionaries only because Darnay, a more important victim, has been imprisoned. In none of Darnay's three trials is he able to clear himself of suspicion. Sydney Carton saves Darnay by a trick of evidence; Dr. Manette saves him on the authority of his own reputation, and, finally, Carton substitutes himself for Darnay in prison. When we last see Charles Darnay, he has become a drugged body lying on a carriage floor being transported out of revolutionary Paris.

The concluding image of Darnay's helplessness confirms a seeming aside Dickens had penned while Darnay was preparing to return to France:

> That glorious vision of doing good, which is so often the sanguine mirage of so
> many good minds, arose before him [Darnay] and he even saw himself in the
> illusion with some influence to guide this raging Revolution that was running
> so fearfully wild. (252)

Neither here nor elsewhere in the narrative does Dickens consider the possibility that progress might occur through revolution itself. Simply put, the
cruel injustices of the *Ancien Regime* provoke the cruel injustices of the Terror. Brutal violence begets brutal violence; any assertion of progress must be
deferred to invoking the future at the close of the novel's last chapter.

Dickens manages to preserve moral justice by questionable national distinctions. Ironically, "doing good" turns out *not* to be a "sanguine mirage" for
all characters. Dr. Manette, Jarvis Lorry, Miss Pross, and Sydney Carton—all
of them apolitical—do good by following the Dickensian virtue of "the faithful service of the heart" through acts of mercy and humanity (100). Only
those middle-class people, mostly English, who work for a living prove able
to act for the good. Darnay, the liberal aristocrat who renounces his heritage
in order to salvage his own purity, is rendered helpless amid revolutionary
violence, no matter how decent or well-intentioned he may be. Pushkin and
Scott, despite their different perspectives, could ascribe no such merit to a
middle class that had, in their time, not yet fully risen to power.[29]

Unlike Flora MacIvor, Burleigh, Claverhouse, or even Pugachev, Madame
Defarge is a fanatic with no political cause. Her motive is revenge for personal family wrong (rape and murder), revenge that she directs first at the
Evrémonde family, then at all aristocrats. Furthering the Rights of Man into
a progressive republican future means nothing to her. She is not even concerned with abolishing the *droit du seigneur* and the *lettre de cachet* that have
been legally used to destroy her family. Through her knitting she commits
herself to the principle that revenge exacted through the silent condemning
of secret names serves as an implacable rule of fate. Her knitting links her to
Lachesis, the Knitter among the three Greek Fates. But she also presages the
fanatic compiling of secret lists that was to recur in the mid-twentieth century
in Russia, in Germany, and in the House Un-American Activities Committee,
to mention only major world powers.

Madame Defarge is personally responsible for the conviction of Charles
Darnay, but Darnay never meets or recognizes her. Dickens's waverer and
his fanatic are such total opposites that their direct interaction is inconceivable. To Dickens, Madame Defarge is a fit symbol of fanatical revenge in part
because she has turned herself into a monster of gender perversion.[30] On the
simplest level, Madame Defarge is linked to La Guillotine, which Dickens
repeatedly refers to as "that sharp female newly born" (262). When Madame
Defarge leads the women of St. Antoine to attack the Bastille, she becomes

male: "her resolute right hand was occupied with an axe, in place of the usual softer implements, and in her girdle were a pistol and a cruel knife" (223). When she sets off in final pursuit of the Manette family, "her dark hair looked rich under her coarse red cap. Lying hidden in her bosom was a loaded pistol. Lying hidden at her waist was a sharpened dagger" (376).

Scott had kept the "purity" of Flora MacIvor's fanaticism entirely apart from any suggestion of dehumanization. Madame Defarge's end suggests that a woman's fanaticism transforms her into a cross-gender monstrosity that can nonetheless be brought down by the courage of a loving moral, middle-class woman. During her fight with Miss Pross, the pistol Madame Defarge hides in her bosom delivers the blow that kills her. Nonetheless, Madame Defarge has lived on. Generations of high school students have enjoyed a *frisson* at the memory of Madame Defarge; generations of critics and scholars have condescended to the simplicity of Dickens' characterization. Such responses cloak the needed self-defense of the reader; rarely has any author created a fanatic so silently implacable, so instantly memorable, in so few words.

NAPOLEON AND PIERRE: 666

Among the sustained criticisms Tolstoy levels at historians is the folly of the nineteenth-century predilection for the "Great Man" theory of history. To assume that the "collective will" of the people (an updating of Rousseau's "General Will") could ever have been embodied in any one person is, from Tolstoy's perspective, a mere grasping at straws, a lazy resort to mono-causal explanations of complex, controversial events. The Second Epilogue to *War and Peace* assembles three examples of this particular folly that are particularly appropriate to this study:

> If power be the collective will of the people transferred to their ruler, was Pugachev a representative of the will of the people? If not, then why was Napoleon I? Why was Napoleon III a criminal when he was taken prisoner at Boulogne, and why, later on, were those criminals whom he arrested?[31]

Napoleon I is, of course Tolstoy's chief target here, not only because he is the central historical figure in *War and Peace* but because by the 1860s Napoleon was assumed to represent the will of the French people, the legacy of the revolution, or whatever universal forces, progressive or regressive, that the historian chose to emphasize.

Recent biographies by Alan Schom and Paul Johnson concentrate on Napoleon's need, after 1804, to pursue ever-expanding warfare for the glory of France, the Grand Empire, and himself.[32] Victory, defeat, or draw, one

battle had to be followed by planning another until the Emperor's need for
conquest and adulation became obsessive. Tolstoy's window upon Napoleonic times is necessarily limited to the Russian campaign, but his characterization of Napoleon is a precursor of Johnson's and Schom's. Rarely do
any of the three writers dwell upon the Napoleon who furthered religious
toleration, the Napoleonic Code, and meritocratic institutions. Instead, we
see Napoleon as a brilliant but erratic military strategist, a battlefield presence, volatile commander of his Marshals, and treacherous egoist among rival
monarchs—a military genius and sometime revolutionary turned fanatic egoist. Tolstoy displaces the predominately heroic portraits of Napoleon penned
by his near contemporaries—Hazlitt, Emerson, and Carlyle—by developing
the symbiotic relationship between Napoleon as an historical fanatic and
Pierre Bezuhov as a fictive bumbling waverer.[33]

Napoleon is introduced in *War and Peace* at the height of his career just
before the Battle of Austerlitz, gazing down from Pratzen Heights with "con-
fident, self-complacent happiness" upon the Russians whom he has duped
into abandoning their superior strategic position (237). Tolstoy immediately
belittles Napoleon's achievement by likening Napoleon's delight to "the
face of a boy happily in love" (237). Victory at Austerlitz is followed by
Napoleon's finest moment when he tours the battlefield, pauses before the
seemingly dead body of André Bolkonski, sensitively declares "that's a fine
death," and then, when André moves his leg, orders André to be removed to
the dressing station, thereby saving his life. Eventually, André will indeed
endure "a fine death," just as his closest friend Pierre Bezuhov will live a fine
life, but Tolstoy will not allow Napoleon's gesture to be regarded as salvific
or wholly admirable. After gazing up into the infinite (and perhaps empty)
blue sky, the wounded André, "looking into Napoleon's eyes," sees there the
Emperor's "paltry vanity and joy in victory" and thinks of "the insignificance
of greatness, the unimportance of life, which no one could understand, and
the still greater unimportance of death, the meaning of which no one alive
could understand or explain" (254). No comforting Emersonian bromides
here.[34]

As Napoleon begins stirring up the diplomatic crises that will justify the
Grande Armeé's 1812 invasion of Russia, Tolstoy portrays him from close-
up perspectives as a mere man of diminishing powers. Tsar Alexander's gentility grates upon Napoleon, as does Alexander's refusal to allow a Corsican
adventurer to marry into the Romanov family. Napoleon rarely pauses for
any reply to his barrage of questions, resorts angrily to pinches of snuff, and
becomes enraged when crossed, proclaiming "I know everything . . . I know
everything" (553). He increasingly resorts to the false analogy that warfare
is a chess game of demonstrable rules in which the winner will be the master strategist who by free will controls the entire game board. As Napoleon

prepares to invade Russia, he is visualized as sinister and pudgy: "rotund stomach," "fat thighs," "short legs," "plump white neck," relying upon "Eau de Cologne" (549). Tolstoy's description recalls the figure of Jacques Louis David's portrait *Napoleon in his Study* (1812), not the virile Napoleon-on-horseback of David's world-famous *Bonaparte at the Saint Bernard Pass* (1800).

At Austerlitz, looking down from above the clearing fog, Napoleon retains the illusion of knowledge and control. At Borodino, however, he cannot command anything because he can neither see the battlefield nor communicate with his troops. To Tolstoy, this change in circumstance should have led Napoleon to a new understanding of the limits of free will:

> And it was not Napoleon who directed the course of the battle, for none of his orders were executed, and during the battle he did not know what was going on before him. So the way in which these people killed one another was not decided by Napoleon's will but occurred independently of him, in accord with the will of hundreds of thousands of people who took part in the common action. It *only seemed* to Napoleon that it all took place by his will. (699)

Each man among the "hundreds of thousands" retains some measure of free will, but no one individual controls even a skirmish, and the sum of all the free wills is unknowable because there is no communication among them, no common denominator. Cavalry regiments gallop back and forth without direction, infantrymen bolting in scattered groups, all trying to save their lives by firing at a barely seen enemy, while artillery units deal random death indiscriminately upon them all (713–714). Although Napoleon's eyes see these details, it still *seems* to Napoleon that the Battle of Borodino "all took place by his will" (727). By this time in Napoleon's career, his fanaticism, egoism, and insanity have become inseparable. Because of his international stature, Napoleon's fanaticism has becomes a salient mark of his revolutionary era.

No matter how often Tolstoy may insist that one action is the sum of unknowably many actions, that "nothing is the cause" (538), and "the higher men stand in the social hierarchy the less are they free" (607), Tolstoy cannot refrain from holding Napoleon chiefly responsible for the 800,000 deaths caused by the invasion of Russia. After the mutual slaughter of Borodino has ended in Russian withdrawal, Napoleon reverts to his "artificial realm of imaginary greatness and, as a horse walking a treadmill thinks it is doing something for itself, submissively fulfilled the cruel, sad, gloomy and inhuman role predestined for him" (727). In the following paragraphs, Tolstoy denounces Napoleon as a man never able to "understand goodness, beauty or truth, or the significance of his actions" no matter how strenuously he had once sought a "European system" of equal laws and revolutionary justice

(727–728). As the defeated Napoleon races to escape from Russia, leaving the remnants of his army behind, Tolstoy dismisses him from the novel with the Fieldingesque reminder that "greatness" is not "goodness" (946). To be sure, Tolstoy's rendering of Napoleon's demise reflects a surge of Slavophile nationalism; it also demonstrates how fanatical pursuit of glory, expanding one's ego across the universe, will subvert progressive revolutionary ideals.

Among all the waverers in historical novels, there can never be a more engaging and likeable bumbler than Pierre Bezuhov. While his intelligent uncertainties make it difficult for him to act, his immense privileges render action unnecessary. His instinctual decency leads him to waver before ordinary human venality, except when he flies into a deserved rage at its meanness. His own mind, he well knows, usually works like a stripped screw, turning endlessly around the same few tentative and disconnected phrases, ending in nonconclusion (303). Many take advantage of him, but not more than once, Vasilii Kuragin excepted. Pierre is open to all of life, forever in search of life's answer. In the characterization of Pierre, the waverer first becomes a comedic figure, in part because Pierre soon discovers how insignificant his decision of allegiance is in the immensity of historical time.

Pierre's sensitivity, intelligence, and capacity to grow emerge through his changing responses to the French Revolution in general, and to Napoleon in particular. We first meet Pierre at Anna Schérer's St. Petersburg salon soon after Genoa and Lucca have become "family estates of the Bonapartes" (3). Amid the aristocratic guests striking attitudes of trendy contempt toward everything associated with the name Bonaparte is the richest potential heir in Russia, Count Pierre Bezuhov, newly returned to St. Petersburg from Paris, and an admiring devotee of Napoleon. Pierre is eager to make the basis of his admiration clear: "Napoleon is great because he rose superior to the revolution, suppressed its abuses, preserved all that was good in it—equality of citizenship and freedom of speech and of the press—and only for that reason did he obtain power" (17). We should remember that in 1805 Pierre's opinion was still widely shared among the citizens of Napoleon's recently "liberated" city-states as well as in France. The greatness of Napoleon, Pierre is sure, lies in his pursuit of revolutionary ideals of liberty and equality, for which military conquest is the necessary means—not the other way around. Napoleon seeks power only for the sake of revolutionary "ideas": "the rights of man, emancipation from prejudices, and equality of citizenship" (17).

Pierre refuses to compromise the purity of his heroic ideal merely because Napoleon ordered the execution of the Duc d'Enghein, a Bourbon émigré, on a probably false charge of conspiracy. "Almost all the aristocracy" in France are joining Napoleon, Pierre claims, not because Napoleon has cynically bought them, but because the aristocrats themselves have become true believers in liberty and equality (16). Tolstoy describes Pierre's outburst ("the Revolution was a grand thing") as a "desperate and provocative proposition" of "extreme youth" (17). Simultaneously, however, Tolstoy discredits the snobbery of the royalists by voicing their fears through the vain, effete Vicomte de Mortemart. As a youth, Pierre thinks in binary oppositions of good and bad. The onset of revolutions, the novel's opening scene implies, encourages such simplistic responses, especially from a distance.

As Pierre's countrymen, including André Bolkonski, prepare to fight Napoleon, Pierre joins the Masons. Liberty, Equality, and Fraternity, the Masons claim, once embodied in associations of high-minded professionals and aristocrats, will leaven a lethargic people by peaceful means, not by conquest. Pierre never considers *why* he has been seduced by the Masons, but he soon recognizes, to his credit, the absurdity of Masonic rituals that claim to be a substitute for active, public commitment. Once Napoleon Bonaparte, symbol of Pierre's liberal ideals, becomes his country's declared enemy, Pierre has nowhere to turn, amid his broken marriage, except to his inconclusive thoughts, his dissolute pleasures, and his failed efforts to reform the condition of the serfs on his vast estates.

Amid his vacillations, Pierre learns from living. Trying to determine whether he or Hélene is responsible for their failed marriage, he seeks an answer by an analogy to revolutionary history:

"Louis XVI was executed because they said he was dishonorable, and a criminal... and from their point of view they were right, as were those who canonized him and died a martyr's death for his sake. Then Robespierre was beheaded for being a despot. Who is right and who is wrong? No one! But if you are alive—live." (277)

Napoleon too was presumably neither wrong nor right. This major shift in Pierre's thinking prompts him, not toward a flabby relativism, but toward two complementary responses: to live life to the fullest and to learn "to laugh at himself" (277). To have worried about the meaning—and possible meaninglessness—of the swift overturns of the revolutionary era has contributed significantly to both realizations. To be able to laugh at one's own confusions offers the waverer a way through, if not a way up.

Soon Pierre is telling a despairing André "if there is a God and future life, there is truth and good, and man's highest happiness consists in striving to attain them. We must live, we must love, and we must believe that we live not only today, on this scrap of earth, but have lived and shall live forever, there in the Whole" (340). The kind of theism Pierre here advances is not dissimilar to the theism of Napoleon's counterpart and opposite, General Kutuzov, who falls on his knees on the battlefield at Borodino, publically kisses an icon, falls asleep at strategy meetings, believes not one word of theology, and retreats in order to wait for Napoleon to destroy himself.

Pierre's gradual understanding of the difference between the image and reality of Napoleon helps him to discover his own values. In 1805 he had thought himself a seeker and a planner, perhaps of a Napoleonic significance; by 1811, he is half willing to be, by comparison, "a retired gentleman-in-waiting": "Had he not at one time longed with all his heart to establish a republic in Russia; then himself to be a Napoleon; then to be a philosopher?" (476). To be the gentleman-in-waiting, however, does not satisfy him for long. Without engaging to fight against Napoleon, he trusts a brother Mason's "revelation" that the number 666 in *Rev. 13:18* implies a connection between Napoleon, the Beast of the Apocalypse, and *L'Russe Bezuhov* that will somehow bring about Napoleon's downfall in 1812. At this moment Pierre is *not* planning to kill Napoleon; he simply aggrandizes himself by claiming scriptural connection with his former idol, now identified with the Beast. Tolstoy is providing his reader comedy of great psychological insight, rather than narrative foreshadowing. Scott, Pushkin, and Dickens would have thought their waverers diminished by so absurd a self-identification as 666. To Tolstoy, Pierre's comic illusion opens up a familiar stereotype for further development.

Dressed in a green swallow-tail coat and white top hat, Pierre comically wanders the battlefield at Borodino, first trying to view warfare as a sublime painting, then descending into the Raevski redoubt where he is nearly blown apart by a French shell. Pierre has, in theory, already abandoned his pacifism when he agreed with André that the French deserve death because they are devastating the Russian homeland (690). But his experience at Borodino provides incontrovertible evidence of Napoleon's murderousness, provoking Pierre into an angry patriotism fueled by despair.

Tolstoy never ennobles Pierre's plan to assassinate Napoleon. Pierre forms his resolve to kill when he discovers that Kutuzov will not defend Moscow. It is prompted by two partially self-destructive impulses: (1) "a feeling of the necessity of sacrifice and suffering in view of the common calamity" and (2) a "quite Russian feeling of contempt for everything conventional" (800). Pierre's resolve plunges him, Tolstoy declares, into "a state of excitement bordering on insanity" (800). A meeting between Pierre and Napoleon would at this juncture be a confrontation between two partially insane men; fanaticisms of opposed kinds suddenly give promise of conjoining.

Pierre's resolve to kill Napoleon is soon diverted into paths both comic and heroic. Because his pistol has already been discharged, he pursues Napoleon with only a dagger. Rather than killing Napoleon, Pierre saves a little girl from burning and then, in a "transport of rage," saves an Armenian woman from rape (825). As Pierre ruefully admits, he "never saw Napoleon, never heard about him" (988). The historical novel, as practiced by Scott, Cooper, Balzac, and Pushkin, had not accentuated such chancy ironies during a climactic battle moment. No predecessor had heaped such comic humiliation on the waverer's head and then persuaded the reader to admire him as a savior of ordinary defenseless lives. The waverer figure has acquired a complexity it might later equal, but could never surpass.

Through the influence of Platon Karataev, Pierre experiences the spiritual soundness of simple decency. A shoeless prisoner of the retreating French army, Count Pierre Bezuhov, the richest man in Russia, discovers in Platon Karataev and in himself a revolutionary faith definable in Enlightenment terms. Freedom and the pursuit of happiness are, to a considerable but not unlimited degree, within reach of every man:

> Pierre had learned not with his intellect but with his whole being, by life itself, that man is created for happiness, that happiness is within him, in the satisfaction of simple human needs. . . . He had learned that as there is no condition in which man can be happy and entirely free, so there is no condition in which he need be unhappy and lack freedom. He learned that suffering and freedom have their limits, and that those limits are very near together. (937)

Whether there is progress or decline between eras, whether a monarchy, a republic, or an empire is best suited to advance human rights, are considerations secondary to the truth of Pierre's new understanding. Here, if anywhere, is wisdom. Despite the phrase "Freedom and the pursuit of happiness," the intellect of a Thomas Jefferson is not necessary to the forming of Pierre's new convictions, but Platon Karataev's peasant simplicity is. Unlike Scott's, Cooper's, or Pushkin's protagonists, Pierre can therefore be a waverer who survives but never fires a gun in battle. Had the rapidly retreating Napoleon happened to overhear prisoner Pierre voicing his new convictions, Napoleon would have expressed contempt for them as the rationalizations of a loser. Tolstoy evidently knew he was reworking literary conventions to lead the historical novel into new ground.

GAMELIN'S BLOODTHIRST: ISOLATING THE FANATIC

Historical novels that center upon an ideological fanatic but lack the balance wheel of a sensitive waverer are likely to dead-end in the darkest corners of the revolutionary mentality. Anatole France intended The *Gods Will Have Blood* to be titled *Evariste Gamelin* until he discovered the phrase *"Les Dieux Ont Soif"* in a letter by Camille Desmoulins denouncing the Terror. Evariste might have become a waverer, but when the reader first encounters him in July of 1793, he is already a member of the military committee of his Paris section, a nominee for the Revolutionary Tribunal, and signer of a petition demanding the exile of all Federalists (Girondists) as traitors. His adolescent kindness has already been effaced by a "serene fanaticism."[35]

A tyro in revolutionary government, Evariste at first has no hunger for personal power. His fanaticism derives from adolescent idolization of Marat's self-rectitude. After Marat's assassination, Evariste transfer his idolization to Robespierre because he wishes to share in the aura of incorruptibility. Given the historical circumstances of depreciated Assignats, countrywide counterrevolutions, and the Prussian invasion, Evariste supports increasingly repressive policies: a mighty army, higher taxes, fixed food prices, private warnings, death to all speculators, and public display of the guillotine to inspire fear.

Liberty and Natural Rights for the individual are never Evariste's concern. Extreme measures, he believes, are not extreme in an extremity: "Perhaps it will be best if the workers in the army do march on Paris and massacre the remaining patriots that the famine's not destroying quick enough! There's no time to lose" (38). Conceiving of himself as a republican, he sincerely believes he is opposed to the death penalty, and yearns like Robespierre to abolish it, "but that won't be possible until the last enemy of the Republic has perished beneath the sword of justice" (75). In the meanwhile, death to every enemy of republican virtue.

There proves to be nothing "serene" about Evariste's growing fanaticism. As a magistrate on the Revolutionary Tribunal, he condemns three victims during the first week, twenty the second week, and sixty-three the third. Food speculators adept at double speak are released; failed elderly generals and impoverished prostitutes are guillotined with scant hearing. Evariste is unable to separate the judicial satisfaction of passing a wise sentence from the emotional satisfaction of receiving the plaudits of the crowd. As the pressure of the trials mounts, Evariste begins to imagine "conspirators and traitors everywhere he looked" (153). A bread vendor is guillotined because she has shouted out "Vive le Roi" (146). Personal vendettas begin to intervene. Because he suspects his sister's aristocratic lover of counterrevolution, and because he suspects Jacques Maubel of having seduced his mistress Elodie, he has them both executed.

Evariste's exhaustion requires ever-new energy that he summons from sado-masochistic sexual encounters with Elodie. The dark pleasure of bloodletting at the Revolutionary Tribunal leads directly to the dark pleasure of bloody lovemaking in the bedroom. Both Evariste and Elodie enjoy recognizing that that their linked political and sexual activities have become increasingly "monstrous" (153, 178). As Revolution turns unavoidably into Terror, Terror arouses perverse sexual desire, "drowning in a strangely mixed flood of horror and ecstatic lust."[36]

The Terror that emerges from the Jacobin Club's ways of enacting the "general will" becomes Evariste's religion. On two occasions he exclaims "Oh Beneficent Terror! Saintly Terror! Holy Guillotine! At this very moment last year, the Republic was torn by opposing factions, the hydra of Federalism threatened to devour her. Today a united Jacobinism spreads its might and wisdom throughout the Republic" (226). Evariste does not recognize that his exclamation is a prayer, just as he perceives no incongruity between pursuing revolution as both a religion and an aphrodisiac. He has descended into the madness of seeing enemies of the republic everywhere; constant vigilance is necessary because the enemy is protean in shape-shifting and Hydra-headed in number.

Evariste's shifting politics illustrate Crane Brinton's model: revolutions move inexorably toward a climax of leftist Terror. Yesterday's leader must be expunged in order to demonstrate today's progress and tomorrow's purity. Before becoming a Revolutionary judge, Evariste had privately condemned Mirabeau, Lafayette, Bailly, and Petion; since becoming a magistrate, he has publically denounced Danton, Desmoulins, Pere Duchesne, and Hébert. Faithful to the joys of self-righteous accusation until the end, Evariste condemns Robespierre and then himself. Dragged to the guillotine in a tumbrel, he is fully convinced that "We have deserved our fate. Even Robespierre, pure and saintly as he was, sinned by being too mild, too merciful; his faults are wiped out by his martyrdom. By following his example, I have betrayed the Republic; she perishes; it is just that I die with her. I did not shed enough blood: let my own blood flow! Let me perish! I have deserved it" (242). To relish martyrdom for insufficient killing becomes the summit of Evariste's revolutionary ecstasy. The purest form of fanaticism is the most insane, the most deadly.

Gamelin's descent into the insanity of endless killing can and should be seen as an historical reality of 1793 as well as a premonition of the purges of Hitler and Stalin. Readers of the novel, however, are unlikely to grant Anatole France's characterization of Evariste Gamelin needed suspension of disbelief. The problem is not that Gamelin's tormented, paranoid psychology is itself implausible. Nor is it the intermittent hyperbole of Anatole France's diction. The problem is rather that Anatole France has created Evariste Gamelin less as a character than a case study in fanaticism that increasingly dominates the world of the novel. As the waverer figure recedes and disappears, so does the balanced capaciousness of historical viewpoint we associate with Scott and Tolstoy.

"VERBAL INCONTINENCE": THE LANGUAGE OF REVOLUTION

Doctor Zhivago keeps the defining events of the Russian Revolution at literary distance. Two chapters refer to the overturn of 1917, but seven chapters immerse the reader in the Civil War of 1918–1920. "Bloody Sunday 1905" is rendered from the innocent viewpoint of young Pasha Antipov. Yurii Zhivago hears about the February 1917 overthrow of the Tsar while he is a doctor on the western front. He then hears of the Bolsheviks' seizure of power while reading a newspaper on a Moscow street. To all members of the genteel Gromeko household, the first days of the Bolshevik revolution are experienced as a sudden explosion witnessed through house windows. The viewpoint is of a privileged apprehensive outsider. Once the household collapses, there will be no distancing oneself from revolution's consequences.

From Pasternak's perspective, the Revolution arises from national suffering and national disgrace (Russia's defeat in World War I). Secretly planning the overturn from outside Russia, the Bolsheviks seize the moment. Only in hindsight is Yurii able to perceive that Marxist socialism may be the Bolsheviks' public creed but seizure of power is their end. The essence of the revolution is to be found, not in the *Communist Manifesto*, but in prolonged civil war. Revolution is swift and unexpected, brutal and promising. Although the Bolsheviks have anticipated the future, the populace as a whole have continued to live their daily lives, setting politics aside until revolt turns into revolution. The anticipatory footsteps portending cataclysm, so important to Dickens, have no place in Pasternak's view of revolution. The name of Vladimir Lenin is not mentioned by any of Pasternak's characters nor by the narrator, until 1919, in the fifteenth of the novel's seventeen chapters.

Revolution to young Yurii Zhivago is a matter of metaphysics not rifles. He has been deeply influenced by his uncle Nikolai's apolitical but revolutionary ideas. To Nikolai, "the idea of free personality and the idea of life as sacrifice" are "the two basic ideals of modern man" that have their root in the Gospels.[37] When Yurii graduates from the University in 1911, he plans to become a doctor because medicine is of immediate service to others as well as "socially useful in his practical life" (64–65). Yet Yurii is also, given his "still helter-skelter" mind, intensely drawn to the freedom and creativity of writing poetry (64). Although Yurii's early years therefore resemble Pasternak's, Yurii's literary origin as a protagonist lies immediately in Tolstoy, ultimately in Scott. Both doctor and poet, Yurii retains the sensitivity of the observing waverer figure. Both his vocation and his avocation lessen his need to make an immediate decision between the old order and the new. True identity and the resurrection of the soul, he believes, can be found only by discovering "you in others," "your life in others," as Yurii tells Tonia's dying mother (68). Sensitivity to one's immediate world, love of women and children, love of nature, and love of Russia are for him transcendent values that render faith in political systems a secondary concern to which he seems almost indifferent. When revolution breaks out, he has already embraced values more firmly grounded than either Waverley or Pierre.

Nonetheless, Yurii is, like Pasternak, excited by the hope that the revolution promises for Russia, beaten down by three years of war and a directionless, tyrannical monarchy. The end of the Romanovs, Yurii exclaims, means "Freedom! . . . freedom dropped out of the sky, freedom beyond our expectations," a release recalling "the days of the apostles," when ordinary men prophesy and "speak with tongues."[38] Perhaps because of the momentary prominence of Kerensky, Yurii conceives of "freedom" and "socialism" as two separate streams flowing into the rising sea of revolution, "the sea of life, the sea of spontaneity" (146, 147). Exactly how "Freedom" and "Socialism" could become compatible Yurii does not pause to consider. He is, of course, unaware that, at that very moment, Lenin was writing *The State and Revolution*, a book which insists that a true understanding of Marxism demands the "smashing" of state institutions as well as strict "accounting" and "control" to further the dictatorship of the proletariat.[39] Yurii does, however, know the personal reason for his political hope: he recognizes that his attraction for revolution is based, not upon present realities, but upon his image of the 1905 revolutionaries as idealistic, middle-class students, genteel constitutional republicans, and "followers of Blok" (160)—that is, moderates who recall the Girondists.

Conditions of daily life in post-revolutionary Russia lead Yurii to turn against not only the Bolsheviks, but revolution itself. Amid a typhus epidemic, control over his Moscow hospital is suddenly assumed by self-interested party bureaucrats. The streets of "silent, dark, hungry Moscow" are plagued with thuggery (175). Vodka, rather than the inflated Bolshevik "credit slips" (so like the French Assignats), becomes the preferred medium of exchange. Abandoned houses are pulled down for fuel to survive the winter. The Gromekos are ordered to live in three rooms of their house, while the other rooms are put to nondescript government misuse. The Gromeko family flees Moscow only when they experience revolution as starvation.

The Gromeko's train trip to the Urals immerses them in much the same dysfunctional brutalities that, for previous historical novelists, had ravaged the neutral ground. Fifty miles on either side of the train track, anarchy reigns; the peasant populace shifts sides depending on whether the Reds or the Whites have the temporary upper hand. The travelers believe their journey will have a hopeful destination, but cattle-car conditions prevail for all. The new circumstances of Soviet life encourage rapacity and indifference, not the compassion Yurii seeks.

Along with hope for freedom through Marxist revolution, Yurii has internalized uncle Nikolai's premise that "only individuals seek the truth" (9). The realities of Bolshevik Russia lead him to conclude "those who inspired the revolution aren't at home in anything except change and turmoil": "for them transitional periods, worlds in the making, are an end in themselves"

(297). Truth and Progress soon disappear into mere change. Marxism, Yurii concludes, pretends to be a science, but its leaders are so self-centered, so "removed from the facts," that they will "do their utmost to ignore the truth" (259). "Politics doesn't appeal to me," Yurii adds, "I don't like people who don't care about the truth" (259).

Among historical novelists, no writer has been as resentful of the falsifying power of revolutionary words as Pasternak. Dickens had described the French Philosophes decorating Monseigneur's salon as "unbelieving Philosophers who were remodeling the world with words" but Pasternak is relentless by comparison.[40] While delivering a pompous recriminatory speech to World War I deserters, Commissar Gintz is deservedly humiliated by falling into a rain-barrow; he is then shot dead by the incensed troops he was trying to recall to the battlefield. Reporter-observers of the War who concoct new theories of the "soul of the Russian people" are said to be engaging in "linguistic graphomania, verbal incontinence" (121). At a political meeting, Yurii is revolted by the "meaningless dullness of human eloquence," "all those sublime phrases," "a torrent of words, superfluous, utterly false, murky, profoundly alien to life itself" (139).

By 1919, newly arrived in Yuriatin, Yurii has consciously rejected the "uncompromising language and single-mindedness" that had once "filled him with enthusiasm" (381). For two years he has been hearing "unchanging, shrill, crazy exclamations and demands, which became progressively more impractical, meaningless and unfulfillable as time went by" (381). As an example, Yurii quotes an official Soviet speech that includes language reminiscent of the Jacobins: "Only terror applied in all its harshness, down to the shooting of speculators on the spot, can deliver us from famine" (381). Through such language, memory of the 1793 Terror becomes, two centuries later, a self-fulfilling prophecy.

The question remains: why does Pasternak so emphasize the destructive power of the word in revolutionary discourse? He is, of course, insisting upon an historical truth: the millions of wasted or murderous revolutionary words expended during two centuries. But Pasternak also belies that revolutionary language, initiated by individuals, soon emerges from groups as resolutions, then as slogans. If, as Nikolai and Yurii both believe, only individuals pursue the truth, then political resolutions are group-speak of the kind familiar to readers of George Orwell's "Politics and the English Language." Soviet Marxism may have been especially prone to such hegemonic language ("capitalists vs. workers," "class struggle," "dictatorship of the proletariat," "withering away of the state" etc.), but Yurii does not restrict his accusations to the legacy of 1917. At issue here is the entire current postwar world in which totalitarianism was evidently thriving on the impoverishing of language.

Yurii is an especially credible spokesman for such Orwellian apprehensions because he is a poet, dedicated to individual expression in which symbolic words have an identifiable referent. In the language of politics, he observes, words no longer correspond to things. Accordingly, the "Poems of Yurii Zhivago," which form the novel's last chapter, avoid politics altogether. *Doctor Zhivago* may be "about" revolutionary Russia, but among great historical novelists, Pasternak alone would like to dismiss the language of politics altogether. Viewed in this way, Pasternak's novel seems to bring one aspect of Scott's legacy to a close.

The fanaticism of Flora MacIvor, Balfour, Claverhouse, Pugachev, Madame Defarge, Napoleon, and Evariste Gamelin originates in individual character and has gradually grown through historical circumstance. In keeping with the fairy-tale quality of Pasternak's novel, Pasha Antipov is suddenly transformed from ingénue to fanatic. Although Pasha is born the son of a working-class labor protestor, his defining qualities as a young man are earnestness to do right, love of Greek and Roman literature, and adoration of Lara Guishar, whom he subsequently marries. A scant three years later, Pasha is said to have become a dedicated Russian soldier—"intelligent, very brave, taciturn and sarcastic"—seemingly possessed, Galiulin says, by "something beyond, an idea that had taken firm hold of him" (114). Antipov's controlling "idea" is however left undefined.

Antipov later erupts into the narrative as Strelnikov "the shooter" (aka, the "executioner"), an implacable military agent of the Bolsheviks assigned to stop desertion and stamp out White insurrection from his special armored express train. Zhivago, momentarily detained by Strelnikov, surmises that Strelnikov must have refashioned himself into "the self he resolved to be" (248). "This man was entirely a manifestation of the will" (248). Decisive, energetic, a whirlwind of competence, Strelnikov has become, Yurii wrongly believes, a dedicated Marxist revolutionary: "his revolutionary fervor, equally unbridled, was remarkable for its genuineness. His fanaticism was not an imitation but was his own, a natural consequence of all his previous life" (250). From Yurii's baffled perspective, Strelnikov appears to have suddenly materialized as his communist opposite; moreover, they love the same woman. But in fact Yurii Zhivago cannot possibly know what has caused the transformation of Strelnikov. Because Strelnikov is terrifying in his furthering of the revolution, Yurii assumes that the unspecified "idea" driving Strelnikov must be his newfound commitment to Bolshevism.

Pasternak treats the cause of Strelikov's fanaticism with remarkable regard for its complexity. Knowing his life is about to end, Strelnikov travels to Varykino in search of Lara and Zhivago. He explains to Zhivago, at length, why he believes that "the birth of socialist thought" in Marxism "gave unity to the nineteenth century" (460):

Revolutions, young men dying on the barricades, writers racking their brains in
an effort to curb the brute insolence of money, to save the human dignity of the
poor. Marxism arose, it uncovered the root of the evil and it offered the remedy.
It became the great force of the century. (460)

Images of the July Monarchy and 1848, of the Second Empire and 1870, of
Karl Marx and the International, here merge into a blur of historical memory
pointing toward 1917. Strelnikov claims that Yurii could never have seriously
entertained the Marxist faith because Zhivago had grown up in the privileged
world of the wealthy and well-educated, not in the railway slums. Class-
consciousness, Strelnikov implies, will always control political motivation.

In the context of knowingly making a final testament, Strelnikov's self-
accounting seems eminently plausible. Only on this last day of life, however,
has he disclosed his longstanding Marxist commitment. Other equally plausible explanations have already been advanced. Why is it that Strelnikov is
repeatedly described as a nonparty agent of the Red military, always acting
as a force of one? Certainly not because Strelnikov's tactics are less ruthless
than those of the communists. Pasha Antipov had joined the Russian Army
in 1914 because he felt unworthy of Lara and trapped in a failing marriage.
Lara later tells Zhivago that Strelikov has "immense integrity," "a wonderful,
upright shining personality" (396). Moreover, Lara believes that in revolutionary times men feel "the need to surrender to some ultimate purpose," "the
need of committing yourself to something absolute—life or truth or beauty—
of being ruled by it in place of the man-made rules that had been discarded"
(127). She makes no mention of Marxism.

The possibility thus arises that Strelnikov's Marxism is the late-life rationalization of a man who needs to believe in the power of the will to transform
an unworthy self by adherence to a cause. In this interpretation, Strelnikov
is, like Zhivago, a man above adherence to any kind of party, but a man of
inhuman activism rather than humane passivity. Although the novel leaves
Strelnikov's motivation unresolved, Pasternak allows for the possibility
that true fanaticism transcends apparent commitment to any cause or group.
Fanaticism is a temperament only superficially definable by creed. Its essence
is the self-determined will, the reckless power of energy expended to hide
emotional failure.

Hated by the Whites, pursued by the Bolsheviks, his wife Lara lost to
him, Strelnikov commits suicide in Zhivago's near presence. By so doing,
he melodramatically plays out the ultimate end of the fanatic temperament.
To be sure, Balfour of Burleigh, Claverhouse, Pugachev, Madame Defarge,
Evariste Gamelin, and Strelnikov all die. Napoleon Bonaparte and Flora
MacIvor, opposite though they be, end their days in imprisonment. Fanatics
ultimately fail, but none quite so dramatically as Strelnikov. The waverers

and the bumblers, men who are too decent or too uncommitted to act decisively, live on at novel's end to share the mixed happiness of marriage and children. Such is the author's way of salvaging hope for the cultural future, of asserting a progress that is historically difficult to substantiate.

The great exception to the pattern is Yurii Zhivago. Yurii's post-revolutionary life seems at first glance to conform to type. He survives the death of his fanatic counterpart. He resumes his medical practice and his writing; he forms a household, and becomes father to two additional children. However, Yurii's career as doctor soon fails, his writings dwindle to pamphlets for the few, his domestic life turns seedy and impoverished, his family life emotionless. He dies from a heart attack on a squalid, overheated tram—a life's end bordering on both the tragic and the merely pathetic.

Pasternak's break with the convention of the hopeful survivor owes much to the shadowy suppressions of postwar Stalinist Russia. But it is also true that Yurii Zhivago too often lacked the inner will to act decisively and responsibly (failing to respond to Tonia's letter; encouraging Lara to leave with Komarovsky). Unlike Waverley or Pierre, Yurii Zhivago does not change. His final years, set beside the stable futures that Waverley, Piotr, Darnay, Pierre et. al, are said to enjoy, imply that the recovery of the genteel man of goodwill is not as easy, not as sure, as Pasternak's great predecessors had believed.

NOTES

1. Helene Cixous, "Character of 'Character'") *New Literary History* 5 (1974), 387. Quoted in Brian Rosenberg, *Little Dorrit's Shadows: Character and Contradiction in Dickens* (Columbia: University of Missouri Press, 1996), p. 10. Rosenberg's study of Dickens provides concise summaries of theories of characterization to which I am indebted.

2. Terry Eagleton, *Literary Theory: An Introduction* (Minneapolis: University of Minnesota Press, 1983), passim, especially the concluding chapter titled "Political Criticism."

3. Martin Price, *Character and Moral Imagination in the Novel* (New Haven: Yale University Press, 1983), p. 37.

4. Baruch Hochman, *Character in Literature* (Ithaca: Cornell University Press, 1985), p. 7.

5. Jonathan Arac, "Hamlet, Little Dorrit, and the History of Character," *South Atlantic Quarterly*, 87(1988), 314.

6. Sir Walter Scott, *Waverley; or, 'tis Sixty Years Since*, ed. Andrew Hook (New York: Penguin Books, 1985), p. 168.

7. George Dekker succinctly summed up the contrast between the two protagonists' kinds of choices: "Henry Morton is repulsed by both Covenanters and royalists; Waverley is attracted to both Jacobites and Hanoverians" (*James Fenimore Cooper:*

the American Scott [New York: Barnes & Noble, 1967], p. 25. Henry Morton's distrust of religious politics may explain why, among Scott's novels, Karl Marx especially admired *Old Mortality* (See S.S. Prawer, *Karl Marx and World Literature* [Oxford: Oxford University Press, 1978], p. 396.

8. Walter Scott, *Old Mortality*, eds. Jane Stevenson and Peter Davidson (New York: Penguin Books, 1993), p. 155).

9. Ann Rigney argues that recurring attacks upon Scott's presumably demeaning characterization of the Covenanters ignore the hybrid nature of Scott's form by presuming that historical accuracy—even if Scott was inaccurate—is the only valid standard of judgment. As Rigney shows, Scott's historical footnotes to the Magnum edition exist in uneasy relation to his fictional narratives. (Rigney, *Imperfect Histories: The Elusive Past and the Legacy of Romantic Historicism* [Ithaca: Cornell University Press, 2001], pp. 43–56). On Thomas McCrie's attack on Scott's "burlesque" of Covenanter preachers, see Ina Ferris, *The Achievement of Literary Authority*, pp.140 ff. The findings of Rigney and Ferris suggest that, for assessing an historical novel, verisimilitude is a more illuminating standard than historical verification.

10. Scott, *Old Mortality*, p. 144. Bruce Lenman shows that the legendizing of the Jacobite cause over the entire preceding century took shape during the years following the conclusive disaster of the battle of Culloden. Claverhouse's death during his victory at Killiecrankie in 1689 became a central link in a claimed legacy of tragic, noble loss: "The death of Claverhouse was remembered, if only to help people to forget the shameful final rout of the Jacobite army. It reinforced an ideology of royalism and sacrifice assiduously built up around the memory of the Great Marquis of Montrose" (Lenman, *The Jacobite Risings in Britain*, p. 284). In 1689 Claverhouse had been the first to raise the Stuart standard in preparation for battle. The wars of Montrose became the claimed point of origin of "Jacobite" rebellion.

11. Jane Millgate observes that Morton's "freedom of action is severely restricted; he cannot change the historical circumstances, his own family heritage, or the attitudes of those with whom he must contend" (*Walter Scott, the Making of the Novelist*, 119). David Brown ascribes Morton's ineffectuality to the particular brutality of the Killing Time: "Henry Morton's moderate Presbyterianism in religion, his liberalism in politics, and his general abhorrence of fanaticism are portrayed sympathetically by Scott, but at the same time are shown to be quite incapable of resolving the conflicts of the period" (David Brown, *Walter Scott and the Historical Imagination*, 182). Perhaps the underlying cause of the moderate man's ineffectuality lies in Scott's view of the extremity of revolution itself.

12. *A History of Pugachev* was Pushkin's intended title. At the insistence of Tsar Nicholas I, the published title was altered to *A History of the Pugachev Rebellion*. See *Alexander Pushkin: Complete Prose Fiction*, translated and edited by Paul Debreczeny (Stanford: Stanford University Press, 1983) p. 532.

13. Pushkin, *A History of Pugachev*, tr. Debreczeny, pp. 373, 396, 413–414, 425; John T. Alexander, *Emperor of the Cossacks; Pugachev and the Frontier Jacquerie of 1773–1775* (Lawrence, KS: Coronado Press, 1973), pp. 162, 164–166.

14. Paul Debreczeny concluded, "The research Pushkin had done for *A History of Pugachev* is behind every line of *The Captain's Daughter*" (Debreczeny, *The Other*

Pushkin: A Study of Alexander Pushkin's Prose Fiction [Stanford: Stanford University Press, 1983], p. 255.

15. Alexander Pushkin, *The Captain's Daughter and Other Stories*, translated by Natalie Duddington (New York: Random House, 1936), p. 55.

16. Pushkin, unpublished note written in 1822, *The Critical Prose of Alexander Pushkin*, translated and edited by Carl R. Proffer (Bloomington: Indiana University Press, 1969), p. 19.

17. Pushkin, quoted in Mark Altschuller, "The Rise and Fall of Walter Scott's Popularity in Russia" in Murray Pittock, ed., *The Reception of Sir Walter Scott in Europe* (London: Continuum, 2006), p. 216, 217. Pushkin's grudging admiration for Scott resembles Carlyle's twenty years later.

18. See Svetlana Evdokimova, *Pushkin's Historical Imagination* (New Haven: Yale University Press, 1999), pp. 74–84. Pushkin's self-consciousness about literary influences emerges in his account of his bachelor existence in St. Petersburg: "I dress carelessly if I am invited out, with all possible diligence if I am lunching at a restaurant, where I either read a new novel or the newspapers; if Walter Scott and Cooper have written nothing and if there is not some criminal trial in the papers, then I order a bottle of champagne on the ice" (Robin Edmonds, *Pushkin; the Man and His Age* [New York: St. Martin's Press, 1994], p. 118). As Pushkin was completing *The Captain's Daughter*, he remarked in letters to his wife Natalya; "I'm reading Walter Scott and the Bible and I keep on thinking of you" (9/20/1834); "I'm reading Walter Scott's novels which I'm in rapture over" (9/25/1835). See *Letters of Alexander Pushkin*, 3rd edition, translated and edited by J. Thomas Shaw (Los Angeles: Charles Schlacks, Jr., 1997), pp. 696, 725.

19. On the figure of the Pretender in the historical novel, including Pugachev, see Richard Maxwell's informative chapter "Pretenders in Sanctuary" in *The Historical Novel in Europe*, pp. 115–170. Some pretenders sought sanctuary, others kingship.

20. Pushkin, *The Captain's Daughter*, p. 65. Michael Katz has kindly informed me that the Russian phrase *uzhasnaya komoediya* is literally translated "horrible comedy." Pushkin's phrase suggests the grotesque, the border region where the horrible and the comedic meet.

21. *Redgauntlet* (1824), an epistolary novel, composed of letters presumably written in the long-ago present of 1765, is the important exception among Scott's Scottish novels.

22. A biographical, rather than literary explanation for the difference in Pushkin's two characterizations of Pugachev hinges upon Pushkin's presumed fear of censorship. Because Tsar Nicholas secured power of censorship over Pushkin's writings after 1826, Pushkin may have feared that any sympathetic rendering of Pugachev in his *History* would have made its publication vulnerable. "The Captain's Daughter," a fiction published anonymously in a literary journal, would presumably be exposed to less risk of censorship. Another kind of explanation lies in literary influence. Scott had ascribed similar moments of mercy, grace, and chivalry both to Fergus MacIvor and to Claverhouse.

23. *The Captain's Daughter*, p. 15. On Piotr's dream, see Michael R. Katz, *Dreams and the Unconscious in Nineteenth Century Russian Fiction* (Hanover and London: University Press of New England, 1984). pp. 51–54.

24. A possible reason for Pushkin's decision to omit the last half of the first draft of chapter 13 is that Piotr is uncharacteristically active in trying to save his family and the family estate, even though the final rescue is performed by Zurin's cavalry.

25. Pushkin's probable borrowing of this scene from Scott's *The Heart of Midlothian* only increases the irony. Scott's Jeanie Deans journeys to London to plead to Queen Caroline for the life of her sister Effie, who has been falsely convicted of child murder. Marya and Jeanie are both to be admired for selfless endurance, but there is a significant difference in the honor of their appeals. Marya rescues her helpless fiancé from military exile; hers is a journey of love without moral complication. Jeanie rescues Effie from the wrongful sentence of murdering her bastard child, while knowing that she has herself endangered Effie's life by refusing to lie under oath. The moral stakes for Jeanie Deans's sense of self-worth are immeasurably higher.

26. Charles Dickens, *A Tale of Two Cities*, edited with an introduction by Richard Maxwell (New York: Penguin Books, 2000), p. 65, 72.

27. Dickens use of select passages and set-pieces of Carlyle's *History* to establish a British perspective on the French Revolution has become one of the most thoroughly rehearsed of literary source studies. I shall not attempt to add to it. See, for starters, Michael Goldberg, *Carlyle and Dickens* (Athens: University of Georgia Press, 1972), pp. 100–128 and many of the essays in *Dickens Studies Annual* 12 (1983).

28. Avrom Fleishman's chapter titled "Dickens: Visions of Revolution" argues convincingly that "Dickens, in common with most of his contemporaries, sees political engagement as an antithesis to, not an expression of, personal fulfillment" (*The English Historical Novel* [Baltimore: Johns Hopkins Press, 1971], p. 124). For variants of this argument, see John P. McWilliams Jr. "Progress without Politics: *A Tale of Two Cities*," *Clio* 7 (1977). 19–31 and Barton Friedman, "Antihistory: Dickens's *A Tale of Two Cities*" in *Fabricating History: English Writers on the French Revolution* (Princeton: Princeton University Press, 1988), 145–171. Dickens's characterization of Darnay may be read as a sign of the author's own political confusion. In letters written before *A Tale of Two Cities* was published, Dickens had declared himself a "Liberal" in 1842, a "Reformer" in 1855, and a "Radical" in 1857 even though he remained, like most middle-class Whigs, a constitutional monarchist. Dickens publicly supported the Six Points of the People's Charter, yet denounced the methods of Physical Force Chartists.

29. Both in Paris and in London, Tellson's Bank plays a crucial role in the survival and prosperity of the characters Dickens persuades us to admire. The power of Tellson's Bank is a sign of new times. Niall Ferguson's *The Ascent of Money* substantiates the immense economic and political power that the Rothschilds suddenly acquired in post-Napoleonic Europe and Victorian England through international banking and the underwriting of securities. See Ferguson, *The Ascent of Money: A Financial History of the World* (New York and London: Penguin Books, 2008), pp. 83–97, 293–294. Tellson's Bank is an essential link binding together the Paris and London of Dickens's novel.

30. The extremity of Madame Defarge's fanaticism emerges by comparison with her historical contemporaries. See Dominique Godineau, *The Women of Paris and their French Revolution*, translated by Katherine Streip (Berkeley: University of California Press, 1988).

31. Leo Tolstoy, *War and Peace*, the Maude translation, ed. George Gibian (London and New York: W.W. Norton & Co., 1996), pp. 1051–1052. Napoleon III was Emperor of France while Tolstoy was writing *War and Peace*. In the mid-1860s Napoleon III had not yet endured the total defeat of the Franco-Prussian War, a disgrace that Zola renders vividly in *La Debacle*. Tolstoy's passage can also be read as a criticism of Hegel's "world-historical individuals."

32. See Alan Schom, *Napoleon Bonaparte* (New York: HarperCollins, 1998), p. 202, 308, 390, 527, 655–666, and especially the epilogue; Paul Johnson, *Napoleon: A Life* (London and New York: Penguin Books, 2002), pp. 7, 49–72, 186.

33. The historicity of Tolstoy's Napoleon begs the larger question of genre. Tolstoy was not willing to confine *War and Peace* within the already familiar category of "Historical Novel." He referred to it consecutively as "this work," "my work," "not a tale," "not a novel," "still less an historical chronicle" and then wrote in summation: "*War and Peace* is what the author wished and was able to express in the form in which it is expressed" (Tolstoy's letters and drafted introductions. Maude edition, pp. 1083–1096). The last of these statements suggests that war and peace, taken together, *are* human life. In 1880 Turgenev was to call *War and Peace* "a historical novel," but almost immediately to observe, most perceptively, "The manner in which Count Tolstoy works out his theme is as new as it is original. This is not the method of Walter Scott, and it goes without saying, it is not that of Alexandre Dumas either" (Maude edition, p. 1108). *War and Peace* instinctively reminds Turgenev of Scott's precedence in writing the "historical novel," even as Turgenev recognizes important differences between them.

34. Emerson had recently reclothed Napoleon as a progressive middle-class democrat: "I call Napoleon the agent or attorney of the middle class of modern society; of the throng who fill the markets, shops, counting-houses, manufactories, ships, of the modern world, aiming to be rich. He was the agitator, the destroyer of prescription, the internal improver, the liberal, the radical, the inventor of means, the opener of doors and markets, the subverter of monopoly and abuse. Of course the rich and aristocratic did not like him" ("Napoleon, Man of the World," *Representative Men* [1850], in *The Complete Works of Ralph Waldo Emerson*, ed. Edward Emerson [Boston: Houghton, Mifflin and Co., IV, 252]).

35. Anatole France, *The Gods Will Have Blood*, translated with an introduction by Frederick Davies (New York and London: Penguin Books, 2004), p. 31.

36. *Les Dieux Ont Soif*, p. 178. Disparaging the sensationalism of the novel, Harry Shaw argued that Anatole France "depicts public life and historical process only to show their unimportance" (*The Forms of Historical Fiction*, p. 103). Whether a "strangely mixed flood of horror and ecstatic lust" had historically been an important part of the French revolutionary process will surely never be reliably known.

37. Boris Pasternak, *Doctor Zhivago*, translated by Max Hayward, Manya Harari, and Bernard Guerney, introduction by John Bayley (New York: Pantheon Books, 1991), p. 10. Nikolai's ideas resemble those of the aging Tolstoy.

38. *Doctor Zhivago*, p. 146. In a letter of 1922, Pasternak had written "the stage of revolution closest to the heart and to poetry is its morning, its explosion" (quoted in Ronald Hingley, *Pasternak: A Biography* [New York: Alfred A. Knopf, 1983], p. 61).

39. V.I. Lenin, *The State and Revolution*, Introduction and translation by Robert Service, first published 1917 (New York: Penguin Classics, 1991), pp. 33–34, 44, 90–92. In the 1950s Pasternak strove to maintain balance when writing about Lenin: "With the fervour of genius and unhesitatingly, he took upon himself responsibility for bloodshed and breakage such as the world had never seen. He did not fear to cry out to the people and summon them to realize their most cherished hopes" (Christopher Barnes, *Boris Pasternak: A Literary Biography* [Cambridge: Cambridge University Press, 1989] I, 326). Pasternak's qualified praise of Lenin may contain an implied criticism of Joseph Stalin.

40. Dickens, *A Tale of Two Cities*, p. 110. The reading list Yurii and Tonia undertake while in seclusion at Varykino indicates important literary influences on *Doctor Zhivago*: "We read and reread *War and Peace*, *Evgenii Onegin*, and Pushkin's other poems, and Russian translations of Stendhal's *The Red and the Black*, Dickens's *Tale of Two Cities*, and Kleist's short stories" (280). There is no work of political philosophy on Yurii's list: no Plato, no Aristotle, no Machiavelli, no Locke, no Montesquieu, no Rousseau, no Proudhon, no Marx, and no Lenin.

Chapter 5

Revolution and Battle Honor

"The transformation of the art of war resulted from the transformation of politics."

—Carl Von Clausewitz, *On War* (1833)

"Gentlemen, my honor lies in no-one's hand but my own, and it is not something that others can lavish on me; my own honor, which I carry in my heart, suffices me entirely, and no-one is judge of it and able to decide whether I have it. My honor before God and men is my property."

—-Otto von Bismarck, 1881

Most of the historical novels that have popularly defined the genre—from *Waverley* and *Ivanhoe* through *The Last of the Mohicans, War and Peace* and Hugo's *1793,* to *Gone With the Wind, Doctor Zhivago,* Vidal's *Lincoln,* and Marquez's *The General's Labyrinth,* have centered upon war, usually upon a revolutionary war, and often upon questions of honor in revolutionary warfare. No influential recent thinker could be less concerned with individual honor on the battlefield than Michel Foucault, yet Foucault's "Society Must Be Defended" (1975–1976) provides a persuasive argument as to why war has been the central lens of historical memory, especially in its written forms. War, Foucault declared, has remained the most compelling means of analyzing power relations in history. As the practice of warfare has changed from interpersonal to international combat, (and more recently to terrorism) wars have defined the conditions out of which new institutions of governmental power grow. Accordingly, historical discourse has sought to trace the ways in which the brutalities of war, affected by chance happenings, have turned into rebellions and revolutions, hopefully to emerge into some principle of governing "rationality." In order to lend coherence to historical time, "the dark, elliptical god of battles must illuminate the long days of order, labor and peace." In words that ironically recall Coleridge's tribute to Scott's balancing of the Old Order against the New, Foucault writes that history has had to become "a discourse that will be able to carry both the nostalgia of decaying aristocracies and the ardor of popular revenges." "The dried blood of the codes of war" had to be shaped into "the traditional mythical forms (the lost age of great ancestors, the imminence of new times and millennial revenge, the coming of a new kingdom that will wipe out the ancient defeats)." The "progress" in which the nineteenth century wanted to believe, thoroughly discredited by Foucault, remains only an illusion that the discourse of history has left forever waiting in the wings. That discourse, however, is sure to continue; society, after all, must be defended.[1]

If war reveals the workings of power and shapes the institutions of government, what then can be the function, within the historical novel, of the lingering concern for the honor of the individual (usually male) who finds himself caught up in such impersonal forces? Before responding, we must acknowledge the validity of the scholarly consensus that, by the end of World War I, and perhaps earlier, the very concept of honor had become so discredited as to have become obsolete, no longer applicable to the anonymous mass slaughters of twentieth-century warfare.[2] Why honor should linger as a concern for historical novelists must therefore be addressed on both literary and historical grounds. If the Waverley Novels form the prototype for the historical novel, then we must recognize the importance of Paul Henderson Stewart's observation, "In the seventeenth century honor was probably more important in England than ever before or after."[3] For Walter Scott personally, Alexander Welsh has argued, "this sense of honor [served] not merely as a measure of fame or status but as a kind of moral imperative."[4] But why was honor to remain a vital concept for Cooper, Tolstoy, Hugo, Zola, Melville, and even Lampedusa, during times when more modern conditions of warfare prevailed and the expectation that an aristocrat should demonstrate battlefield valor had markedly lessened? This chapter will consider not only the changed nature of warfare, but also the need for the historical novelist to balance the ever-increasing deadliness of the battlefield against some measure of redemptive honor to be achieved by those young men who represent a better future.

Sir John Falstaff's famous catechism reduces "honour" to a mere "word" consisting of "air," but for at least the next two centuries men of rank, whether of military or noble title, were brought up to believe and behave differently.[5] Seventeenth- and eighteenth-century warfare pursued limited objectives by conventional tactics, in part so that soldiers, especially officers, could survive with honor. Although capture of strategically located medieval fortresses remained important, possession of Vauban's new "bastion forts" (also called "star forts") came to be more important. The object of warfare was not to destroy the enemy's army but to secure strategic advantages for purposes of negotiation. As the reader of *Waverley* will recall, local military units were raised by local nobility at the king's command and hopefully at the king's expense. Officers were drawn from the aristocracy and professional classes while enlisted men were drawn from the peasantry, free-holding farmers and tradesmen. An officer's claim to honorable authority rested upon his continuing care for the soldiers he had enlisted. An officer knew he was likely to encounter the soldiers of his regiment throughout later life; his soldiers customarily worked farms or practiced trades on or near his lands.[6]

Whatever the reality of the battlefield may have been, warfare during the Enlightenment was supposed to be conducted in reasoned, even geometric ways for limited territorial objectives. For purposes of military advance, straight lines of uniformed infantry, flintlock musket in hand, preceded by artillery bombardment, and flanked by cavalry units, were to move forward firing in alternative rows until they met the enemy in hand-to-hand fighting. For purposes of defense, infantry in the open field were to form into a massed square, hopefully with artillery behind them and a star fortress in the vicinity. Wars were to be fought in summer, followed by retreat to winter quarters. Officers were expected to lead their men into battle; flag bearers carried both a monarchical and a provincial or a clan flag.[7] In these ways, limited war, visible in its clarity and conducted by reason, could conserve resources for future benefit or the next war.

Unwritten war conventions held certain kinds of conduct to be honorable and others dishonorable.[8] Greek city states were presumed to have discovered the morality of warfare: wars should be declared, truces held inviolate, civilians exempted from warfare, enemy surrender respected, prisoners ransomed, and treaties upheld. St. Augustine had argued that, despite Christ's insistence on loving your enemy and turning the other cheek, Christians should engage in a war if it is determined to be "just" by human standards. God's standard of a just war remained forever unknowable to man. The evil of war, Augustine contended, lies not in killing itself, but in the sinful attitudes ("love of violence, revengeful cruelty, fierce and implacable enmity") with which an individual pursues victory.[9]

No recent writing on the morality of war had greater influence on eighteenth-century military theory than Hugo Grotius's *On the Law of War and Peace* (1625). Grotius contends that there are only "three justifiable causes" of engaging in war: "defense, recovery of property and punishment." Christian war should always be defensive: "the law of love, especially as set forth in the gospel, which puts consideration for others on a level with consideration for ourselves, clearly does not permit the injuring of the innocent." Although a war may have just cause, honor should always supersede law in determining what constitutes just cause. "A sense of honour may be said to forbid what the law permits." Honor is, moreover, a Greco-Roman as well as Christian value. Grotius quotes passages from Hesiod, Plato, Plutarch, Josephus, Justinian, Seneca, and St. Paul, all of whom explicitly argue that a man's sense of "honor"—and not merely what the law permits—must impose moral restraint on human enmity.[10]

By the time Emmerich de Vattel wrote *The Law of Nations* (1758), enlightened international standards of battle conduct had advanced still further. Vattel anticipates that wars will henceforth be conducted with frequent truces, passports for safe conduct, prompt exchange of prisoners of equal rank, and return of disarmed prisoners who had surrendered.[11] Behind this conception of war, Vattel claims, lies the standard of aristocratic honor, upheld by officers, that in itself derives from the chivalry claimed by a medieval knight. Accordingly, what we now call "guerilla warfare" was in 1760 thought to be unworthy of a civilized man or a civilized nation. An outnumbered enemy was not to be massacred; a sniper who killed an unarmed man was committing murder.

Eighteenth-century military theory thus assumed territorial integrity and measurable limits. Borders between separate states and separate cultures, commensurate with linguistic borders, were assumed to be discernible. After territories were won or lost, they could be acquired or forfeited by mutual agreement. Sensible treaties, even those reached under duress, would promote international and intranational peace. If wars were not to release animal barbarity, reason must govern their conduct and outcome. But why, the reader might now ask, has a summary of eighteenth-century war practices been needed here? Because the very assumption of the enlightened progress of civilization was at stake. The neutral grounds recreated by Scott, Cooper, and their followers were to describe warfare as the near opposite of everything that war had, until very recently, been expected to be.

SURVIVAL WITH HONOR: SCOTT AND COOPER

As Scott and Cooper look back across the Revolutionary and Napoleonic eras, the underlying purpose of military conflict, even in the seventeenth and eighteenth centuries, seems not to have been limited territorial gain; it was rather to provoke a revolution or a counterrevolution that was likely to develop into the nationalistic total warfare of recent memory. When Walter Scott describes the Jacobite army marching south from the Scottish lowlands toward London, led by regimental units of semi-independent lairds, the army's purpose is not to take Stirling, Carlisle, or Derby, but to overthrow the Hanoverian government. In *The Last of the Mohicans*, the French and the

Hurons seek to drive encroaching white English settlers from western New England and western New York, if not from the North American continent. Because the stakes quickly rise to treason and even genocide, the likelihood of dishonorable conduct in war also rises. As Scott and Cooper look back upon the mid-eighteenth century, they perceive that revolutionary military situations were already subverting expectations of honorable, aristocratic practice.

Edward Waverley is appointed captain in Colonel Gardiner's regiment of dragoons with no military experience and no military training whatsoever. An accomplished horseman who delights in reading Froissart's accounts of knightly tourneys, Waverley is only vaguely aware, even in mid-1745, of the impending Jacobite rebellion. Sent into the military to see the world, Waverley is commissioned a captain in the English army because he is the nephew of Sir Everard Waverley, an English Jacobite Baronet, as well as the son of Richard Waverley, a rising politician in Hanoverian court circles. Outfitted with "gold-laced hat, jack-boots and broadsword," Waverley gathers "twenty young fellows" from his uncle's estate and reports with them to Dundee; he hopes to embark from the Scottish coast for the Low Countries and somewhere beyond.[12] Imagining himself a cavalryman, he does not believe he needs to master infantry field training, and apparently does not carry a musket. Whether he is more naïve than other newly commissioned English officers of privileged backgrounds, Scott does not say. A gentleman tourist as well as a gentleman officer, Waverley anticipates that any warfare he encounters will be conducted by traditional values.

Although circumstances beyond Waverley's control contribute to his dereliction of duty, so does his obliviousness to military reality. Courteous to his twenty recruits, he makes little effort to train them; his superior social class as well as his rank impedes familiarity. Shortly after arriving in Dundee, he requests to visit Lowland relatives and to see the Highlands as if he were leaving on tour. Entranced by the MacIvors and by Highland culture, Waverley never considers that Colonel Gardiner might not have intended to grant him a continuing furlough. He gives no thought to the well-being of his recruits back in Dundee, thereby exposing them to be suborned by Donald Bean Lane. When Waverley is finally cashiered for being absent without leave, his shame centers on his disgrace in the newspapers, not on the substance of what he has failed to do. He feels the loss of what Paul Henderson Stewart has defined as "outer honor" (reputation) rather than "inner honor" (honorableness).[13] From Scott's perspective, a fully admirable man of rank must possess both kinds of honor.

Waverley's achieving of honor is determined during one decisive day at the Battle of Preston Pans. Like Aeneas experiencing the sacking of Troy, the scales suddenly fall from Waverley's eyes. He sees the Jacobite army as it truly is, divided by jealous clans, virtually without artillery or cavalry, composed of well-clad chieftains leading poorly armed peasants, held together by bravery, bravado, and unwilling conscription. Waverley then witnesses the gruesome death of his loyal Sergeant Humphrey Houghton, who has been shot by the English and imprisoned by the Jacobites, after being cashiered for confusedly trying to follow his captain in changing his allegiance. Houghton's repeated cry, "Ah, squire, why did you leave us?" continues to ring "like a knell" in Waverley's ears (331). When Waverley draws near the British army, he sees his former regiment in their familiar uniforms, speaking comprehensible English, led by the publicly honored Colonel Gardiner. As if he were awakening from "a dream, strange, horrible and unnatural," Waverley mutters "am I then a traitor to my country, a renegade to my standard and a foe . . . to my native England?" (333–334). To complete his day of horror, he is forced to witness the slaughter of Colonel Gardiner and the mutilation of Gardiner's body by Highlanders "furious and eager for spoil" (340–341). For weeks thereafter Waverley will be haunted by the seemingly accusatory gaze Gardiner fixes upon Waverley as he dies.

Whether or not Gardiner's accusatory glance is Waverley's psychological projection, the guilt Waverley feels over Gardiner's death is intense. He struggles to save Colonel Gardiner ("this good and brave man") but reaches Gardiner's side a moment too late (340). Similarly, he struggles to save Captain Talbot, whom he knows only as "an English officer, apparently of high rank," from a similarly brutal death at the hands of Fergus MacIvor's clansmen (339). Even though Waverley is a Brevet Major in Charles Edward Stuart's army, he neither fires a gun nor draws his sword against any Englishmen at the Battle of Preston Pans. Instead he acts to save the lives of *English officers* who are purportedly his enemies.

Scott's description of Waverley's rescue of Colonel Talbot is a narrative about the achieving of honor, even though the word "honor" is never used:

Struck with [the English officer's] tall, martial figure, and eager to save him from inevitable destruction, Waverley outstripped for an instant even the speediest of the warriors, and, reaching the spot first, called to him [Talbot] to surrender. The officer replied by a thrust with his sword, which Waverley received in his target, and in turning it aside the Englishman's weapon broke. At the same time the battle-axe of Dugald Mahony was in the act of descending upon the officer's head. Waverley intercepted and prevented the blow, and the officer, perceiving further resistance unavailing, and struck with Edward's generous anxiety for his safety, resigned the fragment of his sword, and was committed by Waverley to Dugald, with strict charge to use him well, and not to pillage his person, promising him, at the same time, full indemnification for the spoil. (340)

Waverley chooses to intervene, but his choice is based upon the imposing stature of the unknown officer he seeks to save. Deflecting the blows of Talbot's sword and of Mahony's battle-axe are entirely defensive actions, designed to save life. Struck by Waverley's restrained, honorable conduct, Talbot admires the "generous" nature of Waverley's bravery. The momentous incident concludes with Waverley's firm insistence upon the rights of a surrendered prisoner, and upon Dugald Mahoney's right to an indemnification that Waverley will willingly pay.

Waverley has acted in accord with highest battle standards of an eighteenth-century aristocratic officer. He has prevented mutilation, taken a prisoner, secured fair treatment, and killed no one. Nobility, honor, perhaps even chivalry, coalesce in ways that both Grotius and Vattel would have approved. Whether Waverley's commitment to saving the lives of Hanoverian officers reduces the chances of Jacobite victory is not to Scott the essential question. Acting honorably toward one's enemy is a higher value than victory. Simultaneously, however, boundaries of social class so important to Scott are being maintained. If Talbot had been an ordinary infantryman, Waverley would not have rushed to save him. John Lynn claims that, in the eighteenth century, officers were expected to have greater personal respect for officers in the opposing army than for the common soldiers they themselves led.[14]

Scott ascribes life-changing significance to Waverley's conduct at Preston Pans, granting his honorable actions a significance Tolstoy or Zola would surely have questioned. Waverley's rescue of Colonel Talbot will prove to be Waverley's salvation. Further shaming, however, must precede recovery. Appealing to patriotism, family heritage, cultural loyalty, constitutional right, and moral consistency, Talbot effectively challenges Waverley's allegiance to the Jacobites. The ironic consequence is that Waverley stands before Talbot "mortified, abashed and distressed in presence of the prisoner, who owed to him his life not many hours before" (352).

After the skirmish at Clifton, a now dispirited Waverley, cut off from the Jacobite army he no longer admires, but hiding from being arrested as a traitor by the Hanoverian army, has nowhere to turn except to flee to Colonel Talbot's house in London. Talbot secures for Waverley a reliable alias, a needed passport, a carriage with horse, and 15,000 pounds from his dead father's estate. In a private interview with the Duke of Cumberland, General of the Hanoverian army, Talbot obtains for Waverley a full pardon. Talbot arranges to repurchase the Bradwardines' estate at Tully-Veolan, recently confiscated and sacked by the Hanoverians. Talbot restores the estate and then re-deeds it to Waverley and Rose Bradwardine, enabling them to marry and settle into the life of the country gentry.

No deus ex machina could possibly perform more. To say that Talbot devotes himself to Waverley's well-being out of gratitude for saving his life rather misses the point. To the extent that Waverley is a *bildungsroman*, Talbot serves as the mentor for Waverley's education. He embodies Walter Scott's will to reward Waverley for the courage and honor Waverley has demonstrated on the battlefield. One fine moment at Preston Pans thus shapes Waverley's future. For Scott's later protagonists, the reward for battlefield honor was not to prove so fully redemptive, perhaps because Scott came to question whether Waverley's way of achieving maturity was historically representative. The achieving of "inner" and "outer" honor was not, however, a value Walter Scott was willing to slight.

Cooper was never less the "American Scott" than when he wrote *The Last of the Mohicans* (1826). The Waverley figure in Cooper's novel is Major Duncan Heyward of the 60th Royal Americans, born in the American South, but the son of an English father and Scottish mother descended from a noble family registered in the Order of the Thistle. Like many protagonists of historical novels, Hayward is educated, genteel, and well-meaning, with no parents to guide him. Heyward identifies himself as a professional soldier, "already sold to my king" who has "no father to expect me, and but few friends."[15] Unlike Waverley or Henry Morton, Heyward has been drawn to the military for motives of outer honor alone, the "unsatiable longings of youth after distinction" (116). Although he survives his ordeal in the American wilderness, marries Alice Munro, and retires to an apparently prosperous life in the American settlements, he never attains the "distinction" in battle for which he once longed.

The causes of Heyward's mediocrity are both circumstantial and innate. The forests surrounding Lake George during the French and Indian War (1756–1763) are a neutral ground in extremis. Major Heyward is trained for eighteenth-century battle conditions that have no place in a world where British troops, French troops, unknown friendly Indians, unknown hostile Indians, colonial settlers, and semiofficial continental "rangers" can suddenly appear in any combination to kill you. Roads are few and exposed; forests are dense and treacherous. Stealth, sniping, surprise attack, and arson are acknowledged realities practiced by those who condemn them. Pitched battles on a visible plain (Culloden Moor) never occur. The English and French armies pride themselves on being civilized, but both armies offer bounties for the scalps of their enemies. Shoot first and save regrets for later is the path to survival. No wonder Cooper's novel was a sensation among European readers who wanted to believe that the Old World had retained a civilization far more advanced than the New.

Before Heyward assumes command of the expedition to escort Cora and Alice Munro from Fort Edward to Fort William Henry, Leather-stocking (here named Hawkeye or "the scout") describes Hayward as "a young gentleman of vast riches, . . . over young to hold such rank . . . a soldier in his knowledge, and a gallant gentleman" (46). As is his military duty, Leather-stocking protects Colonel Munro's two "flowers" from death (54). Major Heyward, however, imagines himself, not unlike Ivanhoe, to be on a mission of quasi-medieval honor (54). When assigned to stand night guard dangerously near Fort William Henry, "the young man sunk into a deep sleep, dreaming that he was a knight of ancient chivalry, holding his midnight vigils before the tent of a re-captured princess, whose favour he did not despair of gaining, by such a proof of devotion and watchfulness" (147). On the Indian frontier, the practice of chivalry, so admired by Grotius and Vattel, is a dream likely to get you killed.

Waverley had demonstrated bravery and earned honor at Preston Pans; Major Heyward sheds neither his illusions nor his incompetence in the forest. Heyward is immobilized by imagining treacherous foes behind every tree (53); he sees beavers as enemy troops building temporary shelter (249). Heyward never acquires the needed forest skills; his impulse to speechify disturbs the silence, endangering his entire party. First Uncas, then Leather-stocking, then Chingachgook must intervene to save Heyward's life. When Heyward inquires of Leather-stocking, "Is there nothing that I can do?" Leather-stocking replies in exasperation "You . . . yes, you can keep in our rear, and be careful not to cross the trail" (213). Nonetheless, Heyward always talks as if he were the gallant, especially when his inabilities endanger others. Book knowledge, gallantry, and foolhardy courage are all he has.

As settlement proceeds westward, Indian culture will not be able to withstand the pressures of white population and white agriculture, but Indian warfare will remain effective as long as the forest remains the forest. Because Cooper considers Europeans and Indians to be peoples of different races, he does not challenge Leather-stocking's insistence that the races have different "gifts." Scalping, torture, and ambush are red man's "gifts" not white man's "gifts"; when practiced by whites, they accrue only dishonor. This neat racial bifurcation cannot, however, solve the paradox of native dispossession Cooper is too honest to ignore. If the dispossession of the Indian and the rise of American empire are to be justified as the spread of Christian civilization, can those goals be achieved without preemptive killing? To subdue the Indian, must the white man become a savage in conduct?

This vexing question is explored to the full in the words and actions of Leather-stocking. Whatever his racial origin may be, Leather-stocking repeatedly prides himself on being white, a "man without a cross" of blood. He is a scout for the English army, currently in service to Lieutenant Colonel Munro, commandant of Fort William Henry. Forest warfare has accustomed him to moral compromises he is often unwilling to acknowledge. Before setting off toward Fort William Henry, Leather-stocking itches to shoot Magua in cold blood, but is ordered not to do so by Major Heyward, who exclaims,

"It will not do. He may be innocent, and I dislike the act" (47). If Leather-stocking had violated white military honor code and shot Magua, he would have saved Uncas's life and the massacre at Fort William Henry would have been far less bloody.

Since the times of Francis Parkman and D.H. Lawrence, Leather-stocking has so often been admired as a un-American hero of frontier integrity and scorn for civilization's "wasty" ways that we readily overlook the battle atrocities he commits. During a British ambush of French troops, Leather-stocking assists in throwing bodies of "the dead, and some say the dying" into the waters known as "Bloody Pond" (154). He declares "with an air of military pride" that there is not "the space of a square mile atwixt Horican and the river, that kill-deer hasn't dropped a living body on, be it an enemy, or be it a brute beast" (154). At times, he seems satisfied to have become a hardened killer. After the Huron attack at Glenn's Falls, "the honest but implacable scout made the circuit of the dead, into whose senseless bosoms he thrust his long knife, with as much coolness, as though they had been so many brute carcasses" (131). Scott's wavering protagonists do not commit such acts.

Compared to Duncan Heyward, Leather-stocking seems to have lost nearly all scruples of honor. His preemptive or retaliatory killings are necessary because they succeed. To kill first protects the innocent. Leather-stocking is well aware that, in accord with eighteenth-century military codes, brutal-ity that would sully the honor of a highborn officer is to be tolerated, even expected, of a lowborn scout. (A lowborn peddler as well as a spy, Harvey Birch had cared greatly about inner loyalty, but very little about outer honor.) Leather-stocking's atypical upbringing among Moravian missionaries is the only explanation Cooper offers for Leather-stocking's fitful but recurrent surges of guilt over dishonor. After arguing that, in the military life, the end justifies the means, Leather-stocking regrets his rationalization. On other occasions, Leather-stocking extends Christian mercy to a helpless enemy, then regrets his lost opportunity to gain victory by killing him.

Psalmodist David Gamut challenges Leather-stocking by insisting that he, David, has remained a true Christian, "an unworthy and humble follower of one who taught not the damnable principle of revenge." Leather-stocking hesitates, then replies:

> "There is a principle in that . . . different from the law of the woods! And yet it is fair and noble to reflect upon! . . . It is what I would wish to practyse [sic] myself as one without a cross of blood, though it is not always easy to deal with an Indian, as you would with a fellow Christian. God bless you, friend; I do believe your scent is not greatly wrong, when the matter is duly considered, and keeping eternity before the eyes, though much depends on the natural gifts, and the force of temptation." (310)

Leather-stocking's statement begins confidently but trails away into circumstantial relativism. The law of the woods is not the law of civilization, red gifts are not white gifts, and today's necessity compromises timeless virtue. Waverley's way of earning honor by an observed act of defensive bravery is impracticable in the wilderness. And yet, one suspects that Cooper is no more able to define "fair and noble" conduct in warfare than Leather-stocking. The only sure conclusion is that conquest of other races and civilizations must sully the Euro-American claim to represent Christian civilization.

Cooper was no more willing than Scott to discard honor in battle as the crucial measure of an officer's merit. Nor would he have accepted Falstaff's claim that honor was a mere word. He confronts the conundrum of honor in the historical centerpiece of *The Last of the Mohicans*, the three-chapter account of the surrender and massacre at Fort William Henry on August 10, 1757.[16] In differing ways both the vanquished and the victor pay the price of lost honor. British Lieutenant Colonel Munro, who is incapable of dishonesty, has grown old in the king's service, respected but little recognized. To Munro, officers remain gentlemen because they honor terms of agreement, especially terms of surrender. Defending a fortress in the American wilderness is not his choice of command, but he will do his honorable best. Although Fort William Henry is a newly built "Star Fort," Munro is sufficiently old-fashioned to be critical of Vauban's "battering system." He remarks to Heyward "the beauty and manliness of warfare has been much deformed, Major Heyward, by the arts of our Monsieur Vauban. Our ancestors were far above such scientific cowardice" (182).

Possession of Fort William Henry is vital to the control of the waterway between French-controlled Montreal and British-controlled New York, but Munro has no chance of successfully defending it. Fort William Henry is made of earthworks, not stone; half its artillery guns have burst; the glacis is unfinished; Munro has few Indian allies; his regulars are outnumbered three to one. Although Munro wishes to resist to the end, he rightly decides to surrender, on grounds of humanity, after he learns that British general Webb, who commands 6,000 soldiers at Fort Edward, has declined to send his troops to relieve Fort William Henry. Munro rightly assumes that the public dishonor for the surrender will soon be his alone, even though Webb outranks him. Webb's cowardice is therefore a violation of outer honor, inner honor, and military "rank honor," but Munro will bear the visible price. "The man has betrayed me!" Munro exclaims, "he has brought dishonour to the door of one, where disgrace was never before known to dwell, and shame has he heaped heavily on his gray hairs" (186).

The Marquis de Montcalm offers Munro generous terms of surrender in accord with the eighteenth-century "Parole of Honour." Munro's forces are to keep their colors, their possessions, and their arms. Protection for surrendered

British civilians and soldiers, Montcalm assures Munro, "shall all be done in a way most honourable to yourselves" (187). According to the code of the Parole of Honour, Munro logically assumes that Montcalm will be true to his word, thereby maintaining the "honesty" increasingly believed to be the essence of honor.[17] Cooper does not specify whether Munro knows that some of Montcalm's Indian allies had promised to join the French army only on condition that they obtain war booty.

As the British leave Fort William Henry on their surrender march to Fort Edward, a variously estimated number of soldiers and civilians were "massacred" (as low as 70, as high as 1,500, Cooper estimates 500). Whether Montcalm intended to betray his own surrender terms remains unknown; in the novel, Montcalm warns the British treaty emissary Duncan Heyward, before terms are finalized, "I find it difficult, even now, to limit them [my red friends] to the usages of war" (175). For Cooper, however, the telling act of dishonor is what Montcalm then chose not to do: while the killing continues, "the armed column of the Christian King stood fast, in an apathy which has never been explained" (202). Cooper judges that the French commander's "cruel apathy" at this particular moment shows him to have been "deficient in that moral courage without which no man can be truly great" (204).

In context of the entire novel, this is a judgment that extends far beyond the person of Montcalm. In a world where rank honor and outer honor are still valued, Cooper judges honor by inner standards of identity and personal integrity that presage Emerson or even Erik Erikson. Greatness depends on "moral courage," not rank or social class. To emphasize the difference, Cooper persistently refers to Montcalm as a Marquis and portrays him as the epitome of a European military aristocracy that equates honor with gesture. Montcalm is said to have been "affable and distinguished, as much for his attention to the forms of courtesy, as for that chivalrous courage, which, only two short years afterwards, induced him to throw away his life on the plains of Abraham" (174). For the reader, however, Montcalm's affability, distinction, courtesy, chivalry, and courage are destroyed in one moment at Fort William Henry, and with them the mystique of rank honor associated with the aristocratic European military.

The ironies of the historical situation continue to compound. Lieutenant Colonel Munro has done nothing dishonorable, yet from the moment he hears of Webb's cowardice, "there commenced a change in his determined character, which accompanied him to a speedy grave" (187). By the time his daughter Cora is buried, he has become, in his own words, "a heart-broken and failing man" (391). To know that he has acted with integrity cannot withstand the loss of outer honor involved in surrender. Conversely, Montcalm's threatened reputation has been salvaged and then enhanced, by his death at the Battle of Quebec. So does a noble death in a losing cause erase the memory of a dishonorable victory? The Marquis de Montcalm dies as a mar-tyred hero; Colonel Munro dies, disgraced and nearly forgotten, in provincial Albany. From Cooper's perspective, the consoling Aristotelian cliché that "honor is the reward of virtue" needs to be doubly challenged.

The ultimate irony is that the actions of neither commander will make lasting historical difference. The novel's opening chapter informs us that the Montreal-New York waterway was the neutral ground where "most of the battles for the mastery of the colonies were contested," a "bloody arena" in which large armies "were seen to bury themselves in these forests, whence they rarely returned but in skeleton bands, that were haggard with care, or dejected by defeat" (16). The novel's historical events take place within "the third year of the war which England and France last waged, for the posses-sion of a country, that neither was destined to retain" (17). For Cooper, true progress can develop only on terms that are both American and republican. Aristocracy must not define military rank; outer honor without inner honor is a sham. Honor and reputation were in evident need of redefinition for the post-revolutionary century.

DEATH WITH HONOR: TOLSTOY AND HUGO

Changed battlefield conditions were to complicate still further the attaining of honor. Napoleon Bonaparte transformed—some would say shattered—the aristocratic honor codes of eighteenth-century warfare. As Emperor of France and General of the Grande Armeé, Napoleon held supreme civil as well as military power, transforming war into an immense international upheaval. Napoleon's object in warfare was to destroy the enemy's army, not to capture strategic locations and forts. As an expert artillery officer, he grouped fifty to hundred horse-driven cannons into a "Great Battery," pulled them close to enemy lines, then bombarded the opposing army for hours before sending in either the cavalry or the infantry. When death rained from the skies long before hand-to-hand combat could even begin, the opportunity for achieving honor became quite literally obscured.

The *Leveé en Masse* decreed in 1793 at the height of the French Revolu-tion had made Napoleon's Grande Armeé possible. Conscription of all male French citizens into a truly national army suddenly became a possibility; appointment and promotion to officer ranks could now be based on merit rather than privilege of birth. Regiments became more uniformly equipped. By commanding a single "Grande Armeé" Napoleon could wait until two enemy armies had drawn near each other, then march his army between them, destroying first one smaller enemy army, then the other. His tactics empha-sized surprise and knowledge of the terrain (he was an expert cartographer).

For purposes of speed as well as plunder, his armies were ordered to live off the land. He cared little for the condition of his field hospitals or the obligations imposed by treaties. The purpose of war was to win a decisive battle, occupy the enemy's capitol, secure the capitulation of the conquered country, and then move on. In the name of international progress, he released a backlash of nationalism in the countries he defeated.

To inspire his troops, Napoleon spoke often of glory, sometimes of honor. The new battlefield conditions, however, made glory and honor increasingly national but impersonal achievements. Rank honor lost its force as meritocracy subverted aristocratic battle codes like the Parole of Honor. The appeal of self-sacrifice for the French Republic may have been more democratic and egalitarian than sacrifice for family, clan, or region, but it was also more distant and abstract, its horizon limitless. When immense armies met under artillery bombardment, could individual instances of battlefield valor even be recognized? As my chapter epigraph from Bismarck shows, the value of honor certainly did not disappear, but public demonstrations of honor became more questionable. By 1881, the greatest of Prussian generals was publically defining honor as an inner not an outer quality.

Clausewitz's *On War* (1832–1837) is both the crucial testament to the contemporary impact of Napoleonic warfare and a harbinger of changes in the conduct of battle as rendered in the historical novel. Citing examples from near contemporary battles, Clausewitz emphasizes practicable strategies for victory, which he defines as disarming the enemy by destroying his forces. Although each battle differs, and warfare can never be reduced to rules, "Genius," "Chance," "Friction" (unexpected impediments of all kinds) and sheer "Guesswork" are timeless factors often overlooked.[18] A man of "Military Genius" will possess four qualities: courage, intelligence, determination, and presence of mind (100–102). A good soldier will also have four qualities: bravery, adaptability, stamina, and enthusiasm. In addition to an army's speed and flexibility, victory depends on tactical factors: "surprise, the benefit of terrain and concentric attack" (360). Just as strategic genius rises above all rules, so sheer will power defines the master commander: "The proud spirit's firm will dominates the art of war as an obelisk dominates the town square on which all roads converge" (119). Surely Napoleon is the shadow figure behind these generalities.

The word "honor" occurs infrequently in Clausewitz's analysis of war. He devotes one two-page chapter to "Moral Factors," defining morality as the spirit that establishes "a close affinity with the will that moves and leads the whole mass of force, practically merging with it, since the will is itself a moral quality" (184). By this definition, the problem of making a "moral" choice becomes synonymous with the "morale" inspired in an army by the dominant will of its leader. Clausewitz correctly predicts that the post-Napoleonic future will belong to what we, in the wake of the American Civil War, the Franco-Prussian War and two World Wars, now call "total war." He looks back at the "limited war" of the eighteenth century with a curious mixture of scorn, regret and relief. As a Prussian military strategist, he fears Napoleon as much as he admires him.

Foucault was to argue that war is the key to understanding the structure of government; Clausewitz argues repeatedly that war is an extension of politics. To both of them, war and politics are inseparable. If, as Clausewitz famously insisted, "war is nothing but the continuation of policy by other means" (69), then Clausewitz is surely correct in arguing that "in war, the result is never final" (75). Many seemingly decisive battles may be fought, but enmity in political policy will be always with us, leading to further wars. As Clausewitz looks back upon the Napoleonic era, he concludes that significant changes in the practices of war "were caused by the new political conditions which the French Revolution created both in France, and in Europe as a whole, conditions that set in motion new means and new forces, and have thus made possible a degree of energy in war that otherwise would have been inconceivable" (610). Energy, technology and political uncertainty will increase together. Major wars will arise between centralized nations led by commanders who understand military technology and know how to arouse the will of the people. The twentieth-century question of whether revolution in the name of equality and/or nationalism inevitably promotes totalitarian ambition lurks in the interstices of Clausewitz's text.

While writing *War and Peace*, Count Leo Tolstoy defended his novel's focus on Russia's upper class by acknowledging "I am an aristocrat because I cannot believe in the lofty mind, the subtle taste and great honor of a man who picks his nose with his finger while his spirit communes with God."[19] This is not the remark of a man who has discarded the possibility of aristocratic honor. Phrases like "sensitive integrity" and "noble honesty" rise readily to mind whenever the reader considers Tolstoy's characterization of Prince André Bolkonski. Tolstoy's portrayal of warfare itself, however, overwhelmingly affirms Clausewitz's findings about recent changes in battlefield tactics brought about by Napoleon. Clausewitz preferred to leave honor out of account, as if it were a chimera; Tolstoy could not and would not do so. How might honor in battle now be redefined? If honor were to retain meaning, who would be able to appreciate it and what lasting benefit could an honorable action henceforth have? What does honor require beyond truthfulness and courage?

Tolstoy's renderings of the Battles of Austerlitz and Borodino convey the technological transformation of eighteenth-century strategic warfare into mass killing. Awaiting his first battle, cavalry cadet Nicholas Rostov, standing dismounted on the bridge at Ens, imagines how "one step beyond that boundary line, which resembles the line dividing the living from the dead, lies uncertainty, suffering and death" (123). "You fear and yet long to cross that line," Nicholas feels, "and know that sooner or later it must be crossed and you will have to find out what is there, just as you will have to learn what lies the other side of death" (123). Nicholas wants to believe there are clear, discernible lines in war, lines beyond which armies strive to advance, lines that separate life from death, honor from dishonor. French grapeshot (one of Bonaparte's most effective innovations) soon whistles around him; he stands still not knowing what to do; no regiment advances anywhere, the shelling simply ends, whereupon Nicholas concludes, "It's all over, but I am a coward—yes a coward" (128). No lines, however, have been crossed; nothing has happened by which cowardice could be alleged. Nicholas's initiation into battle is meaningless save in his mind.

The shooting at the bridge of Ens was merely a skirmish introducing Tolstoy's view of war; the Battle of Borodino was the bloodiest recorded historical battle to date (70,000 dead in one day). Directionless chaos prevails in both. As the Russian and French cavalry rush back and forth, cavalry and infantry are shredded by unseen artillery: "all their rushing and galloping at one another did little harm, the harm of disablement and death was caused by the balls and bullets that flew over the fields on which these men were floundering about" (714). As Clausewitz had emphasized, chance is as great a determinant of survival as strategy, especially for the individual soldier. Victory has no discernible connection with a just cause or honorable conduct. Individual acts of bravery occur without witness; technological and human forces collide indeterminately to constitute total war.

On the evening before the Battle of Borodino, André explains to Pierre his premonition of what is to occur:

> "I would not take prisoners. Why take prisoners? It's chivalry! The French have destroyed my home and are on their way to destroy Moscow. . . . They are my enemies. In my opinion they are all criminals. . . . The aim of war is murder; the methods of war are spying, treachery, and their encouragement, the ruin of a country's inhabitants, robbing them or stealing to provision the army, and fraud and falsehood termed military craft. The habits of the military class are the absence of freedom, that is, discipline, idleness, ignorance, cruelty, debauchery and drunkenness. And in spite of all this, it is the highest class, respected by everyone. All the kings, except the Chinese, wear military uniforms, and he who kills most people received the highest rewards." (690–691)

André may not fully believe his own cynicism, but his summary proves to be generally accurate. Because rank honor still survives, those who direct the slaughter will command respect and be elevated to the "highest class." As long as the French enemy continues to wage war upon civilians, taking prisoners will not only be outmoded chivalry but detrimental strategy. If Prince André were to take no prisoners, he would not, under present circumstances, suffer loss of his outer honor. No Colonel Talbot will be there on the slaughter field of Borodino to admire and reward his honorable behavior.

Despite battlefield experiences to the contrary, Tolstoy's aristocratic characters need to believe in the reality of honor, if not glory. Eighteenth-century military values live on amid war worlds that cannot sustain them. Although André does not share Pierre's belief that Napoleon is a republican, André yearns on three separate occasions to earn a moment of battlefield glory just as Napoleon did when he recaptured Toulon in 1793. André seeks to behave honorably, but his two experiences on the field of battle—among the most memorable scenes of the entire novel—deprive him of the opportunity to do so. At Austerlitz, he seizes the regimental flag, runs ahead shouting "Hurrah" and "Forward lads," then is abruptly shot and left for dead until Napoleon arrives. Whether the infinite "lofty sky" into which André gazes masks God or the Void is left ambivalent, but whatever the lofty sky's ultimate meaning may be, gazing into it fills André with a conviction of the "insignificance of greatness, the unimportance of life, which no one could understand, and the still greater unimportance of death" (254). If the lofty sky masks nothing, what value honor?

At Borodino, André's regiment stands for hours without orders, while 200 men die under sustained French artillery fire. Finally ordered to stand in a "trampled oatfield" upon which French guns are concentrated, hundreds more Russians are killed. André stands there through the afternoon hours: "There was nothing for him to do, and no order to be given. Everything went on of itself" (722). Finally his existential moment arrives when a shell drops "like a bird whirring in rapid flight" two steps away. While "the smoking shell spun like a top," André hesitates, wondering "Can this be death?," then asserts, "I cannot, I do not wish to die. I love life—I love this grass, this earth, this air" (722).

As similes, the bird and the spinning top signify rapid motion arriving without agency and therefore without volition; like "everything" on that day, they simply go on of themselves. André's thoughts suggest, however, that his hesitation is less a sign of despair than of his need to assert that he cannot die because he does not wish to die. Helpless on the battlefield, he still claims the power of free will, even at the price of his own fatal wounding. No dishonor accrues to him; inner honor remains. Twice denied his Toulon, André has spiritually moved beyond equating honor with glory. André also knows, however, that he has been denied the opportunity to demonstrate the outer honor he believes is due to his family's aristocratic heritage. When André left Bald Hills to join the Russian Army, Prince Nicholas Bolkonski bade his son farewell with a rebuke: "if I hear that you have not behaved like a son of Nicholas Bolkonski, I shall be ashamed!" (94). André's firm reply, "You need not have said that to me, Father," is deserved but regrettably wasted. Although General Kutuzov, speaking to André as a substitute father, rightly assures him "I know your path is the path of honor" (661), Kutuzov's reassurance cannot overcome the ironies of circumstance. As André dies, his inner honorableness has been thoroughly tested, but is known to precious few. As narrator, Tolstoy risks no general conclusion about the survival of aristocratic honor in a time of total war; as so often, Tolstoy appears to know how things happen, but refrains from determining their causes.[20]

An aristocrat appointed a cadet, Nicholas Rostov represents, for good and for bad, the ordinary man in battle. Unlike André, he cannot conceive of honor apart from glory. Rank honor remains a consummate value to him. An honorable reputation is bestowed by others; it does not emerge from one's highest inner values. Because Nicholas has been seen hesitating on the bridge at Ens, he assumes he is a coward. Shortly thereafter, during Nicholas's first battle charge, his horse is shot and falls upon his leg. As a French soldier bears down upon him, Nicholas in confused terror flings his pistol at the Frenchman and flees to the bushes like "a hare fleeing from the hounds" (163). At no point, however, does Tolstoy apply the word "cowardice" to Nicholas's actions. Instead, Tolstoy's interest is in Nicholas's need to concoct a narrative for his peers. "His hearers expected a story of how, beside himself and all aflame with excitement, he had flown like a storm at the square, cut his way in, slashed right and left, how his saber had tasted flesh and he had fallen exhausted, and so on. And so, he told them all that" (210). Nicholas is envisioning his body as if it were moving visibly in an eighteenth-century battle. His invented honor is therefore an immediate psychological necessity. Anticipating the reader's likely response, Tolstoy challenges the charge of imposture: "Rostov was a truthful young man and would on no account have told a deliberate lie" (210).

After a few retellings, Nicholas believes his own fabrication; his remembered narrative becomes the recorded past, and he salvages glory, reputation, and, with them, apparently, outer honor. By similar distortions of memory, other ordinary, truthful young men will successfully make their way, though André Bolkonski will not. After wintering in Moscow on leave, Nicholas returns to his regiment, pleased because in the military life "all was clear and simple . . . everything was definite . . . there was nothing to think out or decide" (345). When a superior officer criticizes the Tsar's strategy, Nicholas bangs the table and shouts out "It's not for us to judge. . . . If once we begin judging and arguing about everything, nothing sacred will be left! . . . Our business is to do our duty, to fight and not to think" (364–365). Rank honor, divorced from morality, has now been reduced to unthinking duty, which is justified as "sacred."

On the battlefield at Ostravna, Nicholas strikes a French dragoon from behind with his saber, gazes into the Frenchman's terrified, dimpled, "ordinary, homelike face," takes the Frenchman prisoner, but is suddenly overcome with "an unpleasant feeling of depression." As soon as Nicholas receives the St. George's Cross, however, he concludes that he must have performed a "brilliant exploit," even while admitting, to himself alone, "I can't make it out at all" (581, 582). Nicholas's confused experience in taking the Frenchman prisoner bears no resemblance to Waverley's honorable way of taking Talbot prisoner at Preston Pans. Although Tolstoy does not describe Nicholas's later actions on the battlefield, Nicholas clearly retains a reputation that allows him to be, at novel's end, a respected gentleman-farmer and firm disciplinarian of his serfs, a traditionalist who likes to be seen hard at work in his fields or reading books of history. Nicholas's ordinary sense of honor is not rendered contemptible; it has become the way of the world. Lasting commitment to inner honorableness, by contrast, seems to pass from the novel with André Bolkonski.

Victor Hugo wrote his long-deferred historical novel on the French Revolution, *Quatrevingt-Treize (Ninety-Three)* in 1872–1873, soon after experiencing the Franco-Prussian War, first in Paris, then in Brussels. He chose a surprising segment of the revolution's history. Since the 1840s, the French Revolution had been, for him, the Niagara Falls in the river of historical time, the cataclysm that would lead to God's providential rainbow, the fall that would enable the progress of humanity. His recent experience of the Franco-Prussian war had immersed him in the sudden dissolution of Louis Napoleon's Second Empire, the desperate defense of Paris against the Prussians, and the equally desperate revolutionary ambitions of the Paris Commune. Hugo's contradictory feelings of hope and betrayal are conveyed by his judging the Commune to have been "an admirable thing, stupidly compromised by five or six deplorable ringleaders."[21] Because hope lingered due to the fall of "Napoleon Le Petit," the establishing of the Third Republic, and his own return to Paris from exile, Hugo's *1793* should logically have centered upon the promise of 1789, Prussia's military threat to revolutionary Paris, the efforts of the National Convention to save the city, and the rise and fall of Terror. Instead, Hugo wrote of unsuccessful counterrevolution in Brittany and the Vendeé. The reader experiences 1793 as a prolonged, brutal civil war in the provinces, relieved by a succinct central section describing revolutionary leaders in Paris. Why the seemingly peripheral subject? In the context of literary history, Hugo may have sought to recast the failed counterrevolutions of Highland Jacobites and Bretonese Chouans into prose that would be even more poetically heightened than the historical novels of Scott or Balzac. A more pressing reason, I suggest, lies in Hugo's desire to restore the possibilities for honor and self-sacrifice to memories of French battlefields. To do so,

however, Hugo needed to look past the disgrace of 1871, past the disappointment of 1848, past the chaotic conditions of Napoleonic warfare (*War and
Peace*), and past the chaotic streets of revolutionary Paris, to a prerevolutionary region where simpler conditions made the morality and immorality of
individual actions clearer, more sharply defined.

The impenetrable thickets, swamps, ravines, and forests of Brittany and the
Vendeé are the perfect neutral ground from which to wage civil war through
guerilla tactics. The Marquis of Lantenac, royalist leader of the counterrevolution, says he is prepared to violate every tenet of the old honor code in order
to restore the monarchy: sharpshooting from ambush, killing the wounded,
killing prisoners, killing women who accompany Republican troops, giving
no quarter. After the initial killings at Herbe-en-Pail, however, Lantenac
rarely practices the brutality he preaches. The untrained, ill-equipped peasants of Brittany and the Vendeé prove adept at surprise attack and brave
in hand-to-hand single-combat, but helpless against the republican infantry
when outside their known terrain.

Hugo values liberty and equal rights, but he is no populist, no social egalitarian. The rebels of Brittany and the Vendeé are described as semiliterate
peasants led by commanding aristocrats and refractory priests. Their loyalty
to king, nobleman, and priest is based upon fear of the supremacy of Paris
and the Republic. "Wretched distracted Brittany" is being forced to emerge
from the "underground, the resource of hunted animals."[22] The intensity of
the rebels' loyalty derives from the unadmitted truth that they have become
reactionary "slaves" forced into modernity out of fear. "When the French
Republic burst forth, Terror, which is a species of rage, was already latent
in human souls, and when the Republic burst forth, the dens were ready in
the woods. Brittany revolted, finding itself oppressed by this forced deliv-
erance—a mistake natural to slaves" (179). In terms of cultural politics, the
Bretonese and the Vendeéans are conceived as blocking forces to the republican progress that must eventually succeed Terror and Thermidor, whenever
they may recur.

Hugo's battle descriptions, ostensibly describing warfare of 1793, read as
if warfare is still medieval. When the Republican Blues attack Lantenac's
fortress La Tourgue, they use clubs, pikes, swords, daggers, muskets, fire,
makeshift ladders, and explosives to besiege, mine, and destroy a feudal
tower twice likened to the Bastille.[23] Hugo contrasts the two man-made
"monsters" that represent two equally inhumane eras (384). La Tourgue, the
iron black monster, symbolizes the unchanging aristocracy of the *Ancien
Regime* dooming itself to its own destruction; the guillotine, the wooden red
monster with a triangular iron blade, symbolizes the murderous absolutism
of a revolutionary ideology that knows no pity.[24] Thus 1793 becomes a cusp
year; the two monsters point in opposite temporal directions, but are oddly

one. At the climactic moment of the siege, we see the red monster just "a few paces off" from La Tourgue—"a monster of stone rising up to hold companionship with the monster of wood" (384).

Detailed description of hand-to-hand combat practices allows Hugo to admire clearly visible instances of heroism and honor. Similarities drawn to Greek and Roman leaders, elevated by the adjective "epic," are repeatedly applied to the combatants. The fictional narratives in Brittany and the Vendeé, unlike the Paris section, are built upon a sequence of courageous, self-sacrificial acts. Halmalo and Tellmarch have opportunities to kill or abandon the Marquis de Lantenac, but they refrain out of respect for his courage. First La Vivandiere, then Lantenac, save the lives of Michelle Fléchard's three children; the children are then nurtured by Sergeant Radoub, the most warrior-like of the revolutionary officers. Ex-priest Cimourdain prides himself on being a remorseless republican absolutist, a staunch supporter of Marat and the Terror, but Cimourdain saves his aristocratic nephew Gauvain at risk of his own life, and then honorably offers himself in exchange for Lantenac (300). At novel's end, Lantenac saves Michelle's three children a second time, thereby surrendering himself to anticipated execution. Lantenac's animalistic, devoted follower Imanus sacrifices his own life so that Lantenac and his "Homeric band" of seven surviving royalists can escape from La Tourgue, presently besieged by some 1,500 republicans (314).

Viscount Gauvain, Lantenac's heir and grandnephew, is the novel's liberal, aristocratic young protagonist, but he is no waverer. Wholeheartedly dedicated to service to the revolutionary army, Gauvain's instinctive sense of honor is defined by his acts of "pity," "clemency," and "amnesty" toward the conquered, the helpless, and the less powerful.[25] Gauvain is, of course, the French spelling of Gawain, exemplary knight of the Round Table and bearer of King Arthur's Excalibur, celebrated by Geoffrey of Monmouth, Marie de France, Chretien de Troyes, Malory, and others. The opposite of Cooper's Duncan Heyward, Hugo's Gauvain embodies the combined spirit of Homeric courage, medieval chivalry, and practicable battlefield honor continuing on into the revolutionary era. When Cimourdain and Gauvin imagine the change of human character that should emerge from the French Revolution, Cimourdain says "I would have man made by the rules of Euclid," but Gauvain replies "I would like him better as pictured by Homer" (377). The warfare of the Vendeé in 1793, brutal though it undoubtedly was, honors redemptive deeds in ways the Franco-Prussian War did not.

After the end of battle, the narrative of *Quatrevingt-Treize* focuses on the interrelated moral dilemmas of three self-sacrificial acts. The Marquis de Lantenac, having escaped from La Tourgue into the forest, returns to his burning tower to rescue Michelle Fléchard's three children, knowing that either his beloved nephew Gauvin or Cimourdain is sure to arrest and execute him. After imprisoning Lantenac and binding him over for trial, Gauvain substitutes himself for Lantenac in prison, enabling his royalist uncle, whose death he has ordered by military decree, to escape. Cimourdain, once Gauvain's loving and fatherly tutor, must then sentence Gauvin to death for violating his own decree and for aiding the royalist commander to escape. Moral complexities accumulate and self-contradict. Lantenac has chosen protection of children over his life; Gauvain has chosen admiration for Lantenac's chivalry over his oath; Cimourdain has chosen military duty and revolutionary principle over his love for Gauvain, whom he has raised and educated. Cimourdain knows that to order Gauvain's death will require his own suicide. These three choices are based upon contradictory formulations of the ultimate value of life; what links them is Hugo's admiration for the honor of self-sacrifice that conquers fear of death.

Gauvain expresses Hugo's paradoxical conclusion explicitly: "When the guilty acknowledges his fault, he saves the only thing worth the trouble of saving—honour" (369). At the exact moment Cimourdain orders that Gauvain be guillotined, Cimourdain shoots himself. All three men, none of them guiltless and two of them dead, have redeemed their honor. As the guillotine blade descends and Cimourdain's pistol rings out, the novel ends with the remarkable sentence: "And those two souls [Cimourdain and Gauvain], united still in that tragic death, soared away together, the shadow of the one mingled with the radiance of the other."[26] Hugo here glorifies a double resurrection based on values more akin to Shelley's *Prometheus Unbound* than to the New Testament. Neither bodily resurrection nor heaven's rest is anticipated; the twinned souls, shadow and light, ascend into the unknown. For Hugo, the possibility of noble self-sacrifice can never be closed off, despite the betrayals of 1793, 1848, and the Franco-Prussian War. Whatever the future may bring, honor and self-sacrifice are eternal.

The ironic battle experiences of André Bolkonski, Nicholas Rostov and Pierre Bezukov do not belong in the world of Victor Hugo's novel. Hugo is searching for a principle of justice that ultimately transcends any political formulation whatever. Gauvin has understood that "above the justice of revolutions is the justice of humanity" (344). Lantenac and Cimourdain, like La Tourgue and the guillotine, represent opposed, extreme and aged kinds of justice—the hierarchical aristocratic honor of the *Ancien Regime* and the legalistic honor of cold republican reason. Only Gauvain combines republican politics and battle proficiency with a commitment to clemency, insisting "I do not make war on women," "I do not make war on old men," "I do not make war on children," and "one does not kill a man on the ground" (228, 229). His guiding abstractions never waver; he seeks "the Republic of the absolute" in which equity transcends justice, equality transcends authority, and the citizen transcends the soldier (376–383). Hugo does not criticize

Gauvain for not specifying how to get there. History will prove to be a "constant progression," the climbing of a ladder toward God (380). Literary and cultural admiration for the familiar figure of the high-minded, republican, aristocratic revolutionary can go no further.

Reviewing *QuatreVingt-Treize*, the youthful Henry James chided Victor Hugo for his "passion for the moral enormous," his "pretension to say many things in the grand manner," his walking "between the sublime and the ridiculous as resolutely as his own most epic heroes."[27] It is easy to ridicule the melodrama of triple self-sacrifice and the grandiosity of Gauvin's principles as evidence of "ego Hugo" or of Jean Cocteau's quip that "Victor Hugo was a madman who believed he was Victor Hugo."[28] Before condescending to Hugo's presumed naiveté, however, it is necessary to consider the novel's neglected second section titled simply "In Paris." Given Hugo's steadfast opposition to capital punishment, one might expect Dickensian portrayals of tumbrils and the guillotine. Instead, Hugo provides a remarkably detailed listing of exactly who comprised the Mountain and the Gironde and then concludes that the National Convention was controlled by temporizers and cowards who made up the Plain and the Marsh.[29] Hugo portrays Robespierre, Danton, and Marat meeting in a backroom to appoint Cimourdain as the agent of the Committee of Public Safety commanding the Republic's troops in the Vendeé. None of the three is a visionary or even a committed republican; all are quarrelsome, jealous, ordinary men anxious to survive but controlled by events beyond them. None is concerned with better, orderly government, let alone any "Republic of the absolute"; they quarrel about which one of their conspiracy theories (foreign, domestic, or urban) poses the ultimate danger. Hugo judges them to be "conflicting thunderbolts" but "three terrible men" (131). Consequently, Gauvain's hope for progress and human rights must be deferred to an indefinite future. The French Revolution is said to shine with "rays of truth," but the rays forever disappear at the future's horizon. Gauvain's ladder is only a ladder *toward* God. Faith in the eventual emergence of revolutionary ideals must be maintained even though history has repeatedly betrayed them.

SLAUGHTER AND SURVIVAL: ZOLA AND PASTERNAK

During the immediate aftermath of the Vietnam War, Michael Walzer observed "notions of honor and chivalry seem to play only a small part in contemporary combat." "Chivalry, it is often said, was the victim of democratic revolution and of revolutionary war: popular passion overcame aristocratic honor."[30] As we have seen, "democratic" revolution, fervid nationalism, and the *leveé on masse* arose together in the late eighteenth century, and total war followed soon thereafter. Unlike a willing volunteer, a conscripted man must struggle to summon any kind of inner-directed "honor." The impersonal killing of mass battles forces the individual soldier to dwell upon his insignificance. Appeals to national glory lessen attachments to the local associations that define one's identity. Taken together, historical novels by Scott, Cooper, Tolstoy, and Hugo show, however, that the nineteenth century relinquished the value of honor quite reluctantly. From the novelist's perspective, to feel guilt or pride in one's sense of honor lends conflict, complexity, and the possibility of true deserving to the human condition. The salvaging of honor was, however, becoming almost impossibly difficult as the nineteenth century drew to its close.

Zola's *La Débacle*, like Tolstoy's *War and Peace* and Stephen Crane's *The Red Badge of Courage*, challenges the hope that inner and outer honor can be achieved simultaneously. For 370 of its 430 pages, Zola's novel immerses the reader in the details of a catastrophic national war. We follow the 106th brigade from the French-German front along its panic-driven retreat to Rheims, only to be summoned back, exhausted, to the front. Without military justification, the 106th is marched to the hill-ringed city of Sedan, where an entire French army is surrounded, decimated by Prussian artillery, and swiftly surrenders. Survivors are herded onto the peninsula of Iges, from which the few living members of the 106th eventually escape. Dispiriting circumstances are fully detailed: the total breakdown of supplies, incompetence of officers, rain, heat, and famine, endless names of forgettable villages, deserters, men standing asleep, men stealing sheets to bandage shoeless feet, men craving liquor and laudanum. Zola's metaphors for the marching French army include "a drove of panic-stricken cattle, with the dogs worrying and snapping at their heels" and "a file of manacled galley-slaves, in terror of the lash."[31] Scott, Cooper, and Tolstoy had avoided such recurrent animal imagery; Hugo had applied animal imagery to the Chouans, but not to the three aristocratic protagonists for whom honor remains an actionable reality.

The officers of the 106th attempt to rally their troops through patriotism, not honor, but only a few infantrymen are inspired to fight for the dissolute Second Empire against the Prussian enemy. Bravery is born of desperation when battle circumstances leave little hope of survival. None of Zola's fictional characters, however, summons the kind of bravery that derives from desire for glory or the dictates of honor. Heroism cannot be seen beneath the smoky, random death delivered by the big guns of the Prussian artillery. Moreover, there is no leader to embody a cause worth fighting for. On at least eleven separate occasions, French troops catch glimpses of Emperor Louis Napoleon, motionless near the battlefield but commanding nothing, pallid, wordless, and groaning with dysentery, following his cumbersome entourage, but unable even to convince his own generals to honor his tendering of the white flag.[32]

The longest, sustained military sequence in *La Débacle* transpires in the makeshift field hospital of Major Bouroche, one of two doctors who exhaust themselves performing amputations on factory tables that are slippery with blood, vomit, and entrails. The sickening waste of human life continues without known purpose or result. Within one hour, four French cavalry units are decimated, one after the other, by the fire of the massed square of Prussian infantry. Like André Bolkonski's unit at Borodino, the 106th at Sedan stands without orders while it is shot to pieces.

After the worst of the fighting is over, Maurice and Jean seek a moment of peace in the forest, only to find it filled with the wounded:

> Maurice and Jean saw a Zouave, nearly disemboweled, propped against the trunk of an oak, who kept up a most terrific howling, without a moment's intermission. A little way beyond another man was actually being slowly roasted; his clothing had taken fire, and the flames had run up and caught his beard, while he, paralyzed by a shot that had broken his back, was silently weeping. Then there was a captain, who, one arm torn from its socket and his flank laid open to the thigh, was writhing on the ground in agony unspeakable, beseeching, in heartrending accents, the by-passers to end his suffering. . . . But the dead and wounded had ceased to count; the comrade who fell by the way was abandoned to his fate, forgotten as if he had never been. (243)

To comment on such a passage is superfluous, but it is useful to note that *La Débacle* contains many like it. The textbook importance claimed for Hemingway's World War I as a new revelation of the horrors of war pales beside Zola's cumulative account of the Franco-Prussian War. Surely, the sparsity of adjectives with which Hemingway describes soldiers' wounds does not arouse greater horror merely because Hemingway raises terse understatement to stylistic perfection.

Zola's major characters, Corporal Jean Macquart and Private Maurice Levasseur, save each other's lives twice but not, like Hugo's heroes, for the sake of a code of honor. More by instinct than by choice, they instinctively save the life of a fellow soldier they have come to love. Jean Macquart is content to remain an ill-educated provincial farmer who, as a noncommissioned officer, dutifully supports his men; Maurice Levasseur is an ambitious, excitable, privileged Parisian lawyer who hides his failings beneath criticism of the army he has half-unwillingly joined. After the two men vent their resentments, they develop a friendship based upon genuine care for each other. By novel's end, it makes no difference that the peasant corporal can give orders to the aristocratic private. Rank honor disappears along with desire to save the glory of *la patrie*.

After the surrender of the French army and separate escapes to Paris, both men rejoin military units. Jean joins the French national army gathering at Versailles to suppress the revolution in Paris; Maurice joins the National Guard defending the Paris Commune. To adopt opposed allegiances is a familiar, effective literary representation of the "senseless, atrocious fratricide" of civil war, but Jean and Maurice have become military enemies for the same inglorious reason (410). Both men are consumed by an overwhelming sense of humiliation at the defeat they have endured. Some kind of group restitution has become essential to them. Jean joins the Versailles army, not because he is a constitutional monarchist, or a republican, or because he supports Adolphe Thiers, but because he wants his life in France to somehow become whole again. Maurice, who is far more articulate, redirects his grandfather's faith in the exemplary power of Napoleon's victories for empire. Maurice now longs to see "the empire overturned and swept away amid a howl of universal execration, the republic proclaimed with an outburst of patriotic fervor, while the legend of '92 would incite men to emulate the glorious past, and flocking to the standards, drive from the country's soil the hated foreigner with armies of brave volunteers" (299).

While the barricades are being built, Maurice becomes convinced that "the Commune was to be the avenger of all the wrongs they had suffered, the liberator coming with fire and sword to purify and punish" (397). "He was not quite clear in mind about it all," Zola comments, because Maurice's inchoate craving for revenge is driven by his need for an apocalyptic end (397). He would gladly support a new Committee of Public Safety because he accepts "the necessity of the Terror" (396). A renewal of the glory days of 1792 would, Maurice believes, redeem France from its shame, especially if the redemption should end in total destruction. As Paris burns and the last fighting Communards are executed, Maurice and his sister Henriette wonder "was it not indeed the last act, the inevitable conclusion of the tragedy, the blood-madness for which the lost fields of Sedan and Metz were responsible, the epidemic of destruction born from the siege of Paris, the supreme struggle of a nation in peril of dissolution, in the midst of slaughter and universal ruin?" (421). The energies needed for sustaining such a doomed revolution, they believe, must arise from wellsprings of instinct that are deeper than politics.

A month before the "Bloody Week" that ended the Commune in May of 1871, Zola had written a press report attesting that in Paris "Terror reigns supreme" and ideologues are staging an "abominable parody of '93."[33] Understanding the excesses of the Paris Commune required attention to the national past, not the international future. To Maurice, to Jean, and surely to Zola as well, the rise of the revolutionary Commune in no way substantiates Karl Marx's claims that "the glorious working men's Revolution of the 18th of March took undisputed sway of Paris," and that "the Commune annexed to

France the working people all over the world." Zola may have shared some articles of late-nineteenth-century socialist faith but, as Lukacs knew, Zola did not share Marx's conviction that, in 1871, "The French working class is only the advanced guard of the modern proletariat."[34] To Zola, the angry, defeatist psychology emerging from France's horrific present, not the proclaimed goals of Marxist socialism, had fueled the revolt of the Paris Commune.[35] The Communards had then been put down with a savage totality that hostility to Marxist socialism could not adequately explain.

In the twentieth century, a sense of honor is at least as likely to emerge from one's professional occupation as from aristocratic lineage or military service. As World War I turns into the Bolshevik Revolution, Yurii Zhivago is serving as a medical student turned army doctor. His medical duty—surely an honorable undertaking in Pasternak's eyes—is to save lives, not to take them, to cure the wounds of politics not to fight for mankind's better future. After the October Revolution, however, Zhivago is kidnapped into the Forest Brotherhood, a semi-military unit of the Red Army fighting the Whites in the desolate outposts of Western Siberia. After two years of inconclusive guerilla warfare, no atrocity has become too brutal not to be committed by the "Brothers" on both sides. Zhivago hopes to be protected by his status: "According to the Red Cross International Convention, the army medical personnel must not take part in the military operations of the belligerents."[36] As a noncombatant, questions of cowardice or copping out would seem not to pertain to Zhivago as they had to Waverley, Nicholas Rostov, and Maurice Levasseur. Zhivago's honor, like the honor of ambulance drivers in World War I literature, will consist in not fighting.

Battle conditions soon bring the circumstantial dilemma of the honor/dishonor of killing to a personal crisis. A small group of Red Partisans, Zhivago unwillingly among them, are attacked by a wave of White cadets, "youngsters, first-year students from the universities," who advance according to eighteenth-century tactics "in extended formation and excelling the parade ground smartness of the Imperial Guards" (333). "The bullets of the Partisans mowed them down" like the grass on which the Partisans lie belly downward (333). At such a moment, Zhivago's class instincts take precedence over the fading promise of socialist revolution. He wishes the White youth the "success" of victory, or at least survival, because "their expressive, handsome faces seemed to belong to people of his own kind . . . to families who were probably akin to him in spirit, in education, in moral discipline and values" (333). Unlike Zola, Pasternak emphasizes the continuing influence of social class amid revolutionary conditions.

Yurii's class instincts and his revulsion at killing collide with the necessities of the moment. He wishes to run out onto the field and give himself up as a neutral, but immediately realizes he would be shot down by both sides.

Instinct prevents him from remaining passive. "The laws of what went on around him" dictated that "you had to do what everyone was doing." As the gunfire of the Whites draws near, he picks up the rifle of a dead Red telephonist, and fires repeatedly at a dead tree in order to avoid shooting at any human target. Like many fictional protagonists before him, Yurii bumbles through his battle experience, hitting the tree but accidentally wounding two of the Whites, and seemingly killing a third, before the wounded Whites are "knifed in the field" and all White prisoners are executed.

Yurii's immediate response to his ordeal is to try to avoid thoughts of cowardice and honor. When he sees the handsome innocent face of the White boy he has recently shot, Yurii asks himself the metaphysical question "Why did I kill him?" (335), not the tactical question, "Why did I shoot him?" nor the moral question, "Did I shoot him honorably?" Yurii is astonished by the coincidence that both the telephonist and the White soldier carry the 91st psalm next to their chest as an amulet of protection. The possibility that the 91st Psalm's reassurance ("Thou shalt not be afraid for the terror by night nor for the arrow that flieth by day") might have provided divine protection to the bearer of the amulet never occurs to him. Yurii simply notes that his bullet had been deflected by the gold case into which the mother of the White soldier had inserted the words of the Psalm.

The telephonist dies and the White cadet survives, but there is no judgment passed on the honor or dishonor, courage or cowardice, of any of the three men. Because soldiers are constantly deserting from both Red and White forces, Yurii knows that, if he were to put the telephonist's clothing on the White soldier he has wounded, the White soldier would survive due to the disguise. So it happens. The wounded boy returns to the White army and is never heard from again. Nothing is or can be concluded from this incident, except the important fact that, for Yurii Zhivago, killing is always the violation of the very principle of life. Preservation of life has become for him the essence of military "honor," but Yurii cannot assimilate this idea within the ironic connotations that the word "honor" traditionally bears. Pasternak's compelling account of this brief battlefield moment has the complexity of a novella compressed into four pages.

A NOTE ON TRANSCENDERS

Revolution has historically led to the battlefield, but historical novelists are drawn to imagining honorable behavior that memorably transcends it. The juxtaposition of waverer to fanatic remains at the novel's structural center, but at its periphery—and sometimes near its center—are characters whose moral values are either above or apart from the divided loyalties of the old and new eras. By attending to moral values beyond their politicized surroundings, these characters are relieved of much, though not all, debilitating uncertainty.

These characters—call them transcenders—vary greatly in beliefs, gender, practicality, and personal power. Some are central figures like Cooper's Harvey Birch and Vidal's Abraham Lincoln, nonmilitary men who shun war but are compelled by circumstance and by love of nation to pursue duplicitous wartime strategies toward admirable ends. Others, like Scott's Jeanie Deans and Pushkin's Masha Mironov, are women whose spirit leads beyond political and military allegiance altogether; they bravely undertake dangerous solitary journeys to save those they love through personal appeal to their queen. There is a third category: *Rob Roy, The Last of the Mohicans, War and Peace, Ninety-Three, La Débacle,* and *Les Dieux Ont Soif* all contain peripheral characters whose apolitical simplicity links them to literature's holy fools. Tolstoy's Platon Karataev is the essence of the type. Never able to move history, peripheral but memorable, such characters elicit the admiration, pity, and reluctant condescension of author and reader.

In their highest manifestations, these transcendent characters seem an unrealizable hope for the future. They move beyond and outside the warfare that, as Foucault argued, is the truest gauge of history. The loving and gracious Princess Mary Bolkonski, a precursor of Tolstoy's late-life Christian idealism, marries Nicholas Rostov, bringing forth the best qualities in Nicholas's limited self. Melville's Billy Budd, sacrificed to Captain Starry Vere's sense of revolutionary necessity, ascends the yardarm only to offer a final, possibly Christ-like blessing "God Bless Captain Vere!"[37] Sydney Carton, who cares nothing for the French republic or the English monarchy, goes to the guillotine to save the lives he loves. The genteel waverer, holy pragmatist, earthly pilgrim, and mortal pilgrim finally coalesce in the figure of Yurii Zhivago, whose late-life defeat, rather than victory, spells the possible end of a worthy tradition.

NOTES

1. Michel Foucault, "Society Must Be Defended" in *Ethics: Subjectivity and Truth,* ed. Paul Rabinow, translated by Robert Hurley (New York: New Press, 1994), pp. 59–65.

2. My thinking about the concept of honor is particularly indebted to the following: Peter Berger, "On the Obsolescence of the Concept of Honor" (1970) in *Revisions: Changing Perspectives in Moral Philosophy,* ed. S. Hauerwas and A. MacIntire (Notre Dame Ind: University of Notre Dame Press, 1983); James Bowman, *Honor: A History* (New York: Encounter Books, 2006); Paul Henderson Stewart, *Honor* (Chicago and London: University of Chicago Press, 1994); Michael Walzer, *Just*

and Unjust Wars: A Moral Argument With Historical Illustrations (New York: Basic Books, 1977); Alexander Welsh, *What is Honor: A Question of Moral Imperatives* (New Haven and London: Yale University Press, 2008).

3. Paul Henderson Stewart, *Honor* (Chicago and London: University of Chicago Press, 1994), p. 31.

4. Alexander Welsh, *What is Honor: A Question of Moral Imperatives* (New Haven and London: Yale University Press, 2008), p. ix.

5. Reluctantly raising a regiment of foot to fight for King Henry IV, Falstaff rationalizes away his cowardice with a comic parody of Christian catechism: "What is honor? A word. What is in that word honor? What is that Honor? Air. A trim reckoning! Who hath it? He that dies a Wednesday. Doth he feel it? No. Doth he hear it? No. 'Tis insensible then? Yes, to the dead. But will it not live with the living? No. Why? Detraction will not suffer it. Therefore I'll none of it. Honor is a mere scutcheon—and so ends my catechism." (*King Henry The Fourth, Part One*, vi, i, 133–139).

6. On the history of western warfare, see the following: Robert L. Holmes, *War and Morality* (Princeton: Princeton University Press, 1989); John Keegan and Richard Holmes, *Soldiers: A History of Men in Battle* (New York: Viking Press, 1986); John A. Lynn, *Battle: A History of Combat and Culture* (Boulder, CO: Westview Press, 2003); Larry May, Eric Rovie and Steve Viner, *The Morality of War: Classical and Contemporary Readings* (Upper Saddle River, NJ: Pearson Prentice-Hall, 2006); Michael Walzer, *Just and Unjust Wars: A Moral Argument With Historical Illustrations* (New York: Basic Books, 1977).

7. See "Linear Warfare: Images and Ideals in the Age of Enlightenment," chapter four of John A. Lynn's *Battle: A History of Combat and Culture*, pp. 111–144.

8. Michael Walzer observes that the definition of proper moral conduct during battle (*Jus in Bello*) has always been primarily a matter of agreed-upon convention, not of written military law: "The war convention must first be morally plausible to large numbers of men and women; it must correspond to our sense of what is right" (Walzer, *Just and Unjust Wars*, p. 133). The conventions that most directly affect a soldier's battle behavior are often unwritten.

9. Augustine, letter *Contra Faustum*, quoted in "St. Augustine on War" chapter four of Robert L. Holmes, *On War and Morality*, p. 128. Although Augustine argues that whenever there is "an unrighteous command on the part of the king, . . . the soldier is innocent because his position makes obedience a duty," we need to remember that for Augustine the term "innocent" refers only to the flawed standards of earthly justice (133).

10. Hugo Grotius, *On the Law of War and Peace* (1625) in Larry May, Eric Rovie, and Steve Winer, *The Morality of War*, pp. 71, 72, 75, 76. Grotius's opposition to the immoralities of war led him to contend that, if the cause of a war is unjust by Gospel standards, all acts that contribute to the prosecution of that war must also be unjust even if they are legal (76). None of the novelists under consideration in this book would support so absolute a proposition.

11. See John A. Lynn, *Battle: A History of Combat and Culture*, pp. 125–137. Vattel was a staunch advocate for what he regarded as the highest duties of humanity among nations. He criticized Grotius, whom he greatly respected, for establishing too permissive a standard for defining a just war.

12. Sir Walter Scott, *Waverley; or 'Tis Sixty Years Since*, ed, Andrew Hook (New York: Penguin, 1985), pp. 62, 65.

13. Stewart, *Honor*, p. 18.

14. "Aristocratic disdain for the enlisted ranks constituted a prejudice that legitimated the great privilege enjoyed by the nobility" (John A. Lynn, *Battle: A History of Combat and Culture*, p. 124). Lynn's word "disdain," however, applies more accurately to Fergus MacIvor's politic calculations than to Waverley's innate generosity of spirit. Harry Shaw argued perceptively that Scott is "at his best" when describing how "individual behavior shades over into social and cultural norms and practices seen as a specifically historical phenomenon" (Shaw, *The Forms of Historical Fiction*, p. 128). Waverley's admirable conduct at Preston Pans is a telling example of Shaw's generalization. James Bowman's *Honor: A History* claims that Scott was "The man who did the most to resuscitate honor for the modern era," then later claims that Scott had a "sentimental regard for democracy, tolerance and sincerity of heart" that led him to promote a "glittering, pseudo-chivalric ideal" (Bowman, *Honor; A History* [New York: Encounter Books, 2006], pp. 75, 80, 88). Since the late nineteenth century, cursory readers have been prone to misremember Scott, especially those who have relied on a youthful reading of *Ivanhoe*. There is nothing "sentimental," "democratic," "glittering," or "pseudo-chivalric" about Scott's treatment of honor in the Scottish novels.

15. James Fenimore Cooper, *The Last of the Mohicans*, ed. John McWilliams (Oxford and New York: Oxford University Press, 1994), p. 116.

16. The history of the defense, surrender, and massacre at Fort William Henry is carefully recounted in Ian K. Steele, *Betrayals: Fort William Henry and the 'Massacre'* (Oxford: Oxford University Press, 1990). See also John McWilliams, "The Historical Contexts of *The Last of the Mohicans*" in the Oxford University Press edition of *The Last of the Mohicans*, pp. 399–425.

17. See Stewart, *Honor*, pp. 46–54.

18. Carl Von Clausewitz, *On War*, translated and edited by Michael Howard and Peer Paret (Princeton, NJ: Princeton University Press, 1984), pp. 85, 100, 119.

19. Tolstoy, from a discarded chapter of Part One of *War and Peace*, quoted in Kathryn Feuer, "The Book that Became *War and Peace*," *The Reporter*, 1959, pp. 33–36 reprinted in *War and Peace*, the Maude translation, ed. George Gibian (New York: Norton Critical Editions, 1996), second edition, p. 1146.

20. While immersed in *War and Peace*, Tolstoy wrote "The aim of an artist is not to solve a problem irrefutably, but to make people love life in all its countless, inexhaustible manifestations. If I were told that I could write a novel whereby I might irrefutably establish what seemed to me the correct view on all social problems, I would not even devote two hours to such a novel" (letter to P.D. Boborykin, July 1865 quoted in A.N. Wilson, *Tolstoy* [New York: W.W. Norton, 1988], pp. 267–268).

21. Graham Robb, *Victor Hugo* (New York: W.W. Norton, 1997), p. 465.

22. Victor Hugo, *Ninety-Three (Quatrevingt-Treize)*, translated by Frank Lee Benedict, Introduction by Graham Robb (New York: Carroll & Graf, 1988), p. 179.

23. On the fall of the Bastille as the historical prototype for castle sieges in nineteenth-century fiction, see "History on the Walls," chapter four of Richard Maxwell's *The Historical Novel in Europe*, pp. 171–229. Maxwell does not consider *1793*,

perhaps because the technology of the siege of La Tourgue seems so deliberately to antedate 1789.

24. The color symbolism in this passage suggests an intended reference and compliment to Stendhal's *The Red and the Black*. Hawthorne's "My Kinsman, Major Molineux" (1852), probably not known to Hugo, contains a striking description of the divided red/black face of a sinister leader of a tar-and-feathering procession in prerevolutionary Boston.

25. Hugo, *Ninety-Three*, pp. 220, 227, 232.

26. Hugo, *Ninety-Three*, p. 390. The translator has taken liberties with the French original. The opening clause of Hugo's sentence is "Et ces deux ames, soeurs tragiques, s'envolerent ensemble." It is femininity of soul that ultimately transforms Cimourdain and Gauvin into "tragic sisters," not merely the fact of their shared death.

27. Henry James, "Hugo's *Ninety-Three*," (*The Nation*, April 9, 1874) in *Literary Reviews and Essays By Henry James* ed. Albert Mordell (New York: Twayne Publishers, 1957), pp. 138–144.

28. Jean Cocteau, quoted in Victor Brombert, *Victor Hugo and the Visionary Novel* (Cambridge, MA: Harvard University Press, 1984), p. 4.

29. Hugo did extensive research in order to make the novel's historical details, especially the many names of individuals and places, historically accurate. See Judith Wulf's "Le Role de la Fiction" in the "Présentation" for Hugo's *Quatrevingt-treize* (Paris: GF Flammarion, 2002), pp. 18–25.

30. Michael Walzer, *Just and Unjust Wars: A Moral Argument with Historical Illustrations* (New York: Basic Books, 1977), pp. 34, 35.

31. Emile Zola, *The Downfall (La Débacle)*, translated by E.P. Robbins (New York: Mondial, 2008), pp. 87, 88.

32. Few historical figures have endured such relentless disparagement by diverse important writers as Emperor Louis Napoleon. Thiers, Hugo, Marx, Flaubert, and Zola all at various times denounced him. Even if their condemnations are just, Louis Napoleon served as a vehicle into which writers could project the most glittering, manipulative, and demeaning forces of the era.

33. Quoted in Frederick Brown, *Zola: A Life* (New York: Farrar, Straus, Giroux, 1995). p. 219. Commenting on the historicism of his novel, Zola was later to write "*La Debacle* is a document on the *psychology* of France in 1870" (xxx, italics mine).

34. Karl Marx, "Address. . . . on the Civil War in France," delivered May 30, 1871 in Karl Marx, *The Civil War in France*, introduction by Frederick Engels (New York: International Publications, 1940), pp. 48, 65, 80–81.

35. Rupert Christiansen observes that the legislature of the Paris Commune elected in March 1871 consisted of twenty-five Jacobins, twenty Proudhon Socialists, nineteen Members of the National Guard, nine Blanc-quistes, and two Marxists. Many of the legislators were professionals or artisans, some were politicians, but very few were from the working class. There were no industrialists and no nobility among them (*Paris Babylon: The Story of the Paris Commune* [New York: Viking, 1995], pp. 295–305).

36. Boris Pasternak, *Doctor Zhivago*, translation by Max Hayward and Manya Harari, introduction by John Bayley (New York: Random House, 1986), p. 332.

37. Herman Melville, *Billy Budd, Sailor (An Inside Narrative)*, edited by Harrison Hayford and Merton M. Sealts, Jr. (Chicago: University of Chicago Press, 1962), p. 123.

Chapter 6

Men under Trial

Revolutionary Justice

Cesare Beccaria concluded *On Crimes and Punishments* (1764) with words of long-remembered, often-quoted hope: "In order that punishment should not be an act of violence committed by one or many against a private citizen, it is essential that it be public, prompt, necessary, the minimum possible in the given circumstances, proportionate to the crimes, and established by the law."[1] Two centuries later, writing in the aftermath of the Algerian war and World War II, Albert Camus reflected on the continuation of guillotine justice in words that imply a blunt reply to Beccaria: "The age of enlightenment, as people say, wanted to suppress the death penalty on the pretext that man was naturally good. Of course, he is not."[2]

Albert Camus was as unyieldingly opposed to the death penalty as Marquis Beccaria, but times had changed. Beccaria anticipated a reformed criminal justice system based upon strict enforcement of minimally punitive laws that would better society by deterring crime. Camus had no faith that the criminal system was a deterrent nor that material progress could reform it. Instead he denounced the atrocity of the death penalty in a modernist world in which nothing was certain, neither the guilt of the accused, nor the infallibility of the court. And yet, there is continuity between their two eras as well as change. The uncertainty of justice during the Enlightenment was neither less nor more than the uncertainty of justice in the modernist world. The nineteenth-century historical novel mediates between them, looking backward at 1688, 1776, or 1789 in order to provide a context for the novelist's own era and beyond.

Among the historical novels we are considering, four describe the workings of a military inquiry or a tribunal; three others describe civil or military trials that lead to the guillotine. In all seven novels, the male protagonist faces the death penalty, either for high treason (treason against the king), for mutiny, for spying, or for espionage linked to expatriation. His trial in civil or military court, rather than his participation in battle, is often the climax of the narrative. Amid the shifting fault lines between the dying *Ancien Regime* and the unborn progressive republic, the fictive trials reflect the authors' troubled search for revolutionary justice in a world where timeless standards no longer can be presumed to exist.

The judicial situation in all novels is far more complex than what the Coleridgean opposition of the Old and the New would suggest. Trials take place at a time when it is uncertain whether a people are in the middle of a revolution, a counterrevolution, a civil war, or a transient rebellion. The military need to put down any form of rebellion conflicts with Enlightenment hope that an emerging world of reason and commerce would further the rise of peaceful republics. In the midst of armed conflict, however, the Articles of War, dating from the Cromwellian and Scottish wars, remain very much in effect, Beccaria notwithstanding. Whether passed by authority of Charles I, James II, George I, or the Continental Congress, the Articles of War distinguish between honorable codes of warfare due to a declared enemy, and swift retaliation imposed upon a rebel. An enemy officer condemned to death merits the honor of being shot, but a common spy is to be disgraced by public hanging.

The conditions of civil war further complicate these contrasts. Is your neighbor who is in arms against you a rebel to whom no quarter need be given, or an enemy entitled to soldier's rights in a declared war, or a misguided fellow countryman who deserves more humane treatment than the Articles of War permits? What kind of intelligence gathering, under what circumstances, could require you to condemn your rebellious countryman as a spy deserving death? The French Revolution complicates the canons of punishment even further. The guillotine, intended to make the death penalty more humane, becomes the terrifying symbol of random public injustice. If revolution justifies the eliminating of aristocracy, men of differing social classes no longer merit equal treatment under law. Is an aristocrat retaining title and political privilege now to be treated as a betrayer of the newly discovered rights of man or as an honest believer in traditional distinctions?

In all seven novels, the threat of warfare in the neutral ground creates growing urgency to reach surety of judgment. Circumstantial evidence is likely to be accorded determinative weight, while a claim to ignorance of circumstance is mistrusted. Innocence of intent, impossible to prove, is either ruled out of evidence, or set aside as a reason for mitigating a guilty sentence. A judge like Melville's Captain Vere, who considers intent as well as deed, who acknowledges the existence of judgmental standards beyond and above revolutionary times, is rare indeed. Yet the judges in these novels are not hardened autocrats, nor are the accused pitiable victims. Even the judges presiding over the Terror of '93 are swept up by forces that do not emanate from their reason or their will. The complexity of revolutionary conflict is mirrored in the criminal trial of the single individual; clarification of often irresolvable issues of judgment becomes the historical novelist's most plausible goal.[3]

Why, however, do the narratives of canonical historical novels about revolution so often culminate in a court trial? The conditions of the neutral ground demand it, of course, but there are deeper reasons. Enlightenment thinking seeks to advance the natural rights of the individual while evolving a united polity that would further republican progress. But the murderous confusion of revolutionary times aggravates the need to specify how justice could possibly serve individual liberty and social order simultaneously. Scott approached the question within a legal, historical framework, Cooper within a military context, Dickens within a code of humanitarian morality, and Anatole France within the psychological context of the Terror. By century's end, the irresolvability of the simultaneous demand for liberty and order would lead Melville to surround Billy Budd's Drumhead court trial with the broadest possible spectrum of historical, political, and metaphysical considerations, from Plato to Calvin, from Burke to Paine, and from the Fall of Man (*Genesis* 2–3), to Christ's crucifixion (*Luke* 23). The unfinished state of Melville's text is the fitting counterpart to its unresolved, perhaps unresolvable, complexities.

HIGH TREASON?

What degree of collusion with armed forces committed to overthrowing the government qualifies as high treason? Shortly after Edward Waverley is cashiered as the captain of Gardiner's English regiment, he writes an indignant letter of resignation, and then sets off from the MacIvor estate at Glennaquoich toward Edinburgh, hoping to clear his name of intent to mutiny, so that he can then join the newly gathered Jacobite army with a clear conscience. Travelling through the border village of Cairnvreckan, a village bitterly divided between Jacobites and Hanoverians, he accidentally shoots the town's staunchly Whig blacksmith, and is brought before the local laird and justice of the peace, Major Melville, who must decide whether to indict Waverley for trial before the Supreme Criminal Court of Scotland.

Major Melville summarizes the military and civil charges against Waverley in legal detail:

> "The charge, Mr. Waverley, I grieve to say, is of a very high nature, and affects your character both as a soldier and a subject. In the former capacity, you are charged with spreading mutiny and rebellion among the men you commanded,

and setting them the example of desertion, by prolonging your own absence from the regiment, contrary to the express orders of your commanding officer. The civil crime of which you stand accused is that of high treason and levying war against the king, the highest delinquency of which a subject can be guilty."[4]

Waverley has never intended to spread mutiny, nor desert his troops, nor disobey Gardiner, nor commit high treason. Nonetheless, he has thoughtlessly committed acts that have brought about precisely those results. If the Jacobites are the recognized enemies of the English army, then, according to the Articles of War, Waverley deserves cashiering and death many times over: "If an Officer shall without leave be absent from his Quarters. . . . longer than a week, he shall be discharged from his Command and Place, as a man unfit to bear Office in the Army"; "Whosoever shall be found to have any intercourse with the Enemy without permission from the General, shall die as a Traitor"; "Whosoever concealeth any mutinous Speeches, shall die"; "Whoever is enrolled, if he go away without licence from the Army, Garrison or Camp, or shall attempt to go over to the Enemy, shall die."[5] Such swift, sure punishments were designed to maintain rank honor ("unfit to bear Office") and to strengthen the allegiance through which high treason could be enforced.

Major Melville then recounts, accurately and sequentially, the circumstances leading to the warrant for Waverley's arrest: Waverley's unexplained absence without leave in the Highlands, the suborning and desertion of Waverley's troops in Dundee, Waverley's failure to answer Colonel Gardiner's letters of inquiry, Waverley's sojourn at the MacIvor estate, and Waverley's presence at a gathering of Jacobite forces planning sedition and armed resistance. Waverley's acquiescence attests to the helplessness of confused feelings: "This was too much. Beset and pressed on every hand by accusations, in which gross falsehoods were blended with such circumstances of truth as could not fail to procure them credit—alone, unfriended, and in a strange land, Waverley almost gave up his life and honour for lost, and leaning his head upon his hand, resolutely refused to answer any further accusations" (248).

Waverley cannot grasp the complexity of the situation. Scottish Jacobites are supposedly rebelling against English Hanoverians, but he is now being apprehended by a *Scottish* major, retired from the *English* army, who, as a justice of the peace, is remanding him for trial to the Supreme Criminal Court of *Scotland*. Such are the paradoxical crosscurrents of the revolutionary situation within the nominally United Kingdom. Major Melville, Waverley discovers, fully understands these paradoxes. A scrupulous Lowland Scot, loyal to the terms of the 1707 Act of Union and the Act of Hanoverian Settlement, Major Melville is treating Waverley not as a recent adherent of the *de jure* Stuart king, but as an officer who has deserted the army of the de facto Hanoverian king. Unlike Major Melville, who assesses the facts of the present situation, Waverley has acted as if he were outside of time, assuming he could leave his troops, consort with the enemy, and then resign his commission, all without personal consequence. Waverley's inability to defend himself demonstrates that conditions of counterrevolution and civil war will drive able, well-meaning youth into helpless indecision.

Scott will not allow Major Melville to have the unquestioned last word. He introduces a Reverend Morton to engage Major Melville in a balanced debate about Waverley's guilt. While admitting that Waverley performed acts legally and militarily defined as criminal, Morton argues for leniency, if not release, on the bases of Waverley's innocence of intent, the quality of mercy, and the presumed goodness of the human heart. Scott, himself a lawyer, does not attempt to resolve the differences between the two viewpoints. The moral issues of Waverley's alleged "high treason" remain as many-sided as the jurisdictional issues. Passing appropriate sentence must therefore proceed from a prior choice of judicial perspective.[6]

How justice should be accorded to Henry Morton of *Old Mortality* proves no easier to determine. Virtually abducted into the Covenanter army, Morton fights bravely and effectively in both the Covenanter victory at Drumclog and the Covenanter defeat at Bothwell Bridge. As a gentleman of honor, Henry Morton has, like Waverley before him, saved the life of a royalist officer, Lord Evandale, and has protected the lives of the royalist Bellenden family. Captured as an enemy in arms by royalist commander John Grahame of Claverhouse, Morton is forced to view the decapitated heads of Covenanters while the royalists ride triumphantly into Edinburgh. "In a bewildered and stupefied state," Morton is brought by Claverhouse before the Scottish Privy Council to be tried, as Waverley had been, for high treason, for "the said Henry Morton's accession to the late rebellion . . . under penalty of life and limb."[7]

The Scottish Privy Council functions very like the Tudor/Stuart Court of the Star Chamber. It is both a military court and a civilian court. Vested with "great judicial powers, as well as the general superintendence of the executive department," the Scottish Privy Council of 1679 would have granted no merit to Montesquieu's separation of powers even if the principle had been known to them (365). Combining military, civilian, and ecclesiastical powers, it seeks to enforce what it believes to be in the Scottish and/or monarchical interest at the particular moment. Its presiding judge and defining spirit is the venal and repellent bully John Maitland, Duke of Lauderdale.

Before Morton is tried, Scott describes the judgments brought by the court against two individuals who cannot hope for leniency based upon social class. Morton's mentally limited servant Cuddie is freed because, although he has served with the Covenanters, he is of no political or military consequence. Reverend MacBriar, an extreme Covenanter who had harangued the rebels with Old Testament demands to obliterate the Ungodly, is tortured inside the Council Chamber, before the eyes of the court, in hopes he can be made to reveal the whereabouts of Balfour of Burley. Although "the boot" is applied to MacBriar five times, bringing forth screams of agony, MacBriar refuses to inform on Burley, and dies a brave death denouncing the cruelty of the court without a trace of mad biblical rhetoric.

The culminating irony of Scott's historical verisimilitude is that Henry Morton is never tried at all. Before Cuddie and MacBriar are examined, Claverhouse and Evandale, both of them noblemen, have put up bail to make certain that, upon his release, Henry Morton "should go abroad and remain in foreign parts, until his Majesty's pleasure should be better known" (365). A private agreement, privileging gentlemanly honor (or is it merely birth?) above military allegiance, has evidently been arranged before the trial commences. Unlike MacBriar, Cuddie, or the many Covenanters whose heads now rest on the pikes, Henry Morton had been one of the Covenanters' military commanders at Bothwell Bridge. Claverhouse's influence clearly trumps military fact. It apparently does not matter, in Morton's case, that the conventions of *The Articles of War*, specifically designed for use by "the Government of his Majesties' Forces Within the Kingdom of Scotland," stipulate that no quarter shall be given to rebels.

Henry Morton meekly accepts "the King's mercy," replying to Judge Lauderdale's offer, perhaps inaccurately, "I have no other choice, my lord" (366). Reverend MacBriar, about to be tortured, calls out before the Council that Morton has proven himself "A fallen star! A fallen star . . . by owning the carnal power of the tyrant" (366). The narrator passes no judgment either on Morton's acquiescence or on MacBriar's condemnation of him. Henry Morton will live the next ten years in the Netherlands as an appointee of William of Orange, returning to the Lowlands after the 1688 Revolution to marry Edith Bellenden and assume the apolitical life of a Whiggish Presbyterian gentleman whose strongest belief is in religious tolerance. Because of Claverhouse's influence, Henry Morton has received a full measure of mercy from the corrupt Scottish Privy Council. Reverend MacBriar, hanged and decapitated after being tortured, received no mercy at all. Whether either of them can be said to have committed high treason or to have received "justice," Scott once again will not presume to say. In a revolutionary context, retaliatory "justice" seems to Scott to have no satisfactory definition. There is no known scale according to which punishment could be made commensurate to the crime—as Beccaria had demanded. There are only individual cases that fallible men decide according to circumstances and their own predilections. Such restrained silence is, arguably, the height of realism.

TO HANG A SPY

According to codes of eighteenth-century warfare, a man in uniform serving behind enemy lines in order to learn enemy positions was an honorable spy; he was an army scout fulfilling his official duty. But a civilian or military man out of uniform behind enemy lines, especially if paid, was regarded as a "common spy," a vulgar blackguard secretly carrying out a dishonorable necessity.[8] To scout out enemy secrets and to successfully return to reveal them was thought courageous and admirable (Odysseus' night raid in the tenth *Iliad*) but a disguised commoner caught in an act of betrayal deserved death by public hanging. A gentleman spy, however, crossed over these overly neat distinctions in troubling ways. No gentleman should himself be a spy, but if he were, his status as an officer was thought by many to entitle him to the honor-saving dignity of being shot by a firing squad. Under such circumstances, it was thought best not to inquire too carefully into the role that commanding officers on both sides had played in the hiring and/or directing of spies, be they gentlemen or commoners. In this regard, an expeditious spy trial could be of great political service.

In September 1780 British major John André, the gracious gentlemanly Adjutant General of Sir Henry Clinton's army in New York, was caught behind American lines carrying plans for the fort at West Point, plans procured from American general Benedict Arnold, who was immediately branded as a traitor to the Patriots' revolution. After André's trial and conviction by court-martial, General George Washington sentenced André to be publicly hanged as a spy. The sentence disclosed a compromising divide in American values. Executing André as a spy may have been a military necessity, but was it not carried out in a manner degrading not only to André, but also to his executioners? Unlike Arnold, André was no turncoat; he was serving his king. André had confessed to espionage immediately upon detection. Most importantly, André's shame and mortification upon learning he was to be hanged, not shot, was commonly known. Nearly a decade before David Ramsay was to write at length of the Arnold-André conspiracy in his *History of the American Revolution* (1789), the betrayal of Arnold and the execution of André had become one of the historical moments by which, in memoirs, essays, poems, songs, and plays, the significance of the American Revolution was popularly defined.

More than the end of John André's life was therefore at stake. For decades, sensitivity to British slights that Americans were boorish provincials would compel post-revolutionary Americans to remember the republic's forefathers as enlightened honorable gentlemen, committed to public service, in no way inferior to their British counterparts. George Washington, father of his nation, served as the revered figurehead of this fusion of republican politics with gentlemanly honor. Could it be admitted, then, that General Washington might have sentenced André dishonorably? When Fenimore Cooper, son of a Federalist Congressman, determined to write a self-consciously American historical novel to be titled *The Spy*, he wrote from within this filiopietistic perspective, not only because his readership would expect him to do so, but because he himself believed in it.

The fate of John André is discussed or debated no less than thirteen times in *The Spy*. In recounting history, Cooper sought to scrupulously adhere to known fact, while remaining skeptical of current accounts pitying André as a gentlemanly victim who had honorably taken the fall for Benedict Arnold. Within the novel, André was to serve as the historical example against which the alleged spying of fictional characters, Harvey Birch and Edward Wharton in particular, could be judged. How would the recent hanging of André affect the judgment passed by an American military court-martial upon Captain Henry Wharton during his trial as a British spy? How would the notoriety of André affect the reader's response to Harvey Birch as the spy of the novel's title? If spying is dishonorable, might not the father of his country also have been tainted? Was George Washington not a spy when, in the novel's opening chapters, he passes below American military lines in disguise to visit the Wharton household as "Mr. Harper?"

Detailed historical facts are needed here.[9] As an officer, Major André was required, whenever he was behind enemy lines, to carry an enemy pass, to be in uniform, and to carry a white flag. Although André was carrying a pass from Benedict Arnold, he travelled under an assumed name with his uniform hidden under a greatcoat. When apprehended by three unknown civilians, André claimed to be, first a British officer, then an American patriot, all the while carrying the hidden military plans given him by Benedict Arnold, using a false name, and remaining in disguise. What existing statutes were applicable to André? The *Articles of War* passed by the Continental Congress in 1775, like the British *Articles of War*, required the appointment of thirteen officers to a board of court-martial or a tribunal, including a judge advocate. To try André, George Washington appointed no less than fourteen officers, including Judge Advocate General John Laurence. No calling of witnesses for the defense was needed because André had admitted to all charges of spying in his prepared statement. The fourteen officers were required by the Articles of War to submit a report with a recommended verdict. Their unanimous recommendation was that André be *executed* as a spy. Two historical conclusions are inescapable: if George Washington had passed any sentence other than death he would have violated the Articles of War and military convention; he would also have given encouragement to a still powerful enemy.

After André's conviction, the remaining question was the mode of his execution. André pleaded in a letter to the court to be shot as a gentleman and an officer, a plea with which American officers Nathanael Greene, Alexander Hamilton, and Benjamin Tallmadge all agreed. Because of a countervailing regard for, in David Ramsay's words, "public safety" and "the contagious nature of treachery," George Washington chose to follow centuries of military custom.[10] John André was hanged from the gibbet within sight of General Washington's farmhouse. Baron von Steuben, a member of the board of court-martial, could not imagine any other proper outcome: "André was a spy and in the army was any other death than by gibbet awarded to a spy?"[11] Old ways of capital punishment were not yet giving way to new, Beccaria notwithstanding. Gentleman or not, honorable or not, André was a spy and, as such, was to be hanged. Practical considerations—perhaps those Ramsay was to specify—took precedence over both rank honor and enlightened reservations about capital punishment.

The Spy opens in the late fall of 1780, a scant month after André had been hanged. In the minds of the entire Wharton family, as well as the American military, John André remains a ghastly historical presence. "On the subject of the death of André," says Captain Henry Wharton, "we are all of us uncommonly sensitive" (48). The execution of André reveals fault lines between political belief and social class, old loyalty and new promise, the appearance of honor and irreducible military fact. As a British Captain, Henry Wharton wishes to believe that André represents "all that was brave, that was accomplished, that was estimable" yet Henry is troubled that neither his sister Frances, nor his friend, Major Peyton Dunwoodie of the Continental army, shares his generous appraisal.

There is no consensus of judgment among Cooper's major characters. Henry's sister Frances is determined not to allow her commitment to American independence, and her belief in the integrity of George Washington, to be overswayed by family admiration for British gentility. Their father Colonel Wharton, a closet loyalist trying through feigned neutrality to preserve property and family, regards André as an example of the imminent danger of false appearances. The leader of the Skinners believes André was nothing more than a highborn fool to have revealed himself as a British officer to his three captors. British colonel Wellmere, who assumes that pretending to royalist loyalty is his path to prominence, regards the captors and judges of André as vulgar provincials hungry for an aristocratic victim. And Harvey Birch, secretly committed to counter-spying for the Patriots, lives in terror that the fate of genteel spy John André will soon await him also, especially because he is a mere lowborn peddler. For all these characters, André serves as the mirror of their own values and situation. Outside the courtroom, justice is clearly in the eye of the beholder.

In his last preface to *The Spy*, Cooper insisted that he had chosen "patriotism for his theme" (6). After Henry Wharton is arrested by Major Dunwoodie and remanded to Washington's headquarters for trial as a spy, this claim is put to the test. The recent memory of Major André literally hangs over the trial of Captain Henry Wharton. Although Harvey Birch exemplifies the highest form of patriotism any American could attain, true patriotism as well as honor also depends upon just treatment of the enemy. Dunwoodie quite properly refuses Henry Wharton's parole because Wharton is being arrested as a spy not as an officer-prisoner of war (71).

The judge presiding over Wharton's court-martial, Colonel Singleton, pronounces a charge that is in strict accord with the facts of Wharton's arrest:

> "It is an accusation against you, that being an officer of the enemy, you passed the pickets of the American army at the White Plains, in disguise, on the 29th of October last, whereby you are suspected of views hostile to the interest of America, and have subjected yourself to the punishment of a spy." (301)

Singleton's charge omits one undisputed, doubly incriminating fact; as a British captain, Henry Wharton was carrying a forged pass from General George Washington. The circumstantial evidence against Henry Wharton is almost identical to the evidence against Major John André with the crucial exception that there is no proof to show that Wharton had acquired, or had sought to acquire, any American military secrets. By passing the line of pickets, Wharton like Washington has committed the acts of a spy without the purpose of spying.

All members of the Wharton household, as well as the reader, know that Captain Wharton had travelled to the Wharton estate in the middle of the neutral ground in order to see his family. He had put love of family over divided family politics. The judges at Wharton's court-martial, however, can verify no facts about the British captain's motivation. If the court were to free Wharton even though his innocence of intent remains unproven, the court would cast even more retrospective doubt on the controversial hanging of André. If Captain Wharton is now to be freed, should not Major André have deserved more leniency than to be hanged?

The trial's proceedings follow a convincing sequence of rationalizations. One of the judges, perhaps anxious to display the court's republican credentials, announces that "although we are a court of martial law, yet, in this respect, we own the principles of all free governments" (301). The court soon reverts, however, to an evidentiary principle severe even within martial law, warning Captain Wharton that "the labour of proving your innocence rests with yourself" (304). The court knows that Wharton can never prove his innocence of intent. Presiding Judge Singleton, a "benevolent" elderly man who has long known the Wharton family, nearly breaks into tears because he knows that his associate judges will judge Captain Wharton with "dispassionate integrity" on the sole basis of provable circumstances (311). A deeper, darker motive for conviction is voiced at the trial's outset by one of the associate judges: because Westchester County is "a neutral ground . . . unauthorized by law . . . wherever an army goes, it carries its rights along, and the first is the ability to protect itself" (302). Lawless conditions would seem to justify any and all measures of military self-protection.

The court remains sufficiently uneasy about pronouncing a guilty verdict that it grants great weight to extraneous circumstantial evidence prejudicial against Captain Wharton. Frances testifies that, during her brother's visit to the family estate, Henry had communicated with only one person who was not a member of the Wharton family—Harvey Birch—from whom Henry had obtained his disguise. Because of Birch's notoriety as a British spy, Dunwoodie rightly exclaims that Henry Wharton is now wholly "lost." Even Colonel Singleton is sure that Harvey Birch is an "artful, delusive, and penetrating" British spy who "would have saved André" (307, 308). "According to the laws of war," Wharton is unanimously condemned and sentenced to be hanged as a spy; the ironies of misjudgment compound. Harvey Birch is in fact not a British spy, but an American spy acting as a double agent. An American court-martial is condemning a British captain to be hanged as a British spy even though he is secretly associated with the most selfless of American patriots. George Washington's presence at the Wharton estate on the same day of presumed spying is conveniently overlooked. A major purpose of Washington's visit had been to meet, incognito, with his spy Harvey Birch. If George Washington, in disguise and passing as Mr. Harper, had been apprehended by the British, could they not, by the same circumstantial reasoning, have sentenced George Washington to hanging as a spy?

The conclusion of Henry Wharton's trial remains troubling by any reckoning. As the commanding general of the American army, George Washington rejects Colonel Singleton's plea that Henry Wharton be pardoned, and publicly reaffirms the court's sentence to hang him. General Washington needs to make a clear display of firmness and legality.[12] But he is also honor bound by his pledge to Frances Wharton that he would protect Henry Wharton's life—with Harvey Birch's help. Evidently, the Patriot commander in chief and the gentleman who places honor above country are two separable selves within one skin, two opposed identities both of which Cooper believes to be admirable. Washington's necessary duplicity suggests that Cooper knew far more than he revealed about the extensive spy network General Washington had maintained in British-held New York City until shortly before the British evacuation.[13]

Washington's use of spies was the kind of fact that in the 1820s could neither be publicly admitted nor plausibly denied. In his novel, Cooper could intimate that Washington, through subordinates, had held quasi-military dealings with criminals like the Skinners, but insofar as spying might be suspected, Washington should be visualized employing only a loyal patriot-spy like Harvey Birch. Focusing on Harvey Birch, in turn, enabled Cooper to rise above judgment by social class in order to convey equalitarian feelings of merit. The image of honorable General Washington can be slightly tainted as long as Harvey Birch, the unkempt distrusted peddler, sacrifices his reputation, his family, and ultimately his life for his country. By refusing all payment, the lowest-born colonial becomes the highest revolutionary patriot. Harvey possesses inner honor in fullest measure because his entire outer honor has been lost in patriotic service. When Harvey is last seen during the Revolutionary War, he is covering his ears in terror at the sight of the Skinner leader twisting in the wind, his body hanging from the gibbet. The Cow-boys' hanging of the Skinner chieftain is entirely extralegal, whereas the hanging of André had been legal by statute if not by custom. To Harvey Birch, however, the outcome is the same; the gibbet does not discriminate.

Near the end of *The Captain's Daughter*, Piotr Grinyov, like Harvey Birch, is tried by court-martial to determine whether he has been a "spy" guilty of "Treason."[14] The "Commission of Inquiry into the Pugachev Uprising" proceeds with few if any scruples about use of evidence. Although Piotr had rescued Pugachev, accompanied his revolutionary army, admired his personable qualities, and been rescued by him, Piotr had never acted as a spy for Pugachev, never committed treason, and never considered himself to be anything but a gentleman officer in the Russian army. No allegation of espionage or treason had been raised against Piotr until the Commission of Inquiry begins its search for traitors. As a gentleman officer, Piotr assumes that honorable judges will discern the truth. At the beginning of the inquiry, Piotr muses "My conscience was clear; I was not afraid of the trial" (114).

Piotr should have been afraid. Like Waverley, Henry Morton, and Edward Wharton before him, Piotr confronts judges who, at a time when government seems to triumph, are unwilling to challenge cumulative circumstantial evidence that the waverer must have been guilty of rebellion and treason. Piotr's Commission of Inquiry meets in Kazan, where there is no one to vouch for him. Unlike the large, formal court-martial assembled to try Henry Wharton, Piotr's Commission of Inquiry consists of but three drearily ordinary men: an elderly general, a captain and a secretary who acts as clerk. Oral evidence that Piotr is a traitor is limited to the facts that Pugachev once saved Piotr's life and that the two men ate together and exchanged presents. Written evidence is equally substanceless. The General who had presided at the Russian war council, no model of courage himself, had written a vague letter implying Piotr's disloyalty during the siege of Orenburg. The Commission believes the slurs and accusations that Shrvabin, currently in shackles, has leveled against Piotr in order to gain his own release. Piotr can defend himself only by claiming the increasingly outdated standard of rank honor; he is, he insists, "an officer and a gentleman" who could not possibly pursue treason or spy against Russia (116). In the context of the vengeful aftermath of the rebellion, Piotr's continuing association with Pugachev is enough to condemn him. The Commission of Inquiry forwards a recommendation to St. Petersburg that Piotr be executed for treason as a spy; the recommendation is accepted, apparently without further inquiry.

As was true of Edward Waverley, Henry Morton, and Edward Wharton, extralegal intervention is again necessary to save the life of the waverer convicted on circumstantial evidence. After listening to Masha's plea that Piotr is innocent of all treasonable intent, Catherine the Great writes a letter that frees Piotr and declares his innocence. Justice flows from an Empress through an ill-educated country girl to Piotr, but also from woman to woman, apart from male influence, official or unofficial. The contrast between the judgment of the Commission of Inquiry and the judgment of Catherine the Great suggests that women, but not men, believe that, in times of widespread rebellion, allegiance is rarely clear and that acts of clemency should sometimes outweigh apparent disloyalty. Such acts of saving intervention are, however, clearly the exception not the rule. Even if laws of treason could be written to codify such subtlety, few judges would be likely to summon the acuity and the courage to follow them.

THE GREAT MUTINY: REGRET NOT REMORSE

For almost four decades after the beginning of the Melville revival in the 1920s, *Billy Budd Sailor (An Inside Narrative)*, long titled *Billy Budd Foretopman*, opened with the following paragraph of a two-paragraph "Preface":

> The year 1797, the year of this narrative, belongs to a period which, as every thinker now feels, involved a crisis for Christendom not exceeded in its undetermined momentousness at the time by any other era whereof there is record. The opening proposition made by the Spirit of that Age, involved the rectification of the Old World's hereditary wrongs. In France to some extent this was bloodily effected. But what then? Straightway the Revolution regency as righter of wrongs itself became a wrongdoer, one more oppressive than the Kings. Under Napoleon it enthroned upstart kings, and initiated that prolonged agony of Continental war whose final throes was at Waterloo. During those years not the wisest could have foreseen that the outcome of all would be what to some thinkers since [has turned] out to be a political advance along nearly the whole line for Europeans.[15]

When Harrison Hayford and Merton Sealts published their scrupulously edited and annotated edition in 1962, they had discovered that the authority to publish the two paragraphs long printed as Melville's "Preface" rested on a conjecture by Mrs. Elizabeth Melville (not Herman Melville), penciled at the top of three separate leaves of the manuscript, which read "Preface to Billy Budd?" Hayford and Sealts decided to reject the "Preface" on the supposition that it was no longer part of Melville's intended final version when he died. But can we be quite so sure of Melville's intent? Why Mrs. Melville's question mark? If these paragraphs were to be excised, why did Melville not then discard them? For what reason had he apparently determined to set them aside? Might he have revised and reincluded them had he lived to publish *Billy Budd* in a version that satisfied him? We have no definitive answer to any of these questions.

Regardless of the paragraph's inclusion or exclusion, it concisely expresses a three-stage view of the revolutionary era that follows the paradigm of a Hegelian synthesis. The wrongs of the *Ancien Regime* provoked demands that they be rectified, but reform led quickly to revolutionary bloodshed: the Terror, in turn, led to the "prolonged agony" of the Napoleonic era in which the oppressed became the oppressor; the outcome of the crisis was long to remain "undetermined" but, at least for "some thinkers," the cataclysm resulted in political progress, an "advance along nearly the whole line" of European nations. The cultural need to believe that revolutionary crisis must eventually end in progressive synthesis is endorsed but only with qualification; "political advance" remains questionable. Nothing in the paragraph contradicts the darkened view of the immediate post-revolutionary years, and of Napoleon Bonaparte, that Melville sustains throughout the novella itself.

The second paragraph of Melville's "Preface" reaffirms the same three-stage synthesis, now discerned in the history of the British navy:

> Now, as elsewhere hinted, it was something caught from the Revolutionary Spirit that at Spithead emboldened the man-of-war's men to rise against real abuses, long-standing ones, and afterwards at the Nore to make inordinate and aggressive demands, successful resistance to which was confirmed only when the ringleaders were hanged for an admonitory spectacle to the anchored fleet. Yet in a way analogous to the operation of the Revolution at large the Great Mutiny, tho' by Englishmen naturally deemed monstrous at the time, doubtless gave the first latent prompting to most important reforms in the British navy.[16]

Revolt against old abuses led to unjust executions, but the suppression of the "Revolutionary Spirit," now personified, led eventually to lasting reform. "Important reforms" but not revolutionary overturn emerged. Among nineteenth-century novelists, none would attempt a more judicious and comprehensive overview of the Age of Revolution in such little space.

The second paragraph of the Preface presents the mutinies at Spithead and the Nore both as the setting of the novella, and as historical proof of the three-stage progression. In the novel as now printed, however, there remain only scattered references to Spithead and the Nore, one of which asserts that "The Great Mutiny" at the Nore was "a demonstration more menacing to England than the contemporary manifestoes and conquering and proselyting armies of the French Directory."[17] But in the absence of the supposedly discarded "Preface," the significance of the mutinies at Spithead and the Nore ("more menacing" than Napoleon) is now too often and too readily neglected. Without an understanding of the "Great Mutiny," Melville's novella cannot be fully understood.

In 1797, the French Directorate was assembling a fleet at Brest preparatory to an invasion of England. The English fleet was gathering to repel the French fleet, primarily at Spithead (near Portsmouth) and the Nore (at the mouth of the Thames Estuary). To rebuild the navy, the English muster roles had grown from about 16,000 in 1792 to about 100,000 in 1797, forcing press gangs to impress (Billy Budd is impressed) almost any reasonably healthy Englishman, including debtors, thieves, jailbirds, and seditious Irishmen, from age eleven to age forty, in order to meet their quotas. Common seamen slept in hammocks below decks, "14 inches to a man," but there were "narks" (informers like Melville's Squeak) among them. Wages of common seamen had stagnated, food was sometimes inedible, and grog was diluted; seamen were not allowed shore leave because many would immediately desert. The *Articles of War* stipulated that twelve lashes was the maximum permissible in a flogging, but fifty or a hundred lashes were common. The sentence for mutiny was hanging, as it would be for Billy.

In April 1797 the British fleet was ordered to sea to confront the French, but the sailors collectively refused to set sail. On many ships, the union and cross of the British flag were torn away. Other ships ran up the Red Flag, an act Melville describes as "transmuting the flag of founded law and freedom defined into the enemy's red meteor of unbridled and unbounded revolt" (54). The seamen put hated officers on shore. Not knowing when the French fleet might appear, the Pitt government claimed that the mutiny was inspired by Jacobins reading Thomas Paine below decks. Sailors demanded higher wages, shore leave, and revision of the Articles of War.

During scuffles aboard the mutinous ships, seamen were killed and officers wounded. The mutiny at Spithead dissipated after the government agreed to higher wages and promised reforms. The larger fleet at the Nore was not so easily placated. Seamen blockaded all merchant ships bound to London. The government retaliated by blockading its own navy in order to starve out the mutineers, while increasing punishments and offering rewards for the ringleaders.[18] To convey the severity of the Great Mutiny, Melville's narrator remarks "To the British Empire the Nore Mutiny was what a strike in the fire brigade would be to London threatened by general arson" (54).

Probably during the same month Billy Budd was hanged, the crews of twenty-five ships participating in the Nore Rebellion were arraigned for mutiny. 560 men were imprisoned, 412 were tried, and 36 were hanged. Eventually, however, as Melville wrote, "important reforms in the British Navy" were enacted, in part because of the dire threat of recurrence. Between 1806 and 1879, pay was raised, impressments ceased, the Articles of War were revised, and flogging was abolished. But in "the summer of 1797," when Captain Vere believes he must make a decision regarding Billy Budd's killing of John Claggart Master at Arms, Vere was undeniably right to perceive prospective mutiny aboard the *Bellipotent* as a dire revolutionary crisis aggravated by the threat of French invasion (54). Three chapters before Vere is introduced, the narrator asserts "Reasonable discontent growing out of practical grievances in the fleet had been ignited into irrational combustion as by live cinders blown across the Channel from France in flames" (54). Such a claim is not merely part of the "historical background" of *Billy Budd*. It is an inflammatory yet historically accurate claim advanced by Melville as narrator, a claim that is consistent with Captain's Vere's political thought.

When Billy Budd, impressed into the *Bellipotent*, cries out "And goodbye to you too, old *Rights-of-Man*," the reader senses that Billy is being impressed from the hypothetical post-revolutionary future of Thomas Paine back into the real world of the present (49). Nearly a decade after the French Revolution, human governance still proceeds in accord with the Articles of War, not the Rights of Man, regrettable though that fact may be. The upheaval currently transpiring in France does not justify relaxation of naval order in the name of liberty. The narrator, not Captain Vere, denigrates Napoleon as "this French portentous upstart from the revolutionary chaos who seemed in act of fulfilling judgment prefigured in the Apocalypse."[19]

Captain Edward Fairfax "Starry" Vere embodies the best of the Old Order. His family name carries aristocratic seventeenth-century associations with the Civil Wars but also with the poetry of Andrew Marvell. Vere's pondering, bookish, even "pedantic" qualities are offset by his twice-mentioned "gallantry" (60, 61). In an often-quoted passage, Vere's belief in enforcing regulations is likened to "a migratory fowl that in its flight never heeds when it crosses a frontier" (63), but in a neglected, contradictory passage Vere is said to be "intrepid to the *verge* of temerity," not beyond it (60, italics mine). Vere's Burkean belief that all progress must be incremental, built upon past institutions, is entirely "disinterested" in the sense of being without self-interest. Like Burke, Vere has read enough of prerevolutionary progressive thinkers to have developed a plausible opinion of them: "While other members of that aristocracy to which by birth he belonged were incensed at the innovators mainly because their theories were inimical to the privileged classes, Captain Vere disinterestedly opposed then not alone because they seemed to him insusceptible of embodiment in lasting institutions, but at war with the peace of the world and the true welfare of mankind" (62–63). Vere's honesty signifies an inner sense of honor so firm that he does not need to think about it.

When considering Billy Budd's crime in the contexts of the French Revolution and the Great Mutiny, it is inevitable that a British ship's captain of Vere's convictions would honor his sworn allegiance to the king. As a commander, Vere must believe it is especially incumbent upon him to follow the Article of War that specifies "if any inferior Officer or Soldier . . . shall strike, or shall draw . . . against his Superior Officer, upon any pretence whatsoever, he shall suffer Death."[20] Moreover, Vere refers explicitly, not only to the Articles of War, but to the Mutiny Act of 1689, which had specified that soldiers who stir up sedition, as well as those who strike their superiors, shall be "brought to a more Exemplary and speedy Punishment than the usuall Forms of Law will allow."[21] The word "speedy" legally justifies Vere's calling of a Drumhead court. Vere understands the likely outcome of a verdict of innocence. If sailors were to perceive that a midshipman, after killing the Master at Arms, has been released because he was beloved as the handsome sailor, and was innocent of any intent to kill, what would be the practical consequence? In his closing words to the Drumhead court, Vere answers his own rhetorical question: "Will they [the sailors] not revert to the recent outbreak at the Nore? Ay. They know the well-founded alarm—the panic it struck throughout England" (112–113).

As Hayford's and Sealts's study of the successive revisions of the *Billy Budd* manuscript has shown, Melville's first extended draft expressed a degree of admiration for Vere that seems to sanction Vere's judgment that Billy must hang. In Melville's later revisions, however, he changed wording and introduced new material (the ship's surgeon) that cast doubt on Vere's judgment, even upon his sanity. Why should this shift have occurred? Surely because, as Herman Melville grew older, his writings reveal a steadily increasing awareness of multiple points of view and the difficulty of ever resolving them.[22] The ebullient, thirty-year-old Melville who had praised the Rights of Man and excoriated the Articles of War in *White Jacket*, then celebrated American Republicanism in "Hawthorne and His Mosses" as "the unshackled democratic Spirit of Christianity," was not the same author who, forty years later, wrote *Billy Budd*.[23] Nonetheless his early faith, not easily discarded, was still within him; the child, after all, is father of the man. Vere is therefore allowed to know he must make a decision that can be neither wholly right nor wholly wrong. To hold Billy in irons awaiting an admiralty court on shore, even if the details of naval law were clear as to its propriety, would have been, for Vere as well as for Melville, a cop-out.[24] On the other hand, even legality, necessity, and honor taken together cannot demonstrate that Vere's decision is morally right when judged either by democratic, Christian values or by Beccaria's Enlightenment perspective on criminal punishment.

It is altogether too easy to dwell on the manipulative way in which Captain Vere orders his argument to the Drumhead court that Billy must be convicted and hanged. Melville's remarkable achievement is to allow Vere himself to make the counterargument that Billy should be spared. It is Vere who questions "How can we adjudge to summary and shameful death a fellow creature innocent before God, and whom we feel to be so?" (119). It is Vere who draws attention to the crucial distinction between the prisoner's deed and the prisoner's intent, thereby compelling the members of the court to recognize that the "arbitrary" nature of a martial court, proceeding under the Articles of War, precludes consideration of motive (111). And it is Vere who, aware that human law is forever unjust when measured against divine law, declares that "at the Last Assizes" Billy shall be "acquitted" (111). Until Billy kills Claggart, as Thomas Scorza has shown, Vere remains unaware of the extent of Claggart's "Natural Depravity" and of the limitations of Billy "natural innocence" (his stutter).[25] After the killing, however, Vere understands—too late—the ironies that are impelling him toward his deadly decision. His words to the Drumhead court are more than rhetoric deployed for conviction; they acknowledge the limitations of his own Burkean values, even as he defends them.

None of the other officers seems ever to have thought of Vere's counterarguments. Billy cannot begin to understand them. The most the common sailors can muster in Billy's defense is a groundswell of protest, at the moment Billy is hanged, indicating their inchoate feeling that something is somehow wrong. The conflict within Herman Melville is therefore a conflict within Captain Vere, but within Vere only. Vere knows his decision is a military necessity, demanded by law, by historical circumstance, and by the honor of his rank and allegiance, yet Vere also believes his decision is morally unjust, even murderous, in natural and divine terms. This insoluble burden is his alone. The words Vere murmurs on his deathbed, "Billy Budd, Billy Budd," are therefore said to be "not the accents of remorse," but they clearly are the accents of deep sorrow.

Protagonists of earlier historical novels charged with treason or espionage—Edward Waverley, Henry Morton, Henry Wharton, Harvey Birch, Piotr Grinyov—escape military hanging, though barely. Minor characters and historical figures allied to losing causes—Fergus MacIvor, Evan Dhu, Reverend MacBriar, John André, Pugachev—are brutally hanged, their bodies often mutilated for the benefit of a public warning. Billy Budd is an exception to the pattern. Billy is, to be sure, publicly hanged as a spectacle of the need for order. In one way, Vere's immediate, effective command to the crew, "Pipe down the starboard watch" (126), demonstrates how, as Vere claims, "forms, measured forms are everything" (128). And yet, at Billy's death, measured forms disappear. Among previously published fictional descriptions of military execution, only Victor Hugo had written anything remotely like Melville's startling account of the transcendent final moment when Billy is hanged from the main yard: "the vapory fleece hanging low in the East was shot through with a soft glory as of the fleece of the Lamb of God seen in mystical vision"; "Billy ascended; and, ascending, took the full rose of the dawn" (124).

No St. John of Patmos, Herman Melville probably had never shared a believer's faith in the Resurrection, Transfiguration, Ascension, or Apotheosis of any human or quasi-supernatural being, including Jesus Christ and certainly including a handsome sailor. But the evanescence of "soft glory" does not read as chance accident or as delusion. It is a suggestive remnant of Melville's progressive hope, a last omen within a tale whose calculated ambiguities have no end.

To return to the initial question: why might Melville have decided to set aside but not discard his two-paragraph "Preface?" My belief is that Melville discovered that, the more he rewrote *Billy Budd*, the less sure was his confidence that the progressive third stage of his revolutionary paradigm had ever been, or would ever be, realized. He could easily have shown that the Great Mutiny eventually gave "latent prompting to most important reforms in the British Navy," but he declined in his novella's text to do so. His historical, biblical, and philosophic range of reference had already proposed much higher stakes than nineteenth-century naval reform.

More important, there is no sentence in *Billy Budd* that substantiates the claim of the first paragraph of the "Preface" that the revolutionary spirit, so evident in 1797, had in historical fact led to "a political advance along the whole line for Europeans." As *Billy Budd* nears its tragic end, the historical dimensions of the novella recede, replaced by a general sense that revolutionary idealism, Napoleonic vainglory, Nelson's honor, Benthamite utilitarianism, and Burkean neo-Conservatism are all, in differing ways, inadequate to meet life's insoluble complexities. It is a perspective to which particular evidence for "Progress" and "Political Advance" must seem insufficient, if not incidental. Nonetheless, it may have proven difficult for Melville to consign his three-stage paradigm to paper trash. He had written a deft summary of attitudes toward revolution that his late-nineteenth-century contemporaries had cherished, feared, or regretted, but could not entirely dismiss.

CIVIL JUSTICE, MILITARY JUSTICE

Popular culture, as expressed in film, literature, and newspapers, continues to assume that civil courts are far more likely to render justice than military courts. Courts-martial are presumed to proceed with maximum speed and efficiency toward guilty verdicts that will maintain subordination and exonerate military authority. The assumption is that the defense counsel and officers of lower rank fearfully defer to presiding superiors who seek a conviction that will hide military corruption. In a military trial, soldiers are presumed to have few reliable rights, and international terrorists to have none, because legal procedures will be bent to serve the interests of the hierarchy. The accused is assumed guilty until proven innocent. Civilian trials, on the other hand, are usually assumed to be protracted and open to public scrutiny, because equitable criminal procedures are being followed, the rights of the accused are being protected, and the often-heroic defense counsel has no motive not to pursue justice for his or her client. The accused is therefore assumed innocent until proven guilty.

If these popular assumptions are accurate, the contrast between military and civilian trials should be especially apparent during a revolution, when a military crisis is always, to some degree, occurring. Under revolutionary conditions, the pressures of warfare and the exigencies of politics would be likely to oversway strict construction of laws pertaining to individual rights. Logically, it would seem that a military court trying individuals for an act of treason would assume a predominately prosecutorial function whereas a civil court would assume a predominately defensive function, protecting individuals against wartime oppression.

Surprisingly, the historical novels under discussion do not illustrate the hypothetical contrasts of martial and civil courts advanced by popular culture. Instead, differences between the two kinds of courts recede as similar kinds of judicial compromise are disclosed. The approval we expect for the proceedings of a civil court procedure is sometimes powerfully reversed. The reversal cannot, however, ever be total. As we have seen, martial courts are often inclined toward verdicts of guilt based on circumstantial evidence and little concern for the intent of the accused. And yet, during revolutionary times, the spectacle of civil trial arouses equal apprehensions that law will be disregarded, procedures ignored, and verdicts determined by popular hysteria. Just as 1789 has long been the historical fulcrum for political revolution, so 1793 has been the fulcrum for Terror sure to follow. The remainder of this chapter will consider this supposition by examining the civil trials central to the narratives of two canonical novels set in 1793: Dickens's *A Tale of Two Cities* and France's *The Gods Are Thirsty*. Both novels associate the French Revolution with the rising power of mass public opinion based upon maddened revenge, *ressentiment*, and fearful conformity.

Dickens's Charles Darnay, wavering hero, former Marquis St. Evrémonde, now a language teacher in London, is the good-willed man in the middle, suspected by both sides. The reader must uneasily share Darnay's vantage point, because the reader experiences the revolution through his perspective. Darnay is judged no less than three times in civil courts, first in London and then twice in Paris. During all three trials, the sensation-hungry courtroom crowd expects conviction and eagerly awaits the thrill of execution. The charge in the first two trials carries the death penalty, yet Darnay is, to almost everyone's surprise, found innocent. His third trial proceeds without any stipulated charge, yet he is pronounced guilty. In all three trials, the determining force of the judicial outcome is neither the law, nor the presiding judge, nor the jury. It is rather the force of crowd opinion, swayed by one unexpected piece of irrelevant evidence into a fervor that overwhelms the reason of jury and spectators alike.

Darnay is first tried for treason at the Old Bailey in 1780, a moment when anti-French feeling in Great Britain runs high because of the recent French alliance with the American colonies during the Revolutionary War. In the suffocating courtroom, the crowd of human "blue-flies" maintains a "buzzing" that distracts court proceedings when it does not confound them.[26] As a French immigrant, Darnay is suspected of providing British military intelligence to the French enemy because he has been travelling to and fro Paris and London, supposedly carrying "lists" of military fortifications (like John André). Astute cross-questioning by Darnay's lawyers, Stryver and Sydney Carton, indicates that paid British spies are responsible for the "lists" and that Darnay's journeys (like Henry Wharton's) were undertaken for family purposes only.

Because Stryver's and Carton's defense arguments make little impression on the court, Carton shrewdly switches tactics, demonstrating that his physical similarity to Darnay is so exact that no one could possibly be sure of Darnay's identity aboard a packet ship during a night passage five years before. Carton's trick maneuver works perfectly. The crowd relishes Darnay's acquittal because it results from sudden, lawyerly magic. Darnay has rightly been found innocent, but for the wrong reason, and on sensational but shaky evidence. Such legal failings are of no matter to the sensation-hungry crowd. Dickens ends his chapter with a seeming aside: "the baffled blue-flies were dispersing in search of other carrion" (82).

In late 1792, at the onset of the Terror, Darnay returns to France in hopes of benefiting the peasants and trusted servants on the Evrémonde estate, which he has renounced but still legally owns. Dickens makes it clear that the law of September 1791 requiring the property confiscation and death of any émigré who will have returned to France after January 1792 (a law primarily directed at aristocrats) is now fully in effect. Apprehended at the barrier gates of Paris for violation of unspecified "new laws" and "new offences" (262), Darnay is imprisoned in solitary confinement in La Force, and eventually tried as a traitor along with nineteen others by a civic tribunal consisting of five judges, a jury, a public prosecutor—and no public defender. Fifteen of the accused are sentenced to death in ninety minutes, a rate of six minutes per trial and conviction.

Darnay's plea in self-defense is that he is not legally an emigrant because he left France before the evolution and before the new émigré law was passed. Moreover, he is now a middle class man; he has been supporting himself "by his own industry in England" (293). Although Darnay's self-defense, based on an ex post facto appeal, confuses the meaning of the words aristocrat and émigré, it is Darnay's only plausible legal defense because the new émigré law is based upon exactly the same confusion. Darnay is, in fact, as he well knows, a returned émigré aristocrat; logical enforcement of this crudely discriminatory "new law" requires his death. However, when Doctor Manette, revered as a victim of aristocratic oppression, speaks for the excellence and honor of Darnay's character, Manette immediately wins the hearts of the crowd. Suddenly regarded as a crown prince of liberty, Darnay is enthroned in a great chair, a red liberty cap is placed on his head, and he is marched triumphantly around the streets of Paris "in a wild, dreamlike procession" (296). Darnay's acquittal, touted as the humane release of a falsely accused man, is in fact a judicial error based upon extraneous evidence and the passions of the mob.

To recount procedural violations cannot adequately convey the insanity of Darnay's climactic third trial. Three French citizens, Monsieur and Madame Defarge and Dr. Manette, "denounce" Darnay, demanding he be retried (328). It is a trial only by the most superficial definition. The Defarges, bent on revenge, submit before the Tribunal Dr. Manette's long-withheld letter written in 1767 in the Bastille. The letter, read in court, ends with Dr. Manette's "denouncing" the Evrémonde family of aristocrats "to the last of their race" because of Manette's imprisonment without trial, the legal rape of Madame Defarge's sister, and the subsequent murder of her brother (344). Manette's popularity with the crowd, recently the cause of Darnay's being wrongly declared innocent, suddenly becomes the means by which Darnay is wrongly declared guilty.

The only charge ever alleged against Darnay/Evrémonde is that he is "one of a race proscribed" (328). It is of no moment that Darnay has been found innocent of the same vague charge a few days before. "Double Jeopardy" or "Autrefois Acquit" is not in effect in the republic's Revolutionary court system. Darnay is condemned to death, not for committing treason or transgressing a law, but because of a curse applied to the posterity of an entire family. It is as if the Aeschylean curse on the House of Atreus has become the principle of Enlightenment criminal justice. After Dr. Manette's letter has been read, only the presiding judge is allowed to speak. One by one, facing the roaring mob, the jurymen vote, unanimously of course, to send Darnay/Evrémonde to the guillotine. The only legal authority such procedures can have is that the Tribunal of the revolutionary republic is practicing them.

Secretive legal measures enabling aristocrats to violate human rights have been replaced by republican mob rule that violates those same human rights publically. Dickens is intent upon exposing the continuity of injustice, not its novelty:

> Before that unjust Tribunal, there was little or no order of procedure, ensuring to any accused person any reasonable hearing. There could have been no such Revolution, if all laws, forms and ceremonies had not first been so monstrously abused that the suicidal vengeance of the Revolution was to scatter them all to the winds. (327–328)

Revolution will not occur unless preceded by monstrous abuse of the law, but the "suicidal vengeance" of revolution is sure to be succeeded by legal abuse of a different but equally monstrous kind. Dr. Manette's denunciatory letter, like the Evrémonde *lettre de cachet*, is granted legal standing and fully credited according to the values of the new time. A Revolutionary Tribunal that prides itself on progressive judgment is ironically privileging the dead hand of the past.

The immediate context of revolution alters the nature of Dickens's customary mode of attacking legal injustice. The courtroom frenzy of 1793, fed by disregard for procedural order and rules of evidence, is utterly different from the silent delays and sly obfuscations by which, in *Bleak House, Jarndyce vs. Jarndyce* eats up the health and wealth of litigants and their families. More is at issue here than the differences between the legal fictions of an equity case in Chancery, and the melodrama of a criminal case in a public forum. The crowd in revolutionary Paris physically presses into the tribunal, commending Jacques III and the Vengeance for defying the presiding judge to ring the bell for order; Mr. Vholes and Mr. Tulkinghorn, by contrast, say nothing, keep files hidden, and stay out of court. In times of peace, stealth is the way to injustice; in times of revolution, self-righteous hysteria will suffice.[27]

Dickens devotes two chapters to the trial and retrial of Charles Darnay before the Paris Tribunal during the Terror. Almost half the chapters of Anatole France's *The Gods Will Have Blood* describe trial sessions before the Paris Tribunal. Anatole France is less concerned than Dickens with narrative suspense, but more concerned with historical detail and the psychology behind the "thirst for blood." As the cause of revolution, Dickens emphasizes economics of social class: the famine of the urban poor, the luxury of the urban aristocracy, and the feudal oppression of the rural peasantry.

Anatole France focuses on specifics of the historical situation: the desperate condition of Paris, threatened by Prussian and Austrian armies, by the Vendeé Rebellion, and by counterrevolutionary movements in Lyons, Marseilles, and Toulon. Dickens allows his compelling descriptions of courtroom crowds, vengeful jurors, and accommodating judges to convey the chaos resulting from absence of revolutionary procedure. Anatole France emphasizes how the Law of 22 Prairial (June 10, 1794) legitimized indiscriminate mass killing by devising new procedures: limiting the number of witnesses, denying the accused defense counsel, defining the accused as a "public enemy" and restricting the range of sentencing for conviction to death only.[28] Diverse paths toward the same injustices.

Integrating historical research with sensationalist fiction, Anatole France shows why the new numerically ordered systemization of justice cannot by itself cover up revolutionary chaos. The Paris Tribunal consists of four Sections, each composed of fifteen magistrates, selected to form a class-balanced cross section of male citizens from a particular quarter of Paris. An art student with no knowledge of law, Evariste Gamelin is pleased to discover that the other magistrates of his Section—a surgeon, a cobbler, a tradesman, a printer, a *ci-devant* Marquis who professes republicanism—are no more acquainted with the law than he. Court sessions are held in the four separate Sections as well as the Palais de Justice where the entire sixty-magistrate tribunal meets. Three judges are present at each session, and a jury is empanelled to determine guilt, but until mid-1794 citizen justice does not proceed according to stipulated procedures. Magistrates question the accused at will and then consecutively declare their opinions as to guilt. The jury votes (usually by acclamation) and the judges proceed to the death sentence. The Law of 22 Prairial, in Anatole France's view, simply made legal what had already become customary.

Five trials are recounted in detail; four of them try prominent fictional characters (Louise de Rochemaure, Brotteaux des Ilettes, Father Longuemare, Athenais the prostitute) who are questioned individually, then condemned simultaneously as one group. None is charged with violation of a specific law. Because Reason and Virtue are assumed to emerge through spontaneous citizen participation, the magistrates and judges voice their prejudices as the spirit moves them. We see army contractors suspected of embezzlement (found innocent), then two defeated generals (found guilty of being defeated), and then a widowed bread vendor of the streets who shouted "Vive Le Roi" (guillotined).

As 1793 turns to 1794, the Tribunal's judgments reach deeper into the apolitical crannies of society—suspected grain hoarders, merchants who cheat on weight, mendicants, prostitutes, anyone from Brittany—and the Law of 22 Prairial entraps them all. The four fictional characters, three of whom have been living together, are collectively charged with prostitution, patronizing prostitution, corresponding with foreigners, corresponding with aristocrats, and involvement in a prison conspiracy to free themselves. The magistrates of the Tribunal feel no need to distinguish among the four prisoners if all four are to be guillotined anyway. At novel's end, Anatole France describes the downfall of Robespierre, promptly followed by the guillotining, without even the pretense of a trial, of Robespierre's faithful follower, Evariste Gamelin.

Whenever Judge Gamelin cannot make sense of muddled testimony, he votes for guilt. To show clemency to the destitute would, he believes, display favoritism unworthy of the equality of all French citizens. Similarly, personal resentments are thought to validate political suspicions. Gamelin's dislike for Maubel, whom he wrongly believes to be Elodie's lover, leads him to accuse Maubel of being an agent and spy of William Pitt. Disliking his sister Julie's lover Chassagne because he behaves like an aristocrat, Gamelin argues for the death sentence because Chassagne is a returned émigré. As a public speaker, Gamelin discovers that he achieves eloquence only when he contrasts the guilt of the accused to the purity of the republic. Such predilections lead Gamelin to join the many magistrates who, because they "could not be approached by argument, only by appeals to their hearts, . . . always voted guilty" (135).

During the revolution, the ordinary citizen's view of emerging republican politics would seem to be based on the appeal of simple, binary thinking. Anatole France pictures Gamelin visiting the Jacobin Club in November of 1793 when Robespierre is at the height of his influence. Robespierre's "cold self-possession" and "eloquent, logical attack upon the enemies of the Republic" thrill Gamelin's heart in the same way Elodie's sexuality thrills his body. What Robespierre provides for Gamelin is "a philosophy, a metaphysic of revolution":

> Robespierre simplified everything for him, revealing the good and the evil to him in simple, clear terms. Either Federalism or Centralization: Centralization meant unity and safety; Federalism meant chaos and damnation. Gamelin tasted the mystical joy of a believer who has come to know the word that saves. (148–149)

What Gamelin proudly advances as a "metaphysic of revolution" is only the deadly fact that the forced choices of revolutionary times (Federalism *or* Centralization) allow one's judgments always to seem simple, clear, and true. To spread guilt is to promote unity, thereby advancing centralization. To judge according to the "involved and confused" evidence, however, is to weaken the system by promoting division within the judiciary. When Gamelin sees the Montagnards (Centralizers) overcome the Girondists (Federeés), he concludes that his metaphysic of revolution has been vindicated.

A naturalistic pattern of psychological determinism recurs throughout the narrative. Gamelin's anxious search for enemies leads to verdicts of guilt, which lead to the pleasures of bloodshed and sex, which lead to the search for new enemies to be tried. There are but two moments, at the beginning and the end, when it appears that this ever-intensifying cycle might be broken. Shortly before Gamelin is appointed magistrate, he discusses the legitimacy of the death penalty with Brotteaux. Believing in a godless Lucretian world, but deeply distrustful of the Revolutionary Tribunal, Brotteaux will not unreservedly oppose the death penalty because "murder is a law of nature." At the same time, however, Brotteaux warns Gamelin that when fallible men pursue the death penalty from "virtuous and judicial motives," rather than from necessity, innocent blood is likely to flow.

As a self-professed enlightened republican, Gamelin protests against Brotteaux's reasoning:

> "It's only the despots who believe the death penalty is a natural attribute of authority. One day the sovereign people will abolish it. Robespierre was against, and so were all good patriots; a law to abolish it cannot come too soon. But that won't be possible until the last enemy of the Republic has perished beneath the sword of justice." (75)

Gamelin's last words betray his inability to recognize self-contradictions. Beccaria, whom Anatole France commends for his "humane" outlook, would have readily detected the hypocrisy with which Gamelin maintains his belief in abolition of capital punishment while postponing its enactment into an indefinite future (101). As president of the tribunal, Judge Herman, like many of the magistrates, hopes for abolition of the death penalty "except, of course, for cases endangering public safety" (101). The underlying truth, Anatole France remarks, is that "the old monarchical idea of Reasons of State still inspired the Revolutionary Tribunal" (101). Absolute power is being wielded by a tribunal still governed by the principle of divine right, even though the God who sanctions the republic claims sovereignty of a very different kind.

As the Terror reaches its climax, Gamelin considers whether the sequence of executions can, or even should, have an end. From Mirabeau to Danton, revolutionaries have obtained power, have been accused of betraying the republic, and have ascended the guillotine or died in public disgrace; traitors all. What does it mean and how will it end? Gamelin futilely flogs his mind trying to understand by mindlessly repeating at intervals, the self-command to "think" (206). Those who cannot think clearly, Gamelin feels, must judge and act with finality. When next we meet Gamelin, he is voting for the death of his sister's lover. As long as there is another enemy and another Robespierre in whom the crowd can believe, the virtue of the republic will somehow be safe. It is unfortunate that Anatole France's literary reputation remains greatly diminished; the pogroms of the twentieth-century totalitarianism were to begin shortly after the publication of his prophetic novel.

SUBSTITUTIONS IN PRISON

During revolutions, both military and civilian courts must try to achieve justice, but justice seems to elude them. Court verdicts are so manifestly unjust that novelists arrange for the escape of a wrongly condemned prisoner by substituting a disguised person in the jail cell. Harvey Birch persuades Caesar, the Wharton's family slave, to disguise himself and to replace Captain Henry Wharton in prison, thereby enabling Wharton to escape the gibbet. Sydney Carton substitutes himself for Charles Darnay in the Conciergerie, giving up his own life to the guillotine so that Darnay can be freed to marry Lucy. Gauvain substitutes himself in the prison-keep of La Tourgue for his condemned uncle Lantenac, so that Lantenac can receive justice for his self-sacrificial rescue of Michelle Fléchard's three young children. My point is not that Victor Hugo had read *A Tale of Two Cities* or that Charles Dickens had read *The Spy*, though direct influence is certainly plausible. My point is rather that the physical and spiritual courage of individuals acting outside the law is starkly dramatized, in all three novels, for the purpose of emphasizing the legalized injustice of the court. Justice can be obtained only by subverting judicial procedures entirely.

A final conjecture based on admittedly insufficient evidence. Among the seven fictional trials, an unexpected but consistent difference emerges between the workings of military and civil injustice. If a man must be tried during times of revolution, his chances for receiving an orderly hearing conducted according to principles that follow clear written law are more likely in a military than a civilian trial. In civilian trials, judges as well as juries and spectators give way to the retaliatory pleasures of exacting more than an eye for an eye; the voice of the people turns out to be very like the voice of the mob. From the perspective of 1793, the Articles of War must be superseded, but revolutionary justice proves rare indeed, and republican justice remains more hope than reality.

NOTES

1. Cesare Beccaria, *On Crimes and Punishments and Other Writings*, ed. Aaron Thomas, Translated by Aaron Thomas and Jeremy Parzen (Toronto: University of Toronto Press, 2008), 86.

2. Albert Camus, "Reflections on the Guillotine" in *Resistance, Rebellion and Death*, translated by Justin O'Brien (New York: Alfred A. Knopf, 1961), 222.

3. Although scholarly commentary on single trial scenes in historical novels is plentiful in single author monographs, the importance of the criminal trial to the development of the genre as a whole, has received little or no consideration. Among the many general studies of the relation between law and literature centering upon nineteenth-century authors, I am indebted to the following: Jonathan Grossman, *The Art of Alibi: English Law Courts and the Novel* (Baltimore and London: Johns Hopkins University Press, 2002); Dieter Polloszek, *Literature and Legal Discourse: Equity and Ethics From Sterne to Conrad* (Cambridge: Cambridge University Press, 1999); Richard A. Posner, *Law and Literature*, 3rd edition (Cambridge, MA: Harvard University Press, 2009); Jan-Melissa Schramm, *Testimony and Advocacy in Victorian law, Literature and Theology* (Cambridge: Cambridge University Press, 2000); Brook Thomas, *Cross Examinations of Law and Literature: Cooper, Hawthorne, Stowe and Melville* (Cambridge: Cambridge University Press, 1987): Alexander Welsh, *Strong Representations: Narrative and Circumstantial Evidence in England* (Baltimore: Johns Hopkins University Press, 1992). Posner's *Law and Literature* has long been authoritative.

4. Sir Walter Scott, *Waverley; or, 'tis Sixty Years Since*, ed. Andrew Hook (New York: Penguin, 1985), p. 243.

5. *Laws and Articles of War for the Government of his Majesties Forces Within the Kingdom of Scotland* (Edinburgh: Evan Tyler, 1667), pp. 4, 5, 10; *Rules and Articles of War for the Better Government of his Majesties Army in the Kingdom of Scotland* (Edinburgh: Andrew Anderson, 1686), pp. 9, 15.

6. Alexander Welsh observes that Scott has constructed the three-chapter sequence describing Waverley's examination as if it were an informal trial with lawyer-like questionings, first by a counsel for the prosecution, then by a counsel for the defense: "His [Scott's] narrative somehow stops short of finding Waverley not guilty even as it stops short of finding him guilty." Waverley must therefore emerge from his examination feeling a compromised "guilty innocence" (Welsh, *Strong Representations*, pp. 89, 92). These chapters illustrate Scott's remarkable legal acumen.

7. Walter Scott, *Old Mortality*, eds. Jane Stevenson and Peter Davidson (New York: Oxford University Press, 1993), pp. 362, 365.

8. Alexander Rose summarizes late-eighteenth-century attitudes toward common spies as follows: "Permanently embedded in enemy territory and psychologically disguised as "friendlies," they ['the kind of spy that was beneath contempt'] were the sneaky, shifty toadies who informed on Jacobites, Jacobins, and radicals of various kinds. By their masters, cash was earmarked for bribes" (*Washington's Spies* [New York: Bantam Books, 2014], p. 97).

9. For the history of the Culper Spy ring maintained by George Washington in and around New York City, see Alexander Rose's *Washington Spies*, especially chapter seven on André's capture and conviction, pp. 195–212. For informative summaries of Cooper's understanding of the history and legendizing of the Arnold-André affair see the following: James P. Elliott, Historical Introduction to *The Spy* (New York: AMS press, 2002); Wayne Franklin, Introduction to *The Spy* (New York: Penguin Books, 1997); James Pickering, Introduction to *The Spy* (New York: College and

University Press, 1971), James D. Wallace, *Early Cooper and His Audience* (New York: Columbia University Press, 1986). Cooper would devote no less than fourteen pages of *Notions of the Americans* (1828) to an historical narrative of the rise and fall of the Arnold-André conspiracy.

10. David Ramsay, *The History of the American Revolution* (1789) (Indianapolis: Liberty Fund, 1990), II, 523.

11. J.E. Morpurgo, *Treason at West Point: The Arnold-André Conspiracy* (New York: Mason Charter, 1975), p. 158.

12. Compare Alexander Rose's defense of Washington's decision to hang André: "Even had Washington been willing to spare the spy's life, he had his army to think about. As it was, thanks to Arnold, the men were becoming reluctant to trust their officers, and the officers were losing faith in their commanders. Public opinion also had to be appeased. Somebody had to be punished, and punishment had to be seen to be done to restore order" (*Washington's Spies*, pp. 210–211).

13. In addition to Rose's *Washington's Spies*, see G.J.A. O'Toole's *Honorable Treachery: A History of U.S. Intelligence, Espionage, and Covert Action from the American Revolution to the C.I.A.* (New York: Atlantic Monthly Press, 1991). O'Toole describes George Washington as "the chief American spymaster" (18). Robert Morris gave General Washington a bag of silver coins with which Washington paid off spies. As O'Toole and Rose demonstrate, the Culper spy ring in New York City, managed by Benjamin Tallmadge, reported sometimes directly to General Washington. The Culper Spy Ring included such thuggish factotums as Hercules Mulligan, Joshua Merseneau, and Haym Solomon, none of whom seems to have been noted, then or now, for self-less patriotic commitment.

14. Alexander Pushkin, *The Captain's Daughter and Other Stories* (New York: Vintage, 1936), pp. 114, 117, 118. We know Pushkin had been reading Cooper's novels during the 1820s; it is likely, but not proven, that he had read *The Spy*.

15. The "Preface" was printed in the various editions of *Billy Budd* by Raymond Weaver, F. Barron Freeman and others, where it may still be found. My transcription is from Hershel Parker's essential textual study *Reading Billy Budd* (Evanston, IL: Northwestern University Press, 1990), p. 135.

16. Hershel Parker, *Reading Billy Budd*, p. 135.

17. Herman Melville, *Billy Budd, Sailor (An Inside Narrative)*, eds. Harrison Hayford and Merton M. Sealts Jr. (Chicago: University of Chicago Press, 1962), p. 54.

18. My historical summary of the naval mutinies of 1797 is drawn from two sources: James Duggan, *The Great Mutiny* (New York: G.P. Putnam's Sons, 1965); G.E. Manwaring and Bonamy Dobreé, *The Floating Republic: An Account of the Mutinies at Spithead and The Nore in 1797* (London: Penguin, 1935).

19. *Billy Budd, Sailor*, p. 66. Brook Thomas quotes an 1811 speech by Massachusetts chief justice Lemuel Shaw, Melville's father-in-law, in which Shaw had summarized Napoleon's career as "a despotism equally at war with the dictates of justice, the precepts of religion and the rights of humanity" (Brook Thomas, *Cross-Examinations of Law and Literature: Cooper, Hawthorne, Stowe and Melville* [Cambridge: Cambridge University Press, 1987], p. 242).

20. *Rule and Articles of War* (1686), p. 10.

21. Quoted in Joseph W. Bishop, Jr., *Justice Under Fire: A Study of Military Law* (New York: Charterhouse, 1974), p. 7.

22. *Clarel* (1876), the most ambitious and lengthy work of Melville's last period, consists largely of inconclusive debates among its varied pilgrim-characters.

23. Herman Melville, "Hawthorne and His Mosses" (1850) in *Herman Melville: Representative Selections,* ed. Willard Thorp (New York: American Book Co., 1938), p. 339.

24. The direction and pace of Melville's narrative also require that Vere convene the Drumhead court. Richard Posner forcefully argues "That Billy Budd should be tried on the ship is a literary imperative. A delay to rejoin the fleet, followed by the shift of the action to a court-martial in which Vere could play no role, would unhinge the story by eliminating Vere's responsibility for Billy's death" (Posner, *Law and Literature* [Cambridge: Harvard University Press, 2009], p. 214).

25. See Thomas J. Scorza, *In the Time before Steamships: Billy Budd, the Limits of Politics, and Modernity* (Dekalb, IL: Northern Illinois University Press, 1979), pp.104–106.

26. Charles Dickens, *A Tale of Two Cities,* ed. Richard Maxwell (New York: Penguin Books, 2000), p. 71.

27. In a fine analysis of *Bleak House,* Jan-Melissa Schramm observes "Despite the allegations of sensationalism, Dickens's interests were as much evidentiary in nature, and his fear that the professional rhetoric of the law displaces personal narrative was most pronounced when he dwelt upon the plight of the prisoner condemned to death" (*Testimony and Advocacy in Victorian Law, Literature and Theology* [Cambridge: Cambridge University Press, 2000], p. 111). The courtrooms of Dickens's Paris, however, stand in need of more application of the "professional rhetoric of the law," not less. For an informative comparison study of how Chancery procedures functioned both historically and in Dickens's novel, see chapter four, "The Legacy of Incarceration in Dickens's *Bleak House*" of Dieter Paul Polloszek's *Literature and Legal Discourse: Equity and Ethics from Sterne to Conrad* (Cambridge: Cambridge University Press, 1999), pp. 124–202.

28. Anatole France, *The Gods Will Have Blood (Les Dieux Ont Soif),* translated with an Introduction by Frederick Davies (New York: Penguin, 1990), p. 101. Information about the Law of 22 Prairial is taken from William Doyle, *The Oxford History of the French Revolution* (Oxford: Clarendon Press, 1989), p. 275.

Chapter 7

The Appeal of the Old Order
The Threat of the New

For the nineteenth-century historical novelist, progress is desired but distrusted, warily anticipated but needing definition. In the context of failed revolutions, novelists who wrote within Scott's tradition increasingly faced choices. They could sever the connection Scott established between the historical novel and narratives of revolution by selecting classical or medieval eras that would minimize contemporary political reference. Or, after the rise of socialism in mid-century, they could shift the basis for faith in revolutionary progress from legislating the political Rights of Man to supporting a working-class revolution to advance economic equality. A third option was to regard working-class revolution as nearly impossible, and assume that the discourse of 1789 would continue to define the context of subsequent revolutions.

To follow the first alternative was to hollow out the narrative substance of Scott's model; to follow the second meant writing fiction about the rapidly industrializing present (not an historical novel) thereby exaggerating the impact the working class had had upon revolutions before 1848 (lacking in verisimilitude). The third alternative proved to be the preferred path for the canonical novels we are discussing. Novelists chose to follow Scott in balancing the Old Order against the New, in placing a wavering genteel protagonist between them, and in allowing the fate of the fictional characters to project the slow course of historical change. Among the many variants to be wrought upon Scott's paradigm, however, was a marked shift in tone. The balance Scott strove to maintain between the merits and failings of the Old Order and the New would became increasingly unsustainable. As more blood was shed in failed revolutions, as the prospect of the just republic receded into the future, the customs and values of the Old Order acquired greater attraction. This chapter will trace the shift.

Before doing so, we should more fully address the question, why might the third alternative have been preferred? By writing *Ivanhoe*, Scott himself had established the first alternative, which would be followed by Bulwer Lytton (*The Last Days of Pompeii*), Flaubert (*Salammbo*), Victor Hugo (*Notre Dame de Paris*), George Eliot (*Romola*), and many others. The historical trajectory shifted: social change and sometimes warfare occurring in a long-past historical context, yes, but not civil war leading to revolution. The second alternative, to adapt the historical novel to the Marxist conception of revolution, will be the focus of my conclusion, but needs initial mention here. From what social classes did the novelists discussed in this book emerge? Tolstoy was a count and Lampedusa a prince. Pushkin was descended from Russian nobility and attended Tsar Nicholas's court. Scott, Cooper, Balzac, Hugo, Melville, Jewett, Cather, Mitchell, Pasternak, and Vidal were born into genteel mercantile or professional families that provided them with initial material advantages, together with education and personal connections to powerful families with upper-class manners.

Such advantages cast long shadows. When the outcome of a revolution betrays the hope that inspired it, the ways of the Old Order, even if selectively remembered, exert an emotional attraction against will and reason. Because of their lower class birth and modest upbringing, Dickens and Zola would seem to be the great exceptions to the pattern of hereditary attraction to the Old Order. Accordingly, Dickens and Zola would become the historical novelists to whom Marxist critics would look for revolutionary attacks on capitalist economic exploitation—revolutionary attacks that neither novelist could ever quite embrace.

The appeal of the Old Order also suited the late-nineteenth-century development of the historical novel's subgenre. An important variant of the term "The Historical Novel," especially for scholarly studies of American fiction, has been "The Historical Romance."[1] The unclear boundaries of the distinction date back beyond Scott's 1819 essay on romance for the *Encyclopedia Britannica* to Clara Reeve, Horace Walpole, and even to Henry Fielding. Among my reasons for preferring the term "The Historical Novel" is its prevalence in early-nineteenth-century literary discourse and the critical centrality of Georg Lukacs. The term "historical novel" directs attention toward historical realism within the novel form, as developed in Scott's early novels of Scotland. "Romance," however, allows for, even promotes, an admiring view of the past as an implied contrast to today's failings. For many nineteenth-century readers, the term "Romance" came to connote the kind of historical novel that would provide them idealization, nostalgia, and escape from the present. The overlap of the two terms created continued confusion as well as room for creativity. To cherish the Old Order could be regarded as a sign of realism, or romance, or of historical fictions that combined them.

The extent of the overlap becomes a question of historical accuracy. What degree of admiration for the past can be condoned in an historical novel of the kind Lukacs and then Jameson were to claim for "realism"?

Scott's Scottish tales resolve this particular problem with comparative consistency. Unless the Old Order elicits considerable appeal, Scott's reader can have no sympathy with the protagonist who wavers between Old and New. However, any tendency to bedeck the eighteenth-century Scottish past with the full appeal of "Romance" (chivalry, loyalty, spirituality, preindustrial rural purity) is continually held in check both by Scott's historical realism, and by his trust in the eventuality of progress following revolutionary change. The Old Order is, therefore, to be admired, but not to be embraced. As the Old Order passes away, the young waverer emerges into a presumably better future, while the threat of revolutionary opportunists is kept peripheral.

Although Scott, like Adam Ferguson, had Jacobite ancestors, he ascribed continuing progress to the Glorious Revolution of 1689, to the 1702 Act of Settlement, to the 1707 Act of Union, to a balanced economy, and to the leadership of educated men who would further the welfare of both Scotland and England. His Scottish novels contain many a "romantic" description of picturesque mountain crags, waterfalls, and glens, but he does not elegize peasant customs or praise the purity of unchanged rural life. Much as Scott admired Wordsworth's poetry, he did not believe there was spiritual uplift, let alone moral restoration, in contemplating the virtue of an old cumberland beggar, Michael in his sheepfold, or the leech-gatherer on the lonely moor. Long-suffering endurance, simple honesty, and intense love of land and family were, for Scott, not enough. Nor did he share Wordsworth's belief in the greater purity of rural speech.[2] Scott's peasant farmers and rural merchants speak a lively dialect, set apart by quotation marks, that establishes them as people of lower class than the narrator, the protagonist and the presumed reader. Wordsworth idealizes his aged peasants by isolating them from social and historical contexts, removing them from the world that is now "too much with us."[3] To Scott, the loyal, local peasant must be seen in his place within a backward-looking rural economy that must and shall change.

In many of Scott's novels, two contrasted but equally flawed men represent the forces of the Old Order and the progressive present. In *Waverley*, Cosmo Bradwardine and Richard Waverley; in *Old Mortality*, Claverhouse and Burleigh; in *Rob Roy*, Rob Roy and Bailie Jarvie; in *The Heart of Mid-Lothian*, Douce Davie Deans and George Stanton (Robertson); in *The Bride of Lammermoor*, Edgar Ravenswood and William Ashton. Sometimes the opposition of the two is based upon family hostility, sometimes upon religion, sometimes upon social class and occupation, sometimes on wealth, sometimes on politics, but usually on various combinations of them all. None are villains; none are heroes. Such is the complexity of the lives we live.

Young men admire the values of traditionalist elders almost against their will. Waverley cannot help but appreciate Cosmo Bradwardine's comic but selfless loyalty to his *de jure* Stuart king; Henry Morton admires Claverhouse's blunt courage; Frank Balderstone longs to share Rob Roy's mastery of his environment; Pastor Reuben Bright wistfully grants Douce Davie Deans the absolutism of his religious beliefs. There are always certain qualities of the Old Order to be admired: family and monarchical loyalty, personal honor, martial bravery, and acceptance of responsibility toward those below as well as those above you. But these qualities are as often betrayed as they are upheld, especially by those who loudly profess them. Moreover, the merits of tradition are balanced against its failings (class prejudice, refusal to change, quixotic scruples, cruelty in battle) and contrasted to their opposite virtues in the New Order (flexibility, realism, trust in commercial contract, meritocracy). As Scott's narrative unfolds, the protagonist discovers he can make no lasting alignment of virtue and vice between the Old and the New. By novel's end, he prefers to believe in a better future, but its indeterminacy encourages lingering looks backward.

BENEATH KELPIE'S FLOW

No Scott novel more concisely juxtaposes the Old Order to the New than *The Bride of Lammermoor* (1819). Family conflict originates in property dispossession between two flawed men: proud, now titleless aristocrat Master Edgar Ravenswood and ambitious, nouveau riche lawyer, Sir William Ashton. During the Glorious Revolution of 1688, Edgar Ravenswood's father, male heir of a once prominent family loyal to the Stuarts, has lost his title, his castle, and nearly all his lands and tenants to Sir William Ashton, Lord Keeper of the Great Seal of Scotland, and member of the Scottish Privy Council. The novel opens immediately after the 1707 Act of Union,[4] at a time when the Whigs, dominant since 1689, are losing power to Tory ministers serving Queen Anne. From the outset, young Edgar Ravenswood is defined by his fierce loyalty to family tradition, his Byronic hauteur, his embittered pride, and his striking lack of occupation. Ashton, whose father had been a struggling Puritan—a "hypocrite," "miser," and "knave"—has gained money and political power through the disempowering of Jacobites during and immediately after the Glorious Revolution.[5] Ashton is a "cool lawyer and able politician," "politic, wary and worldly," who has stripped Edgar Ravenswood of his properties and his noble title by being adept at mortgages, casuistry, and the accommodating politics of the Scottish Privy Council.[6]

Cultural differences aggravate their visceral hostility. Ravenswood is a Tory and an Episcopalian, Ashton a Whig and a Presbyterian. Ravenswood's associates are of the countryside, mostly Jacobite; Ashton is well-connected in Edinburgh, but ignorant of peasant customs on lands he now owns. In order to reclaim family lineage, Ravenswood strikes defiant gestures; to hide his opportunistic path to success, Ashton strives to appear adroit and flexible. Ravenswood's hatred of Ashton is based upon his barely repressed need for extralegal revenge; Ashton's dislike of Ravenswood is based upon fear that his recent acquisition of Ravenswood lands might be overturned through Ravenswood's right of appeal to England's House of Lords. The complexity of their juxtaposition is vintage Scott.

In all these ways, the decline of a principle of aristocracy based upon family landholding (Master Edgar Ravenswood) furthers the rise of an aristocracy based upon words, contracts, and cash (Sir William Ashton). By novel's end, Ravenswood's instinct to draw his sword seems late medieval compared to Ashton's showily learned remark about power in today's world: "*cedant armae togae* is the maxim of lawyers, you know" (193). In Marxist terms, Ashton would be a petit bourgeois hypocritically climbing to money and power in revolutionary times.

As representatives of the Old Order and the New, Ravenswood and Ashton are historically convincing; quasi-legal dispossession of Jacobite lands and titles was a fact after 1688. The two men are convincing as fictional characters because their opposing traits are qualified, not absolute. Ravenswood understands that the Glorious Revolution has transferred the power of determining monarchical succession to Parliament; he criticizes the Stuart kings and refuses to turn Jacobite or emigrate to France. He admits that his father and grandfather have impoverished their tenants by denying them written leases (259). Ravenswood's few remaining tenants in the struggling village of Wolf's-Hope are ignoring ancestral obligations and taking up artisan trades.[7] The town's cooper voices what Marx was to advocate as the labor theory of value; desiring to be a gentleman of reason, Ravenswood is prepared to swallow revenge and wed the new with the old by marrying Sir William Ashton's daughter Lucy, whom he dearly loves. Resenting the manipulation underlying Ashton's ingratiating manner, Ravenswood nonetheless acknowledges, with a sardonic flourish, "things may have appeared right and fitting to you, a skilful and practised lawyer, which to my ignorant understanding seem very little short of injustice and gross oppression" (171).

Sir William Ashton, for his part, hides a "cautious and timid disposition" beneath his acuity and eloquence (36). Because his title is recently acquired, he knows that his new estate and aristocratic status would be better secured if his daughter Lucy could be married to Ravenswood. Ashton is, however, utterly unable to withstand the force of his wife's ruthless ambition. A second Lady Macbeth, Lady Ashton pursues power by backing Whigs empowered through the Union, be they Scottish or English. Trampling on the vulnerable,

she denounces Ravenswood as a "beggarly Jacobite bankrupt" and deceit-
fully blocks Ravenswood's marriage to Lucy, virtually imprisoning her own
daughter (238).

Which of the two men embodies the needed qualities of leadership for the
United Kingdom now emerging from the Act of Union? The implied answer
is clearly—neither of them. Ravenswood's honesty and honor are admirable
but his rage to revenge his family's decline overpowers his resolve to act
responsibly. Ashton cedes his skills at negotiation to his wife's willpower
and to the money power of contractual law; he silently accepts the horrifying
circumstances of his daughter's death rather than taint his reputation as the
new Lord of Ravenswood. Scott surrounds Ravenswood and Ashton with a
virtual gallery of middle-aged, male trimmers: Bucklaw, Turntiippet, Reverend Bide-the Bent, and the controlling members of the Scottish Councils
in Edinburgh. The chief trimmer, the Marquis of Atholl, warily professes to
support the Jacobite cause, claims to sympathize with his cousin Ravenswood, but wonders "what cards would be trumps next Parliament?" (263).
Edinburgh politicians who follow the Marquis of Atholl are described as
"uniform adherents to the party who are uppermost" (286).

The presentation of revolutionary politics in *The Bride of Lammermoor* is
unrelievedly ugly, especially for a novelist who consistently praised both the
Glorious Revolution and the Act of Union. At novel's end, all male members
of the Ravenswood and Ashton families die without issue. In a grandly realized image of ever-increasing fatality, Edgar Ravenswood and the past he
represents literally disappear into the quicksand and rising tide of Kelpie's
flow, leaving a vacuum of power. Among the major characters, only Lady
Ashton remains alive at novel's end.

Scott's nihilistic ending is an anomaly among his Scottish novels. By
denying the survival of the Old Order, Scott's ending leaves a blank future.
Neither the Old Order nor the New provides persons or values upon which to
build. If, as critics repeatedly contend, T*he Bride of Lammermoor* achieves
a uniquely tragic effect, it is in part because the novel contains no wavering
hero who, at novel's end, can contribute to a better future through marriage
and honorable citizenship. Instead, the entire weight of past and present
evils, transferred through the two male antagonists, is brought down upon
the marriageable heroine, leading her to murder, madness, and suicide. Nothing said in the novel is more cruel than Edgar Ravenswood's last words to
Lucy: "And to you, madam . . . I have nothing farther to say, except to pray
to God that you may not become a world's wonder for this act of willful and
deliberate perjury" (328). No act in the novel is more destructive than Sir
William Ashton's refusal to do anything to lessen the profitable misery his
worldly success has created. Ravenswood, however, remains the novel's central figure. When he sinks beneath Kelpie's flow, we are asked to regret his

political victimization, but not the loss of the culture he represents. Nor can we celebrate the virtues of the mercantile, lawyerly culture that supplants it. As Ravenswood vanishes into quicksand, the sun simultaneously rises in the east, but Scott's juxtaposition of the two images allows for neither historical progress nor nostalgia.

The Scottish novels set in times after the Act of Union point forward toward a more enlightened, prosperous, and peaceful kingdom. Scott invests hope for the future in subsidiary characters who have emerged out of the Old Order but prefigure the New. These figures are practical, resolute, middle-aged males who have achieved success less through personal ambition than through realism, energy, decency, and public service. There is nothing of the avenger or the trimmer about them. Invariably, they provide needed advice and support to the wavering protagonist who remains at the center of the narrative. Just as the protagonist represents the emerging promise of the liberal gentry, so the mentor figure provides a model of public responsibility. Colonel Talbot of *Waverley*, whom we have already considered, is the prototype of this figure. Bailie Nicole Jarvie of *Rob Roy* and the Duke of Argyle of *The Heart of Mid-Lothian* represent its full realization. Their function is complex. They embody admirable character traits of the Old Order, but practice them to further values of the new. As befits their subsidiary status, they represent, not a certainty, but Scott's tentative hope for the progressive course of the eighteenth century.

Born a Scot of the border country, Bailie Nicole Jarvie is thoroughly familiar with the brutality of the clan system, but fond of his cousin, the outlawed cateran Rob Roy, who owes Jarvie a thousand pounds. Emigrating to Glasgow, Jarvie has become a leading merchant, lawyer, and alderman. Jarvie understands the causal connections between the 50 percent unemployment rate in the Highlands, the increasing power of the caterans, and the ready appeal of Jacobitism among those within the clan system.[8] Although the Act of Union has provoked hatred of English excisemen and increased the fervor of Jacobite loyalty, it has also enabled Scottish merchants like himself to sell textiles in European and Atlantic markets, thereby providing employment and a decent living for Highland peasants who have left the land to work in Scotland's port cities. Finance, not family, now underlies political antagonisms. Jarvie knows that land-poor Highland lairds, deeply indebted to Glasgow and London bankers, have been pledging their lands as collateral for debts that they now, in 1714, cannot repay. Bailie Jarvie's grasp of conditions in the entirety of the United Kingdom enables him to predict the near certainty of Jacobite rebellion (the '15 and the '45) and the inevitable decline of the clan system. Needed economic progress would therefore require mutual restraint and compromise for decades to come.

As a magistrate, deacon's son and man of peace, Baillie Jarvie honors
the Presbyterian Church primarily because Presbyterians have opposed both
Catholic and Jacobite absolutism. His convictions about present values recall
Falstaff's catechism: "Honour is a homicide and a bloodspiller, that gangs
about making frays in the street; but Credit is a decent honest man, that sits at
home and makes the pat [pot] play" (297). Jarvie financially supports the University of Glasgow because it encourages universalist thinking, not because
it is a gathering place for the privileged. He has seen how the clan system,
like dueling, encourages distrust for law. A committed Whig and Hanoverian
though Jarvie declares himself to be ("Weel, but there's a new warld come
up wi' this King George. I say, God bless him," p. 305), he is incensed when
English redcoats take law into their own hands within Scotland. Rob Roy is
a cousin Jarvie will never betray, but Jarvie regards Rob Roy's decline from
drover to cateran as a telling example of Scottish cultural self-destruction.
In order not to drive Rob Roy to desperation, Jarvie declines to collect the
thousand pounds Rob Roy owes him, but not before Jarvie forces Rob Roy
to confront the dismal future awaiting his sons, who cannot read, write, add,
or subtract.

Like Talbot in *Waverley*, Baillie Jarvie enables the waverer to survive.
The extrication of Frank Osbaldistone from his many troubles depends more
on Jarvie's acumen than on Rob Roy's broadsword. Jarvie provides bail
for Owen, chief clerk of Osbaldistone and Tresham, when Owen is falsely
imprisoned for debt by Glasgow bankers. Jarvie then provides a large needed
advance, on trust, to the firm of Osbaldistone and Tresham. He prevents probable prosecution of Frank Osbaldistone for having lost papers of credit. He
warns Frank about the villainy of Rashleigh Osbaldistone, Frank's cousin,
who threatens to supplant him. When Bailie Jarvie and Frank Osbaldistone
are captured by Rob Roy MacGregor's followers, Baillie Jarvie stops their
imminent execution by courageously defying the authority of Rob Roy's
wife, the wronged Helen MacGregor, whose implacable vengeance makes
her a precursor to Dickens's Madame Defarge.

Bailie Jarvie rises to deserved local prominence. At novel's end, Scott
takes leave of Bailie Jarvie with the comment "He continued to grow in
wealth, honour, and credit, and actually rose to the highest civic honours in
his native city" (421). Scott's admiration for Bailie Jarvie cannot, however,
negate the reductive implication of the word "actually." As Frank Osbaldistone compliments Jarvie for being both "a keen Scotchman" and "disposed to
think liberally of the sister kingdom," Frank simultaneously defines the limits
of Jarvie's influence:

> Although, like my father, he [Jarvie] considered commercial transactions the
> most important objects of human life, he was not wedded to them so as to

undervalue more general knowledge. On the contrary, with much oddity and vulgarity of manner,—with a vanity which he made much more ridiculous by disguising it now and then under a thin veil of humility, and devoid as he was of all the advantages of a learned education, Mr. Jarvie's conversation showed tokens of a shrewd, observing, liberal, and to the extent of its opportunities, a well-improved mind. (312)

Because Frank is no longer a callow innocent, he cannot extend his praise beyond such qualification. Frank understands that there is a limit to Bailie Jarvie's ability to reach beyond his origins. Jarvie's dialect is sometimes as impenetrable as any Scotsman in the Waverley Novels. His sympathetic understanding of the culture he has discarded leaves a residue of "oddity and vulgarity of manner" that will not enable him to assume authority beyond Glasgow. His bluntness leaves an impression of "vanity" that borders upon the ridiculous. Bailie Jarvie almost represents the merging of old and new into a fully progressive future—but not quite.

In the Scottish novels, there is no influential historical figure more admired than John, Second Duke of Argyle and Duke of Greenwich (1678–1743), who intervenes prominently in *The Heart of Mid-Lothian*. Scott introduces Argyle, admired as MacCallummore in the Lowlands, as a man of equal talent as soldier and statesman. He is said to be "above the petty distinctions of faction," a man of peace whose "voice was raised, whether in office or opposition, for those measures which were at once just and lenient."[9] In implied contrast to Cromwell or Napoleon, Argyle is said to be ambitious, but "without that irregularity of thought and aim, which often excites great men . . . to grasp the means of raising themselves to power, at the risk of throwing a kingdom into confusion" (360). Argyle is fortunate to be "alike free from the ordinary vices of statesmen, falsehood, namely, and dissimulation, and from those of warriors, inordinate and violent thirst after self-aggrandizement" (360). Balanced in judgment, cosmopolitan, and well-educated, Argyle's mind is "so happily regulated" that he prefers not to stir the political whirlwind, nor "direct its fury" (360). Living through an era first of revolution then of counterrevolution, Argyle's just, equable temper would not allow him to become fully committed to either.

The historical policies and loyalties with which Argyle is associated are an index of the moderate political values to which Walter Scott was deeply drawn. Argyle is a Protestant Scot who supports the Act of Union, an owner of vast Scottish lands who lives primarily in London; he is a Duke in both Scotland and in England, as well as a Whig member of the House of Lords. He led Hanoverian regiments during the 1715 rebellion, but urged leniency or pardon for defeated Jacobites. His ancestry, like Waverley's, includes men of both Anglican and Presbyterian, Stuart and Hanoverian persuasions. Argyle will pursue the middle way to a better future, whether the occasion demands steadfastness or compromise.

Unlike Waverley, however, Argyle's divided loyalties never cause him to vacillate. He carefully and consistently distinguishes between Scotland as his "native country" and Great Britain as his "country." By staunchly supporting Scottish rights within the terms of the Act of Union, he declares his support for the rights of Englishmen as well as Scots. His defining moment is his self-justification before Queen Caroline, wife of King George II: "My sword, madam," replied the Duke, "like that of my fathers, has been always at the command of my lawful king, and of my native country—I trust it is impossible to separate their real rights and interests" (381). Unlike the divisive party men who loudly proclaim Whig or Tory, Jacobite or Hanoverian principles, Argyle assumes that one can always discover a progressive policy upon which men of reason can come together. "Real rights and interests" especially after 1689 and 1707, are, he claims, "impossible to separate." A Scott's fealty to England is consistent with independence of belief.

In Scott's novel as in history, Argyle acts with justice and leniency to enhance Scottish/English concord. The separate narratives of the novel are brought together by Argyle's influence in achieving two royal pardons. George II's pardon of John Porteous, which reversed the verdict of the highest criminal court of Scotland, causes the Edinburgh "mob," embittered by recent English tax measures, to riot and fire the Tolbooth, as vividly described in the novel's opening chapters.[10] King, ministry, and members of Parliament then seek to punish the city of Edinburgh by dismissing its Lord Provost, tearing down the city gates, and abolishing the City Guard. Opposing all these measures in the House of Lords, the Duke of Argyle condemns the riot but persuasively argues that the proposed severities violate the rights of Scottish and English citizens (571–572). In Scott's fictional plot, Jeanie Deans, modest daughter of a Scottish cowfeeder and Covenanter, resolves to plead for her condemned sister Effie's life by walking barefoot from Edinburgh to London to seek a pardon from the queen. Urged to seek the Duke of Argyle's help in so seemingly hopeless an endeavor, she earns Argyle's affection, support and aid.

The great Duke treats the peasant girl with an admiration for her sturdy integrity of character that is inseparable from affectionate class condescension. His sense of *noblesse oblige* is void of pride. After Jeanie's plea for pardon succeeds, Argyle supports her return to Scotland, then secures for Jeanie, her father, and her beloved Reuben Butler a parish, a manse, and a cottage on Argyle lands near Glasgow. In the concluding chapters, Scott characterizes Argyle as a landed reformer in two senses: he pursues progressive agricultural practices; he welcomes all men of peace (Highlander and Englishman, persecuted Covenanter and forsworn Jacobite) to take up residence on his lands.

Argyle functions both as an historical hero who quells the Porteus Revolt and as the "benevolent enchanter" who saves the life of Effie Deans. On a national and a personal level, Argyle pursues policies in which lenity and justice coincide. Like Bailie Jarvie, the Duke of Argyle almost, but not quite, represents the merging of old and new into a fully progressive future. Argyle's confidence, self-control, and "happily regulated mind" derive from his sure sense of personal belonging. His vast lands, his position in the House of Lords, and his sense of continuing class distinctions are not yet directly threatened. Argyle's outlook, unlike Bailie Jarvie's, remains as preindustrial, even pre-mercantile, as his manners remain engagingly aristocratic. Given Walter Scott's troubled view of the volatility and tensions in post-Napoleonic England, it is hard to imagine how Argyle's virtues could still exert a prompt, telling effect in the changed world of Scott's present.

In historical novels following Scott, admirable qualities of the Old Order are commonly represented by men even older than Argyle and Bailie Jarvie. Sometimes they are sages, sometimes patriarchs, sometimes witty outsiders, sometimes men of unwavering commitment, sometimes victims of their own loyalty. Balzac's Pere Goriot, Cooper's Tamenund, Leather-stocking in his old age, Pushkin's Captain Mironov, Dickens's Doctor Manette and Melville's Captain Vere, strikingly different though they are, are all variants of one of these subtypes. Two other older men are especially noteworthy. Victor Hugo's Marquis de Lantenac adheres to the late medieval social order of Brittany with a brutal frankness that does not preclude his willingness to sacrifice his own life for three peasant children. Anatole France's *ci-devant* Marquis Maurice Brotteaux, now the powerless Citizen Brotteaux des Ilettes, gains the reader's trust through the acuity of his attacks on the hypocrisy of revolutionaries, his witty Lucretian atheism, his humanity to the unfortunate, and his engaging (rather than sadomasochistic) sensuality. Although most of the young wavering heroes wish to look past these older men to a presumably better future, the young men love and invariably learn from such elders. Novels in which elderly men are accorded admirable self-knowledge do not promote enthusiasm for political revolution.

"RELIC OF THE PAST CENTURY"

The master at creating unforgettable old men faithful to yesterday's values is Tolstoy. General Michael Ilaronovich Kutuzov, the perfect foil to Napoleon Bonaparte, is not the man to follow the newly formulated battle tactics soon to be set forth by Clausewitz, however correct they might be. He attends to the strategy and spirit, not the tactics, of the Russian army. Kutuzov knows that, as long as the Grande Armeé remains in Russia, *"patience and time"* are what is needed.[11] He turns French wisdom against France: "*Tout vient a point a celui qui sait attendre*" (663). Retreat, guerilla warfare, and the enemy's overstretched supply lines are his best weapons. An old man, he dozes through the war council of his subsidiary generals before battle, or reads a French romance, because he knows that his generals' advice, most of it self-serving, will end in disagreement and will not affect the outcome anyway.

Fat, disheveled, and slow-moving, Kutuzov's discolored eye and facial scar, together with his contempt for clever fools, make him an easy target for backbiting among subordinates, allies, or the habitués of Petersburg salons. Kutuzov knows, however, exactly how to make use of his physical limitations. Tolstoy faults Kutuzov for tactical errors at the Battle of Borodino, but there is no suggestion of authorial ridicule when Kutuzov walks painfully and slowly to the forefront of his army, falls on his knees, touches the soil, and kisses an icon before the battle begins. Whether Kutuzov believes that God determines the outcome of battle is far less important than Kutuzov's inspirational ability to persuade his soldiers that their general is a believer.

Like the Duke of Argyle, Kutuzov is the same man in person and in public. Knowing that his aide Prince André is a Bolkonski, Kutuzov asks him to join his personal staff, advising him that "advisers are always plentiful, but men are not" (663). This comment serves Kutuzov as a segue to mention his memory of André carrying the standard at Austerlitz. Although the reader expects that a compliment to André's battle glory will follow, tears spring to Kutuzov's eyes as he says to André "Go your way and God be with you. I know your path is the path of honor!" (661). Kutuzov may or may not sense what André had felt looking into the infinite blue sky; his tears are his sensitive response to André's having been wounded *after* carrying the standard. At the end of the scene, tears still in his eyes, Kutuzov exclaims that he will make the French eat horseflesh; he dismisses André with the words "Goodbye, my dear boy" and returns to reading *Les Chevaliers du Cygne*, by Madame de Genlis.[12]

The effect of this encounter upon André is to convince him that Kutuzov "will hear everything, remember everything, and put everything in its place. . . . He [Kutuzov] understands that there is something stronger and more important than his own will—the inevitable course of events, and he can see them and grasp their significance."[13] To foresee the inevitable course of events is not the same, however, as actively promoting progress as the nineteenth century understood it. André knows that Kutuzov "will not bring in any plan of his own. He will not devise or undertake anything" (664). Kutuzov assumes that best intentions lead to unintended consequences; history does not move through purposive stages. His fatalistic mentality is therefore not adaptable to nineteenth-century values. The generals, statesmen, and thinkers who had been favorable to revolutionary change in 1776, in 1789, or during the Decembrist Revolt did not believe that progress could occur when man does nothing.

On the same occasion, before André can say one word of greeting, General Kutuzov assumes the instant familiarity of a shared sorrow: "Well, sit down, sit down here. Let's have a talk. . . . It's sad, very sad. But remember, my dear fellow, that I am a father to you, a second father" (362). Kutuzov's words show almost preternatural sensitivity to a young officer who has recently lost his father. Kutuzov wishes to be associated with the admired "Old Prince" by becoming a second father to Nicholas Bolkonski's honorable son. Between André and both fathers, however, there must always be a longing for intimacy that can never come to fruition. Kutuzov is the commanding General of the entire Russian army; Old Prince Bolkonski will not permit emotional intimacy.

A cultural divide also separates son from father. To André as well as to Tolstoy, the Old Prince embodies Enlightenment ideals no longer applicable in a new century. His vast library reflects a faith in the advance of knowledge worthy of the Encyclopedists or of Thomas Jefferson. His insistence on constant industriousness, daily routine and constructive planning recalls Voltaire and Benjamin Franklin. Reason is the Old Prince's God. He would liberate his daughter Mary from the constrictions placed upon her sex by schooling her in algebra and geometry. A mathematical world will be a better world; God has had no proven effect on the workings of natural law. The Old Prince raises his two children to believe "that there are only two sources of human vice—idleness and superstition, and only two virtues—activity and intelligence" (75).

The inadequacy of Prince Nicholas Bolkonski's values lies not in their being wrong, but in their being so absolute, so one-sided. His pursuit of Reason is unreasonable; it leads him to issue dicta rather than advance a proposition. His suppression of his essentially kind and loving nature starves the emotional responses of his children while bordering upon patriarchal tyranny. By railing against religious "superstition," he increases Mary's faith in the person of Jesus Christ as the world's savior. His insistence upon a one-year postponement of André's and Natasha's marriage, however appropriate it may be to their difference in age, shows no understanding of the emotional needs of an eighteen-year-old girl. Nor can the Old Prince admit to himself that denying the eligibility of Mary's suitors is his only way of ensuring that Mary will remain with him. His is a cruelty born of love; consequently, Mary can become a fully adult woman only upon the death of her father.

The wonder of Tolstoy's characterization of the Old Prince is that everyone, including the reader, feels deep affection for him despite his failings. His unchanging love surfaces beneath the blunt criticisms and abrupt commands through which he tries to hide it. Mary treasures her memory of his trying to utter the words "forgive," "thank you," and "dearest" to her during his last gruesome moments (638). Tolstoy rightly calls the Old Prince "a relic of the past century" but in a novel set amid the sumptuous town houses, showy salons, and army camps of the Napoleonic era, the library, lathe, and gardens of Bald Hills represent, not the good life perhaps, but the best life we are permitted to see (479). The honor and high striving that the Old Prince embodies must henceforth seek another form, another dwelling that is not yet in evidence.

The novels Fenimore Cooper published in the 1820s are the exception to Scott's (and Tolstoy's) pattern of granting qualified virtues to men of integrity with hesitant loyalist sympathies. Cooper's strong commitment to American republicanism, so explicit in *Notions of the Americans* (1828), led him to grant integrity and courage to former loyalists who had openly supported or joined the British, but also to direct pity and scorn toward men of means and position who had wavered out of self-interest. Such men lack what Cooper calls "moral courage." Mr. Wharton of *The Spy,* trying to safeguard money and family no matter who wins, is the prototype for similar elderly characters in Cooper's other novels of the American Revolution: the temporizing Colonel Howard of *The Pilot,* the devious Mrs. Lechmere of *Lionel Lincoln,* and even, to a lesser degree, the opportunistic judge Temple of *The Pioneers.* In every one of these novels, the foil to the elderly temporizer is a heroic commoner of ordinary birth, lowly occupation, democratic instinct, blunt honesty, and great physical skills: Harvey Birch, Long Tom Coffin, Job Pray, and Leather-stocking. All but Leather-stocking are outspoken revolutionary patriots.[14] Together with America's republican gentry, these commoners of democratic feeling represent the mainstays for the emerging nation.

For Cooper in his later years, the appeal of the Old Order was best embodied in a people wholly unlike the losing loyalists of the American Revolution. Anticipating the "Manifest Destiny" thinking of the 1840s, Cooper foresaw the removal, defeat, and possible extinction of ancient Indian peoples. He knew that the bloody future of Indian demise would be widely interpreted, for purposes of Euro-American self-justification, as "progress," the march of civilization through successive stages. Here was the legacy of Adam Ferguson's stadialism, but with a telling difference. Ferguson had described the evolution of one civilization toward uncertain progress; Americans were defining progress as the beneficial replacement of the Indian (the state of nature) by the white (the state of civilization).

Although Cooper was certainly a racialist, he neither supported nor attacked the racist assumption of his contemporaries that the Indian was inferior to the white Euro-American. Instead he explored this assumption by juxtaposing admirable Indians against villainous ones, and admirable white pioneers against vulgar white plunderers. In *The Leather-stocking Tales* as a whole, the Indian becomes Cooper's vehicle for conveying the worth of old virtues being lost to the so-called progress of civilization. Physical grace, the skills acquired by a life lived in nature, freedom from greed, clarity of language, courtesy to women, and honor due to family and tribe are all ascribed to Indians. Scott had, of course, ascribed similar kinds of virtues to Highland Scots. To be a known member of a Scottish clan or Native American tribe, it would seem, promotes an intense loyalty harder to summon for the citizen of a nation.

Within an American context, Cooper's purpose was not so much to affirm the historical reality of the "Noble Savage," or to rival Scott, as to expose the cruel, crude underside of the pioneer spirit. Westward moving white pioneers, citizens of the republic, were degrading the environment and reverting to savagery as they dispossessed the Indian. Readers accustomed to Scott's way of paying tribute to the best of the Old Regime could re-experience, in Cooper's Indians, a new way of fulfilling a familiar elegiac need. From Cooper's perspective, however, the stark contrast between the Indian and the Euro-American was of greater future significance to the western world than the opposition of Scots and Englishman, Jacobites and Hanoverians. *The Leatherstocking Tales* therefore become less a five-part historical novel, and more a mythic encounter between two incompatible kinds of civilization, one advancing as the other declines. Under such circumstances, Leather-stocking, Tamenund, and Chingachgook, like Old Prince Nicholas Bolkonski who is their cultural opposite, can only pass away as a patriarchal "relic" of unquestioned honesty and integrity.

CENTURY'S END: WOMEN AND PROGRESS

There is good reason why J.B. Bury's long influential and still useful study *The Idea of Progress* (1920) concludes abruptly with reflections on Herbert Spencer's progressive view of Darwinian evolution. During the half century since Spencer's time, continuing evidence of progress had become hard to find. Despite the progressive conclusions of Guizot, Comte, Emerson, Macaulay, John Stuart Mill, and many others, liberal confidence in tomorrow's better world was disintegrating into uneasy hopes. Astonishing technological and industrial advances had not demonstrably improved the living conditions of the poor, but had visibly widened the gap between the privileged and the disadvantaged. David Ricardo's Iron Law of Wages seemed an economic truth to angry Marxists as well as opportunistic capitalists.

Titled aristocrats were still plentiful, but fewer of them assumed responsibilities of leadership. Monarchy continued everywhere except France and the United States. The Prussian Kaisers, like the Hapsburg, Romanoff, and

Hanover-Windsor dynasties, all of them crucial to the outbreak of World War I, pursued policies and pageantries that advanced nationalism and colonialism. Despite the long-ago hopes of Condorcet, Godwin, and Jefferson, republicanism had not been broadly accepted as the future polity of peace. Brutal repression of the revolutionary movements of 1830, 1848, and 1870 aroused discouragement as well as angry memories. Nor had republicanism brought peace and plenty to the New World. Bolivar's *Gran Columbia* had disintegrated into regional fiefdoms. America's "Great Experiment" in New World republicanism had led to the most deadly and protracted civil war in memory.

Equality of human rights, clearly dependent on opportunity, was advancing slowly at best. As a standard of social analysis and judgment, race had eroded the universalist thinking of the revolutionary era. Widespread graduation from public high schools and lyceés (Condorcet's dream) had still not occurred. Women could not vote and almost no women were admitted to the professions. In the wake of biblical higher criticism, informed people who no longer believed in revelation, grace, or the afterlife had lost a key component of their belief in spiritual progress. Doubt and uncertainty of all kinds were rapidly emerging; the darkly ironic world-outlooks of Henry Adams and Oswald Spengler waited in the wings.

Nor was the late nineteenth century, outside of France, a period of recognized achievement for the historical novel. The immense popularity of Scott's novels led to a need for abridgment that eventually created an adolescent market for adventure entertainment fitted upon an historical scaffold, usually medieval.[15] Abridgements of Scott's and Cooper's novels appeared in simplified language versions, then in Classic Comics. *Ivanhoe* furthered the kind of medieval revivalism that, in the Arthurian books of Howard Pyle and Sydney Lanier, prompted adolescent dreams of medieval tourneys. Bestselling adventure melodramas of Terror and the guillotine (Baroness Orczy's *The Scarlet Pimpernel* [1905] and Rafael Sabatini's *Scaramouche* [1921]) lacked historical purpose. Henry James's growing scorn for historical fiction and E.M. Forster's distaste for Scott ("I do not care for him") were motivated partly by reservations about Scott's form, but partly by their awareness of the literary dustbin into which the historical novel then seemed to be headed.[16]

Of the many paths into which the historical novel was to diverge after 1890, this chapter section will consider three historical novels by American women: Sarah Orne Jewett's *The Tory Lover* (1901), Willa Cather's *Death Comes For the Archbishop* (1927), and Margaret Mitchell's *Gone With the Wind* (1936). Diana Wallace's recent critical study *The Woman's Historical Novel* (2005) has shown how Lukacs's model of the "classic historical novel," based almost entirely on Scott, "has actually worked to exclude many forms of the woman's historical novel from critical attention."[17] Wallace studies an alternative tradition of twentieth-century historical novels by women that derives ultimately from the Gothic novel and from shifting models of literary romance and modernism, rather than from Lukacs's insistence on the merits of realism.[18]

I have chosen these three novels because they do not fit into the often subversive tradition of women's historical fiction that Diana Wallace has clearly defined. Jewett, Cather, and Mitchell wrote as women but still within the tradition Scott had established; they maintained their distance from modernism and in no way anticipated postmodernism. All three were regional writers accustomed to rural ways and an agricultural economy. As women of genteel upbringing and scant experience of battle or politics, Jewett, Cather, and Mitchell could have had little, if any, confidence in their ability to portray convincing battlefield warfare. Nonetheless, Scott's juxtaposition of the Old Order and the New, as defined by Coleridge, still resonated deeply for them. Genteel male protagonists, the neutral ground, waverers and fanatics, are still clearly discernible. War may be in the background, but it affects all characters; narratives center on the promise and threat of revolutionary cultural change. There is, however, a shift away from Scott's determination to maintain balance of judgment between successive eras. For reasons that include gender, the authors' disillusionments about the present state of "progress" led to increasingly elegiac evocations of an old order associated with Euro-American gentility.

Jewett's *The Tory Lover* opens with the departure of the newly refitted frigate *Ranger*, John Paul Jones Captain, from Portsmouth New Hampshire on November 1, 1777. The novel describes Jones's meetings with Benjamin Franklin in Paris, then Jones's notorious raid on Whitehaven, and concludes back in New England in 1779 with the end of the Revolutionary War nowhere in sight. As in many a Scott or Cooper novel, hero and heroine of opposing political beliefs marry at novel's end. Landscapes are vividly rendered and treachery proves considerably more villainous than Tory belief. However, no battle on land or sea is ever described. Political exchanges exist as a measure of individual character and of social change, not as potential insight into government-making or revolutionary history.[19]

High-minded Roger Wallingford, the Tory lover of the title, is emotionally divided between his loyalist heritage and his love for Mary Hamilton, patriot daughter of a leading merchant. Like most of Scott's protagonists, Wallingford is "not a hero,—only a plain gentleman, with a good heart and steady sense of honor."[20] A son of the merchant elite inclined to serve province and king, Wallingford's loyalties have heretofore been intensely local and personal. Roger and his widowed loyalist mother are devoted to each other. After spending his adolescent years in London, the comfortable federal-style New England houses crowning the meadows sloping down to the Piscataqua now seem to him an all-sufficient world.

When the revolution breaks out, Roger and his mother are marked as "Tory" sympathizers. Although New England is Roger's "country," his heart tells him never to fight against his British heritage or his king. Consequently, when Mary Hamilton pleads with him to demonstrate allegiance to America, Roger agrees to become an officer aboard John Paul Jones's ship *only* to please his beloved. The complexity of political allegiance that had beset Waverley or Henry Morton does not afflict Wallingford. He tells Paul Jones "When I took my commission, I openly took the side of our colonies against the Crown. I am at heart among the Neutrals; 'tis ever an ignominious part to take . . . I have gone against my principles for the sake of one I love and honor" (125). To be neutral at heart is "ignominious" to him because he is violating "principles" of cultural heritage, not political belief. Whether the thirteen colonies continue to staff the British army is not for him an activating issue, nor is the Declaration of Independence.

Unlike historical novelists before her, Jewett does not fault her protagonist either for his overwhelmingly loyalist "principles" nor for his troubled willingness to violate those principles for the sake of love. Roger Wallingford retains his integrity even though, by the standards of Scott, Cooper, or Tolstoy, he does remarkably little and accomplishes less. The seamen under him gradually abandon their suspicion that he is an English spy; during the raid on Whitehaven, he is captured and imprisoned in England; after his release, he returns to "the great house" of the Hamilton family and marries Mary Hamilton (404).

Jewett's marital ending, superficially the same as the ending of *Waverley*, has no political resonance whatever. Schoolmaster Sullivan, once a Jacobite, now a mentor to Roger Wallingford, knows that Roger's joining the American navy will prove a superficial, passing allegiance:

> "There is something in the boy that holds by the past; he may be a persuaded Patriot, but a Tory ghost of a conscience plucks him by the sleeve. He does not lack greatness of soul, but I doubt if he does any great things except to stand honestly in his place, a scholar and a gentleman; and that is enough." (152)

Roger's very last words to Mary are "I have done nothing that I hoped to do! . . . I have done nothing; but, thank God, I am alive to love you, and to serve my country to my life's end" (404). His self-accounting need not be read as an admission of insignificance. Unchanged by his experiences, Roger has remained the honorable and decent "Tory Lover." In a post-revolutionary world in which old houses and old families still stay in place, "that is enough."

At select moments, Mary Hamilton speaks as if she were, like Cooper's Frances Wharton, a republican maiden turned American revolutionary:

"'Twas not the loss of our tea or any trumpery tax; we have never been wanting in generosity, or hung back when we should play our part. We remembered all the old wrongs; our own timber rotting in our woods that we might not cut; our own waterfalls running to waste by your English law, lest we cripple the home manufacturers. We were hurt to the heart, and were provoked to fight; we have turned now against such tyranny." (314)

Mary does not, however, confirm these sentiments by commensurate action or decision. In Roger Wallingford's absence, her greatest emotional bond is to his loyalist mother, with whom she shares tastes, manners, and a sense of honor. When a Sons of Liberty mob from Portsmouth threatens to burn Madam Wallingford's house, Mary denounces them as cowards avoiding patriotic service, then defends the loyalist lady and her property until other genteel patriots come to her aid (257–259). When in England Mary discovers to her surprised pleasure, as Roger had discovered before her, that England is (to borrow a title from Hawthorne) our old home.

"Home" is the great value that, in Jewett's view, should emerge from the divisive experience of revolution. The novel's last words of dialogue, spoken by Mary to Roger as they disembark at the great house along the riverbank, are "Thank God, we are at home!" (404). Home is a place free from both Parliamentary usurpation and the Sons of Liberty; it is founded upon generosity of mind and feeling, not the written word or the spoken public word. But it is also a place associated with women of a certain social class. The narrator remarks of Mary Hamilton and Madam Wallingford that "often the hearts of both these women, who were mistresses of great houses and the caretakers of many descendents, were full of anxious thought of home and all its business" (289). In both senses of the word, women's "business" depends upon maintaining past tradition.[21]

Jewett grants the family retainer a role beyond the comic extra. The Hamiltons' aged family boatman voices Jewett's conviction about gender politics: "women folks is natural Tories; they hold by the past, same as men are fain to reach out and want change" (79). Beneath Jewett's unassertive tone and restrained diction lies an implied challenge to longstanding male tradition; she brings the values of women's domestic fiction to the Scott paradigm of the historical novel. Revolutionary politics as well as warfare are thereby wished out of a Revolutionary War novel.

When Jewett sent a copy of *The Tory Lover* to Henry James, he responded as if Jewett's novel were a charming, tactful, well-written imitation of an overly familiar genre. James began by regretting that he wished to avoid the "tangle" of telling Jewett "how little I am in sympathy with experiments of its general (to my sense) misguided stamp." But James then proceeded to immerse himself in his own tangle: "The 'historic' novel is for me

condemned, even in cases of labour as delicate as yours, to a fatal cheapness, for the simple reason that the difficulty of the job is inordinate & that
a mere *escamotage*, in the interest of each & of the abysmal public naiveté,
becomes inevitable."[22] *The Tory Lover* has its failings, but "cheapness" and
"*escamotage*" are not among them.

Willa Cather's *Death Comes for the Archbishop* (1927) transforms the
historical lives of French Catholic missionaries, Archbishop Jean Baptiste
Lamy and Father Joseph Macheboeuf, into a fiction that is half historical
novel, half a saint's legend.[23] Cather had never forgotten her mentor Sarah
Orne Jewett's advice, "When a woman writes in the man's character, it must
always, I believe, be something of a masquerade."[24] To Cather, the historical
Archbishop Lamy was "a sort of invisible personal friend" but also a revered
"pioneer churchman" before whose photographs and bronze statue, "one felt
the same thing, something fearless and fine and very very well-bred—something that spoke of race."[25]

To render the "fine," "fearless," and "well-bred" qualities of Lamy, the
directness of first person narrative would have been counterproductive.
Lamy (renamed Latour in the novel) had been a gentleman seminarian from
Auvergne who had gained respect, affection, and power in New Mexico
among Pueblo Indians, Hispanics, and the "crude frontier society" of white
American pioneers.[26] He must negotiate among three racial groups, but his
commitment to European Catholic values never wavers. However admirable
the novel's individual Hispanics, Indians, and Anglo-American frontiersmen
might be, the preeminence of a man of Archbishop Lamy's "race" needed to
be invoked and implied, never expressed as his personal conviction.

Revolution is not the primary subject of *Death Comes to the Archbishop*,
but two failed racial revolts are crucial to its meaning. The successful but
short-lived 1680 revolt of the Pueblo peoples against Spanish occupation,
referred to three times, provides historical grounding for the racial hostility
of Indians and Hispanics that threatens Archbishop Latour's pacifist mission. The recent revolt led by Padre Antonio José Martinez of Taos in 1846
against the new American government, resulting in the killing of Governor
Brent, is the subject of an entire chapter whose opening section is titled "The
Old Order."[27] Father Latour wishes to reduce the Martinez of history into a
"picturesque and impressive, but really impotent" relic of "the day of lawless
personal power."[28] By referring to these events as "revolts" not rebellions,
Cather seeks to close revolution off into the past, leaving the future of New
Mexico in Euro-American, predominately Catholic hands.

Although Bishop Latour and Father Vaillant struggle to make Catholicism
convincing to the Pueblo people, their missionary efforts are only moderately
successful. The dominant image Cather associates with the Indian is a high
solitary rock, notably the Shiprock at Canyon de Chelly, and the rock cliff

beneath Acoma. Latour's Pecos Indian guide Jacinto saves Bishop Latour's life by leading him into a sacred cave during a snowstorm, but the cave proves as frighteningly incomprehensible to Latour as the Marabar caves in Forster's *A Passage to India* (1924). Imagery of "the rock," Latour reflects, should establish a link between Indian and Christian spirituality (St. Peter as "the Rock"), but it does not. For Cather, rock connotes strength and timelessness, but also impenetrability, a culture of ancient origin that can no longer evolve and cannot be shared.

Father Latour cooperates with American authorities but often regrets the results. Drifter and hunter Buck Scales, almost the first Anglo-American Latour meets in New Mexico, is a robber and serial killer who brutalizes his Mexican wife until he is hung as a "degenerate murderer" (77). The greed and decadence of the Colorado Gold Rush arouse Latour's disgust. Kit Carson seems an admirable scout, very much in the Leather-stocking tradition, until Carson leads the American military into Canyon de Chelly in order to destroy cornfields, orchards, and lay waste to "all that was sacred" to the Navajos (291).

During his last days, Latour reflects that his life in New Mexico has spanned the transition between the bison and the railroad, but signs of progress in Santa Fe are few and disheartening:

In the old days, it [Santa Fe] had an individuality, a style of its own; a tawny adobe town with a few green trees, set in a half-circle of carnelian-coloured hills; that and no more. But the year 1880 had begun a period of incongruous American building. Now, half the plaza square was still adobe, and half was flimsy wooden buildings with double porches, scroll-work and jack-straw posts and banisters painted white. Father Latour said the wooden houses, which had so distressed him in Ohio, had followed him. (268)

Like many a saint of legend, Bishop Latour has had good reason to be discouraged. Three years after coming to New Mexico, sleepless before Christmas, Latour first felt "the sense of failure clutching at his heart" (211). At that time he ascribed his sense of failure to the fact that "his great diocese was still a heathen country," in which Indians "traveled their old road of fear and darkness" and Mexicans were "children who played with their religion" (211). Nearing his life's end, Latour has little reason to believe that American culture and the practice of American Christianity will offer anything to revitalize or better the Pueblo/Spanish heritage.

What remains for Father Latour? There is his abiding Catholic faith, with strong ties to Rome, a faith that Willa Cather respects but does not share. There is Latour's lifelong friendship with Father Vaillant, who lacks Latour's "fine" qualities, but devotes to pastoral service an unflagging energy Latour

cannot match. There are Latour's memories of the ancient and fruitful beauty
of Auvergne, memories that sustain him when the carnelian and golden-ochre
brightness of New Mexico becomes momentarily overwhelming.

Most important of all is the climactic symbol of Archbishop Latour's life's
work, the building of Santa Fe's Cathedral of St. Francis of Assisi. Although
the Cathedral is built with local stone, it is designed by an architect from
Toulouse in the style of Latour's beloved cathedral of Clermont-Ferrand.
Latour's "fineness" of character, his aristocratic values, derive from his long-
ago French past, not his New Mexico experiences. He advances the aestheti-
cally dubious proposition that "our own Midi Romanesque is the right style
for this country" (240). Willa Cather never questions Latour's underlying
assumption that the traditions of French culture are needed to redeem New
World crudity and redirect New World energies. Progress resides, if anywhere, in the persistence of European cultural and churchly traditions within
a transatlantic context. Nonetheless, a sense of disappointment underlies
Lamy's life of saintly accomplishment. The remarkable clarity of Cather's
elegiac prose describing the air and landscape of New Mexico suggests that
only the oldest order of all, the geological laws of Nature, has ever been truly
godly.

Margaret Mitchell's *Gone With the Wind* (1936) has now sold more than
30 million copies in twenty-five languages. Although these statistics show
that it remains the most universally readable of long historical novels, for
most of us *Gone With the Wind* has become its film version. The reading of
the book has become a dim, late-adolescent memory; book copies purchased
after seeing the film may never be read. Undeserved condescension toward
mere popularity is the likely outcome, especially when academic critics recall
that *Gone With the Wind* and Faulkner's *Absalom! Absalom!* were published
in the same year. The familiar contrast of Faulkner and Mitchell, a contrast
based upon commonality of subject matter, compares an apple to an orange.
Faulkner's novel applies high-modernist narrative form to a regional historical legend retold through conventions of the Gothic novel; by contrast, Margaret Mitchell's brother recalls that his sister was eagerly reading Scott and
Dickens before twelve years of age.[29]

The film version opens with an over-script, not written by Mitchell, invit-
ing the audience to share in nostalgia, even bathos, for the Lost Cause: "There
was a land of Cavaliers and Cotton Fields called the Old South. Here in this
pretty world gallantry took its last bow. Here was the last ever to be seen of
Knights and their Ladies Fair, of Master and of Slave." From its first page,
Margaret Mitchell's novel is more complex in its rendering of history, more
divided in its social and human values. In 1926, Mitchell began writing her
novel with full awareness of the sentimentality of the magnolia tradition of
Southern Literature, and of the dangerous attraction of the newly resurgent

KKK.[30] More than half of her novel was to concern Reconstruction, not the "Old South." As representative Southerners, Ashley Wilkes is contrasted to Rhett Butler, and Melanie Hamilton to Scarlett O'Hara, but the two survivors among these four major characters, Scarlett and Rhett, prove to be deeply self-conflicted. Three years before the film made its appearance, Mitchell wrote, "if the novel has a theme, the theme is survival. What makes some people able to come through catastrophes and others, apparently just as able, strong and brave, go under?" Mitchell's response to her own question was "I don't know."[31]

In order to sentimentalize the Lost Cause, the film version leaves out historical facts important in Mitchell's novel: the significant numbers of Confederate deserters, of corrupt Confederate army contractors, and of confiscations by Confederate commissary officials. The film allows its audience to assume that Atlanta was heroically defended. Mitchell tells her reader otherwise. Despite General Joe Johnston's gritty strategic retreats to defend the city, Johnston was replaced by General John Bell Hood, who foolishly attacked Sherman's larger forces, then ordered the Confederate army to evacuate the city rather than defend it. In order to align the plantation tradition with genteel protestant aristocracy, the film entirely excludes Will Benteen, repeatedly identified as a "Cracker," who skillfully and honestly manages Tara after 1865 and eventually marries Scarlett's sister Suellen. Gerald O'Hara's Irish-Catholic qualities, briefly referred to in the film, are repeatedly cited by Mitchell to explain Scarlett's volatility, passion, courage, and sheer "gumption."

As many readers have noticed, often with distress, Mitchell wrote an unresolved open ending. In order to provide a hopeful resolution, the film ends by reprising Gerald O'Hara's faith that land (Tara) is the only thing that lasts, the only constant source of human strength and virtue, especially in the American South. Scarlett's famous last line "tomorrow is another day," thus implies that Scarlett will regain Brett's love and that they will return to Tara and to Atlanta. Mitchell's book shows us that Rhett has no such intentions, nor does Scarlett suggest she intends to return "home" permanently. She is returning once more to Tara to recoup her strengths: Tara is now only "a quiet place to lick her wounds, a haven in which to plan her campaign" (958).

At issue here is the prevailing attitude Margaret Mitchell assumes toward the Old Order of the South. Throughout Part One and deeply into Part Two of the novel (mid-1862), its tone is more accurately described as fond satire than cloying nostalgia. The fussy formalities of barbecues, balls, and receptions show that distinctions among the privileged, de-emphasized in the film, are maintained because they are a source of unadmitted snobbery. The appeal of the Old Order relies upon a combination of winsome exterior qualities: "good family," grace of appearance and manners, opulence of surroundings, a sure sense of belonging. The shallow societal forces that encourage Scarlett O'Hara to play the risky game of being the Belle of Clayton County are constantly in evidence. Irony is directed at the consequences of Scarlett's self-assurance: "Life had not taught her that the race was not to the swift. She lay in the silvery shadows with courage rising and made the plans that a sixteen-year-old makes when life has been so pleasant that defeat is an impossibility and a pretty dress and a clear complexion are weapons to vanquish fate."[32] More insulated than the aristocracy of Scott's or Cooper's border country, Scarlett's world knows outer reality through newspapers: "the first two pages of the paper were always devoted to advertisements of slaves, mules, plows, coffins, houses for sale or rent, cures for private diseases, abortifacients [sic] and restoratives for lost manhood" (234). These kinds of details do not belong to the world of the film.

After the burning of Atlanta and the collapse of the Confederacy, the New Order mushrooms into power: from the North, carpetbaggers, radical republican politicians, ex-military officers, and fortune seekers; from the South, scallawags, opportunistic overseers, freed desperate blacks, landless white trash, and still more fortune seekers. The keynote to Mitchell's evaluation of all these types, except for ex-slaves loyal to white families, is *nouveau riche* vulgarity. The New Order consists of peoples without a family past whose sense of self-importance is based on vulgarity not elegance: "overdressed women, overfurnished houses, too many jewels, too many horses, too much food, too much whisky" (814). Even Scarlett, who seeks money and security through business deals with the *nouveau riche*, calls them, in a moment of honest rage, "buzzards," "nigger lovers," "dirty Scallawags," and "lousy trashy poor whites" (507).

A telling reversal occurs. As Mitchell weaves her narrative through the dark era of Reconstruction, the venality and corruption of the New Order lead her to increasingly admire those who remained faithful to the Old. Scarlett concludes that her O'Hara heritage, which includes Catholic Jacobites and Irish nationalists (entirely omitted in the film), "had not been crushed . . . not been broken . . . not whined, they had fought" (401). Within the old families gathering in Mrs. Elsing's tattered Atlanta drawing room, Scarlett now perceives "an ageless dignity, a nameless gallantry . . . they were a soft-spoken, fierce, tired people who were defeated and would not know defeat, broken yet standing determinedly erect" (569). There is no irony in such passages. As Scarlett's guilt over profiting from ventures with the *nouveau riche* grows more troubling, her opinion of the Old Order softens toward understanding and admiration.

Mitchell's difficulty in resolving her attitudes toward the Old South centers upon her characterization of Ashley Wilkes. Ashley understands the dangers of a one-crop economy, the hollowness of Southern war rhetoric, and the illogic in arguing for supremacy of states rights, yet loyalty to region prompts him to enlist. Brave in battle, Ashley proves a "coward" in peace (497). His aristocratic grace, honesty, and sense of honor render him ineffectual in the postwar South, "as helpless as a turtle on his back" (670). Ashley's superior education and his love of books and music, which would have allowed him to remain a "studious country gentleman" in the antebellum world, have by 1865 left him stranded in historical melancholy and crippling fears of an unknown world (212, 498–499). No cultural hope resides in such a man, even when old family Southern Democrats return to power. Rhett Butler, unknowingly speaking as a Social Darwinist, contends that it is a "natural law" that people like Ashley, who "have neither cunning nor strength . . . should go under" even as the "hardy few . . . come through" (719).

Nonetheless, Ashley's voice retains a lyric resonance unique among the novel's characters. He explains to Melanie "the reason why I am fighting":

I see Twelve Oaks and remember how the moonlight slants across the white columns, and the unearthly way the magnolias look, opening under the moon, and how the climbing roses make the side porch shady even at hottest noon. . . . And there's the long view down the road to the river, across the cotton fields, and the mist rising from the bottom lands in the twilight. And that is why I'm here, who have no love of death or misery or glory and no hatred for anyone. Perhaps that is what is called patriotism, love of home and country. But Melanie, it goes deeper than that. For Melanie, these things I have named are but the symbols of the thing for which I risk my life, the symbols of the kind of life I love. For I am fighting for the old days, the old ways I love so much, but which I fear are now gone forever, no matter how the die may fall. For win or lose, we lose just the same. (212)

When Ashley speaks in this vein, venturesome sixteen-year-old Scarlett may thrill to the rhythm of his voice, but she does not understand the meaning of his words. Melanie Hamilton, however, thoroughly understands them, and their true author, Margaret Mitchell, seems to deeply appreciate them half against her will.

At novel's end, Ashley's words as well as his voice fill Scarlett's being, precisely because she is now guiltily immersed in the emerging industrial order of the New South. As Ashley speaks of the old ways Scarlett ought to remember, the narrator summarizes her response to his words:

She could hear the gay jingle of bridle bits as they rode under the dogwood trees to the Tarleton's picnic, hear her own careless laughter, see the sun glinting on his silver-gilt hair and note the proud easy grace with which he sat his horse. There was music in his voice, the music of fiddles and banjos to which they had danced in the white house that was no more. There was the far off yelping of possum dogs in the dark swamp under cool autumn moons and the smell of eggnog bowls, wreathed with holly at Christmas time and smiles on black and white faces. . . . Over it all rested a sense of security, a knowledge that tomorrow could only bring the same happiness today had brought. (857)

Scarlett's remembrances, centered on Ashley as well as Tara, are even more sensual than Ashley's, but the appeal of both passages depends upon the same plangent cadences. In the midst of turmoil, be it 1861 or 1867, both evoke the consolation of a changeless peace that, presumably, once existed. Like Gatsby's search to recreate the past, Scarlett's and Ashley's yearning can never be satisfied, which is surely one source of its power for millions of readers.

The last section of *Gone With the Wind* magnifies and deepens self-conscious nostalgia for the Old Order.[33] Mitchell's narrative ends, not with Rhett's and Scarlett's divorce, nor with any concern for Scarlett's two neglected living children (Wade Hampton Hamilton and Ella Lorena Kennedy), nor with the fate of the two symbolic houses at Tara and in Atlanta, but with the death of Melanie Hamilton and the seeming end of all she represents. Throughout the narrative, Rhett and Scarlett change and survive, Ashley disintegrates, but Melanie Hamilton steadily grows in stature.[34] She is, as Rhett repeatedly says, the only true lady, the woman who rises above life's pains, believes the best of others, loves family and friends, and, yes, maintains decorum. Ashley says of Melanie "she is the only dream I ever had that lived and breathed and did not die in the face of reality" (938). After years of scorning Melanie's seeming helplessness, Scarlett recognizes that "Melly is the only woman friend I ever had . . . the only woman except Mother who really loved me" (937). To cynical, often brutal Rhett Butler, Melanie represents "the passing not of a woman but a legend—the gentle, self-effacing but steel-spined woman on whom the South had builded its home in war and to whose proud and loving arms it had returned in defeat" (949). Although an historical novelist raised on Walter Scott has finally centered the appeal of the Old Order in a symbolic woman, all three tributes are directed toward a "dream" and a "legend" that is declared to be past.

Paradoxically, however, neither dream nor legend utterly dies. Consider the future plans of former blockade-runner, speculator, Byronic cynic, and scallawag Rhett Butler. He will use his ill-gotten gains to go to England, to Paris, or perhaps back to Charleston to search for "the calm dignity life can have when it's lived by gentle folks, the genial grace of days that are gone" (956). To author and reader, his new resolve is meant as a hopeful sign that Melanie's virtues and Ashley's dream will somehow live on in Rhett Butler, who has consistently scorned everything Ashley represents. By affirming the gumption necessary to survive, the ending of *Gone With the Wind* has it both ways; it deepens the appeal of futilely searching for a lost past, even as it undermines it.

CODA: REVOLUTION CLIMBS THE STAIRS

In 1957 and 1958, Giangiacomo Feltrinelli—socialist, then communist, then ex-communist, then publisher of Castro, Che Guevara, and Ho Chi Minh— published a novel by a gentleman of aristocratic taste (Pasternak's *Doctor Zhivago*) and then a novel by a fifteenth-generation Sicilian prince (Lampedusa's *The Leopard*). The European world of the 1950s had good reason to repeat Robert Graves's valedictory wish, "Goodbye to All That." World War I had shredded the authority of monarchy, aristocracy, and genteel diplomacy. Approximate numbers can only suggest the increasing horror; World War I: 35 million casualties and 17 million dead, including three million Russians and one million Italians. The 1917 Battle of Caporetto, in which Giuseppe Tomasi di Lampedusa fought, ended in 45,000 Italian dead or wounded, 265,000 captured Italian soldiers, and no less than 350,000 Italian deserters. During the trench warfare at the Somme, at least one million German, British, and French were killed, achieving an Allied advance of seven miles.

The slaughter was only a prelude.[35] World War II: at least 60 million dead, including 23 million Russians, 6.3 million Germans, and nearly half a million Italians, English, and Americans. Such numbers numb the mind, still tempting us, in moments of confused outrage, to overlook the multiple causes of the casualties: the failure of the League of Nations, inflation, the Depression, the decline of socialism, the rise of fascism, the Spanish Civil War, appeasement, the fear and adoration of dictators like Mussolini, Hitler, and Stalin, complicity, conscription, concentration camps, many European cities in ruins. The vastly increased powers of a central national government, a predicted legacy of the French Revolution, was everywhere apparent for good and for bad. For Pasternak, under the eye of Stalin, and for Prince Lampedusa, his inheritance gone and his Palermo palazzo bombed, the attractive way of life of their nineteenth-century aristocratic forbears aroused futile longing as well as respectful condescension. For them no less than for Margaret Mitchell, the appeal of a belle époque depended upon awareness of what was to follow.

To Yurii Zhivago, even as a young boy, the days when there had been "a Zhivago factory, a Zhivago bank, Zhivago buildings" are imagined as "a fairy-tale kingdom" that he never knew.[36] For Yurii, unlike Tolstoy's Pierre Bezukhov, "suddenly all that was gone" and he found himself "poor" (5). Until the outbreak of World War I, however, Yurii feels fortunate to be raised in the wealthy Moscow home of chemistry professor Alexander Gromeko. In the loving Gromeko household, he enjoys an apolitical, comfortable, and sophisticated life centered on academic achievement and the arts, especially music—an upbringing very like the youth of Boris Pasternak. Merit, skill, and aesthetic sensitivity are Alexander Gromeko's measures of character; he is pleased that his daughter Tonia will marry a promising medical student and a poet, not an industrialist.

Unlike Yurii, who is initially enthusiastic about socialism and the revolution, Professor Gromeko is skeptical about the motivations of both revolutionaries and the nobility, even though, as a professional who married the daughter of a wealthy ironmaster, he stands to lose greatly at the hands of both. Aboard the train to the Urals in 1918, he reminds Yurii that, during the early days of any revolutionary movement, stated goals have a "single-mindedness" and "original purity" that must promptly fade. "Next day, the casuistry of politics has turned them inside out" (241). The consequence can only be, for people such as he and Yurii, that Bolshevik "philosophy is alien to me, their regime is hostile to us" (241). The retreat of the Gromekos and the Zhivagos to the Urals is their futile attempt to say 'goodbye to all that.' Farewell to Bolshevik Moscow also demands farewell to the high culture they have known in pre-War Russia. Only a few books, including *War and Peace* and *A Tale of Two Cities*, will remain with them.

In Pasternak's view of the revolution, people like the Gromekos—unlike the Bezhukovs, the Bolkonskis, and even the Rostovs of *War and Peace*—lose everything except their integrity. Their Moscow house is taken over by the Bolshevik government, subdivided into apartments, and degraded. Eventually the Gromekos, like other apolitical professionals, are deported to Paris, taking precious few assets with them. Knowing that Yurii has fallen in love with Lara Guishar, Yuri's wife Tania, who is about to be deported with their two children, writes Yurii a heartbroken letter of farewell, full of grief but free of blame. Yurii never sees his first family again. When he returns to Moscow after the civil war is over, all traces of the Gromekos' way of life have disappeared into a tawdry urban world of bureaucracy, opportunism, and near poverty. For the second time in Yurii's experience a life remembered as a fairy tale irredeemably collapses. A third will follow.

The Leopard, narrated almost entirely from the perspective of the aging Don Fabrizio Corbera, Prince of Salina, sustains the impression that the world of aristocracy, and the historical novel with it, have ended. Although neither of these impressions is true, they seem plausible because of Lampedusa's command of metaphor, subtlety of psychology, and vivid renderings of the sensual realities of his remembered Sicilian world. The novel sums up an entire tradition in small compass and few pages. Convinced that his life was a failure, his aristocratic heritage a faded memory, Lampedusa relinquished all material things in his last letters except his unpublished book. *The Leopard*, he wrote with excessive modesty, is "not without its elegiac poetry"; "each word has been weighed up and many things are not made explicit but only hinted at."[37]

The phrase "elegiac poetry" did not mean that the end of the Sicilian aristocracy was to be an occasion for nostalgic sentimentality. Lampedusa intended to convey "how the degeneration of the family becomes ever more marked until it reaches almost total collapse" (xi). Don Fabrizio contributes greatly to the family's "degeneration." To Lampedusa's great credit as a novelist, he persuades the reader to share the prince's outlook, without forgetting the prince's failings, and without turning him into an icon of the lost past.

Don Fabrizio understands that mid-nineteenth-century Sicilian life, still dominated by noble families and the Catholic church, had been built on the premise that the purpose of maintaining power was to prolong idleness (22). As family money dwindles, Don Fabrizio knows he should not forgive his peasant tenants their rent, but he feels genuine affection for them, even if they cheat him. The complementary appeal of his Palermo palazzo and his country estate, of his vineyard and the hunt, of the brothel and the bath, of presiding over family table and local reception, are as overpowering as the Sicilian sun.

The prince knows that he is living at the historical moment, 1860, when the essential oils of his way of life have been refined to simultaneous perfection and evaporation:

> The wealth of many centuries had been transmitted into ornament, luxury, pleasure; no more; the abolition of feudal rights had swept away duties as well as privileges; wealth, like an old wine, had let the dregs of greed, even of care and prudence, fall to the bottom of the barrel, leaving only verve and color. And thus eventually it cancelled itself out; this wealth which had achieved its object was composed only of essential oils—and like essential oils, it soon evaporated." (30)

The sensual power of such writing matches the lethargic appeal of Don Fabrizio's life. A sense of inevitability, not blame, hovers over Lampedusa's summary comment that "Prince Fabrizio lived in perpetual discontent under his Jovelike frown, watching the ruin of his own class and his own inheritance without ever making, still less wanting to make, any move toward saving it" (9).

Insofar as such a life has a public crisis, it comes about through the arrival of the Risorgimento when Garibaldi's Redshirts besiege Palermo. Politically, Don Fabrizio is revealed to be an uneasy aristocratic waverer familiar to readers of Scott or Tolstoy. Fabrizio has been cooperating with the "Kingdom of the Two Sicilies," ruled by Bourbon King Ferdinand II, but he is not opposed to unseating the Bourbons and establishing a Sicilian legislative assembly. He avoids commitment because he has little faith that the Liberals, even if they gain power, could significantly change Sicilian life anytime soon. He listens carefully to the plausible warnings of his trusted Jesuit friend Father Pirrone, who contends that the Liberals will first sell church lands with the complicity of the nobility, but will then placate the outraged peasantry by confiscating lands held by the nobility (38–39). So it had happened in France seventy years before.

Fabrizio's self-interest and his principles are at variance, but he is not especially troubled by the contradictions between them. He does not waver because he feels he ought to commit himself; he prefers to do nothing because he believes that, in the long run, he need do nothing. Lampedusa implies, but never states, that many an honorable nobleman of Fabrizio's position, tastes, and beliefs would remain equally passive.

Political revolution directly enters Fabrizio's life only on occasions that he can too easily dismiss. Against his self-interest, Fabrizio votes "yes" on the plebiscite for the unification of Italy. In part, he is yielding to the public pressure of fellow citizens at Donnafugata, his country estate; in part, he is languidly submitting to what he regards as historical necessity. After learning that the vote in Donnafugata was 512 to 0 in favor of unification, he discovers that the mayor not only pressured citizens to vote "yes," but had also falsified the election returns to make the vote unanimous. Fabrizio's feeling that an "evil fairy of unknown name" has been hovering over Sicily since the arrival of Garibaldi's troops has its measure of truth (110).

Cavaliere Chevalley arrives at Donnafugata to offer Fabrizio the position of senator in the newly formed national legislature at Turin. Fabrizio acknowledges that, at this "decisive moment," it is the "duty" of all citizens to support the newly founded Italian State, and to give no public sign of disloyalty, but he then proceeds to decline the honor of being a senator:

> "In these last six months, since your Garibaldi set foot at Marsala, too many things have been done without our being consulted for you to be able now to ask a member of the old governing class to help develop things and carry them through. . . . In Sicily it doesn't matter whether things are done well or done badly; the sin which we Sicilians never forgive is simply that of 'doing' at all."
> (176, 177)

In order graciously to excuse his personal refusal, Don Fabrizio defines his lassitude as a Sicilian cultural principle. He wrongly describes himself as both negligible and "old" simply because he prefers not to participate.

Lampedusa makes it clear that, if the Turin Senate ever acquires the same stature as the Roman Senate of antiquity, Fabrizio might well agree to serve (175). But Fabrizio has seen enough vulgarity and hypocrisy among Redshirts and Liberals not to be persuaded. Neither to Fabrizio in 1860, nor to Lampedusa in 1957, were pride of family, pride of region, and pride of nation the same thing. The conflicts among the separable loyalties of the Old Order had never been resolved.

Although Don Fabrizio can ignore national political change without immediate consequence, social and economic revolution comes upon him in the form of Don Calogera Sedara, the new mayor of Donnafugata, soon to be the richest landowner in the county and a consummate vulgarian without taste or manners. Mayor Sedara is shrewd enough to keep his crude peasant wife out of the public eye, to send his beautiful daughter Angela to attend finishing school in Florence, and to work energetically at problems of local governance, including the rigging of elections. Before offering his daughter in marriage to the Salina family, Sedara shrewdly buys a title of Baroness for her. In the context of traditional Sicilian class structure, the vulgarity of Sedara's ambition is expressed through arranged marriage, not through the banknotes readily seized and eagerly displayed by Margaret Mitchell's carpetbaggers.

When Don Fabrizio sees Don Sedara ascending the Salina family staircase, at Donnafugata, dressed in tails for an informal reception, but ready to arrange for his daughter's marriage, Fabrizio recognizes that he is witnessing "the bourgeois revolution climbing his stairs in Don Calogero's tailcoat" (93–94). Against the vehement protests of his wife and Father Pironne, Fabrizio allows the courtship between Angelica Sedara and his beloved nephew Tancredi to continue toward betrothal and marriage. To Fabrizio, allowing Mayor Sedara into his palazzo and then into his family is the swallowing of a toad (124). The Salina family's need for new money is not, however, a sufficient explanation for his passivity. Fabrizio's authority as a nobleman depends on good manners he cannot be seen to violate. The rise of bourgeois vulgarity, he rationalizes, need not be an historical necessity simply because it now threatens to occur.

From Lampedusa's mid-twentieth-century perspective, the Old Order preferred passivity to any acknowledgment of its increasing vulnerability. As Sedara stands at the foot of the stairs, Don Fabrizio tries to think of himself as the Salina family's heraldic Leopard "preparing to tear a timid jackal to pieces." This image is immediately replaced, however, by Fabrizio's visualizing a French history painting in which Sedara, surrounded by plumed marshals, figures as the crowd's admired but "ironic Napoleon" (122). It is a moment of consummate historical illusion. Opposition to today's Napoleon, Fabrizio would like to believe, must remain conveniently futile, no matter how vulgar today's Napoleon might be.

The more an historical novelist dwells on the appealing qualities lost in the demise of the Old Order, the more crass and opportunistic seem those who supplant them. During the first half of the twentieth century, as the certainty of progress becomes increasingly untenable, the pattern becomes especially marked. In *The Debacle*, the greedy factory owner Delaherche rises as the region around Sedan is wasted. In *The Gods Are Thirsty*, Citizen Blaise and Desmahis rise after Brotteaux is guillotined. In *Gone With the Wind*, Rhett Butler and Scarlett O'Hara rise as Ashley Wilkes and Melanie Hamilton pass away. Don Sedara ascends to power as Don Fabrizio declines to death.

Writing *Doctor Zhivago* during the decades when Scott's fictional legacy seemed exhausted, Pasternak is the most explicit in his contempt for new men on the rise. Yurii Zhivago is first dismayed, then angered, to discover that the Moscow hospital to which he has returned in 1918 is now run by a new breed of "suppliers, concessionaires and authorized agents":

> They were not former men of substance or dismissed heads of old firms—such people did not recover from the blow they had received. They were a new category of businessmen, people without roots who had been scooped up from the bottom by the war and the revolution. (198)

"Scooped up from the bottom"; the more the Old Order is associated with the good life, the darker the rendering of social overturn is likely to be. War and revolution, Yurii feels, allow the scum of society to rise to the top.

NOTES

1. See especially Richard V. Chase, *The American Novel And Its Tradition* (Garden City, NY: Doubleday & Co., 1957); George Dekker, *The American Historical Romance* (Cambridge and New York: Cambridge University Press, 1987); Joel Porte, *The Romance in America: Studies in Cooper, Poe, Hawthorne, Melville and James* (Middletown Conn: Wesleyan University Press, 1969); see also John McWilliams, "The Rationale for the American Romance," *Boundary II*, 17 (1990), 71–82. This scholarly tradition has yielded continuing insight into individual novels; it could not resolve the centuries of overlap among the terms "novel," "romance," and "epic."

2. See William Wordsworth, "Preface" to the Second Edition of *Lyrical Ballads* (1800) in *Selected Poems and Prefaces*, ed. Jack Stillinger (Boston: Houghton Mifflin, 1965), p. 446.

3. Wordsworth "The World Is Too Much With Us," *Selected Poems and Prefaces*, p. 182.

4. Jane Millgate argues persuasively that the first edition of Scott's narrative opened shortly before the 1707 Act of Union and that, while revising the novel for the Magnum Opus edition of the Waverley Novels, Scott altered many passages to shift the opening to shortly after the Act of Union (Millgate, *Walter Scott: the Making of the Novelist,* pp. 169–184). Fiona Robertson, editor of the Oxford World's Classics text followed here, reprints the Magnum Opus version, with many clarifying footnotes. As Millgate argues, a pre-Union opening makes both Ravenswood and Ashton seem more vacillating and insecure because both are "in some sense out of step with the times and thereby rendered largely powerless" (173). Sir William Ashton thus

becomes "the pre-Union opportunist" who needs to secure his gains before Scotland ceases to exist (174). The effect of the difference is one of degree only. The years after 1707, when the terms of the Union were being institutionalized, were to be equally insecure, especially for those who had always thought the Scots and the English were separate peoples and nations. Whether the action occurs immediately pre-Union or immediately post-Union, the inner qualities of the two men, and the cultural shift they represent, remain the same.

5. Sir Walter Scott, *The Bride of Lammermoor*, edited with an introduction and notes by Fiona Robertson (Oxford and New York: Oxford University Press, 1990), p. 191.

6. Sir Walter Scott, *The Bride of Lammermoor*, edited by Fiona Robertson, pp. 27–28, 41. Scott's portrayal of the venality of the seventeenth-century Scottish Privy Council, here and in *Old Mortality*, should disabuse anyone of the lingering notion that Scott was a romantic, aristocratic reactionary.

7. David Brown observes that the village of Wolf's-Hope "formerly part of the Ravenswoods' domain, is a microcosm of bourgeois Scotland emerging from the shadow of feudalism" (Brown, *Walter Scott and the Historical Imagination*, 1979, p. 146).

8. Sir Walter Scott, *Rob Roy*, edited by Ian Duncan (Oxford: Oxford University Press, 2008), pp. 296–309.

9. Walter Scott, *The Heart of Mid-Lothian*, edited with introduction and notes by Tony Inglis (London and New York: Penguin, 1994), pp. 360–361.

10. Scott's description of the motives and methods of the mob's attack on the Edinburgh Tolbooth is very like the descriptions of the attack on the Bastille later written by Michelet, Carlyle and Dickens. Scott probably had the assault on the Bastille in mind as he wrote about the Tolbooth. The black and red imagery Scott associates with a prerevolutionary urban mob may have influenced the portrayal of the Boston mob in Hawthorne's great short story "My Kinsman, Major Molineux."

11. Leo Tolstoy, *War and Peace*, the Maude translation, 2nd edition, edited by George Gibian (New York: W.W. Norton and Co., 1996), p. 663.

12. *War and Peace*, p. 664. Tolstoy seems to be dismissing *Les Chevaliers de Cygne* as mere entertainment. However, without referring to Tolstoy, Richard Maxwell has described Madame de Genlis as an early proponent of the term *roman historique* who believed that "historical fiction is more difficult to write than tales of pure invention" (Maxwell, *The Historical Novel in Europe*, p. 43).

13. *War and Peace*, p. 664. Like Prince André, Isaiah Berlin would struggle to express the essence of Kutuzov's rare virtue. Because Berlin cannot convey it through one word, he evokes it by negative definition: " It is not that they [people like Kutuzov] are more knowledgeable . . . not their deductive or inductive reasoning that makes them masters . . . not merely clever, not a victim to abstract theories or dogma. . . . They see the way the world goes, what goes with what, and what will never be brought together" (Isaiah Berlin, *The Hedgehog and the Fox* [1953] quoted in *War and Peace*, ed. Gibian, p. 1133). Kutuzov seems to sense the will of the world, a quality altogether beyond time.

14. Leather-stocking had served British major Effingham with loyalty and enthusiasm during the French and Indian War. If Cooper had written a novel about

Leather-stocking during the Revolutionary War, as he once planned to do, he would have faced the problem of whether or not he could convincingly describe Leather-stocking's conversion to the Patriots. See Wayne Franklin, "'One More Scene': The Marketing Context of Cooper's 'Sixth' Leather-Stocking Tale" in *Leather-Stocking Redux; or, Old Tales, New Essays*, ed. Jeffrey Walker (New York: AMS Press, 2011), pp. 225–252. For a collective interpretation of Cooper's six novels of the Revolutionary War, see John McWilliams, *Political Justice in a Republic; James Fenimore Cooper's America* (Berkeley: University of California Press, 1972), pp. 32–99.

15. Richard Maxwell, *The Historical Novel in Europe, 1650–1950* (Cambridge and New York: Cambridge University Press, 2009) part III, pp. 233–273. See also Avrom Fleishman, *The English Historical Novel* (Baltimore: Johns Hopkins University Press, 1972) chapter six.

16. E.M. Forster, *Aspects of the Novel* (New York: Harcourt, Brace and World, 1954), p. 30. Originally published in 1927. Constructing a straw man for the premodernist novel, Forster will grant Scott only the power to tell a good story at excessive length. Scott's kind of novel, Forster misleadingly concludes, cannot depend on realism and must therefore depend on "passion" that turns into mere sentimentality: "But passion—surely passion is low-brow enough, and think how all Scott's laborious mountains and scooped-out glens and carefully ruined abbeys call out for passion, passion and how it is never there!" (30–31).

17. Diana Wallace, *The Woman's Historical Novel: British Women Writers, 1900–2000* (New York: Palgrave Macmillan, 2005), p. 3. Distinguishing Wallace's formation of a tradition of women's historical fiction from Scott, Jerome de Groot has written "Wallace posits a different genealogy for the woman's historical novel, arguing that it develops from the hybrid potentialities of the Gothic novel rather than the rationality of Scott" (Jerome de Groot, *The Historical Novel* [Routledge: London and New York, 2010], p. 67. De Groot distinction is just, as long as one recalls that few novels of Scott lack some element of Gothic fiction.

18. The tradition Wallace traces begins after World War I with the romances of Georgette Heyer, and continues through Daphne Du Maurier, Mary Renault, Sylvia Townsend Warner and many others to Pat Barker. Sometimes Wallace criticizes Lukacs and his followers (chiefly Avrom Fleishman and Harry Shaw) for their omissions of women; at other times, she presents women's historical fiction as a separable tradition. Consider some of the recurrent terms and concerns through which Wallace defines and analyzes the woman's historical novel: gender identity created through performance and social construction, escapism and fantasy-space; victimization and empowerment, adultery and illegitimacy; homosexual and lesbian; subgenres known as the "erotic-historical" and the "bodice-ripper"; cross-reading, cross-writing, and cross-dressing; queens as opposed models of womanhood (Elizabeth I and Mary Queen of Scots), regency nostalgia and romantic Toryism, There is little here, except the last two couplings, that brings the *Waverley Novels* to mind. Wallace does not present evidence that the twentieth-century women novelists were concerned to oppose the overwhelmingly male legacy of Scott. Perhaps, in the context of the decline of Scott's reputation from 1920 to 1960, women historical novelists were suddenly in a position to go their own way.

19. *The Tory Lover* begs to be read as a revision of Cooper's *The Pilot* (1823) and Melville's *Israel Potter* (1854), both of which characterize John Paul Jones and describe Jones's raid on Whitehaven in detail. None of Cooper's interest in nautical description, no lowborn patriot hero like Long Tom Coffin, enters into *The Tory Lover*. Melville's grim focus upon the suicidal brutality of the battle of the *Bon Homme Richard* and the *Serapis* ("Intrepid, unprincipled, reckless, predatory, with boundless ambition, civilized in externals but a savage at heart, America is, may yet be, the Paul Jones of Nations") bears little resemblance to the glory-seeking, Byronic courtesies of Jewett's John Paul Jones. Melville's Benjamin Franklin is a confidence-man; Jewett's Franklin is an honest, plainspoken citizen (Melville, *Israel Potter: His Fifty Years of Exile* [Evanston, Ill: Northwestern University Press, 1982], p. 120).

20. Sarah Orne Jewett, *The Tory Lover* (Boston and New York: Houghton, Mifflin and Company, 1901), p. 55.

21. As Jewett completed *The Tory Lover*, she wrote Horace Scudder she was pleased that her admittedly ambitious novel had preserved admirable qualities of colonial life: "*The Tory Lover* . . . has taken more than a solid year's hard work and the dreams and hopes of many a year beside. . . . It has been the happiest year of work that ever came to me as well as the hardest. A good deal of the 'tone of things' which existed in those earlier days had survived into my own times; the fine old houses, the ladies and gentlemen of colonial days were not all gone" (Sarah Orne Jewett, letter to Horace Scudder, July 12, 1901 in *Sarah Orne Jewett Letters*, ed. Richard Cary (Waterville, ME: Colby College Press, 1956), p. 95.

22. Henry James, letter to Sarah Orne Jewett, October 5, 1901 in *Critical Essays on Sarah Orne Jewett*, ed. Gwen L. Nagel [Boston: G.K. Hall, 1984], pp. 41, 42).

23. Shortly after *Death Comes for the Archbishop* was published, Cather wrote that her novel was "a conjunction of the general and the particular, like most works of the imagination. I had all my life wanted to do something in the style of legend, which is absolutely the reverse of dramatic treatment. . . . In the legend, the martyrdoms of the saints are no more dwelt upon than are the trivial incidents of their lives. . . . The essence of such writing is not to hold the note, not to use an incident for all there is in it—but to touch and pass on"(letter to *The Commonweal*, November 23, 1927 in *Willa Cather: Stories, Poems and Other Writings*, notes by Sharon O'Brien [New York: The Library of America, 1992], p. 959).

24. Letter of Sarah Orne Jewett to Willa Cather, 1908 in *Letters of Sarah Orne Jewett*, ed. Annie Fields (Boston and New York: Houghton Mifflin Co., 1911), p. 246.

25. Willa Cather, letter to *The Commonweal*, November 23, 1927, p. 959.

26. Willa Cather, letter to *The Commonweal*, p. 960.

27. Willa Cather, *Death Comes For The Archbishop* (New York: Vintage Books, 1990), p. 139.

28. *Death Comes For the Archbishop*, p. 141. Neither in Lamy's nor Cather's eyes does Padre Martinez seem "impotent." Martinez's body arouses fearful, sexual revulsion: "His [Martinez's] mouth was the very assertion of violent, uncurbed passions and tyrannical self-will; the full lips thrust out and taut, like the flesh of animals, distended by fear or desire" (140–141).

29. Darden Asbury Pyron, *Southern Daughter: The Life of Margaret Mitchell* (New York and Oxford: Oxford University Press, 1991), p. 48. Unlike Faulkner, but

Chapter 7

very much in the Scott tradition, Mitchell insisted upon the verifiable accuracy of her novel's historical details.

30. See Helen Taylor, *Scarlett's Women: Gone with the Wind and Its Female Fans* (New Brunswick: Rutgers University Press, 1989), pp. 54–62.

31. Margaret Mitchell, autobiographical sketch for the *Wilson Bulletin* (1936) in Richard Howard, ed., *Gone with the Wind as Book and Film* (n.p: University of South Carolina Press, 1983), p. 38.

32. Margaret Mitchell, *Gone With the Wind* (New York: Scribner, 2011), p. 89.

33. Lawrence Buell shrewdly notes that *"Gone With the Wind . . .* refuses to disown the old order it seems to undo" (Buell, *The Dream of the Great American Novel* [Cambridge, Mass: Harvard University Press, 2014], p. 305). The importance of this paradox refutes those who would dismiss the novel as a gathering of sentimental clichés.

34. Margaret Mitchell referred to Melanie as "my heroine" (Helen Taylor, *Scarlett's Women*, p. 78). Her comment reflects a response to the completed novel. A reader who has finished only parts 1 and 2 of the novel would have difficulty perceiving Melanie as its heroine.

35. See Nicola Chiaromonte's *The Paradox of History* for a telling description of the continuity of disillusionment between World War I and World War II. In his last chapter, "An Age of Bad Faith," Chiaromonte expands upon the familiar truth that "Faith in Progress was severely shaken by the outbreak of the First World War" by summarizing the consequences of the Great War for subsequent decades: "The whole of Western society had been completely devastated by the cataclysm and no political idea, no technological resourcefulness, no traditional wisdom, no ideology and no belief was capable of withstanding it" (*The Paradox of History*, Foreword by Joseph Frank, Postface by Mary McCarthy [Philadelphia: University of Pennsylvania Press, 1985], p. 142).

36. Boris Pasternak, *Doctor Zhivago*, Introduction by John Bayley (New York: Pantheon Books, 1991), p. 5.

37. Giuseppe Tomasi di Lampedusa, *The Leopard*, translated by Archibald Colquhoun, foreword by Gioacchino Lanza Tomasi (New York: Pantheon Books, 2007), pp. xi, xii.

Chapter 8

Women, Children, and the Progressive Ending

The intent of the title of Jeffrey Eugenides's *The Marriage Plot*, an academic novel cum *Bildungsroman* set at Brown University in the early 1980s, is indicated in its first chapter. Madeleine Hanna, an inveterate reader and an English major, enrolls in a Junior Honors Seminar ("The Marriage Plot: Selected Novels of Austen, Eliot, and James") taught by K. McCall Saunders, "a seventy-nine year old New Englander":

> In Professor Saunders's opinion, the novel had reached its apogee with the marriage plot and had never recovered from its disappearance. In the days when success in life had depended on marriage, and marriage had depended on money, novelists had had a subject to write about. . . . Marriage didn't mean much anymore and neither did the novel. Where could you find the marriage plot nowadays? You couldn't. You had to read historical novels.[1]

For Madeleine, academic buzz about the New Novel, postmodernism, and French literary theory have persuaded her that nineteenth-century novels built upon the marriage plot and the happy ending must be fusty and irrelevant. Nonetheless, Madeleine loves "The Great Tradition" and, in fact, would like emotionally to live within its parameters. Madeleine knows that tacit yearning for the marriage plot persists, especially among historical novel readers, despite the objections raised, ironically, by George Eliot, by Henry James, and by select late nineteenth-century historical novelists. This chapter will trace the literary and historical causes of this slow, reluctant but decided reversal.

Scott is the exemplar and chief practitioner of the happy marital ending in the historical novel. The bases for Scott's marital plots lie in gender roles that had prevailed during the seventeenth and eighteenth century, had continued throughout Scott's era, and had remained normative for at least half a century thereafter. Fictional plots leading to a concluding marriage needed to substantiate the social construction of gender within the historical novel's chosen period—and vice versa. For admirers of Scott, the historical novel was to long remain an overwhelmingly male occupation, an endeavor associated with the male worlds of property, politics, and war. Women needed men, society needed marriage, and progress needed enlightened children. But recurrent historical subjects based on revolutionary conflict did not easily yield the desired marital resolutions. Revolution brought the worlds of property, politics, and war together in ways that made change, destruction, and death fully visible, but progress difficult to discern.

In the closing chapters of historical novels, evoking marriage and children became a consoling proxy for the unprovable emergence of a better world. Although a wavering hero might assume a position of influence in the post-revolutionary new order, keen memories of carnage and compromise, honor and dishonor, military trial and unjust conviction, remained behind. Under such circumstances, the heroine fulfilled a crucial function despite her limited political power and secondary role in the narrative. As the source of temperate compassion, she needed to be both the wife to the maturing protagonist and, somehow, the mother to a better future. By mid-twentieth century her dual role was to prove, as aged Professor Saunders complains, an unsustainably tall order.

The single strongest influence upon our ideas of literary endings has surely been Frank Kermode's provocative, essentialist study, *The Sense of an Ending*. Citing the Bible as the exemplary human text, Kermode argues that all writers and all human beings, caught forever "in the middest" between the beginning and the end, neither of which we will ever know, must project a final Revelation that partakes of literary apocalyptic.[2] The drive to closure in Shakespearean tragedy is Kermode's supreme example. From Shakespeare, Kermode leaps to the twentieth-century open ending in order to demonstrate three proclivities of literary modernism: dissatisfaction with closed endings, the need of the novel to continuously redefine itself, and the desire of writers to allow for continuities of time (Kermode's "Tick-Tock" metaphor) without claiming knowledge of the end. In Kermode's model, Enlightenment and romantic writers are, however, left almost entirely out of account. His model of literary endings is based upon the deaths of Shakespearean tragedy, not the marriages of Shakespearean comedy, which are not mentioned. Kermode's only reference to Scott is to denigrate his characters in "the land of fiction" as "stereotypes which ignore reality" (128). The modernist perspective of breaking with all conventions to reveal the underlying chaos of life, "cannot work with the old hero, or with the old laws of the land of romance" (129).

If the happy marital ending of pre-Modernist fiction is to be ruled out of consideration, then it is idle to complain, as critics since Hazlitt have done, that the heroine of many an historical novel is often an insipid remake, or a pale imitation, of her fair-haired, sensible, and compassionate predecessors leading back through Walter Scott to the heroines of Shakespeare's comedy and ultimately to Una of Spenser's *The Faerie Queen*. The marriageable maiden of the historical novel is not so much an individuated person as the representative of a healing force associated with womanhood. It is not her inner character that matters, but her function as the herald and progenitor of a better world emerging during a time of crisis. After the honor-driven ravages of the male political world lie exhausted, woman is evoked as the agent of reconciliation, the origin of new life.

Scott's resolution of his narratives through a marriage reconciling families of opposed loyalties became formulaic because it proved so satisfying to his readers. After experiencing civil war, revolution, or counterrevolution, a young waverer and his beloved, freed of the absolutist convictions of their parents' heritages, marry and settle on one of their two ancestral estates. Although the couple maintains an aristocratic life shrunk in political power, they have learned that tolerance, reason, and compassion create a better world than intransigence. Scott's variant of the marriage plot recalls the familial conflicts of *Romeo and Juliet* with a marital ending out of *As You Like It*. Regional hostilities dissolve into an emerging national identity. A Scottish daughter of royalist, High Church or Catholic heritage marries a Whig Presbyterian from London or its environs; the couple determines to live on her family estate, newly saved and rebuilt by his English money. Jacobite and Hanoverian, Catholic and Protestant, rural and urban interests are reconciled in a union that flourishes under male legal and financial control, but also under the healing force of woman's domestic management.

The progressive course of Scottish-English history since the accession of James I is implicitly reinforced through such marriages. Edward Waverley marries Rose Bradwardine; they then inherit Baron Bradwardine's refurbished Tully-Veolan (*Waverley*). Henry Morton marries Edith Bellenden; they then inherit Lady Bellenden's estate Tillietudlem (*Old Mortality*). Frank Osbaldistone marries Diana Vernon; they then inherit Osbaldistone Hall, which has served as Diana's refuge after the failed Jacobite Rebellion of 1715 (*Rob Roy*). Markham Everard marries Alice Lee; they then inherit Woodstock, a Crown estate built by King Henry I (*Woodstock*). All four brides have but one living parent, who long serves as a blocking force to marital happiness. The bride's living parent is a royalist devoted to the Stuart cause, either High Church Anglican or Catholic, sometimes refined and sometimes boorish, but usually eccentric in ways that are rendered both endearing and anachronistic.

The parents of the wavering hero, by contrast, are conspicuously absent, the mother usually dead and the father removed, leaving the waverer fully open to the experience of civil war and to the influence of male mentors who are paired opposites (Fergus and Talbot, Claverhouse and Balfour, Rob Roy and Bailie Jarvie, Oliver Cromwell and Henry Lee). The male worlds of war and politics preoccupy the young man as he matures, but his growing awareness of the value of toleration, reason, compromise, and compassion is prefigured in the woman he marries. She will share with him the refashioned estate, which represents both his regained authority and his best self.

The repetition of these particulars illustrates the strength of an unprovable need, not mere literary carelessness. After the Postscript to *Waverley*, Scott became extremely wary about citing details of fact that would declare historical progress. Instead, he allows the happy marriage of representative individuals, with whom the reader identifies, to imply betterment for society as a whole. It is a literary device very like Kermode's explanation of the "Principle of Complementarity," derived from physics, in which the laws governing a wave of light can be determined by the complementary laws of the individual particles that compose it (59). Two forms of metonymy.

Cooper and Pushkin follow Scott's convention: marriage and progress are presumed to follow civil war or revolution. After helping to save Henry Wharton from hanging as a British spy, Peyton Dunwoodie marries Frances Wharton (*The Spy*). After being freed from the charge of treasonable association with Pugachev, Piotr Grinyov marries Marya Mironov (*The Captain's Daughter*). Both couples live contentedly on ancestral estates, finding satisfaction in their posterity and prosperity. But there are revealing differences. Scott's regard for the *de jure* plausibility of the Stuart cause, added to his love of Scotland, made a coming together in marriage of Jacobite and Hanoverian essential. Compromise, to Scott, is of the essence. Much as Cooper admired the personal qualities of loyalists, he could not approve of British policies during the Revolutionary War. American patriots embodied the republican future, not the British. Similarly, Pushkin granted Pugachev moments of integrity and compassion, but Pushkin could not condone the tactics or goals of Pugachev's rebellion.

For Cooper and Pushkin, the redemptive marriage must therefore occur between partisans of one progressive cause, rather than a uniting of opposed forces. Cooper's progressive ending marries an American military officer to a young American woman of outspoken republican principles. In like fashion, Piotr Grinyov serves in the Russian Army and then marries his Captain's daughter. Instead of refashioning a half-destroyed ancestral estate on which the happy couple will begin their married life, Cooper and Pushkin remove their newly married couples from the scene of conflict entirely. In the last chapters we leave the neutral ground and the Russian steppes far behind; the reader imagines that the children of both couples will be raised in a world no longer torn apart by war. Scott's marital ending, at its most convincing, acknowledges that former differences will likely linger, but be resolved in time. By contrast, the marriage plots of Cooper and Pushkin seem too orderly, more than a little perfunctory.

The recurrent problems of Scott's progressive ending are already apparent in *Waverley*. Scott's "Postscript Which Should Have Been A Preface" asserts that, since the defeat of the 1745 Jacobite Rebellion, "there is no European nation which, within the course of half a century, or little more, has undergone so complete a change as this kingdom of Scotland."[3] Because of "the destruction of the patriarchal power of the Highland chiefs," feudal land tenures have disappeared in the Lowlands as well as the Highlands. Waning desire to retain traditional Scottish customs suggests that a return of Scottish nationalism is unlikely.[4] "The gradual influx of wealth, and extension of commerce" have created a people averse to continuing counterrevolution. Scott celebrates incremental Burkean progress, asserting that the change "though steadily and rapidly progressive, has nevertheless, been gradual." "Rapidly progressive" and yet somehow "gradual." Unlike Victor Hugo, who was to see the river of time falling into revolutionary cataclysm only to rise again, Scott affirms a continuously visible gradualism, at least for the United Kingdom: "like those who drift down the stream of a deep and smooth river, we are not aware of the progress we have made, until we fix our eye on the now distant point from which we have drifted" (492). In 1814, as Napoleon and Wellington were heading toward cataclysmic confrontation, Scott's tidy celebration of history's continuity must have been deeply consoling.

Where does Scott's notion of the steady flow of progress leave newly wedded Edward Waverley and Rose Bradwardine? They will live on their estate at Tully-Veolan, far from the centers where "the gradual influx of wealth and extension of commerce" are occurring. If they seek to reform the land practices that have made the village of Tully-Veolan a hovel of degraded peasantry, Scott does not mention it. We are not told that Waverley will ever engage in commerce or in politics, either in England or in Scotland. Waverley in no way shares the activism of Bailie Jarvie or the Duke of Argyle. He is not engaged in promoting national wealth or pursuing reform; he lives a privileged and contented family life at Tully-Veolan and Waverley-Honour. His estates evidently continue to be self-sustaining. Progress happens around him but not, apparently, because of him.[5]

As a married man, Waverley proves to be less of a British nationalist, more of a nostalgic Jacobite, than his creator. When attesting to personal political belief, Walter Scott consistently supported the settlements of 1689 and 1707, urged clemency for Jacobites, but criticized Jacobitism. Waverley's mature feelings for his country are not cut from the same cloth. In the reception room at Tully-Veolan, there hangs "a large and spirited painting, representing Fergus MacIvor and Waverley in their Highland dress" at the time they served together in the army of Bonnie Prince Charlie. "Beside this painting hung the arms which Waverley had borne in the unfortunate civil war" (489). "Unfortunate," we wonder, for whom? Acute memory of a disastrous rebellion is being transformed by art into a *picture* of fraternity.

By hanging this painting, Waverley is falsifying his own experience, turning his disillusionment with Jacobitism into a misleading romantic memory of Highland nationalism. As George Dekker has observed, the reader encounters the painting only ten pages after Scott had visualized the heads of Fergus and Evan Dhu spiked over the gate of Carlisle Castle.[6] In domestic memory, however, Fergus is henceforth to be remembered simply as a man of "ardent, fiery and impetuous character" (489). Fergus has become his portrait; his calculating, ambitious, and deceptive qualities, which Waverley had once deeply resented, are apparently forgotten.

To promote the past represented by this painting reveals the hopeful, accommodating qualities of Waverley in his maturity. When Waverley's devotion to Bonnie Prince Charlie had been at its height, Flora MacIvor had predicted to Rose Bradwardine, Waverley's future bride, what Waverley's future will be:

> "I will tell you where he will be at home, my dear, and in his place,—in the quiet circle of domestic happiness, lettered indolence, and elegant enjoyments of Waverley-Honour. And, he will refit the old library in most exquisite Gothic taste, and garnish its shelves with the rarest and most valuable volumes; and he will draw plans and landscapes, and write verses, and rear temples, and dig grottoes;—and he will stand in a clear summer night in the colonnade before the hall, and gaze on the deer as they stray in the moonlight, or lie shadowed by the boughs of the huge old fantastic oaks; and he will repeat verses to his beautiful wife, who will hang upon his arm,—and he will be a happy man." (370–371)

Even allowing for Flora's Jacobite fanaticism, her prospective assessment of Waverley's character, tinged though it is with condescension, seems remarkably astute. Within Waverley's domestic circle lies an alternative world of taste, artistry, security, and happy memory for which the painting of himself and Fergus is entirely appropriate.

The question posed by this well-known, exquisitely written passage is one of proper response to distortion of history. Does Scott intend his reader wholeheartedly to celebrate Waverley's peaceful future—or to see in it an anodyne of escapism? If the latter, did Scott calculate that the reader of 1814, enmeshed in the deadly, glory-seeking aftermath of the French Revolution, might well, like Waverley, wish the wider world of political and technological progress entirely away? Or is the viewer of the painting to recognize that its owner, Edward Waverley, has now become a loyal Englishman prepared to honor the fact, still controversial in the 1750s, that he had recently been a Jacobite rebel? I opt for the latter view. We know only, however, that the usual explanation of problems in Scott's endings—that he was in a hurry to sew up the threads of his narrative—does not answer these questions. Perhaps Scott was sufficiently self-divided between Hanoverian principle, Jacobite memory and contemporary turmoil, that he could not have satisfactorily answered them himself.

The same unanswerable questions can, in varying degrees, be asked of the marriages of Henry Morton and Edith Bellenden, Frank Osbaldistone and Diana Vernon, Markham Everard and Alice Lee. Historical progress is implied when it is not invoked; the marriage of hero and heroine ends the novel on a unifying note that seems to affirm a progressive reading of history. But the happiness of the married couple is a happiness in retreat from the post-Napoleonic world in which the novels are written. The dwellings and occupations that constitute happiness are built upon the defeat of the Old Order, even though they incorporate the New. Neither the counting room, nor the manufactory, nor the political conference room has any part in them. There are no angry workers promoting change, like those then gathering not far from Abbotsford. Instead of visible progress, such endings express relief from the *menace* of counterrevolution. During the first Jacobite rebellion (1715), Scott declares, "The diversions of Whig and Tory then shook England to her very centre, and a powerful party, engaged in the Jacobite interest, menaced the dynasty of Hanover."[7] The disappearance of Jacobitism by 1800 allowed Scott to trust that the times when "every alehouse resounded with the brawls of contending politicians" were now past (97).

Two of the later Scottish novels resolve the marriage plot quite differently. Lucy Ashton dies horribly, forced into marriage and toward suicide by the deceit of her parents, both of them still living (*The Bride of Lammermoor*). Jeannie Deans and Reuben Bright, neither of them members of the gentry, live a happy but circumscribed local life on the Duke of Argyle's lands (*The Heart of Mid-lothian*). However, in his last novel dealing with seventeenth-century revolution (*Woodstock*), Scott returned to the marital convention of *Waverley*, amplifying it to determine whether its problematic qualities could be plausibly resolved. Having repeatedly sent his newly married gentry into happy historical limbo, Scott ventured to explore the political reality of their postmarital future.

In *Woodstock*'s lengthy denouement, Markham Everard and Alice Lee, long devoted to each other but separated by family political allegiances, happily marry once Charles II has escaped Cromwell by fleeing to the Low Countries. Markham and Alice retire from public life to live on Lee family lands. Everard, a moderate Presbyterian, who has served in Cromwell's New Model Army, will neither openly oppose nor openly condemn Cromwell's ascent to become Lord Protector. Because Everard has suffered Cromwell's fitful tyrannies, he will no longer serve in Cromwell's New Model Army. The Stuart cause, however, appears equally flawed to him. Although Everard supports Charles II's return by clandestinely providing money, Everard will not publicly act on Charles's behalf. The consequence is that, after the mid-1650s, "Markham had given up all concern in public affairs, disapproving of the forcible dismissal of the Parliament, and submitting to Cromwell's subsequent domination, rather as that which was the lesser evil, than to a government which he regarded as legal."[8] It is not Markham Everard's nature, as it had been Waverley's nature, to become apolitical. Markham has instead been forced to give up "all concern for public affairs" for two complementary reasons: (1) a Stuart restoration may be *de jure* legitimate but its intolerance and venality pose as great an evil as Puritan absolutism, and (2) neither Cromwell nor Charles II possesses the integrity and stature of a true national leader.

Colonel Markham Everard is an admirable man, temperate and humane in character and deeply concerned for the welfare of a Great Britain that does not yet quite exist. He is a public servant left with no honorable place to turn. His wife Alice forcefully defines the values in which they both believe. For them, happiness is not dependent on grottoes, well-furnished libraries, and deer in the park, but on sensible distrust of the world outside. When Sir Henry Lee had threatened to renounce his daughter because she has fallen in love with a Roundhead, Alice retorts "Accursed be these civil commotions; not only do they destroy men's bodies, but they pervert their souls; and the brave, the noble, the generous, become suspicious, harsh and mean!" (19). If you would preserve your integrity, Alice believes, avoid rebellion and the "civil commotions" that give rise to them.

Subsequently, it will be Alice, not Sir Henry nor Markham Everard, who defines the virtues a good king must exemplify for his people (267–268). Her standard for a king's virtue ("benevolence, love of his people, patience even of unpleasing advice, sacrifice of his own wishes and pleasures to the commonweal") is one to which neither of the two Stuart monarchs to whom her family has been so loyal can rise. Why should Markham Everard, formerly misused by Oliver Cromwell and by Charles II, but now married to so able a woman, offer his services to bettering the commonweal? In his experience, public service exposes one to treachery. Everard has already seen enough of the revolutions of 1640, 1652, and 1660 to find no progress in them. He now fully shares his wife's belief: if you would retain your integrity, avoid restoration no less than rebellion. By the time Scott wrote *Woodstock,* he no longer assumed that the life of the happily married genteel couple could by itself contribute to the well-being of society. Scott does not explicitly subscribe to Markham Everard's disillusioned withdrawal; by ending Woodstock as he did, however, he sympathetically explored its principled, dispiriting complexity.

As a spokesman for New World republicanism, Fenimore Cooper was determined to link marital happiness to social progress. Accordingly, *The Spy* strives to fill in the often-vacuous future of Scott's marital endings by adding a final chapter, an epilogue that takes place in 1814, thirty-three years after the novel's narrative. A young American officer stands "on the tablerock, contemplating the great cataract" of Niagara Falls.[9] Physically, he is almost a hermaphrodite. His "proud expression," "deep black eyes," and pure white complexion collectively "partook of feminine beauty"; "His hair shone in the setting sun like ringlets of gold" (401). The inference of Cooper's characterization is political, however, not sexual. The young man's name, Wharton Dunwoodie, suggests that the son of Peyton Dunwoodie and Frances Wharton embodies the reconciliation, the blood union, of patriot and loyalist family hostility. To contemplate the sublimity of Niagara Falls is to demonstrate his sensitivity to the treasured symbol of America as Nature's nation. To the exclusion of other races and ethnicities, Wharton Dunwoodie represents Young America facing its grand future. The river of time still leads over an immense fall but without the cataclysm that Victor Hugo was soon to find in the same metaphor.

The sudden appearance of Wharton Dunwoodie is clearly meant to compensate for the battlefield death of Harvey Birch, the novel's model of disinterested patriotism. For Harvey, his only reward has been his secret letter of tribute from General George Washington, a letter long carried next to Harvey's heart, now disclosed on his dead body. For the general public and for the reader, however, Washington's conveniently belated tribute to his unacknowledged counter-spy must suffice for a memorial. Revising Scott even as he imitates him, Cooper implies that the marriage of hero and heroine is not by itself an adequate resolution. Evidence of true revolutionary patriotism must live on through a marriage that produces a child who appreciates and receives nature's grandest blessing.

Master of melodrama, Dickens outdoes Cooper in elaborating Scott's progressive marital ending. Harvey Birch endured self-sacrifice for the patriotic purposes embodied in Wharton Dunwoodie; Sydney Carton welcomes self-sacrifice in a spirit of Christian love that achieves secular cleansing. The closing pages of *A Tale of Two Cities* describe Sydney Carton's ascending the guillotine to die in place of the unjustly condemned Charles Darnay, the former Marquis Evrémonde. Without a trace of irony, Dickens renders Carton's death as a contemporary *Imitatio Christi*, a fulfillment of the supreme Christian virtue "Greater love hath no man than to give up his life for another" *(John* 15:13). After a frail nameless seamstress, strengthened by Carton's compassion, has gone to her death just ahead of him, Carton murmurs "I am the Resurrection and the Life, saith the Lord; he that believeth in me, though he be dead, ye shall he live; and whosoever liveth and believeth in me shall

never die" (*John 11*: 25).[10] By giving his life for another, Carton has redeemed
himself from a parasitical lawyer's life of alcoholism and despair. His unforgettable last words ("It is a far, far better thing that I do, than I have ever
done; it is a far, far better rest that I go to than I have ever known") imply that
climbing the steps of the guillotine is his ascension to some unknown form
of eternal life (90). His description of death as a "rest" surely conveys more
than mere oblivion.

Carton's self-sacrifice is rendered in accord with nineteenth-century denial
of providential intervention. Although the Revolutionary Tribunal passes
judgment very much as the Sanhedrin and the crowd of Romans and Jews had
done, there are for Sydney Carton no disciples, no designated God, no rend-
ing of the veil, no resurrection of the body, and no assurance of heaven. Christ
gave his body and blood so that all men might live; Sydney Carton gives his
life, not primarily for Charles Darnay, and certainly not for all men, but for
Lucie Manette. In London he had voiced his hope that she might "think now
and then that there is a man who would give his life to keep a life you love
beside you" (159). To Sydney Carton as to Dickens, Lucie Manette serves
as "the golden thread" that binds together all the characters who are capable
of compassion (218). The value for which Carton dies is "the faithful service
of the heart," but the faithful service of the heart is the special province of
woman, as it had not been for Cooper (100). Its source lies not in a woman
comparable to the Biblical Mary, but in the kind of womanhood associated
with the fair heroine who has married the wavering hero. Although neither
Lucie Manette nor Charles Darnay may seem worthy of Sydney Carton's
self-sacrifice to today's reader, mankind's undeserving has always been
essential to the meaning of Christ-like death. None of us is worthy of the
ultimate self-sacrifice of another.

Through the redemptive force of woman's heart, Dickens's ending celebrates the social progress that will follow Revolutionary Terror. As in *The
Spy*, self-sacrificial death, marriage, family descendants, and a better future
are rendered finally inseparable. At the moment of death, Carton's silent,
peaceful face is perceived by the crowd to be "sublime and prophetic" (389).
Through indirect discourse, Dickens summarizes Carton's vision of the
future:

> "I see Barsad, and Cly, Defarge, The Vengeance, the Juryman, the Judge, long
> ranks of the new oppressors who have risen on the destruction of the old, per-
> ishing by his retributive instrument, before it shall cease out of its present use.
> I see a beautiful city and a brilliant people rising from this abyss, and in their
> struggles to be truly free, in their triumphs and defeats, through long long years
> to come, I see the evil of this time and of the previous time of which this is the
> natural birth, gradually making expiation for itself and wearing out." (389)

The opening sentence of this passage restates the last sentence of the opening paragraph of the last chapter: "Sow the same seed of rapacious license and oppression over again, and it will surely yield the same fruit according to its kind" (385). The tyranny and license of the Revolutionary New Order are the "tortured" consequence of the tyranny and license of the Old (385).

So do the evils of one era beget the same evils, albeit in different form, in the next generation. But there is a gap of logic in the transition to Carton's next sentence in which he sees "a beautiful city and a brilliant people arising from this abyss" (389). The beauty of mid-nineteenth-century Paris may be visible evidence of progress, but how did progress occur if the sins of one generation continually recur in the next? Carton does not say; he does not even conjecture. He is sure only that it is through an entire people's "struggles to be truly free" that progress will come about. Only the goal—"freedom"—is specified, not the political, economic, or institutional process of achieving it.

Dickens use of the term "expiation" at the end of this passage lends a religious significance to the secular progress he has just described.[11] The expiatory legacy of Sydney Carton will somehow complement the increasing beauty and brilliance of the urban world. As the title of the last chapter indicates, the fated footsteps that have brought the weight of the revolution upon Darnay and Lucie must die out. Accordingly, Carton envisions the blessed future of the married couple he has saved:

> I see the lives for which I lay down my life, peaceful, useful, prosperous and happy, in that England which I shall see no more. I see her [Lucy] with a child upon her bosom who bears my name. . . . I see that I hold a sanctuary in their hearts, and the hearts of their descendants, generations hence. . . . I see that child who lay upon her bosom and who bore my name, a man winning his way up in that path of life which once was mine. . . . I see him, foremost of the just judges and honoured men, bringing a boy of my name, with a forehead that I know, and golden hair, to this place [the Place de la Revolution]—then fair to look upon with not a trace of this day's disfigurement. (389–390)

Dickens even surpasses Cooper in heightening the marital and familial imagery that affirms intergenerational progress. Like the Dunwoodies and the Whartons, Carton and Darnay will remain united in the name of the son who bears both their surnames. There will soon be two Sydney Carton Darnays, not one. Lucie Manette will be father to a lawyer who, redeeming Carton's lost career, will be recognized as "foremost of the just judges and honoured men," And then there will succeed yet another Sydney Carton Darnay. Lucie will be grandmother to a golden-haired son, occupation unspecified, who presumably lives in the present day of the reader. She is "the golden thread" indeed.

As in Cooper's novel, the linking of familial happiness to societal progress leaves formidable questions. There is more than a hint of Arian prejudice in the evocation of a golden-haired son and grandson. Wharton Dunwoodie is, literally, a stick figure. Dickens did not customarily view the chosen profession of Lucie's male descendants, the civil law, as civilization's road to progress. The courtroom of the Old Bailey in 1780, so unforgettably described in the second book of *A Tale of Two Cities*, will need complete transformation if it is to become a place where "just judges and honoured men" like Sydney Carton Darnay will be able to display their lawyerly virtue.

All we are told of Lucie's and Darnay's future life in England is that it will be "peaceful, useful, prosperous and happy." They will apparently continue to live as they did in the quiet domestic circle of Soho, hoping to avoid the footsteps of revolution that come ever nearer. Could Darnay and Lucie maintain their happiness in any way of life other than yet another genteel retreat? Lucie and Darnay, we discover, will be "prosperous" not because they engage in commerce or politics, nor because of Darnay's wage earnings as a tutor of French, but because that "good old man" Jarvis Lorry dies "enriching them with all he has" (367). Long live the fairy tale benefactor![12] The problems of Scott's marital ending have not been resolved by Cooper or Dickens; the problems must resurface until the novelist finds plausible evidence that family bliss and social progress are one.

No novelist would strive harder than Tolstoy to make the progressive marital ending of the historical novel convincing. The first epilogue of *War and Peace*, some fifty pages, is devoted to doing so. On the last page of the narrative, at the end of book 15, Natasha exclaims to Princess Mary "Think what fun it will be when I am his [Pierre's] wife and you marry Nicholas!"[13] Shortly after Napoleon's Grande Armeé is driven from Russia, Nicholas Rostov marries Princess Mary Bolkonski, and Count Pierre Bezukhov marries Natasha Rostov. True to Scott's prototype, Nicholas and Mary live on her family's estate at Bald Hills. Natasha and Pierre travel among their various houses and estates, but spend much time visiting the Rostovs. The entirety of the epilogue consists of a remarkably static description of the married life of the two couples and their households. Other than the birth of their children and the superintending of their estates, nothing of note happens to them or through them. Tolstoy therefore faces a problem of extended fictional anticlimax.

Too many happy wedding bells had rung down the curtain of previous historical novels, however, for Tolstoy to suggest that marriage is unalloyed bliss. Throughout the first epilogue, he qualifies the happiness and progress he would seem to be affirming.[14] To remain landlord to many serfs provokes intermittent money anxieties for Nicholas and intermittent moral guilt for Pierre. Scott, Cooper, and Dickens had implied that the newly married couple would somehow be young forever. To Tolstoy, aging must be recognized as a universal fact. Sonja has become a *"sterile flower"* (1035). The constant presence of the now shriveled and querulous Countess Rostova in Nicholas's household reminds everyone that, money or no money, "we must all become like her" (1028). Recurrent moments of boredom on one's country estate prefigure Chekov. The two couples lead contented lives but Natasha's expectation of a life of continuing "fun" greatly overstates the reality.

In a time of Peace, the major characters seem less significant, even to themselves, than during a time of War. Nicholas Rostov—Tolstoy's portrayal of an ordinary, respectable man—proves to be an excellent farm manager, fair though stern to his serfs, and a good father to his family, but without one imaginative idea. Although Nicholas dutifully reads books by Montesquieu and Rousseau, his books grace his shelves rather than stir his mind. Anything but a progressive, Nicholas seems to have been unaffected by the Napoleonic experience in which he played an active military part. Living through the revolutionary era has not changed him (or presumably the many who are like him), in any essential way. Nicholas's later life thus challenges the assumption, common among Scott's generation of historical novelists, that men and women learn through historical experience.

Princess Mary's tender understanding of her husband's limitations shades her marital happiness with melancholy. Mary's spiritual yearning is beyond Nicholas's stolid mind; he cannot share her grasping after intangible realities. While Mary watches Nicholas playing with their daughter, she reflects "I should never, never have believed that one could be so happy," then sighs with "quiet sadness," reflecting "that there is another sort of happiness unattainable in this life" (1019). Tolstoy's point—an insight Scott or Cooper would not venture—is that unacknowledged spiritual difference between husband and wife can increase, rather than hinder, their mutual conciliation. Nicholas's "steady tender and proud love of his wife rested on his feeling of wonder at her spirituality and at the lofty moral world, almost beyond his reach, in which she had her being" (1036). Princess Mary returns Nicholas's "steady tender and proud love" with a touch of inevitable condescension: "She felt a submissive, tender love for this man who would never understand all that she understood, and this seemed to make her love for him still stronger and added a touch of passionate tenderness" (1036, 1038). Through such characterization, Tolstoy brings to the gender politics of the historical novel a literary realism still based on the importance of family feeling as the basis of social stability.

The appeal of Natasha Rostov rests upon her instinct to live the life of the moment. It is not a quality likely to wear well for a mother dedicated to sustaining the well-being of an aristocratic household in semiretirement from social gatherings. By 1820, aging and maternal duty have dulled the "ever-glowing animation" that once filled her face. "Her soul was not visible at all; all that struck the eye was a strong, handsome, and fertile woman. The old fire very rarely kindled in her face now" (120). Whatever minimal interest Natasha had ever had in politics or progress has vanished, including any interest she ever had in Pierre's ideas: "There were then as now conversations and discussions about women's rights, the relations of husband and wife and their freedom and rights, though these themes were not yet termed *questions* as they are now; but these topics were not merely uninteresting to Natasha, she positively did not understand them" (1021). Neither Scott, nor Cooper, nor Pushkin, or Dickens would have entertained the notion that the happily married life with which their historical novels end would, through its very nature, have *precluded* marital discussion of such "questions."

The world beyond the withdrawn lives of the two couples comes to consciousness only through the resurgent rebellious ideals of Pierre Bezukhov. Republicanism is no longer a threat posed by Napoleonic empire; instead it poses an opportunity for Russia's liberal intelligentsia. To Nicholas's discomfort, Pierre denounces the present government as a betrayal of both Enlightenment values and the patriotism that had defeated Napoleon:

> "Well, everything is going to ruin! Robbers in the law courts, in the army nothing but flogging, drilling and Military Settlements, the people are tortured, enlightenment is suppressed. All that is young and honest is crushed! Everyone sees that this cannot go on. Everything is strained to such a degree that it will certainly break. . . . Something else is needed. When you stand expecting the overstrained string to snap at any moment, when everyone is expecting the inevitable catastrophe, as many as possible must join hands as closely as they can to withstand the general calamity. . . . What I say is widen the scope of our society, let the *mot d'ordre* be not virtue alone, but independence and action as well!" (1033)

Pierre is a Decembrist in the making, but the only one we see.[15] Like the Decembrists, Pierre desires to participate in a revolt of gentleman and nobility against oppressions of the Tsarist Regime, rather than a revolt of peasants against nobility. He will join hands with other gentlemen of virtue for two purposes: "for the public welfare and the general safety" and "to prevent some Pugachev or other from killing my children and yours" (1034). He has become the quintessential nineteenth-century liberal nobleman advocating revolutionary action for the sake of popular "freedom" and "general welfare," neither of which he can exactly define. His sympathies leave an unanswered question: can liberal gentry of ability and good will summon the sustained commitment necessary to achieve the changes they advocate?

True to later historical example, Tsar Nicholas I would brutally suppress the Decembrist Revolt. Its progressive, even revolutionary impulse nonetheless persists, not only within Pierre, but also within Prince André Bolkonski's fifteen-year-old son Nicholas, with whom Tolstoy's narrative ends. To young Nicholas, his dead father André is "a divinity who could not be pictured." Nicholas loves his blood uncle and namesake Nicholas Rostov "with just a shade of contempt," but he adores "uncle" Pierre beyond measure. The first epilogue ends with Nicholas trying to unite his two models of male virtue, exclaiming that Uncle Pierre is "a wonderful man" and vowing that, to honor his father's memory, "I will do something with which even *he* would be satisfied . . ." (1042). The ellipses that end the first epilogue suggest that neither young Nicholas, nor Tolstoy, nor the reader can possibly know what that "something" might be, or if that "something" will ever materialize. In this detail, as in the first epilogue as a whole, Tolstoy writes as the realist expanding and reshaping the simplistic finality of the traditional marital ending. His success in doing so remains a remarkable achievement. He had opened up the closed marital ending in deliberate, convincing ways.

LONELINESS, LOVELESSNESS, CONVENIENCE

The famous first sentence of *Anna Karenina* (1877), "All happy families are alike; each unhappy family is unhappy in its own way," suggests that, for the future of the novel, marital happiness will be of less interest than marital unhappiness.[16] Even after Tolstoy, however, a blissful marriage reconciling the Old with the New could continue to draw down the curtain of a fine historical novel. Jewett's *The Tory Lover*, for example, follows the Scott formula scrupulously, ending in the marriage of the Tory lover, Roger Wallingford and the Patriot maiden, Mary Hamilton, and their settling into the "home" of the Hamiltons, "the great house" along the Piscataqua.[17] Now that the American Revolution is over, neither the dockside mob nor intransigent Tories will reappear; moderation and comfortable security prevail, while the cultured gentry of New England continue to receive social deference. Jewett was willing to risk the anachronism of a static view of history for the greater benefit of communal good feeling.

By 1900, however, Scott's ending had become, as the colloquialism now has it, literary déjà vu all over again. Henry James's "The Art of Fiction" (1884) ridiculed critics and readers who assume that a "good" novel "depends on a 'happy ending,' on a distribution at the last of prizes, pensions, husbands, wives, babies, millions, appended paragraphs, and cheerful remarks."[18] Marriage bells ceased to peal in the last chapter of fictions, especially so in historical novels emanating from Scott. After Tolstoy's qualifying elaboration, the happy marital ending was challenged by Hugo and Zola, then literally upended by Anatole France, Margaret Mitchell, Pasternak, and Lampedusa. As the Old Order came to seem increasingly irrecoverable, the happy marital union disappeared along with it. For the historical novelist, however, the happy ending did not readily give way to the experimental open ending of the modernist novel. Instead, early-twentieth-century historical novelists closed off the promise of marriage, replacing it with historical pessimism and images of loneliness and lovelessness. Contemporary sociological developments, always pertinent to historical fiction, lent credence to the demise of the happy marital ending: widespread public prostitution in large cities, slowly rising divorce rates, and an increased willingness, in journalistic writing, to confront the realities of marital failure and marital misery.

Victor Hugo eliminates courtship and marriage from the Parisian and Vendéean worlds of *1793*, but not the force of the feminine. The novel contains only a single woman character, the illiterate peasant Michelle Fléchard, usually referred to simply as "the mother," who wanders the Vendéean countryside in desperate search for her three young children, who have been carried off, she knows not where, as potential hostages by the royalists. Modeled on the biblical Rachel, Michelle Fléchard must wander without end, a symbol of the wrongs women suffer during times of revolutionary struggle.

Motivated by guilt as well as mercy, the Marquis de Lantenac, who had ordered the abduction of the three children, surrenders himself to the revolutionaries in order to save the lives of Michele's children and restore them to their mother. Nothing is written, however, about the future of mother or children; they are saved and then they disappear. As the novel concludes, the value of femininity is transferred from the marriage of hero and heroine to Gauvin's idealistic hopes for an indeterminate republican future.

The final conversation between Cimourdain and Gauvin culminates in their opposed definitions of the republic for which both have been fighting. Gauvin, who prides himself in not making war on women or children, praises "this marvelous '93" because "beneath a scaffold of barbarism a temple of civilization is building":

> "Yes," replied Cimourdain. "From this provisional will rise the definitive. The definitive—that is to say, right and duty—are parallel; taxes proportional and progressive; military service obligatory; a leveling without deviation; and above the whole, making part of all, that straight line, the law,—the Republic of the absolute."
>
> "I prefer," said Gauvin, "the ideal Republic. . . . In all which you have just said, where do you place devotion, sacrifice, abnegation, the sweet interlacing of kindnesses, love? To set all in equilibrium is well; to put all in harmony is better. Above the Balance is the Lyre. Your Republic weighs, measures, regulates man; mine lifts him into the open sky."[19]

Gauvin is granted the better of the argument, as well as its last word, but there is no indication that his republic will be realized. Cimourdin assumes that a progressive civilization based upon strict obedience to law, upon military service and upon straight, leveled lines will be "definitive" because it is rigorously mathematical. In Gauvin's view, Cimourdain's model leaves out the values associated with femininity in general and Michelle Fléchard in particular: "devotion, sacrifice, abnegation, the sweet interlacing of kindnesses, love." Gauvin's view of a republic based upon the lyre, not the balance, is therefore not only more "ideal." Hugo would have his reader believe that Gauvin's republic is more realistic because more complete: it fuses the feminine with the masculine in a vision that foregoes the risks of Cimourdain's geometric absolutism. No model republic could be more abstract; Hugo is clearly reluctant to admit that it is unrealizable.

Zola invites his reader to expect a happy marital ending, then denies it. Amid the apocalyptic burning of Paris with which *La Débacle* concludes, it seems likely that Jean Macquart and Henriette Levasseur, Maurice's sister, will emerge from the ruins, marry, then return to a life that will exemplify France's phoenix-like recovery. After the death of Henriette's husband and after Jean Macquart's wounding, Henriette has nursed Jean Macquart back to life and fallen in love with him. Jean's resilience, good will, and common sense, repeatedly shown throughout the battle narrative, make Jean a credible symbol for slow, steady national rebirth. But Zola denies Jean and Henriette a marital future. Because Jean has shot and killed Henriette's twin brother Maurice on the Communard street-barricades, the couple must acknowledge their love but renounce their future union. Jean Macquart has become convinced that "Maurice's grave would be there, a yawning chasm, to part them [he and Henriette] as long as they should live." "The love thus openly expressed could have no other fruition than an eternal farewell."[20]

Is Zola's terminal parting of the lovers gratuitous, a reversal undertaken merely to challenge literary convention? Whether killing your beloved's twin brother would have posed a greater impediment to marriage in 1870 than today remains an open question. Zola does not end the novel, however, by passing judgment upon the couple's mutual renunciation. Jean Macquart makes his way back to his "neglected field" and "ruined house," "his face set resolutely toward the future, toward the glorious and arduous task that lay before him and his countrymen, to create a new France" (428).

Jean Macquart's resolution creates a further problem. In France's present condition, Jean can see only "defeat treading on the heels of defeat, their provinces torn from them, an indemnity of milliards to be raised, a most horrible civil war that had been quenched in blood, their streets cumbered with ruins and unburied corpses, without money, their honor gone, and order to be re-established out of chaos" (426). In predicting the national future, however, he invokes seasonal change to substantiate society's regeneration. There will always remain the "hope of imperishable humanity," "the harvest that is promised to him who sows," "the tree throwing out a new and vigorous shoot to replace the rotten limb that has been lopped away" (428). As in Cooper's *The Spy* and in Hugo's *1793*, natural metaphors are advanced to do the work of political and economic specificity.

Meta-reference among troubled endings was becoming a tradition. In a gloss on Dickens's timid, pure seamstress who precedes Sydney Carton to the guillotine, Anatole France pictures Brotteaux des Ilettes sitting in the tumbrel beside Athenais the defiant prostitute. Instead of Sydney Carton's consoling certainty ("it is a far, far better rest that I go to"[21]), Brotteaux gazes regretfully at Athenais' white breasts, while murmuring Lucretius's "When we shall have ceased to be" (*Sic ubi non erimus*). The ironies are of a piece with the relentless cynicism of Anatole France's ending. To spill the blood of presumed conspirators, en masse, has become Evariste's revolutionary aphrodisiac. Because he can never succeed in purifying his ideal republic from ever-multiplying traitors, he eventually seeks his own martyrdom. As Robespierre is shot, Evariste exultingly attempts suicide. Nothing will suffice but a death dedicated to pseudo-Roman republican virtue, a death very like those he so admires in the paintings of David.

The novel's final chapter belongs, however, to the surviving women. After her husband is sent to the guillotine by her brother, Julie Gamelin becomes a milliner's assistant gathering new suitors. Rose Thevenin, actress, has taken a new lover. Citizenness Blaise helps maintain the stock of trendy art objects in her husband's store, the *Amour Peintre*; she now rents a room to Evariste Gamelin's mother, who spends her days disconsolately murmuring over rosary beads. Above all, the ending belongs to Elodie Blaise, who has taken a new lover, the venal opportunist Desmahis. Already bored with Desmahis, Elodie looks beyond his caresses to enjoying those of Henry the Dragoon. No young woman seeks to marry or bear children; all are concerned with sensual pleasure and monetary survival. They could care less about La République.

No sentence in Anatole France's ending extends the novel's time frame beyond the counterrevolutionary world of Thermidor. In January 1795 the weather and temper of Paris are described as frozen in place. The *jeunesse dorée*, with whom Rose and Julie would like to associate, speak only about wigs, hats, grottos, gothic chapels, busts, theaters, and restaurants (246–247). Prefiguring the popularity of Napoleon without being aware of it, purchasers in the art market are beginning to prefer large canvases with military subjects. The novel ends with Elodie dismissing her lover from her apartment with the exact same words she had once used to Evariste Gamelin. Except to denounce dead Jacobins, no one now speaks of politics. To mention even the possibility of "progress" would be regarded as absurd naiveté. *The Gods*

Will Have Blood thus subverts the conventional ending of historical novels by refusing to consider the future at all. Neither Hugo nor Zola had gone so far. We can plausibly conclude that Anatole France's view of the incomprehensible passage of time was Stoic or Lucretian. Alternatively, we can surmise that he sensed the disaster in which France and the European world would be immersed a scant two years after his novel was published. His rendering of crazed nihilistic killing informs today's fears of terrorism.

Pasternak sets marital defeat within the context of political and cultural catastrophe, drawing appropriate connections between them. Yurii Zhivago arrives back in Moscow in the spring of 1922 shortly after Lenin has inaugurated the National Economic Plan (N.E.P) in a failed attempt to revitalize the Russian economy by minimal legalization of private commerce and manufacturing. The first words of Pasternak's "Conclusion" specify that "the last eight or ten years of Zhivago's life, during which he went more and more to seed," were to be defined by "long periods of indifference to himself and to everything in the world."[22] He practices medicine fitfully for a time, and then gives it up. He still writes a few poems and short essays, but his major literary project, a volume of imagistic poems about the atomistic life of the modern city, comes to nothing. He makes little effort to contact Tonia and his children; Lara is irrevocably gone. His daily life is evidence of Russia's indifference to high culture and overturn in social class. He lives in the house of Markel, the Gromeko's former family servant, in quarters consisting of "a derelict bathroom, a room with a single window adjoining it, and the dilapidated, crumbling kitchen and back entrance" (476). "After he had moved in, Yurii Andreievich gave up medicine, neglected himself, stopped seeing his friends and lived in great poverty" (476). His will to struggle is gone.

At various times, Markel, Yurii's half-brother Evgraf, and Yurii's lifelong friends Misha Gordon and Dudurov try to lift him out of his indifference, but all fail. When Yurii begs water from the Markels, Markel calls him a "poor fish" and a "wet rag" (476). Agafia Markel scorns Zhivago's passivity, attributing it to the weakness of his privileged upbringing: "The money that was spent on you!" she exclaims: "All that learning, and where has it got you? I'd like to know?" (477). In a grotesque parody of the happy marital ending, Yurii allows Marina Markel to live with him and to take care of him, even though they are not legally married; Zhivago and Marina beget two daughters, Kapka and Klazhka, to whom Yurii pays no attention and for whom he has no emotional concern. Marina and Zhivago share neither a legal nor a spiritual marriage; they merely exist together in animal convenience, day by day.

Yurii dies because of the failure of the communist transportation system. He collapses ignominiously on the streets of Moscow after the trolley car in which he is riding breaks down on a stifling August day. Lest the connection be missed, Pasternak insists upon the details of mechanical failure. Like Zhivago's heart, the trolley's motor is defective; electrical short circuits cause it to stop functioning. The trolley line backs up and the city rail system, its life's blood, comes to a halt. The trolley image redounds back through the novel: Komarovsky's train to eastern Siberia, Strelnikov's military express, the slow train Zhivago and the Gromekos took to the Urals, the train in which Yurii had returned from the front after World War I, and the train from which Yurii's father had jumped to his death in the novel's opening scene. All movements forward seem to have been brought to a final standstill in the airless, tawdry Moscow streetcar.

Boris Pasternak suffered economic decline, marital difficulties, and censorship problems, but he never underwent anything like the degradation and degeneration of Yurii Zhivago. Why would Pasternak have wished to bring a man of such humanity, intelligence, ability, and love of life so very low? To be sure, the betrayal of Russia's revolutionary promise, the terrible carnage of civil war, the failure of Soviet collectivization, the emotional loss first of Tonia and then of Lara, Yurii's separation from three of his children, and his ultimate failure of will are all contributing causes. Whether they can collectively account for Zhivago's pathetic end is another question. None of the privileged, educated, liberal, and genteel heroes in Scott's legacy of the historical novel had declined so far and so completely. Insofar as Pasternak is rewriting Tolstoy, he may have emphasized Zhivago's degraded lonely end in order to contrast it to the afterlives of the Rostovs and Bezukhovs. Yurii Zhivago's final years may also represent Pasternak's imagining of the worst that might have befallen Pasternak himself, but fortunately never did. As Tolstoy had discovered, it is easier to answer the "how" of life than the "why."

Although Tonia Gromeko and Yurii Zhivago had made a good marriage, Lara Guishar and Yurii Zhivago are said to be soul mates from the outset. In a passage that Nabokov was to scorn as sentimentality, Lara reflects at Zhivago's funeral that "they loved each other because everything around them willed it, the trees and the clouds and the sky over their heads, and the earth under their feet" (501). Lara then elaborates on the source of their irresistible will to love one another: "Never, never, even in their moments of richest and wildest happiness, were they unaware of a sublime joy in the total design of the universe, a feeling that they themselves were a part of that whole, an element in the beauty of the cosmos" (501).

Lara here voices a romantic pantheism, akin to Wordsworth, Emerson, or Heine, that Pasternak affirms through the novel's many renderings of nature's splendor. But Lara's tribute to "the beauty of the cosmos," "this unity with the whole" leads a scant two pages later to the final paragraph of the "Conclusion," in which Pasternak describes the reality of Lara's remaining years:

One day Larisa Feodorovna went out and did not come back. She must have
been arrested in the street at that time. She vanished without a trace and probably died somewhere, forgotten as a nameless number on a list that afterwards
got mislaid, in one of the innumerable mixed or women's concentration camps
in the north. (503)

At the end, "the beauty of the cosmos" no longer exists for her; there is only
the world of the Gulag and the concentration camp. Pasternak's paragraph is
built upon phrases conveying oblivion: "must have been," "without a trace,"
"probably died somewhere," "a nameless number," "a list that got mislaid,"
and "innumerable mixed or women's concentration camps." After Yurii
urges Lara to depart from Varykino with Komarovksy (who probably ordered
her arrest), she will never see Zhivago again; far worse, he rarely seems,
after moving to Moscow and "marrying" Marina, to have thought about his
beloved Lara. Soul mates forever they are not to be, even in spirit.

Despite the sorry state of postwar Russia and the ultimate disintegration
of Zhivago's relations with women, children, and family, Pasternak was not
quite prepared to abandon all notions of a better future. For the historical
novelist, hope of progress dies especially hard. The novel's four ending paragraphs leave the reader with contrasting prophecies. Misha Gordon initially
concludes, "it has often happened in history that a lofty ideal has degener-
ated into crude materialism. Thus Greece gave way to Rome and the Russian
Enlightenment has become the Russian Revolution" (518). Misha is sure
that the time when men could think of political change as "sent from above,
apocalyptic" has now passed. "Now the metaphorical has become literal,
children are children and the terrors are terrible" (518). Experience has led
him to dismiss all metaphors by which historical novelists try to order or to
control history.

Gordon voices these convictions amid the darkness of 1943. The novel's
three concluding paragraphs, however, picture Dudurov and Gordon in the
mid-1950s expressing tentative hope that "portents of freedom filled the air
throughout the postwar period, and they alone defined its historical significance" (519). "Freedom of the soul" once again seems a reality to them; they
feel around them "the *unheard* music of happiness" (519, italics mine). More
than the brightening prospect of the end of Stalin's era may be involved here.
It may not be possible for an author who has expended the energy to create
a book of the length and quality of *Doctor Zhivago* to abandon all hope of
historical progress. Metaphor returns in the "music of happiness."

The inadequacy of marital compromise has become social custom in *The
Leopard*. Because the structure of Sicilian society is built upon marriage,
Don Fabrizio must somehow continue the prominence of his fading aristo-
cratic lineage by promoting the influence of the next generation. By marrying

Angelica Sedara, daughter of the parvenu mayor, Don Fabrizio's nephew Tancredi marries for beauty, lust, money, and civic position. Although both Tancredi and Fabrizio know that Tancredi will be marrying down socially, they need Sedara's new money. Moreover, the marriage promises to contribute to both family renewal and a more modern Sicily still outwardly respectful of tradition. Politically, Tancredi supports Garibaldi and the Risorgimento. Doing so proves to be a gesture of Tancredi's ever-adaptable ambition; Garibaldi is today's road to power.

Before their marriage, the engaged couple explores the once sumptuous, now half-vacant rooms of the Donnafugata palazzo, luxuriating in anticipation of their sexual and social happiness. With characteristic understatement, Lampedusa summarizes their melancholy afterlife:

> These were the best days in the life of Tancredi and Angelica, lives later to be so variegated, so erring, against the inevitable background of sorrow. But that they did not know then; and they were pursuing a future which they deemed more concrete than it turned out to be, made of nothing but smoke and wind. When they were old and uselessly wise their thoughts would go back to those days with insistent regret; they had been the days when desire was always present because it was always overcome.[23]

In later decades, Tancredi and Angelica will gain their full measure of money, power, and the good life. To Lampedusa, however, their success, like Sicily's progress, is an illusion. When there is more pleasure in anticipation than in reality, when defining traditions collapse, "happiness" becomes the chimera we are condemned to seek in the past.

Lampedusa's lost world is rendered almost entirely from Don Fabrizio's sensitive and convincing perspective. Alone among celebrated historical novels in the Scott tradition, *The Leopard* is from the outset an aging man's book. "Nearing fifty," Don Fabrizio politely endures the presence of his wife Stella who has become "too bossy as well as too old" (24). Regard for the mother of his children lingers, but Stella has become little more to him than a presence fulfilling her wifely role as Princess of the House of Salina. His erotic needs, of which he is neither proud nor ashamed, are periodically satisfied with a Palermo prostitute. In all things, he has learned to accept compromise in the hope that passivity will enable the pleasures of aristocratic tradition to continue.

"The Death of the Prince" is the novel's climactic chapter. By 1888, Stella is dead, Father Pironne is dead, and a grandson Fabrizietto will inherit the Don's title as well as name. Don Fabrizio is no longer close to Angelica and Tancredi. He has laid aside the telescopes with which he had sought regularity and cyclical return (the Copernican meaning of *revolution*) in the universe. Lampedusa denies him the comfort of dying either at Donnafugata or at his Palazzo in Palermo. Instead, Fabrizio dies on a balcony of the Trinacria Hotel, overlooking the bay, transforming his watery surroundings into metaphor: "All he had of his own now was this exhausted body, those slate tiles under his feet, that surging of dark water toward the abyss. He was alone, a shipwrecked man adrift on a raft, prey of untamable currents" (248).

Don Fabrizio's death is the most superbly rendered moment in a novel of superbly rendered moments. After dimly perceiving the "little crowd" of relatives gathered around his bed as "a group of strangers staring at him with frightened expressions," Fabrizio slips into unconsciousness:

> Suddenly amid the group appeared a young woman, slim, in brown traveling dress and wide bustle, with a straw hat trimmed by a speckled veil which could not hide the sly charm of her face. She slid a little suede-gloved hand between one elbow and another of the weeping kneelers, apologized, drew close. It was she, the creature forever yearned for, coming to fetch him; strange that one so young should yield to him; the time for the train's departure must be very close. When she was face to face with him she raised her veil, and there, modest, but ready to be possessed, she looked lovelier than she ever had when glimpsed in stellar space.
>
> The crashing of the sea subsided altogether (254).

So does Fabrizio's life end in silence. The young woman is the same anonymous women he had "glimpsed even yesterday at the station of Catania in a brown traveling dress and suede gloves" (252). She is Death come to "fetch" him, "ready to be possessed" in the form of a woman. She is "the creature he forever yearned for" but has never found. At the very last he realizes that he "glimpsed" her only in the "stellar space" revealed through his telescope. He cannot possess her; she can come to him only as his body dies. Compared to her perfection, the Prince's alien family, his ruined properties, and Italian politics are no longer of importance. The futuristic concerns of Scott's and Dickens's marital endings ebb away in the Keatsian perspective of an old man "half in love with easeful Death."[24] Metaphoric writing of the highest subtlety here displaces history.

Because the long rise of anti-progressive attitudes in historical fiction culminates in *Doctor Zhivago* and *The Leopard*, one would expect their resolutions to confirm Frank Kermode's sense of an ending. Both novels affirm a tragic, not comic view of life; marriage proves to be restorative in the narrative of neither. And yet, Kermode's model does not fully apply. Although both novels record the complete dissolution of the Old Order, there is in their endings no form of apocalypse, no revelation beyond the personal. To use Kermode's Greek terminology, there is *chronos* ("passing time") aplenty in these two texts, but no *kairos* ("a point in time filled with significance, charged with a meaning derived from its relation to the end"[25]). The two aging protagonists die, exhausted by a lifetime of experience they cannot reduce to meaningful order. The Bolshevik revolution and the Risorgimento are now far past, belonging to another lifetime. History conceived as the chronology of events beyond the self is no longer their concern. If there is no happy union in marriage, no hope in children, then is there only silence? For my scholarly purpose, the issue here is not nihilism or indifference, or inscrutability. It is rather the arriving at a prospective, at novel's end, in which the underlying progressive assumptions of Scott's paradigm of the historical novel have been quite literally emptied out.

After the Waverley Novels, the solacing close of the fictional curtain upon a dawning marriage became increasingly untenable. Cooper and Dickens strove to support it by expanding upon it; Tolstoy qualified the happy marital future by placing it within realistic contexts of time and place; Victor Hugo tried to supplant it with abstractions of republican spirit; Anatole France subverted it; Pasternak and Lampedusa demolished it. Its credibility as a harbinger of the better future continued to decline along with expectations of political progress and lasting harmony among peoples and nations. As technology evolved, so did the power of the single successful individual; accordingly, the importance of maintaining educated landed families as cornerstones of social and political stability dwindled. By the 1950s, the facts of European and American history made marrying the conservative maiden to the once-wavering patriot seem the flimsiest possible support of progressive hope. It had itself become an historical "fiction" in the demeaning sense of the term. Accordingly, such happy marriages have now been relegated to the "romance" sections of bookstores, supermarkets, airport kiosks, and websites, where anonymous brain candy is always readily available. Closure needed a new turn if Scott's legacy were to survive.

Nonetheless, Scott's ending speaks to a longing not easily destroyed by the numbing repetition of literary cliché. Ask readers who have just finished *Waverley* how they remember Flora MacIvor and they will recall Flora's encounter with Waverley at the waterfall. Ask them how they remember Lucie Manette, and they will recall Lucie caring for her father, or looking up to catch a glimpse of Darnay at a window of the Conciergerie. Ask them how they remember Natasha Rostov, and they will recall a thirteen-year-old girl bursting delightedly into the Rostov social gatherings or grieving at the wrong she has done to André Bolkonski. Ask them how they recall Lara Guishar, and they will remember the winter idyll at Varykino and the metaphor repeatedly applied to her, "a candle burned."

Readers do not wish to contemplate Flora MacIvor aging in her convent, Rose Bradwardine or Lucie Manette in late life, Natasha Rostov as an unimaginative middle-aged mother, or Lara Guishar reduced to namelessness in one of Stalin's concentration camps. Since the Enlightenment, something deep within western-educated man wants to believe in the continuities of early adulthood, family and future progress, no matter how many times the hope has been betrayed. That hope, Scott recognized, was a mainstay of the kind of historical novel he popularized. As a literary convention, the happy marital ending was to prove increasingly ineffective because historically untenable. Nonetheless, the yearning for it lies deeper than the reservations and cynicisms we outwardly express.

NOTES

1. Jeffrey Eugenides, *The Marriage Plot* (New York: Farrar, Straus and Giroux, 2011), p. 21, 22.

2. Frank Kermode, *The Sense of an Ending* (Oxford and New York: Oxford University Press, 2nd edition, first published 1967), p. 29. Kermode repeats the unusual phrase "in the middest" many times to very great effect; his phrase vividly conveys where mankind stands in time.

3. Sir Walter Scott, *Waverley; or, 'Tis Sixty Years Since*, edited by Andrew Hook (London and New York: Penguin Books, 1985), p. 492.

4. Since Scott's time, his belief that Scottish political nationalism would gradually weaken has seemed–depending on the historical period—to be particularly misguided. Distinguishing among nationalisms is essential here. No writer had more fully conveyed the attractions of Scottish *cultural* nationalism than Scott.

5. Alexander Welsh's summary of the values of Scott's "passive hero" ("prudence, restraint, suppression, precaution, reason, principle and masculine self-denial") applies accurately to the temperament of Scott's heroes at novel's end. Welsh does not take full account, however, of the conflicting values the hero has felt and acted upon during revolutionary crises, nor of the international uncertainties of 1814–1820, the years when Scott's Scottish novels were being published (Welsh, *The Hero of the Waverley Novels*, p. 167).

6. George Dekker, *The Fictions of Romantic Tourism* (Stanford: Stanford University Press, 2005), p. 139.

7. Sir Walter Scott, *Rob Roy*, edited by Ian Ducan (Oxford and New York: Oxford University Press, 1998), p. 97.

8. Sir Walter Scott, *Woodstock, or The Cavalier* (Boston: Indypublish.com, 2011), p. 448.

9. James Fenimore Cooper, *The Spy*, Introduction by Wayne Franklin (London and New York: Penguin Books, 1997), p. 401.

10. Charles Dickens, *A Tale of Two Cities*, edited with an Introduction by Richard Maxwell (New York: Penguin, 2000), p. 389.

11. Avrom Fleishman argues for the reverse emphasis. For Dickens as well as Carton, secular progress is being affirmed by the terminology of Christian salvation:

"this is the mark of a translation of Christian redemption into a historical process" (*The English Historical Novel*, p. 122). Either way, the steps of secular process are not specified.

12. Consider George Orwell's sardonic summary of Dickens's values: "He [Dickens] has an infallible moral sense, but very little intellectual curiosity. . . . He has no ideal of work. . . . In the last resort, there is nothing he admires except common decency. Science is uninteresting and machinery is cruel and ugly. . . . Really, there is no objective except to marry the heroine, settle down, live solvently and be kind. . . . That is the spirit in which most of Dickens's books end—a sort of radiant idleness" ("Charles Dickens" [1939] in *Orwell: A Collection of Essays* [New York: Doubleday and Co., 1954]. p. 94).

13. Leo Tolstoy. *War and Peace*, the Maude translation, edited by George Gibian (New York: W.W. Norton & Co., 1996), p. 996). In the first Russian edition, there was no separation of the epilogue into two parts.

14. Marianna Torgovnick rightly observes, "The familial ending of *War and Peace* still retains a quality of blithe Dickensian belief that a happy family solves all significant problems." She also concludes, however, that "a general pattern of strong resolution, followed by a hint of irresolution, exists throughout the familial epilogue" (Torgovnick, *Closure in the Novel*, [Princeton: Princeton University Press, 1981] pp. 63, 67). There are, however, so many complicating "hints of irresolution" in the first epilogue that I believe Tolstoy should perhaps be regarded as a pioneer of the open ending, rather than a follower of Dickensian convention.

15. Pierre is speaking in 1820 just after the revolt of the Semenovsky Regiment, at a time when groups who were to lead the 1825 Decembrist Revolt were gathering in protest. Some Decembrists followed British revolutionary tradition in demanding a constitutional monarchy with a widened suffrage; others followed French revolutionary tradition in demanding a republic and the abolition of serfdom. To bring about these changes, privileged Russian westernizers, continuing the tradition of the Freemasons and the German *Tugendbund*, created groups very like the "society of gentlemen" Pierre plans to found (1034). As is well known, Tolstoy started an historical novel to be called *The Decembrists,* then abandoned it in favor of the work eventually titled *War and Peace*.

16. Leo Tolstoy *Anna Karenina*, translated by Richard Pevear (London & New York: Penguin Books, 2000), p. 1. I owe this insight to Marianna Torgovnick, *Closure in the Novel*, p. 69.

17. Sarah Orne Jewett, *The Tory Lover* (Boston and New York: Houghton, Mifflin and Co, 1901), p. 404.

18. "The Art of Fiction" in *Henry James: The Future of the Novel*, edited by Leon Edel (New York: Vintage Books, 1956), p. 8. E.M. Forster would turn James's ridicule into unfair generalization: "Nearly all novels are feeble at the end. This is because the plot requires to be wound up. . . . Usually the characters go dead while he [the novelist] is at work, and our final impression of them is through deadness" (Forster, *Aspects of the Novel* [New York: Harcourt, Brace, World, 1957] p. 95).

19. Victor Hugo, *Ninety-Three*, translated by Frank Lee Benedict, Introduction by Graham Robb (New York: Carroll & Graf, 1998), p. 377.

20. Emile Zola, *La Débacle*, translated by E.P. Robbins (New York: Mondial, 2008), pp. 426, 427.

21. Anatole France, *The Gods Will Have Blood*, translated by Frederick Davies (London and New York: Penguin Books, 1990), p. 225.

22. Boris Pasternak, *Doctor Zhivago*, translated by John Bailey (New York: Pantheon Books, 1991), p. 465.

23. Giuseppe di Lampedusa, *The Leopard*, translated by Archibald Colquhoun, forward by Gioacchino Lanza Tomasi (New York: Pantheon Books, 2007), p. 162.

24. John Keats, "Ode to a Nightingale," *Complete Poems and Selected Letters* (New York: Odyssey Press, 1935), p. 351.

25. Frank Kermode, *The Sense of an Ending*, p. 47.

Chapter 9

New Directions

In the late 1950s and 1960s, after the achievements of Pasternak and Lampedusa, the *Waverley* model of historical fiction had become so attenuated as to seem no longer of use. Its literary conventions no longer needed to be criticized, but could simply be set aside, viewed as no longer relevant to modernist attitudes and postmodernist assumptions. Fredric Jameson's criticisms of Scott's historical novel enter critical discourse at this time. These kinds of intra-genre judgments (favoring Balzac, condescending to Scott; favoring Tolstoy, condescending to Dickens) may, however, in time be proven premature. Important historical novels centering upon revolution have continued to be written by celebrated authors who are commonly described as modernists or postmodernists, but whose connection to the *realism* of Scott's legacy is essential. I select novels by Gore Vidal, Gabriel Garcia Marquez, and Hilary Mantel to suggest promising new directions that the realist historical novel of revolution has recently pursued. No prediction about collective trajectory can be conclusive, but the possibilities to be offered here are, I believe, all plausible, all worth consideration.

What new emphases do Vidal's *Narratives of Empire*, Marquez's *The General in His Labyrinth*, and Mantel's *A Place of Greater Safety* share? Their authors bring no apriori assumptions to the contemplation of history. Any felt need to affirm the surety of progress or decline between the Old Order and the New disappears, no matter how intently the novel's historical characters may continue to worry the question. In these novels Marxist economic assumptions do not lead to affirmation of the Marxist model of revolutionary history. Time is conceived as a sequence of man-measured days and years upon which the human imagination tries to impose order by selection and omission. Like a Waverley novel, the recounting of the passing days immerses author and reader in realistic detail, but unlike a Waverley novel, there is no assumption that the details could ever be made to fit consistently into a holistic view of how past develops into present.

For these novelists, any decision of allegiance reached by a wavering protagonist seems of little consequence measured against the fragmented contradictions of a wide, unknowable world. Honor is a gesture to be made on a dueling ground or a revolutionary battlefield. Freed from protected domestic retreat, women emerge as mates, lovers, thinkers, coconspirators, or ambitious materialists; they exert no force, maternal or spiritual, that could by itself substantiate progress. Gentility, family, and property convey no security for the future. Novels conclude with the death of an important historical individual (Vidal's Burr, Marquez's Bolivar, Mantel's Danton) but without arriving at an end point in time or at closure of meaning.

EMPIRE WITHOUT REVOLUTION

In response to a question about lifetime reading, Gore Vidal told his literary executor Jay Parini that, presumably during late adolescence, "I worked my way through a shelf of Scott."[1] Recalling his writing practices during the early sixties, Vidal said "I often thought of Sir Walter Scott. He had a desk in his study with two sides, so that he could have two novels boiling at the same time. I was doing the same."[2] Vidal's interconnected seven-volume series of historical novels, *Narratives of Empire* (1967–2000) assumes that Scott's way of balancing fiction and history needs to be altered.[3] Whereas Scott begins with a politically divided fictional family, then brings his thorough knowledge of Scottish history to them, Vidal begins to write after formidable historical research, conceives an historical grid, then situates his fictional characters within it as observers of political and cultural change. Scott builds his novels around a marital plot upon which history intrudes, and then lavishes his descriptive powers upon anything or anyone suitable. Vidal, by contrast, has told Parini "If I'm working on an historical novel, then history provides the outline."[4] (284). Vidal's title term for his *Empire* series ("narratives" not "novels") suggests the equal importance of history and fiction, as well as a postmodernist conception that written history is always a selective narrative. Because Vidal believes that "description is usually boring," he moves his novels forward through witty, sharply pointed dialogue, minimizing the sequences of physical movement that had served Scott so effectively (284). Scott's characters journey through landscapes; Vidal's characters confront each other in offices, committee rooms, restaurants, and reception halls.

Their opposed priorities suggest contrasting literary strengths. Within any era of American history from the Revolution onward, to post World War II, Vidal can summon up a wide range of historical figures, imbedding statements from the historical record into crackling fictive dialogue that compels suspension of disbelief. The Afterwords that Vidal has written for his novels distinguish between an historical novelist's obligation to remain true to known facts and the novelist's freedom to invent a plausible range of motives for historical persons. Vidal's accuracy in rendering fact and dialogue convinces the reader that satirical or condemnatory historical characterizations with which the reader is likely to take exception (notably George Washington, Thomas Jefferson, Theodore Roosevelt, and Woodrow Wilson) might have been historically valid.

Although most historical characters in novels by Vidal's predecessors seem wooden by comparison, Vidal pays a price for this great literary/historical merit. Whereas Scott depended, often successfully, upon the reader's identification with his wavering fictional protagonist, Vidal has difficulty enlivening Charlie Schuyler (*Burr*), David Herold (*Lincoln*), Charlie and Emma Schuyler (*1876*), and Caroline and Blaise Sanford (*Empire*), each of whom seems meant to function as a Jamesian central intelligence. We care about what they see, but we do not care about who they are; they remain windows through which we see only outward.

In the concluding paragraph of his "State of the Union" essay, a companion piece to his bicentennial novel *1876*, Vidal prophesied a forthcoming American revolution:

> True revolution can only take place when things fall apart in the wake of some catastrophe—a lost war, a collapsed economy. We seem headed for the second. If so, then let us pray that the somber, all-confining Bastille known as the consumer society will fall, as the *first* American revolution begins! It is long overdue.[5]

With a glance at Yeats's "The Second Coming" ("Things fall apart, the center cannot hold"), Vidal unfolds his often restated, neo-Marxist argument about American consumerism, American power, and American decline: The privileged few with money control the many without money. Locked in a class system where "the myth of upward social mobility dies hard," the rich hoodwink consumers into struggling to retain jobs they dislike in order to consume surplus goods they do not need (936). Contrary to American populist myth, power does not accompany the vote. Instead, the big money buys and elects politicians who control Congress. Congress taxes consumers in order to support foreign wars that increase national and private debt. To continue to sell surplus goods, as well as to buy needed, cheaper goods abroad, America must export "democracy" at gunpoint to any would-be dictator who can be bought. America's class system thus demands an ever-expanding empire to sustain it. As America ages and declines, the system of American empire has become one immense, still unfallen Bastille imprisoning rich and poor alike.[6]

The "catastrophe," when it occurs, will be "the *first* American revolution." Vidal's italics emphasize his subversive conviction that 1776 had in fact witnessed no "American Revolution" at all. *Burr* must be read as an affirmation of this hypothesis. Vidal's Aaron Burr rises to military fame without patriot political conviction:

> "I confess to not having listened to a word of the Declaration of Independence. At the time I barely knew the name of the author of the sublime document. I do remember hearing someone comment that since Mr. Jefferson had seen fit to pledge so eloquently our lives to the cause of independence, he might at least join us in the army. But wise Tom preferred the safety of Virginia and the excitement of local politics to the discomforts and dangers of war."[7]

Burr fights for personal glory, for separation from England, and because he is the son and grandson of presidents of Princeton, not because he is committed to Man's Natural Rights to "life, liberty and the pursuit of happiness." His "sacred honor" is defined through his reputation; "Equality" is not on his revolutionary horizon.

Ambitious though Burr is, he will neither lie, nor cheat, nor steal to advance his opportunities. Vidal must have relished describing the legendary traitor as an honest thinker, first among his lawyerly associates: "Burr was the more effective in a courtroom because his mind was swifter than Hamilton's; also, of an entire generation of public men, Burr was free of cant; he never moralized unless to demonstrate a paradox. As a result the passionate believers thought him evil on the ground that the man who refuses to preach Goodness must be Bad" (136). Clearly, Aaron Burr functions as Gore Vidal's kindred spirit. Avoid cant and moralize only in the service of paradox, but be aware that you will therefore be thoroughly misunderstood.

The pantheon of American founding fathers receives a deft drubbing. Vidal's George Washington, repeatedly described as slow-witted, is an incompetent military general but a coony politician alive to the value of inertia and the importance of an impressive appearance. Vidal's Jefferson twice deceives Burr at turning points in Burr's political career. Burr describes Jefferson as "ruthless," "a hypocrite," "the most charming man I have ever known, as well as the most deceitful."[8] Alexander Hamilton, who stops at nothing to best Burr in New York politics, is far more secretive than Burr in his dealings with mistresses and prostitutes. As president, John Adams proves to be too jealous, rigid, and moralistic to survive more than one term amid Washington D.C.'s ever-shifting nest of vipers.

These characterizations make a clean sweep of the supposedly revolutionary founding fathers, Madison excepted. All of them save John Adams are at least as interested in acquiring western lands as they are in establishing good republican government. None of them thinks in terms of the appeal of the *Ancien Regime* versus the hope of libertarian progress. Their patriotic energies are devoted to national expansion into Quebec, Kentucky, Ohio, East Florida, West Florida, and Louisiana. In Vidal's rendering, Aaron Burr's trial for treason was motivated by President Jefferson's desire to exact retaliation for Burr's scheme to gather armed followers to free Mexico from Spanish misrule. Earlier, Burr had summed up his feelings about Jefferson by remarking about the Louisiana Purchase, "had Jefferson not been a hypocrite I might have admired him. After all, he was the most successful empire-builder of our century, succeeding where Bonaparte failed" (160). In Vidal's view, the founding fathers needed no tutelage in the arts of achieving national expansion through waging wars of "liberation."

The overturn Vidal sees in American history is not the political revolution of 1776 but the hardening of republic into empire. The land hunger, public and private, that Burr witnesses in 1803 is witnessed again in the 1830s by Charlie Schuyler, when expansion toward and into Mexico develops in earnest (*Burr*). The military and legal bases for empire are then put in place by Abraham Lincoln through wide expansion of federal powers, including the draft, suspension of habeas corpus, and military and railroad contracting (*Lincoln*). By the centennial year, bosses controlling powerful parties determine the outcome of corrupting elections (Hayes-Tilden) while conspicuous consumption and large national corporations expand in tandem (*1876*).

The nation's transformation openly emerges at the turn of the twentieth century in the novel titled *Empire*. The Spanish-American War, the annexation of the Philippines, John Hay's "Open Door" policy toward China, and the posturing of Theodore Roosevelt coalesce in Vidal's narrative, amassing a collective power no individual successfully resists. Brooks Adams, not Henry Adams, is portrayed as the intellectual force behind the McKinley-Roosevelt presidencies: Brooks Adams's Social Darwinism convinces republican administrations that forthright American imperialism, based upon the need to surpass Great Britain in naval power and colonial trade, will lead eventually to a worldwide struggle between the United States and Russia.

Henry Adams, who, like Gore Vidal, promotes himself as the satirical iconoclast who speaks truth, delivers the *coup de grace* to the revolutionary republic that might have been, but never was. When Secretary of State John Hay delivers a Kipling-esque appeal to Henry Adams that "Surely, we have a moral—yes I hate the word, too—duty to help less fortunate nations in this hemisphere," Henry Adams replies:

"John, it is empire you all want, and it is empire that you have got. . . . The American republic. You've finally got rid of it. For good. As a conservative Christian anarchist, I never much liked it." Adams raised high his teacup. "The republic is dead; long live the empire."[9]

No other historical character in the novel, except possibly Henry James, could or would credit Adams's sardonic toast, but for Vidal and his reader, it supplies the novel's informing title.

Always wary of clichés, Vidal is unwilling to limit the meaning of "Empire" to military, territorial and economic conquest. Throughout the novel, Teddy Roosevelt, usually assumed to be the representative of his era, is contrasted to William Randolph Hearst. Roosevelt proves to be anything but the forceful progressive his admirers describe him to be. Vidal introduces Roosevelt as "the thick small restless shrill-voiced man who was marching about the room like a toy soldier that someone had wound up but forgot to point in any particular direction" (126). Vidal sustains the simile throughout the novel. Vidal's Teddy Roosevelt is only fitfully aware that Admiral Mahan, Brooks Adams, and New York City's Boss Platt have wound him up; Teddy remains unsure whether to march off to bust the trusts or to defer to the capitalists who warily support his political career. What President Roosevelt will not admit is that "Teddy Roosevelt," hero of the Spanish-American War and leader of the Rough Riders, is the creation of William Randolph Hearst's yellow press. The money interests behind the press now create the news, determine the elections, and shape the nation's remembered history. Hearst's intermittent socialism, as Vidal sees it, is nothing more than sensational posturing designed to maintain Hearst's celebrity. Media moguls will support the forces of empire as long as the forces of empire provide the money, whether through payoffs or newspaper sales.

Empire ends with a dramatic one-on-one confrontation in the White House between President Roosevelt and William Randolph Hearst. For the first time, Roosevelt is reduced to spluttering or to silence by the truth of Hearst's one-liners: "I made you up in Cuba"; "I bought the country"; "You're just an office holder"; "The world becomes what I say it is"; "I can usually make the market rise or fall," and then, in parting, "True history is the final fiction. . . I thought even you knew that" (485). Within what Henry James ruefully refers to as "our newspaper democracy," the media have become as strong a force for empire as the battleship or the stock exchange (24). Such a conclusion leads directly to the next novel in Vidal's series, *Hollywood,* describing a brave, new world in which, for the credulous populace, reality beyond one's immediate surroundings is created by the celluloid image.

In 1980, Gore Vidal said he would like to be remembered as "the person who wrote the best sentences in his time."[10] His skill at terse satirical summary is unsurpassed; the closing sentence of many a paragraph resembles Jonathan Swift or Alexander Pope in its biting concision. Moreover, if Vidal's view of American empire—and of America's forthcoming revolution—prove to be correct, Vidal will be remembered for a great deal more than stylistic mastery. As an historical novelist, however, questions remain. Because his history is so much more compelling than his fiction, the whole of a Vidal novel is less than the sum of its parts. The United States of America is considerably more than the New York—Washington—Hollywood geographical axis within which the scenes of the *Narratives of Empire* unfold. How can an author whose characters, historical as well as fictional, come almost exclusively from the educated, propertied, and powerful urban classes justify such repeated generalizing about the entirety of "America"? Nonetheless, Jay Parini has made a persuasive case for Vidal's place within Scott's legacy of historical fiction: "He [Vidal] took the old-fashioned historical novel in fresh directions with Julian, Burr and Lincoln, foregrounding the figure in the title, digging into the texture of their lives, examining motives, giving a rounded sense of their accomplishments, their needs, their weaknesses, their public self-renderings."[11]

PLOWING THE SEA

If Scott, Cooper, Dickens, Tolstoy, or Hugo had attempted an historical novel centered on Simon Bolivar, they would surely have pictured him, first, as a privileged young Venezuelan Creole, ignorant of politics, but well aware that wealthy native-born Venezuelans of Spanish ancestry like himself were regarded, in his own words, as "neither Indians nor Europeans, but a race halfway between the legitimate owners of the land and the Spanish usurpers."[12] A nineteenth-century historical novelist would surely have emphasized the youthful Bolivar's extended visits to Paris and to Rome, where Bolivar not only read Locke, Montesquieu, Rousseau, and Voltaire, but witnessed, with mingled ecstasy and disapproval, Napoleon's crowning of himself as emperor of the French. A chapter describing the most legendary moment in Bolivar's life, his vow atop Monte Sacro in Rome, would have been hard to forego; there, in the presence of his admired tutor Simon Rodriguez, Bolivar had vowed "I swear by my country that I will not rest body or soul until I have broken the chains binding us to the will of Spanish might."[13] The moment became, in memory, Bolivar's personal declaration of independence from colonial misrule.

Whatever wavering Simon Bolivar may have felt as he matured is of no interest to Gabriel Garcia Marquez, whose concern is the historical consequences of a life of military politics. The important facts of Bolivar's life are unobtrusively woven into Marquez's narrative. The aging Bolivar looks back, with pitiless realism, on the failure of his heroic endeavors. For fifteen years, Simon Bolivar had rarely lost a battle. He led his army across the Andes during the height of the rainy season in order to liberate New Granada (Columbia). Influenced by Montesquieu's belief that a successful polity must be adapted to the nature of its people, he insisted that South American republics should adopt neither the United States Constitution, nor the French Rights of Man. In the name of man's natural right to revolt against unjust government, Bolivar demanded the abolition of Spanish imperial power and the institution of a republic based upon separation of powers, checks, and balances, freedom of the press and an independent judiciary.

At various times, Bolivar envisaged one *Gran Columbia* republic that would include not only today's Venezuela, Columbia, Ecuador, and Peru, but all of South America from Panama to Cape Horn. Influenced by Benthamite Utilitarianism, Bolivar was willing, however, to settle for as many as thirteen loosely federated Republics. He was aware that the entrenched powers of local warlords (*caudillos*), regional politicians, and Spanish loyalists would oppose his republicanism. Whenever threatening circumstance made it necessary, he was willing to accept, temporarily, positions as Liberator President of Columbia and Peru, but he often threatened to resign from them, on the grounds that political control by a dictatorial general merely restored monarchy in a different form. For a nineteenth-century historical novelist, the literary advantages of characterizing Bolivar as an admirable, latter day Napoleon free of vainglory and overweening ambition, committed to conquest for the sake of liberty, would have been hard to resist. Marquez resists them entirely.

By restriction of his novel's time frame, and generous use of remembered flashbacks, Marquez subverts such progressive expectations from the outset. The foreground narrative of *The General in His Labyrinth* (1990) takes place during 1830, the last year of Bolivar's life. Wearied unto death by the defeat of his grand revolutionary republic, Bolivar leaves Bogota to sail down the Magdalena River toward self-imposed European exile, only to die of tuberculosis before embarkation.

Bolivar describes himself, with minimal self-pity, as "old, sick, tired, disillusioned, harassed, slandered, and unappreciated."[14] Through the eyes of his loyal valet José Palacios, we are introduced to an exhausted, eighty-eight pound, world-famous but half-delirious general, trying to purge his body through baths and to purge his memory through writing letters that might control the past and the future. As Bolivar's Venezuelan soldiers and political allies defect, he finds himself short of money, without a passport, without a child, without a future, his reputation rapidly disintegrating. In town after town along the Magdalena, he must endure exhausting ceremonies of tribute from hypocritical Columbians most of whom, Bolivar knows, are glad to see him go. The heat, rain, and stench are overwhelming. In the novel's closing chapters, Bolivar compares himself to an old, mangy, wounded, smelly, stray dog; turkey buzzards are five times pictured hovering over street garbage and/ or Bolivar's dying body.[15]

Nonetheless, the narrator of *The General in His Labyrinth* invites the reader to admire Bolivar as both a revolutionary patriot and a politician:

Of all the generation of enlightened Americans who sowed the seeds of independence from Mexico to Rio de la Plata, he [Bolivar] was the most convinced, the most tenacious, the most farseeing, the one who best reconciled the ingenuity of politics and the intuition of warfare. (78)

The problems with which Bolivar was faced, however, have done him in. The sum of Spanish loyalists, local *caudillos*, envious subordinates, rival generals, linguistic and cultural differences, geographical barriers, and lack of democratic traditions have proven too much to surmount. As soon as revolutionary turbulence in one area of *Gran Columbia* quieted down, Bolivar moved on to the next, only to discover that the old problems resurfaced behind him. "It had been proved over and over again, " Bolivar realizes, "that when he abandoned the south to march north, and vice versa, the country he left behind was lost, devastated by new civil wars. It was his destiny" (113).

Bolivar's commitment to universal republicanism has been defeated primarily by the resurgence of separatist forces from within. As regional cultures are liberated to become small republics, they resist being swallowed up into Bolivar's *Gran Columbia*. Bolivar sees this ironic development, not as the beginning of distinctive national cultures, but as the divisive result of a power vacuum caused by the needed disappearance of Spanish authority. He declares to Francisco Iturbide, a royalist family friend, "the damn problem is that we stopped being Spaniards and then we went here and there and everywhere in countries that change their names and governments so much from one day to the next we don't know where the hell we come from" (184). From Marquez's late-twentieth-century perspective, the kind of nationalism Bolivar sees emerging out of revolutionary republicanism in South America is very different in kind and in consequence from the Risorgimento or the unification of Germany. The nationalisms underlying German and Italian unification were empowered to their eventual destruction; South American nationalism would lead immediately to corrupt, local tyranny.

Although the dying Bolivar is never quite willing to abandon all hope of recovering health and power, he predicts that his lifelong republican purpose is doomed. "The immense unified nation he had forged during so many years of wars and sacrifices would break apart," he muses; "factions would divide it among themselves" (142). Bolivar predicts "The only wars here will be civil wars," a historical prophecy confirmed by the narrator's reminder that the successful insurrection in Bogota in 1830 was "the first coup d'état in the Republic of Columbia, and the first of the forty-nine civil wars we would suffer in what remained of the century" (199).

In accord with the novel's controlling metaphor, the labyrinth, the narrator offers no clear explanation for the recurrence of the forty-nine civil wars. Instances accumulate without apparent connection. We may assume, however, that Marquez's scorn for the internal politics of twentieth-century South American nations lies behind his emphasis on the many civil wars of Bolivar's time. We can definitively conclude only that the inner fault lines of multiple regional cultures constantly rise to the surface to destroy progress. Inquiries into the truth of history, like Bolivar's attempt to sort out the flood of his memories, lead to mystery and to inconclusive dead-ends. Bolivar's faithful lover Manuela Saens describes Bolivar as "wandering without direction through the mists of solitude" (153–154). Bolivar himself acknowledges "I've become lost in a dream, searching for something that doesn't exist" (221). His journey down the Magdalena is a forced pilgrimage with no destination, a mission downriver into his variant of the heart of darkness. Bolivar's last utterance is his discovery of the most appropriate metaphor for his entire life: "Damn it," he sighed. "How will I ever get out of this labyrinth!" (267). By phrasing the metaphor as a rhetorical question, Bolivar confirms that he can imagine no exit. His life encapsulates the historical future, at least for South America; grand, unifying purpose ends in fragmentation, enabling local dictators to seize power.

To be lost in a mental and historical labyrinth creates a need to search past experiences for conclusions about a future one cannot change. Marquez describes the dying Bolivar dictating "a series of somewhat disordered notes that did not express his desires so much as his disillusionment":

> America is ungovernable, the man who serves a revolution plows the sea, this nation will fall inevitably into the hands of the unruly mob and then will pass into the hands of almost indistinguishable petty tyrants of every color and race. (257)

These "disordered notes," which the narrator judges to be "lugubrious thoughts," are in fact a revealing revision of an extremely orderly letter the historical Bolivar had written during his last month of life. On November 9, 1830, Bolivar had written to General Juan José Flores:

> You know that I have ruled for twenty years, and I have derived from these only a few sure conclusions: (1) America is ungovernable, for us; (2) those who serve revolution plough the sea; (3) The only thing one can do in America is emigrate; (4) This country will fall inevitably into the hands of the unrestrained multitudes and then into the hands of tyrants so insignificant they will be almost imperceptible, of all colors and races.[16]

What the historical Bolivar thought were "sure conclusions" have become in Marquez's novel "lugubrious thoughts." Bolivar's qualifying phrase "for us" is eliminated. So is the historical inaccuracy of "The only thing one can do in America is emigrate." Whereas Bolivar had written that the future belongs to "unrestrained multitudes" and "insignificant," "imperceptible" tyrants, Marquez changes the terms to "the unruly mob" and "almost indistinguishable petty tyrants." Even after allowing for uncertainties of translation, Marquez's need to temper Bolivar's despairing phrases so as not to foreclose all hope seems evident.

The one "conclusion" Marquez felt no need to change is Bolivar's proverbial declaration "Those who serve the revolution plough the sea." The historical Bolivar had found the perfect metaphor for the futile, directionless confusion into which the service of revolution had led him.[17] The plough was the wrong tool; the future he was entering was not fertile earth, but boundless sea without direction or limit. There can be no better summation of late-twentieth-century disillusionment with the promise of revolution.

FACTIONS: "SPLITTING APART LIKE ROTTEN FRUIT"

After winning the Man Booker Prize for *Wolf Hall*, Hilary Mantel observed that "the boundaries of the term 'historical fiction' are now so wide that it is almost meaningless, so use of the term is beginning to look like an accusation. . . . The accusation is that authors are ducking the tough issues in favour of writing about frocks."[18] Although Mantel believes the truth of history can never be known, the closer we approach it, the more we realize that the past is no "feathered sanctuary . . . suffused by a pink, romantic glow." Her evident animus against women's historical romance is based less on its costumery than on its avoiding the dark recesses of the known past. "History doesn't make you backward-looking; it makes you want to run like hell toward the future." Everyone who writes about the past brings to it "the biases of his training and the vagaries of his personal temperament," but the inevitability of bias does not free the historian or the historical novelist from the responsibility to strive for accuracy. The historical writer must perceive that "much of what we retain about the past is a collection of factoids, received opinions and accumulated moral judgments." He or she must also recognize that "the only requirement is for conjecture to be plausible and grounded in the best facts one can get."

This position is fully consistent with the "Author's Note" preceding *A Place of Greater Safety* (1992), Mantel's 750-page historical novel on the French Revolution. The novel consists of some three hundred, short, separate scenes that follow in strict historical sequence as in traditional film narrative. The novel is preceded by a lengthy "Cast of Characters" most of whom are historical; its narrative is divided into five parts, with an historical climax (the "massacre" of August 10, 1792) at the end of the third part; at least six scenes are written as dramatic dialogue. The reader must provide the links between and among the scenes. All characters speak, clearly and concisely, the language of today's daily life; dialect, costumery, and local color disappear, even from the few scenes that transpire outside Paris.[19]

At no point does the novel's narrator provide any summation of the historical significance of the French Revolution, nor her personal view of it. Verisimilitude lies in details that are true to surviving sources, but unfolded in chronological order without the phony prescience of the historian. Mantel's opening note insists that her novel is "closely tied to historical facts," that she has whenever possible used the "real words, recorded speeches and preserved writings" of her main characters, then "woven them into my own dialogue."[20] "I am not trying to persuade my reader to view events in a particular way, or to draw any particular lessons from them" (x). Accordingly, Mantel's narrative voice is more detached than Pasternak's or Lampedusa's. She has no *Ancien Regime* to regret and no illusions about truth. Considered collectively, these are the familiar standards of late-nineteenth-century literary realism applied to a postmodernist pastiche of genre and pervaded with a postmodernist skepticism about overriding answers of any kind.[21]

Mantel avoids rewriting many of the set pieces recurrent in histories and novels of the French Revolution. We do not see the first meeting of the Estates General, the Tennis Court Oath, the fall of the Bastille, the trial and execution of Louis XVI, the murder of Marat, or, most importantly, the fall of Robespierre. Nor are there any lachrymose scenes of aristocrats in the tumbrils awaiting their turn at the guillotine. We hear of these events, together with many others, as they are discussed in family households or as they are reported in committee rooms.

Unlike characters in the Scott tradition, Mantel's historical characters rarely seem aware that they might become important participants in something soon to be called "history." Desmoulins, Danton, and Robespierre, the three central figures in the novel, are all young men trained in law, estranged from their provincial parents, but determined to make their way in the Paris of the mid-1780s. As Danton puts it, "I just want to be somebody."[22] They are sons of lawyers and civil servants important in towns and small cities, exactly the kind of middle-class fortune seekers who, from Marx's perspective, were to make the French Revolution a bourgeois ascendancy. Among the three, only Desmoulins advocates a republic before 1790; Danton does not favor a republic until after Louis XVI's flight to Varennes. Although they yearn for domestic comfort amid the political turmoil, all three have complicated sexual needs (Desmoulins is bisexual, Robespierre asexual, and Danton a woman-chaser) that make fidelity to a monogamous marriage impossible. Their economic uncertainties and sexual conduct inflict pain upon wives and other women who are often equally unscrupulous. The prospect of daily marital happiness emerging from such relationships soon vanishes.

As in the novels by Vidal and by Marquez, political life is less a search for governing principals and institutions than a jockeying for power. The merits of monarchy, aristocracy or democracy, of statute law or common law, of legislative chambers in a constitutional republic, are crucial issues of political theory for which none of Mantel's revolutionaries has the time. Instead we see factions being endlessly formed and reformed. To have been a member of yesterday's faction renders one instantly suspect. Through print gossip pretending to be periodical journalism, conspiracy theories emerge, swell poisonously, and then are acted upon. Men of political ambition worry about their reputation on today's city streets, not about the crude left-to-right group distinctions (the Mountain, the Plain, and the Gironde) which were to be advanced by historians from Michelet to Crane Brinton and thereafter. Instead, Mantel's revolutionaries worry whether Monsieur X is an Orleanist, a Brissotin, a Rolandist, a Dantonist, an Hébertist, an Ultra, an Enragé, or an adherent of yet another splinter group.

These small groups are defined by their leader's current street status. Today the faction flourishes; tomorrow it flounders; day after tomorrow it perishes. Power accrues through accusing a small group of conspiracy, trying them on evidence of rumors, and then executing them together as individuals comprising a faction. To expedite the purging of factions, the Committee of Public Safety and the Revolutionary Tribunal develop nearly infallible tactics. They ignore differences among the accused, make up rules of evidence, and improvise random questioning. When no one knows exactly what a "Brissotin" is, but everyone knows that Brissotin himself is no longer popular, a "faction" of four or five accused "Brissotins" can be promptly sent to the guillotine with the full approval of a fearful public. Rage against the legal injustices of the *Ancien Regime* is no longer the driving force of rush to judgment within the Paris Tribunal, as it had been in *A Tale of Two Cities*; instead, it is strategizing among today's conspiratorial factions that matters most.

In Mantel's rather Burkean view, French discourse about political change exploded suddenly into declarations of human rights without careful consideration of the institutions necessary to support them. As a member of the National Assembly, Danton sardonically notes that, after July 13, 1789, governmental speechifying, including his own, continued to neglect constitution building. Because France lacks a king, a constitution and legal procedure, baseless self-serving rhetoric will flourish unchecked. To emphasize the rapid growth of faction, Mantel cites two telling, often forgotten facts of revolutionary history. In October of 1793, at the onset of the Terror, the National Convention enacted a resolution of Saint-Just declaring that "the provisional government of France is revolutionary until the peace. . . . Terror is the order of the day."[23] Second, the French Constitution, ratified in June 1793, was never implemented; it was set aside by the Committee of Public Safety. When government is both "provisional" and "revolutionary until the peace," its constitution becomes a piece of paper.

As deadly, unplanned events accumulate, the Revolution's leaders become increasingly rudderless and bewildered. Robespierre carries Rousseau's *Social Contract* in his pocket, but is never able to think beneath today's policy and personnel decisions. Returning after a long day at the National Convention in late 1792, Robespierre admits to Eléonore Duplay that he feels he is "floundering, . . . bogged down in detail": "you are worrying all the time about supplying boots for the army, and you're thinking, *every day I fail at something*—and it begins to look like one gigantic failure" (625). Mantel's Danton exhausts himself making compromise deals that will somehow keep the British army at bay, bolster the French army, maintain popular support for the Mountain, and maintain the reputation of the National Convention. The accelerating pace of daily realities leaves no opportunity for thinking through to truth.

Danton realizes he must act, albeit inconsistently, on the faith he had expressed to Mirabeau: "it is not a government's descriptive label that matters, but its nature, the way it operates, whether it is government by the people" (277). Consequently, Danton is charitable toward individuals, but duplicitous in public policy. With comparable inconsistency, Robespierre condemns capital punishment, then promotes the Terror. Depending on the situation, Robespierre uses the French word *vertu* to mean either virtue or strength (Latin *Virtus*). For both men, the unknown end of the revolution justifies repellent means; they increasingly suspect one another, even while they claim they are proceeding together.

Readers familiar with the historiography of the French Revolution expect that the central historical character of Hilary Mantel's novel will be Robespierre and that the novel will end with Robespierre's fall from power and the end of the Terror. Neither expectation is fulfilled. Camille Desmoulins is Mantel's central character and the novel ends with the successive guillotining of Desmoulins and Danton, leaving Robespierre's execution to be listed in a concluding note that recounts in single sentences the later lives of fifteen historical characters. In a review, Mantel has noted "He [Robespierre] is remembered as the theoretician of the Terror. It is he who bears the blame when blame is handed out."[24] Whenever Robespierre is scapegoated in this manner, Mantel implies, historical complexity and collective responsibility will be conveniently forgotten.

Like the attention Vidal paid to William Randolph Hearst, Mantel's fore-grounding of Desmoulins stresses the importance of the media, journalism in particular, as a growing influence upon post-Enlightenment politics. Danton's oratorical power leads him to surmise, "actions are being manufactured out of speech" and to wonder "How can words save a country?" (442). Desmoulins has been a skilled journalist from the outset. His way with words first brings him to prominence when he urges the crowd in the gardens of the Palais Royal to attack the Bastille. Thereafter Desmoulins's notoriety is maintained by the "black radiance" of his writings and his "magnetic" personality (486). Desmoulins is said to be among the first to advance the possibility that the revolution might lead to a republic, but no specific notion of a republican state ever emerges from him. He is forever performing the gestures of a public personality because he has no inner center. The force of his pen is therefore spent on the shifting defamations of the journalistic moment.[25]

Unlike Danton or Robespierre, Desmoulins undergoes a crushing loss of faith. As editor/publisher first of the *Revolutions de France* and then of *Le Vieux Cordelier*, Desmoulins understands that he is expected continually to outdo himself in arousing revolutionary fervor. As his authority mounts together with the executions, he increasingly questions his role in maintaining the climate for Terror. His finest moment occurs in the winter of 1794, when he finally confronts Robespierre about the purpose of the revolution: "What did we have the Revolution for? I thought it was so that we could speak out against oppression. I thought it was to free us from tyranny. But this is tyranny. . . . Show me another dictatorship that kills with efficiency and delight in virtue and flourishes its abstractions over open graves" (663). Robespierre is reduced to looking away in silence, grasping Desmoulins's arm, and whispering, "Everything you say is true, . . . but I don't know how to proceed" (663). At this moment, neither man can see any future beyond more Terror.

Searching for the compelling phrase under ever-changing circumstances only intensifies Desmoulins's disillusionment. From prison he writes to his wife and sometime political accomplice Lucile: "I dreamt of a republic which the world would have adored: I could never have believed that men could be so ferocious and so unjust."[26] About to die, Desmoulins has found bitter consolation in the assurance that his "dream" of a republic had always been doomed, not by his own actions, but by the ferocity and injustice of human nature.

Mantel implies, however, that Desmoulins is rationalizing after the fact. Desmoulins's shrill denunciations have caused the revolutionaries to continue "splitting apart like rotten fruit" (596). The revolutionary leaders have failed to sustain the integrity of their families as well as the integrity of the state. To fix the blame on mankind's unchangeable ferocity and injustice is too easy, too simplistic. From Hilary Mantel's perspective, it is the totality of historical circumstance, together with the individual failings of able men like Danton, Robespierre, and Desmoulins, which has led France over the precipices of the revolution.

For Mantel, unlike Victor Hugo, there is no rainbow emerging from the fall over the precipice. The last subsection of the novel ends with Robespierre's childhood remembrance of his mother knitting lace, "beneath her fingers the airy pattern, going nowhere, flying away" (747). Robespierre now realizes that "it was the gaps that were important, the spaces between the threads which made the pattern, and not the threads themselves" (747). So it is in the novel. A pattern of history has been woven, but eventually it flies away, and no one can presume to know where it is going. Is there "a place of greater safety" than this clearly treacherous and volatile world? The pertinence of Mantel's title is introduced in only one seemingly throwaway passage. Camille Desmoulins approaches a soldier worriedly guarding the National Convention against conspirators and assassins. The soldier asks if he can provide Citizen Deputy Desmoulins an escort "to a place of greater safety" (559). Desmoulins muses that the "place of greater safety" can only be "the grave. . . the grave," a response the soldier cannot or will not comprehend. For the reader, Mantel's title passage points toward an historical and personal dead-end that counters the liveliness and energies of her characters.

Vidal, Marquez, and Mantel take the form of the historical novel in varied directions, but they share assumptions about the nature of revolutions that are characteristic of the late twentieth century, not of the hopes of the late eighteenth century: No populace and few individuals ever anticipate a revolution. People wish to assume that revolutions happen elsewhere. What we agree to call a revolution is a rebellion that has succeeded at deadly cost. Because revolutions arise from civil dissension, usually civil war, revolutions become terrible, bloody cataclysms. The confused sense of crisis that prevails at the height of revolutionary conflict promotes predictions of both apocalyptic and utopian extremes that will not occur. Instead successful revolutions empower centralizing governments, and the media, often against the will of their leaders. Beyond this single truth, the political outcome of revolution—republic, dictatorship, or something in-between—can never be finally determined because there is no agreement on the time frame by which the outcome can be defined and measured.

NOTES

1. Jay Parini, "An Interview with Gore Vidal" (1990) in *Gore Vidal: Writer Against the Grain*, ed. Jay Parini (New York: Columbia University Press, 1992), p. 281.

2. Quoted in Jay Parini, *Empire of Self: A Life of Gore Vidal* (New York: Doubleday, 2015), p. 152.

3. Rearranged and listed in order of historical time of setting, the seven *Narratives of Empire* begin with the revolutionary era and end after World War II: *Burr* (1973), *Lincoln* (1984), *1876* (1976), *Empire* (1987), *Hollywood* (1990), *Washington D.C* (1967) and *The Golden Years* (2000).

4. Jay Parini, "An Interview with Gore Vidal," *Gore Vidal: Writer Against the Grain*, p. 284.

5. Gore Vidal, "The State of the Union" (1975) in *Essays 1952–1992* (New York: Random House, 1993), p. 937.

6. In length, subject matter, historical coverage, and imagistic concision, the modernist series of historical novels that precedes and most clearly resembles *Narratives of Empire* is John Dos Passos's *USA*. Although there appears to be no anxiety of influence on Vidal's part, Dos Passos's "radical" attack on the nexus of political and economic power in America is a clear precedent for Vidal's prophecies of cataclysm. The connections between the two series deserve more sustained study than they have yet received.

7. Gore Vidal, *Burr: A Novel* (New York: Random House, 2000), p. 58.

8. Vidal, *Burr*, pp. 160, 160, 154.

9. Gore Vidal, *Empire: A Novel* (New York: Random House, 2000), p. 399.

10. Dennis Altman, *Gore Vidal's America* (Cambridge, UK: Polity Press, 2005), p. 111.

11. Parini, *Empire of Self: A Life of Gore Vidal*, p. 404.

12. Simon Bolivar, "Response from a South American to a Gentleman of this Island" known as 'The Jamaica Letter,' written September 6, 1815 in *El Libertador: Writings of Simon Bolivar*, translated by Frederick H. Fornoff, edited by David Bushnell (Oxford and New York: Oxford University Press, 2003), p. 18.

13. Bolivar, "Oath Taken in Rome, 1805" in *El Libertador: Writings of Simon Bolivar*, p. 114. John Lynch's thorough biography renders Bolivar's final phrases in more accusatory diction: "until I have broken the chains with which Spanish power oppresses us" (John Lynch, *Simon Bolivar: A Life* (New Haven and London: Yale University Press, 2006), p. 26. Bolivar told the story of his vow repeatedly; first written down in 1850, it was not published until 1884 (see Lynch, *Simon Bolivar* fn. 13, chapter two, p. 307).

14. Gabriel Garcia Marquez, *The General in His Labyrinth: A Novel*, translated by Edith Grossman (New York: Random House, 1990), p. 205.

15. Marquez, *The General In His Labyrinth*, pp. 100, 168, 228, 230, 230, 237.

16. Bolivar, *El Libertador; Writings of Simon Bolivar*, ed. Fornoff, p. 146.

17. Bolivar's words had long remained in currency. As Conrad's Martin Decould grows from self-protective cynicism toward reluctant progressive commitment, he remarks "As the great Liberator Bolivar had said in the bitterness of his spirit, 'America is ungovernable. Those who worked for her independence have ploughed the sea'" (Conrad, *Nostromo* [Oxford and New York, 2009] p. 135).

18. Hilary Mantel, *The Guardian*, Friday October 16, 2009, http://www.guardian.co.uk/books/2009/oct/17/hilary-mantel-author-booker

19. At the outset of her memoir, *Giving Up the Ghost*, Mantel states her standards for writing, phrasing them as commands no one can quite fulfill: "plain words on plain paper"; "Remember what Orwell says, that good prose is like a windowpane"; "Stop constructing those piffling little similes of yours"; "Don't use foreign expressions; it's elitist" (*Giving Up the Ghost* [New York: Henry Holt and Company, 2003], p. 4). Her sentences emerge from the tradition of minimalist prose influenced by journalism; Scott's legacy in prose is utterly different.

20. Hilary Mantel, "Author's Note" to *A Place of Greater Safety* (New York: Henry Holt and Co., 2006), p. ix.

21. In a recent interview, Mantel has asserted, "there isn't any necessary conflict between good history and good drama." Her research on sixteenth-century England for the Cromwell trilogy has lead her to firm convictions that were implicit in *A Place of Greater Safety*: " I know that history is not shapely and I know the truth is often inconvenient and incoherent. It contains all sorts of superfluities. You could cut a much better shape if you were God, but as it is, I think the whole fascination and the skill is in working *with* those incoherencies" ("Hilary Mantel, *Paris Review Interviews*, vol. 212, [spring, 2015] interview by Mona Simpson http://www.theparis-review.org/interviews/6360/art-of-fiction-no-226-hilary-mantel).

22. Hilary Mantel, *A Place of Greater Safety*, p. 41.

23. *A Place of Greater Safety*, p. 598. On the significance of Saint-Just's Declaration, see R.R. Palmer, *Twelve Who Ruled: the Year of the Terror in the French Revolution* (Princeton: Princeton University Press, 1941, 2005), pp. 72–77. Saint-Just's formulation has its own ironic logic; France was in fact to experience the insecurities of "provisional" government from 1789 through the Napoleonic era until the "peace" of 1815—and conceivably long thereafter.

24. Hilary Mantel, review of *Robespierre*, eds. Colin Haydon and William Doyle in *London Review of Books*, vol. 22, #7, 30 March 2000, pp. 3–8.

25. Mantel's characterization of Desmoulins illustrates Francois Furet's summary of a lasting change brought about by French revolutionary culture: "Thought and speech were liberated not only from censorship and the police, but from the internal inhibition created when voluntary consent is given to age old institutions: the king was no longer the king, the nobility was no longer the nobility, the Church was no longer the church. . . . Language was substituted for power for it was the sole guarantee that power would belong only to the people, that is, to nobody" (Furet, *Interpreting the French Revolution*, pp. 46, 48).

26. Mantel, *A Place of Greater Safety*, p. 736. Simon Schama quotes this moving passage as the first epigraph of his bicentennial history *Citizens* (1989), published three years before *A Place of Greater Safety*. There are many parallels in the citation and rendering of historical facts between the two works, notably Mantel's characterization of Théroigne de Méricourt. Mantel's view of the merit of Schama's history is divided: "In the non-Francophone world, the bicentennial was dominated by Simon Schama's *Citizens*, which does not challenge comfortable preconceptions. Schama uses his narrative skill and his wealth of illustration to confirm people in the belief they already hold, which is that the Revolution was a bloody and nonsensical waste of time" (Mantel, review of *Robespierre*, pp. 7–8).

Conclusion

Scott's Legacy, Flaubert, and the Marxist Revolutionary Novel, 1848

The preceding chapters have shown that there is continuity as well as change within the long legacy of Scott's model of the historical novel. Scott's legacy lasted at least until the 1950s novels of Lampedusa and Pasternak—and perhaps into select later novels. Why then, has this continuing legacy not received greater critical recognition? The high-modernist condescension toward Scott is not a sufficient explanation; Scott has always had his influential admirers. This conclusion, returning to matters raised in my introduction, will offer an explanation. At issue is the well-known, ingenious, and commonly accepted argument of the third chapter of Lukacs's *The Historical Novel* titled "The Crisis of Bourgeois Realism." Marx had called the June days of the 1848 revolution, "the most colossal event in the history of European civil wars."[1] Lukacs followed, identifying "the defeat of the 1848 revolutions" as "the decisive turning point in the history of western literature."[2] To both of them, 1848 was the "crisis" of western history and western literature because it marked the first time in revolutionary conflict that the working-class proletariat had risen up against bourgeois authorities who cloaked capitalist ambition behind the twin façades of republicanism and nationalism.

For substantiating these claims, the events of 1848 posed a series of paradoxes. On the one hand, the revolt of socialists, republicans, and the working class, joining together against the "Bourgeois Monarchy" of Louis Phillipe, was an international, not merely Parisian, revolution. Between February and June of 1848, universal male suffrage, the Right to Work, National Workshops, abolition of imprisonment for debt, and a law shortening work hours had all been legalized by the Provisional Government, with the seeming support of all insurgent parties. A centralized national bank, a graduated income tax, nationalization of railroads and factories, free public education, and even the abolition of inheritance, were possibilities being debated. After the

National Workshops were disbanded in June, however, the bloodshed on the barricades (1,500 killed and 4,000 imprisoned, then deported to Algiers) created a wave of fear in the countryside and among the Parisian middle class; the nationwide fear of socialism was to persist until long after Louis Napoleon became "Prince President" in 1849, then emperor in 1852. In June 1848, republicans and socialists, now divided, fought one another on the barricades, even though the newly elected members of the "Mountain" in the assembly (a name meant to associate 1848 with 1792) tried to hold republicans and socialists together. The National Guard, which had sided with the insurgents against Louis Philippe in February, turned against them. The "Party of Order," (defined by Louis Napoleon as "family, religion, property") first supplanted, then suppressed the voices of reform and revolution. By 1852, most of the progressive enactments of the Provisional Government had been undone, either legally or through neglect.[3]

To Marx and Lukacs, 1848 remained the year of great promise for working-class revolution, but also a year of great defeat. Marx's *18th Brumaire* is a brilliant exercise in historical irony, exposing the hypocrisies of political declarations and political maneuvering, whether legitimist, republican, or socialist. Behind all the hypocrisies lie the constant unacknowledged motives of bourgeois money and political survival, motives for which the adventurer Louis Napoleon figures as the crafty beneficiary and lucky survivor.[4] Compared to the exhortative *Communist Manifesto*, written three months *before* the February uprisings, the *18th Brumaire* expresses sardonic disillusionment controlled by the comedy of the grotesque. Marx's sustained narrative of self-interested human hypocrisy darkens until it reaches the last summary chapter in which "the Executive power," the army, landed proprietors, urban capitalists, and bourgeois bureaucrats combine into "this fearful body of parasites that coils itself like a snake around French society," all the while calling itself the Party of Order (99).

Nonetheless, Marx's faith in future proletarian revolution persists. The paragraph preceding Marx's reference to the triumph of the "parasites" begins as follows: "All the same, the revolution is thoroughgoing. It still is on its passage through purgatory. It does its work methodically" (98). The capitulation of the "Parisian proletariat" in 1851, its acquiescence in repeal of reform measures, may have "proved that the defeat of June 1848 had incapacitated them from resistance for many a year to come," but not forever; "the historic process must again, for the time being, proceed over their heads" (55).

The 1848 revolution must therefore be seen in its totality (a favorite Marxist word) as a working-class revolution against the capitalist bourgeoisie. In historical fact, however, of the eleven leaders of the Provisional Government, four were avowed socialists but five were avowed republicans. Louis Napoleon twice assumed power through plebiscites in which he was elected by an overwhelming majority. Marx's hope must therefore be bolstered by selective omissions. Unlike Marx's characterizations of individual political leaders, the working class of Paris is evoked but never described in detail. Whether the Parisian proletariat consists primarily of factory laborers or unemployed artisans is not directly addressed. Marx coins the word *lumpenproletariat* both to denigrate and to separate ignorant defectors from the revolutionary socialist cause. As industrial capitalism expands, Marx trusts, so will the number of impoverished workers, until the moment arrives when worker organization and recurrent capitalist economic depressions will combine to turn failed insurgency into achieved revolution.

The third chapter of Lukacs's *The Historical Novel* accepts Marx's view of the 1848 revolution as a given, then updates it in even more darkened ways to fit late-nineteenth-century social conditions. Darwinian evolution and then social Darwinism, have commonly been used, Lukacs argues, to justify expansion of laissez faire entrepreneurship and capitalist industrialization. Colonial imperialism has promoted racism and nationalism as well as the production and sale of middle-class goods. The development most pertinent to the historical novel, however, has been the changed conception of history. After the great era of French Revolutionary historians during the 1840s (Thierry, Michelet, Blanc), historians have turned away from realism, from dialectical and diachronic thinking that discerns progress. In the writings of Taine, Burckhardt, and Nietzsche, historical inquiry has embraced relativism and discontinuity, thereby denying the very ideas of progress and of truth. To Lukacs, the consequence is that "History becomes a collection of exotic anecdotes"; "In Western Europe after the 1848 Revolution the writer is alienated from comprehensive social problems."[5]

The effect of these changes upon the historical novel, Lukacs contends, has been to vitiate the realistic achievements of Scott, Balzac, and Tolstoy. The aim of writing the historical novel has become escapism from the "gray" dreary capitalist present into an exotic world of the forgotten, irrelevant past. Even when historical novelists write in opposition to capitalism, they now convey "an intensification in literature of capitalist dehumanization in life" (195). For Lukacs, the prime example of the decline of the historical novel is *Salammbo* (1857), Flaubert's lengthy novel about third century B.C. Carthage. Flaubert's "consistent programme," Lukacs alleges, is "to reawaken a vanished world of no concern to us" (185). Flaubert's novel immerses us in "a world of historically exact *costumes and decoration*"; it projects modern psychological tensions back into a time in which they do not belong (189). The result is a "pseudo-monumentality" a mélange amounting merely to "a compound of outward exoticism and inner modernity" (192).

The darkened Marxist context informing Lukacs's attack on *Salammbo* leads him to condemn with faint praise many of the now canonical novels, written after 1857, that have been central to this book. In *A Tale of Two Cities*, "the events of the French Revolution . . . become a romantic background" (243). Victor Hugo's *1793*, "a last echo of the Romantic historical novel," suffers from "the metaphysical abstractness of his [Hugo's] humanism" (257). Anatole France is unable to move beyond "a defensive superior skepticism" to affirm any prospect of economic change (257). Zola, limited by naturalist determinism, could have made a great contribution to the protest against imperialism and capitalism had he "found real intellectual support in a revolutionary Marxist working-class party" (255).

Behind these individual judgments we discern Lukacs's conviction that the historical novel has become "an inferior form of light reading" because of "the general decline of the era" (250). The realism with which Scott, Balzac, and Tolstoy had confronted the totality of historical change has been undone by a false historicism hidden under escapist romantic entertainment. For Lukacs, the still unrealized promise of the 1848 revolution bifurcates the century, leaving the possibility of the ongoing *development* of Scott's literary conventions out of consideration. *Salammbo* demonstrates the betrayal and the dead-end of the "classic" realist tradition Scott had established.

Even if Lukacs's strictures against *Salammbo* are valid, his argument is undermined by his choosing not to consider a major Flaubert novel of much more lasting influence and pertinence, two thirds of which is set in Paris during the revolution of 1848. No less than eighteen pages of Lukacs's chapter on "The Crisis of Bourgeois Realism" are devoted to *Salammbo*; by contrast Lukacs's fleeting mentions of *Sentimental Education* total at most one long paragraph. The effect is similar to judging Thackeray's historical fictions by *Henry Esmond*, not *Vanity Fair*, or judging Hemingway's war novels by *For Whom The Bell Tolls*, not *A Farewell to Arms*. For Lukacs to have excluded *Sentimental Education* from his critical argument about the Revolution of 1848 is a non sequitur revealing an anomaly. *Salammbo* develops along a vector quite outside the historical novel of revolution that Scott had established; *Sentimental Education* does not.

There are important ways in which *Sentimental Education* must be seen as both a continuation and a challenge to Scott's paradigm. After an adolescence spent, like Edward Waverley, reading Froissart, Frédéric Moreau "nursed an ambition to become the Walter Scott of France"[6]—an ambition for which Frédéric's inner character will prove in every way unsuited. The rapidly growing city of Paris, repeatedly shrouded in mist, arouses the "boundless expectation" and compromising sensuality of those it attracts. Flaubert's Paris, like Balzac's, is an urban variant of Scott's neutral ground, a precedent for the threat of the modern city in Pasternak's Moscow and Vidal's Washington D.C. The sheer multiplicity of Flaubert's characters, even though they are almost entirely middle class, exemplifies the kind of historical "totality" found in Scott, and rightly commended by Lukacs. Supposed waverers are juxtaposed, at least in their public speechifying, to seeming fanatics. Madame Arnoux, a variant of the domesticated fair lady, is contrasted to Roseanette, a courtesan forever in search of needed male money. Two-thirds of the way through the narrative, revolutionary insurgency explodes, turning self-serving debate into civil warfare. The law, martial or civil, cannot quell the instinct of revenge. Consolidation of property through marriage dominates the novel's ending, enabling divisions of social class to continue. These variants of Scott's literary conventions inform the very structure of Flaubert's novel.

There are equally important dissimilarities to Scott's paradigm. Flaubert's reader is never taken to the barricades to see the street fighting. There are no court trials to sort out the legality and morality of political violence. The word "honor" hardly ever appears, though public revenge involving women and money remains a prominent motive. History does not evolve; Flaubert's declared purpose is to write "the moral history of the men of *my* generation"[7] (italics mine). The cast of characters includes no prominent historical figure, no Hegelian world-historical personage, not even an historical member of the Provisional Government, who might have embodied the spirit of the disappearing past or the emerging future. Cisy is the novel's only aristocrat, and he is a frivolous dilettante. Dussardier is the novel's only working-class laborer; his commitment to radical economic change, though genuine, is undermined by his stolid simplicity, which borders upon the obtuse. The novel's one seemingly committed radical Socialist, Sénécal, readily turns police informant the day after Louis Napoleon's coup d'état, and then murders Dussardier.

Satire of human hypocrisy and revolutionary progress remains the dominant tone, as it never does in a Waverley novel. Flaubert's middle-class Parisians are ordinary citizen bystanders, uncommitted to socialism or democracy, hoping to profit, anxious to survive, and ready to trim any conviction at the appropriate moment. The interactions of Flaubert's characters leave an unpleasant aftertaste compelling the reader to wonder whether he or she would prove to be any less selfish, any less venal, under similar circumstances.[8] The bourgeoisie of *Sentimental Education* are petty enough to satisfy any Marxist, but Flaubert leaves his reader no opportunity to believe in working-class integrity among revolutionaries. The speakers advocating revolution at the *Club D'Intelligence* are united only by their dislike of authority and their need to impress an audience with trendy sentiments. For the sake of his Marxist purpose, Lukacs had good reason not to draw attention to Flaubert's cynicism about socialism and the notion of generational progress.[9]

Flaubert's transformation of the *Waverley* tradition centers upon his characterization of Frédéric Moreau, whose perspective we follow, but do not share. Like Scott's protagonists, Frédéric has the advantages of gentility, substantial if tenuous family income, a cultured upbringing, powers of articulation, and personal charm. Like Edward Waverley, Henry Morton, and Frank Osbaldistone, Frédéric is caught up in a revolutionary time that leads him to feel, as he watches the killing on the barricades, "as if he were watching a play" (311). But the differences balance the similarities. Scott's protagonists waver because of political indecision based upon ignorance or upon real divided loyalties. Frédéric Moreau wavers because of innate, political indifference. He will echo most any political opinion that enables him to appear au courant. He has no interest in historical change or the political future. To him, Paris is the world's capital of "art, learning and love"; only in Paris might he find those "three faces of God" that will reveal the "secret riches of his nature" (100–101).

The anticipated emergence of his inner "secret riches" constantly requires moneys that Frédéric must either inherit or marry. Something of a *flaneur*, Frédéric will not be seen working toward achievement in any business or profession. He must remain the bourgeois who scorns the bourgeoisie. Nonetheless, he plans "the life he was going to lead" as the acquiring of "a great abundance of things," that include women, art objects, and sumptuous living quarters. Madame Arnoux, love of his life, is in fact an icon, safely married, toward whom he can project a spiritual longing he cannot feel. As a protagonist in revolutionary times, Frédéric represents a type of rootless arriviste Balzac and Stendhal would have recognized. Walter Scott would have expressed contempt for him.

Instinctive indifference to revolutionary politics is a trait essential to explaining why Frédéric represents, for Flaubert, "the moral history of my generation." Frédéric sees the fighting of the February days as a street play because he lingers near the barricades only in order to consummate his assignation with Madame Arnoux in a rented room. Instead of observing or involving himself in the conflict, he and Roseanette seduce each other in the same room rented for the seduction of his sometime beloved. Frédéric will then spend the June days of the 1848 Revolution touring Fontainebleau with Roseanette, luxuriating in "nostalgic lust" over the "inevitable impermanence of all things," especially royal residences, only to fall peacefully to sleep after hearing that "a terrible and bloody battle was raging at Paris" (347–350). When Louis Napoleon achieves his coup d'état by dissolving the assembly, Frédéric dismisses the news: "Politics left him indifferent, he was so preoccupied with his own affairs," "thinking only of himself and nobody else" (448). One would assume self-interest would eventually lead Frédéric to approve of the emerging power of the Party of Order. In fact, as Frédéric observes the gathering of trimmers and toadies at the salon of Dambreuse the banker, Frédéric enjoys feeling contempt for "the great Monsieur A, the famous B, the intelligent C, the eloquent Z, the wonderful Y, the old stagers of the Centre Left, the paladins of the Right, the veterans of the Middle Way, all the stock characters of the political comedy" (391). At such moments it is impossible not to conclude that Flaubert shares Frédéric's satirical point of view, however self-protective it may be.

In Scott's marital endings, love emerges through revolutionary crises in which the waverer and his bride have had shared experiences. In *Sentimental Education* marriages occur after the upsets of politics have receded and advantageous money arrangements become clear. Martinon marries Cecile Dambreuse, Madame Dambreuse marries an Englishman, and Frédéric's supposed friend Deslaurier, besting Frédéric in the rush to profitable marriage, weds Louise Roque. Frédéric, in pointed contrast to the historical novel's happy marital ending, spends his later days travelling the world, tasting "the boredom of landscapes and monuments," and having affairs with other women: "the years went by and he resigned himself to the stagnation of his mind and the apathy that lived in his heart" (451). Of course, the Parisian cultural custom of maintaining a wife for domesticity and a mistress for love and sex makes Scott's marital ending seem an innocent anachronism. But Frédéric's wasting away means more. Is it misleading to conclude that Frédéric's life, whatever it signifies, amounts to exactly nothing, not even victimization? Does his education consist of ever-changing sentiments only?[10]

By omitting *Sentimental Education* from consideration in *The Historical Novel*, Lukacs ignored an essential transition in the history of the genre. Despite Flaubert's insights into bourgeois hypocrisy, insights very like those of Karl Marx, Lukacs evidently believed that Flaubert's cynicism toward revolution, together with Flaubert's insistence upon stagnation in both history and individual lives, offered no model for the progress Marxists claimed for the 1848 revolution. But Lukacs's emphasis on *Salammbo*, rather than *Sentimental Education*, did more than set the precedent for denigrating the historical novel as escapist entertainment. It severed the connections between Scott's paradigm of the historical novel of revolution and Flaubert's transformation of it, a transformation that could and should have been traced in the historical novels of Dickens, Hugo, Zola, and Anatole France.

Lukacs's opening chapter had argued persuasively that Walter Scott had created the "classic" form of the historical novel for the nineteenth century. Because a "classic" can be established only by determining its continuing legacy, Lukacs's pages on *Salammbo* led him into a failed detour, a dead-end. Searching in the dark year of 1937 for the historical novels that could effectively combat fascism, Lukacs privileged his Marxist faith in working-class revolution over his attention to the development of the literary form Scott had established. In this regard, the key sentence in *The Historical Novel* occurs in Lukacs's last chapter: "The anti-Fascist popular front and the spirit of revolutionary democracy which it has revived have once again made it possible to embody a people's yearning for liberation in positive characters" (340).

A few pages later Lukacs concluded "the liberation of the people from the Fascist yoke, the new social order of democracy, not to speak of the abolition of exploitation, is today at best an object of struggle, in most cases a real, but nevertheless future perspective" (348). At those junctures in *The Historical Novel* where *Sentimental Education, La Debacle, 1793,* and *Les Dieux Ont Soif* might have been considered in detail, Lukacs claims prominence and influence for historical novels by Heinrich Mann, Leon Feuchtwanger, and Romain Rolland. These claims have not worn well; they now seem substitutional, based on political not literary considerations.

Lukacs's hopes for the historical-materialist novel of working-class revolution centered in his later years on Maxim Gorki, especially on the promise of Gorki's *Mother* (1907). Lukacs describes Gorki as a "militant proletarian humanist" who exposes the process of class formation by which industrial capitalism confines workers and capitalists alike within a "self-isolation in a petty-bourgeois individualism." By showing "the effect of Marxism on the working-class movement," Gorki's *Mother* serves as "the great turning point . . . in the whole of literature."[11] Immersed in the European struggles against fascism, Lukacs chose not to write about the leftist American novels of the 1930s, novels that, whether avowedly communist or not, depicted the rising up of a working-class people against industrial capitalism amid the Depression (novels by Robert Cantwell, Clara Weatherwax, John Steinbeck, Josephine Herbst). Beginning with Gorki's *Mother,* this fictional tradition, sometimes referred to as "the proletarian novel," is both Marxist and populist in the ways it analyzes the alienation of labor, the economics of social class, and the revolutionary anger they arouse. But as a literary tradition, it is not primarily historical. There are few dates, few historical characters, and little specificity of place in 1930s proletarian novels. Their narratives, set in the very recent past, encourage an assumption of presentism, because they point toward future revolutionary prospects, not toward the past. They do not show us the past as the prehistory of the present, as Lukacs had rightly claimed for Scott.

The preface to Fredric Jameson's first important book, *Marxism and Form* (1971), begins with a paragraph on Marxist issues of the 1930s: "The burning issues of those days—anti-Nazism, the Popular Front, the relationship between literature and the labor movement, the struggle between Stalin and Trotsky, between Marxism and anarchism—generated polemics which we may think back on with nostalgia, but which no longer correspond to the conditions of the world today."[12] Compared to the complex conceptual issues about history raised by Hegel, by Tolstoy, by emerging postmodernism, and by the recent analysis of consumer capitalism published by Herbert Marcuse, the issues of the 1930s proletarian novel had come to seem simple and one-dimensional, an opposition of admirable laborer to oppressive industrialist that belonged to another era.

Conclusion 275

Jameson retained the framework of Lukacs's thinking but was clearly in search of some newer form of diachronic historical fiction that would retain Marxist perspectives and a Marxist resolution. It has clearly proven to be a vexing search. In "The Case for Georg Lukacs," Jameson mentions that *Education Sentimentale* is "the most illustrious example of the new form," which Jameson calls "the novel of romantic disillusionment."[13] But as a model for the new form of Marxist novel, *Sentimental Education* clearly leads to no progressive resolution based on communal revolt. By then emphasizing Lukacs's *The Theory of the Novel*, rather than *The Historical Novel*, Jameson in effect displaces Scott from the primary position Lukacs had accorded him. Scott's belief in community loyalties maintained through class distinctions within a constitutional monarchy could provide no prototype for Jameson's historical and literary hopes. Accordingly, the great line of novelistic realism now begins with Balzac and proceeds through Flaubert to Sartre.

Jameson's quest continued. *The Political Unconscious* (1981) traces the realist tradition of historical fiction and Hegelian/Marxist dialectic from Balzac through Gissing and Conrad to a conclusion in which "what is wanted here—and it is one of the most urgent tasks for Marxist theory today—is a whole new logic of collective dynamics, with categories that escape the stain of some mere application of terms drawn from individual experience."[14] Behind every historical narrative, Jameson argues, lies the "political unconscious" of writer and reader, an unconscious that must be brought to the surface so as to move western culture beyond the individualistic perspective upon which late monopoly capitalism thrives. Even though all historical political revolutions have admittedly been "failures" by Marxist standards, historical fiction must move toward some kind of collective "untranscendable horizon" that recalls the Hegelian absolute spirit (13). Scott is mentioned in only four sentences, always in comparison to other writers more essential to Jameson's political argument.

Jameson's displacement of Scott from the realist tradition of historical fiction is more explicit yet oddly less assured in *The Antinomies of Realism* (2013). The realist tradition is both elaborated and refined. Still originating in Balzac, it proceeds through Tolstoy, Galdos, George Eliot, and Zola, with insightful remarks on Flaubert, Thomas Mann, and others. No Waverley novel is worth quoting, because Scott's name is now associated, quite unfairly, with the melodrama of opera librettos adapted from his novels.[15] In a curious twist, Jameson makes Scott responsible for having introduced the very same failings Lukacs had associated, not with Scott, but with Flaubert's *Salammbo*: "Scott's historical novel, combining adventure, the past, the romantic costume drama and the great national heroes all together, may be said to be the first form of the successful and influential novelistic apparatus of the nineteenth century" (179). Jameson's next sentences establish the contrast that entombs Scott: "It is within this popular efflorescence that Flaubert marks a break and a decisive restructuration. . . . Flaubert's legacy was the new status of the novelist as an artist." Scott had allegedly devised only the "apparatus" from which others were later to create art.

And yet—to repeat a crucial quotation—it is within *The Antinomies of Realism* that we find Jameson's most convincing tribute to the Waverley novels: "Scott confirms our obscure suspicion that all genuinely historical novels must have a revolutionary moment as their occasion: a moment of radical change, which lifts their content out of the placid continuities of mere custom and of the picturesque daily life of this or that exotic moment of the past" (266). In this sentence, if nowhere else, Jameson reverses the terms by which he judges Scott to be inferior to Balzac and Flaubert. The uplifting power of the historical novel as a genre originates in Scott's having shown that revolution reveals the transformative significance of the past. As I hope to have demonstrated, great historical novels, including near contemporary examples, have indeed centered upon "a revolutionary moment" as the "occasion" for fictions that lift the reader through entertainment into historical awareness. It is a literary legacy originating in Scott, not in Balzac, and certainly not in Flaubert.

If the title of Jameson's last chapter, "The Historical Novel Today, or Is It Still Possible?" is a rhetorical rather than an open question, then Jameson's unwritten answer is "almost surely not." Jameson assumes that the totality of historical awareness he seeks has been vitiated, if not lost, to postmodern fragmentation and to synchronicity, as well as to individual narcissism aggravated by capitalism:

> What kind of historical novel is being reproduced here? Harlequin "histories"
> in which a romantic tale is played out against this or that costume setting?
> *Annales*-school reconstruction of the peculiar mores and customs of a selected
> segment of the past? . . . How to have confidence in the presence and stability
> of any of the allegedly world-historical figures of the past when we have lost
> our own? (259)

Jameson devises a marvelous metaphor for the consumption of such novels today: to read the historical novel is to step into an "immense elevator" moving up and down through time, but opening its doors onto only one floor that serves "the euphoric or dystopian mood in which we wait for the doors to open" (301). The immense elevator suffocates the reader within one disconnected time period, opening onto only a single warehouse floor of half-forgotten names and worn images. No wonder, given such a metaphor, that Jameson concludes that the historical novel has arrived at "a kind of evolutionary dead end" (264), inducing him to turn both toward film and to the "Science-Fictional futures" of David Mitchell's *Cloud Atlas* (2004) as replacements. Whether Jameson fully credits his own pessimism is, however, questionable; his last chapter includes three complimentary pages on Hilary Mantel's recently published *A Place of Greater Safety* as an historical novel decidedly about revolution.

The publication of recent historical novels of revolution written by Vidal, Marquez, and Mantel argues for a more open conclusion. Perry Anderson's essay "From Progress to Catastrophe: The Historical Novel" (2011) provides a balanced overview from Scott through Tolstoy, Dumas, Dickens, Galdos, Fontane, Hugo, and Joseph Roth to Lampedusa's *The Leopard*, which Anderson regards as "the greatest historical novel of the century."[16] To Anderson, Lukacs and Jameson remain the scholar critics of the genre who must be reckoned with today. The terms of Anderson's title, "Progress" and "Catastrophe," serve as bookends for the changed attitudes of historical periods from 1789 to 2000, not as critical judgments attesting to a decline in artistic quality.

Anderson's essay opens up the future of "meta-historical fiction" to Latin American novels beginning with Carpentier and Marquez. He then mentions Egyptian, Indonesian, and Arabic postcolonial novels concerned with imperialism. For thirty years after World War II, Anderson contends, the status of the historical novel had been reduced to "a few antique jewels on a huge mound of trash," but postmodernism has enabled a revival of the form. Sharing a broadly Marxist outlook, Anderson differs sharply here from Jameson. Whether the paradigm of the Scott novel can be plausibly connected to the open forms of non-Western postmodernism lies far beyond my ken. Anderson's essay, however, restores continuity by beginning with Scott, and by refusing to cut off the legacy Walter Scott established. This book has aimed to continue and to develop that restitution.

NOTES

1. Karl Marx, *The Eighteenth Brumaire of Louis Bonaparte* (Rockville, MD: Serenity Publishers, 2009), p. 16. Originally published 1852.
2. Georg Lukacs, "Tolstoy and the Development of Realism" (1936) in *Studies in European Realism* (London: The Merlin Press, 1972), p. 150.
3. For the history of the 1848 revolutions, see Maurice Agulhon, *The Republican Experiment, 1848–1852*, translated by Janet Lloyd (Cambridge: Cambridge University Press, 1983); George Comninel "Revolutionary History: The Communist Manifesto in Context") in Douglas Maggach and Paul Leduc Browne, *The Social Question and the Democratic Revolution: Marx and the Legacy of 1848* (Ottawa: University

of Ottawa Press, 2000), pp. 71–100; Geoffrey Ellis, "The Revolution of 1848–1849 in France," in R.J.W. Evans and H.P. Von Strandmann, *The Revolutions in Europe 1848–1849: From Reform to Reaction* (Oxford: Oxford University Press, 2000), pp. 27–53; Francois Furet, *Revolutionary France 1779–1800*, translated by Antonia Nevill (London: Basil Blackwell, 1992), chapter 9. The essays by Ellis and Furet are especially informative.

4. Marx also calls Louis Napoleon "the Pretender" thus linking him with the long sequence of pretenders in the historical novel. On the pretender figure, see Richard Maxwell, *The Historical Novel in Europe* (Cambridge: Cambridge University Press, 2009), chapter 9.

5. Georg Lukacs, *The Historical Novel*, translated by Hannah and Stanley Mitchell (Lincoln: University of Nebraska Press, 1983), pp. 182, 207.

6. Gustave Flaubert, *Sentimental Education*, translation by Robert Baldick, revised by Geoffrey Wall (London and New York: Penguin Books, 2004), p. 17. Geoffrey Wall's biography records that Flaubert began reading Scott at age eleven and was still reading Scott after *Sentimental Education* was published in 1869 (*Flaubert: A Life* [NewYork: Farrar, Straus and Giroux, 2001], pp. 40, 311).

7. Flaubert, letter to Leroyer de Chantepie, October 6, 1864 in *Gustave Flaubert: Selected Letters*, translated by Geoffrey Wall (London and New York: Penguin, 1997), p. 304.

8. Flaubert's literary restraint and self-discipline while writing a novel contrast sharply to the vitriol released in his letters: "Let us bellow against Monsieur Thiers. Has there ever been a more rampant imbecile, a more abject dimwit, a more turdiform bourgeois! No! Nothing can convey the vomit-inducing equality of this old diplomatic bigwig, spouting his nonsense from the top of that dungheap called the bourgeoisie!" (letter to Georges Sand, 22 September 1866 in *Selected Letters*, translated by Geoffrey Wall, p. 329). Socialists, however, deserved no more commendation than the bourgeoisie: "Modern Socialism stinks of petty authoritarianism" (Wall, *Flaubert: A Life*, p. 294).

9. In an essay on Gorki, Lukacs complained that Flaubert's "pessimism degenerates into nihilism" ("The Human Comedy of Pre-Revolutionary Russia," *Studies in European Realism*, p. 246). Within Lukacs's terms, Sénécal's murder of Dussardier can be seen as an instance of authorial "nihilism." Flaubert has arranged for the radical Socialist theorist and the honest worker to eliminate each other. Victor Brombert concluded "Flaubert felt suspicion and distaste for all Socialist theories. . . . The people is for him the imbecile rabble, and Socialists are, he feels, imbued with a fanatical hatred of freedom" (Brombert, *The Novels of Flaubert: A Study of Themes and Techniques* [Princeton: Princeton University Press, 1966], p. 159).

10. Comparison of *Sentimental Education* with Sylvia Townsend Warner's *Summer Will Show* (1936) confirms the differences between the predominately male model of the historical novel established by Scott and the concerns Diana Wallace uncovers in *The Woman's Historical Novel*. Sophia Willoughby, a privileged, middle-aged English aristocrat, whose two children have recently died, journeys to Paris in 1848 to renew her spiritually empty life by conceiving another child with her estranged husband who is, perhaps pointedly, named Frederick. Instead of reaffirming family values, the freeing experience of revolutionary Paris leads Sophia into fervent physical and

spiritual love for a woman who has a gypsy-like lifestyle and iconoclastic sometime friends. Sophia recognizes that the 1848 revolution has afforded her the opportunity to "run away from . . . sitting bored among the tyrants. From Sunday Schools and cold-hearted respectability and hypocrisy, and prison and . . . domesticity." Until Sophia reads the opening words of the *Communist Manifesto* on the novel's very last page, she displays no knowledge and little interest in socialism or French revolutionary politics: She remarks dismissively, "to me, a revolution means there is a turmoil and after it people are worse off than they were before." Revolutionary Paris serves her as an exotic place that serves as the catalyst for personal inner transformation, not as one's embattled home ground nor as a spur for political inquiry. (Sylvia Townsend Warner, *Summer Will Show* [New York: Viking Penguin, 2009], pp. 179, 219).

11. Lukacs, "The Human Comedy of Pre-Revolutionary Russia" in *Studies in European Realism* (London: The Merlin Press, 1972), pp. 215, 213, 237.

12. Fredric Jameson, *Marxism and Form: Twentieth-Century Dialectical Theories of Literature* (Princeton, Princeton University Press, 1971), p. ix.

13. Jameson, *Marxism and Form*, p. 176.

14. Fredric Jameson, *The Political Unconscious* (Ithaca: Cornell University Press, 1981), p. 94.

15. Fredric Jameson, *The Antinomies of Realism* (London and Brooklyn: Verso, 2015), pp., 109, 124. Scott's *The Bride of Lammermoor* is, needless to say, hardly recognizable within the altered characters, altered relationships, absurd plotting, and stilted diction of Cammarano's libretto for Donizetti's *Lucia Di Lammermoor*. Scott's historical realism is swallowed up in the beauty of Donizetti's bel canto melody.

16. Perry Anderson, "From Progress to Catastrophe; the Historical Novel," *London Review of Books* vol. 33. #15. July 2011, 24–28. & http://www.lrb.co.uk/v33/n15/perry-anderson/from-progress-to-catastrophe

Bibliography

Agulhon, Maurice, *The Republican Experiment, 1848–1852*, translated by Janet Lloyd. Cambridge: Cambridge University Press, 1983.

Alexander, John T. *Emperor of the Cossacks; Pugachev and the Frontier Jacquerie of 1773–1775*. Lawrence, KS: Coronado Press, 1973.

Altman, Dennis. *Gore Vidal's America*. Cambridge, UK: Polity Press, 2005.

Altschuller, Mark. "The Rise and Fall of Walter Scott's Popularity in Russia" in Murray Pittock, ed., *The Reception of Sir Walter Scott in Europe*. London: Continuum, 2006.

Anderson, Benedict. *Imagined Communities*. Revised Edition. London and New York: Verso, 1991.

Anderson, Perry. *A Zone of Engagement*. London and New York: Verso, 1992.

Anderson, Perry. "From Progress to Catastrophe; the Historical Novel." *London Review of Books* vol. 33. #15. July 2011, 24–28 http://www.lrb.co.uk/v33/n15/perry-anderson/from-progress-to-catastrophe

Arac, Jonathan. "Hamlet, Little Dorrit, and the History of Character," *South Atlantic Quarterly*, 87 (1988): 310–322.

Archer, John E. *Social Unrest and Popular Protest in England 1780–1940*. Cambridge and New York: Cambridge University Press, 2000.

Arendt, Hannah. *On Revolution*, introduction by Jonathan Schell. New York and London: Penguin Books, 2006.

Ashley, Maurice. *Cromwell's Generals*. New York: St. Martin's Press, 1955.

Asprey, Robert. *The Reign of Napoleon Bonaparte*. New York: Basic Books, 2001.

Bachelard, Gaston. *The Poetics of Space*, translated by Maria Jolas. Boston: Beacon Press, 1994.

Bagehot, Walter "Sir Walter Scott," *National Review* (1858), in *The Critical Heritage: Sir Walter Scott*, ed. John O. Hayden, 2nd edition. London: Routledge, 1995.

Baguley, David, ed. *Critical Essays on Emile Zola*. Boston: G.K. Hall, 1986.

Bakhtin, M.M. *The Dialogic Imagination*, translated by Caryl Emerson and Michael Holquist. Austin: University of Texas Press, 1981.

Bailyn, Bernard. *The Ideological Origins of the American Revolution*. Cambridge, MA: Harvard University Press, 1967.

Balzac, Honoré de. *The Chouans*. Introduction by Marion Crawford. London and New York: Penguin Books, 1986.

Barnes, Christopher. *Boris Pasternak: A Literary Biography*. Cambridge: Cambridge University Press, 1989.

Benjamin, Walter "Theses on the Philosophy of History" in *Illuminations*, translated by Harry Zahn and Hannah Arendt. New York: Schocken Books, 2007, first printed 1968.

Berg, William J. and Martin, Laurey K. *Emile Zola Revisited*. New York: Twayne-Macmillan, 1992.

Berger, Peter "On the Obsolescence of the Concept of Honor" (1970) in *Revisions: Changing Perspectives in Moral Philosophy*, by S. Hauerwas and A. MacIntire. Notre Dame: University of Notre Dame Press, 1983.

Berman, Sandra. "Introduction" to Alessandro Manzoni, *On The Historical Novel*. Lincoln and London: University of Nebraska Press, 1984.

Bishop, Joseph W. Jr. *Justice Under Fire: A Study of Military Law*. New York: Charterhouse, 1974.

Bolivar, Simon *El Libertador: Writings of Simon Bolivar*, translated by Frederick Fornoff, edited by David Bushnell. Oxford: Oxford University Press, 2003.

Bowman, James. *Honor: A History*. New York: Encounter Books, 2006.

Brinton, Crane. *The Anatomy of Revolution*. New York: Random House, 1965. First published 1938.

Brombert, Victor. *The Novels of Flaubert: A Study of Themes and Techniques*. Princeton: Princeton University Press, 1966.

———. *Victor Hugo and the Visionary Novel*. Cambridge, MA: Harvard University Press, 1984.

Brown, David. *Walter Scott and the Historical Imagination*. London: Routledge & Kegan Paul, 1979.

Brown, Frederick. *Zola: A Life*. New York: Farrar, Straus, Giroux, 1995.

Buchan, John. *Sir Walter Scott*. London: Cassell, 1987.

Burke Edmund. *Philosophical Inquiry into the Origin of Our Ideas of the Sublime and the Beautiful*. Mineola, NY: Dover, 2008. First published 1737.

———. *Reflections on the Revolution in France 1790*, edited by L.G. Mitchell. Oxford and New York: Oxford University Press, 1993.

Burke, Edmund and Paine, Thomas. *Reflections on the Revolution in France and The Rights of Man*. Garden City, NY: Doubleday, 1973.

Buell, Lawrence. *The Dream of the Great American Novel*. Cambridge, MA: Harvard University Press, 2014.

Butler, Bonnie. *Balzac and the French Revolution*. Totowa, NJ: Barnes & Noble Books, 1983.

Carlyle, Thomas. "Sir Walter Scott" (1838), in *Critical and Miscellaneous Essays*, vol. iv. London: Chapman and Hall, 1888.

———. *The French Revolution: A History*, Introduction by John D. Roenberg. New York: Random House, 2002.

Cather, Willa. *Willa Cather: Stories, Poems and Other Writings*, notes by Sharon O'Brien. New York: The Library of America, 1992.

Chandler, James. *England in 1819: The Politics of Literary Culture*. Chicago: University of Chicago Press, 1998.

Chase, Bob. "History and Post-Structuralism: Hayden White and Fredric Jameson" and "Walter Scott: A New Historical Paradigm" in *The Expansion of England: Race, Ethnicity and Cultural History*, edited by Bill Schwarz. London and New York: Routledge, 1996.

Chase, Richard V. *The American Novel and Its Tradition*. Garden City, NY: Doubleday & Co., 1957.

Chiaromonte, Nicola. *The Paradox of History*, Foreword by Joseph Frank, Postface by Mary McCarthy. Philadelphia: University of Pennsylvania Press, 1985.

Christiansen, Rupert. *Paris Babylon: The Story of the Paris Commune*. New York: Viking, 1995.

Cixous, Helene. "Character of 'Character,'" *New Literary History* 5 (1974): 381–394.

Clausewitz, Carl Von. *On War*, translated and edited by Michael Howard and Peter Paret. Princeton, NJ: Princeton University Press, 1984.

Coleridge, Samuel Taylor. *The Friend*, edited by Barbara E. Brooke. Princeton: Princeton University Press, 1969.

Comninel, George. "Revolutionary History: The Communist Manifesto in Context" in Douglas Maggach and Paul Leduc Browne. *The Social Question and the Democratic Revolution: Marx and the Legacy of 1848*. Ottawa: University of Ottawa Press, 2000.

Condorcet, Antoine-Nicolas de. *Sketch for a Historical Picture of the Progress of the Human Mind*, translated by June Barraclough, introduction by Stuart Hampshire. Westport Conn: Hyperion Press, 1979.

Conrad, Joseph. *Nostromo*, edited by Jacques Berthoud and Mara Kalnins. Oxford and New York: Oxford University Press, 2007.

Cooper, James Fenimore. *The Last of the Mohicans*, edited by John McWilliams. Oxford and New York: Oxford University Press, 1994.

———. *The Spy: A Tale of the Neutral Ground*, edited by Wayne Franklin. London and New York: Penguin Books, 1997.

David Daiches, "Scott's Achievement as a Novelist " in *Literary Essays*. Chicago: University of Chicago Press, 1967, 88–121. Originally published 1951.

Debreczeny, Paul. *The Other Pushkin: A Study of Alexander Pushkin's Prose*. Stanford, California: Stanford University Press, 1983.

Dekker, George. *The American Historical Romance*. Cambridge and New York: Cambridge University Press, 1987.

———. *The Fictions of Romantic Tourism: Radcliffe, Scott and Mary Shelley*. Stanford, California: Stanford University Press, 2005.

———. *James Fenimore Cooper: The American Scott*. New York: Barnes and Noble, 1967.

Dickens, Charles. *A Tale of Two Cities*, edited by Richard Maxwell. London and New York: Penguin Books, 2003.

Donoghue, Denis. *Metaphor*. Cambridge, MA: Harvard University Press, 2014.

Duggan, James. *The Great Mutiny.* New York: G.P. Putnam's Sons, 1965.

Duncan, Ian. *Scott's Shadow: The Novel in Romantic Edinburgh.* Princeton: Princeton University Press, 2007.

———."Waverley" in *The Novel: Forms and Themes,* edited by Franco Moretti. Princeton: Princeton University Press, 2006.

Eagleton, Terry. *Literary Theory: An Introduction.* Minneapolis: University of Minnesota Press, 1983.

Eco, Umberto. "Excess and History in Hugo's *Ninety-Three*" in *The Novel: Forms and Themes,* edited by Franco Moretti. Princeton: Princeton University Press, 2006.

Edmonds, Robin. *Pushkin; the Man and His Age.* New York: St. Martin's Press, 1940.

Elliott, James P. "Historical Introduction" to *The Spy.* New York: AMS Press, 2002.

Ellis, Geoffrey. "The Revolution of 1848–1849 in France," in R.J.W. Evans and H.P. Von Strandmann. *The Revolutions in Europe 1848–1849: From Reform to Reaction.* Oxford: Oxford University Press, 2000.

Emerson, Ralph Waldo *Representative Men* [1850], in *The Complete Works of Ralph Waldo Emerson,* vol. IV, edited by Edward Emerson. Boston: Houghton, Mifflin and Co., 1883.

Eugenides, Jeffrey. *The Marriage Plot.* New York: Farrar, Straus and Giroux, 2011.

Evdokimova, Svetlana. *Pushkin's Historical Imagination.* New Haven: Yale University Press, 1999.

Ferguson, Adam. *An Essay on the History of Civil Society,* edited by Fania Oz-Salzberger. Cambridge and New York: Cambridge University Press, 1995.

Ferguson, Niall. *The Ascent of Money: A Financial History of the World.* New York and London: Penguin Books, 2008.

Ferguson, Priscilla Parkhurst. *Paris as Revolution: Writing the Nineteenth Century City.* Berkeley: University of California Press, 1994.

Ferris, Ina. *The Achievement of Literary Authority: Gender, History and the Waverley Novels.* Ithaca: Cornell University Press, 1991.

Flaubert, Gustave. *Selected Letters,* translated by Geoffrey Wall. London and New York: Penguin, 1997.

———. *Sentimental Education,* translated by Robert Baldick, revised by Geoffrey Wall. London and New York: Penguin Books, 2004.

Fleishman, Avrom. *The English Historical Novel.* Baltimore: Johns Hopkins Press, 1971.

Foner, Eric. *Tom Paine and Revolutionary America.* Oxford: Oxford University Press, 1976.

Fontane, Theodor. *Before the Storm,* translated and edited by R.J. Hollingdale. Oxford and New York: Oxford University Press, 1985.

Forbes, Duncan. "Introduction" to Adam Ferguson, *Essay on the History of Civil Society.* Edinburgh: Edinburgh University Press, 1966.

———. "The Rationalism of Sir Walter Scott" in *Critical Essays on Sir Walter Scott,* by Harry E, Shaw. New York: The Gale Group, 1996.

Forster, E.M. *Aspects of the Novel.* New York: Harcourt, Brace and Co., 1927.

Foucault, Michel. *Ethics: Subjectivity and Truth*, edited by Paul Rabinow, translated by Robert Hurley. New York: New Press, 1994.

France, Anatole. *The Gods Will Have Blood (Les Dieux Ont Soif)*, translated with an Introduction by Frederick Davies. New York: Penguin Books, 2004.

Frank, Joseph. *The Levellers*. New York: Russell and Russell, 1969.

Franklin, Wayne. Introduction to *The Spy*. New York: Penguin Books, 1997.

——. *James Fenimore Cooper: The Early Years*. New Haven: Yale University Press, 2007.

——. "'One More Scene': The Marketing Context of Cooper's 'Sixth' Leather-Stocking Tale" in *Leather-Stocking Redux; or, Old Tales, New Essays*, by Jeffrey Walker. New York: AMS Press, 2011.

Friedman, Barton. *Fabricating History: English Writers on the French Revolution*. Princeton: Princeton University Press, 1988.

Furet, Francois. *Interpreting the French Revolution*, translated by Elborg Forster. Cambridge: Cambridge University Press, 1981.

Gilpin, William. *Observations Relative Chiefly to Picturesque Beauty*. London: R. Blamire, 1789.

Godineau, Dominique. *The Women of Paris and their French Revolution*, translated by Katherine Streip. Berkeley: University of California Press, 1988.

Goldberg, Michael. *Carlyle and Dickens*. Athens: University of Georgia Press, 1972.

Goodwin, Doris Kearns. *Team of Rivals*. New York: Simon and Schuster, 2006.

Grant, Elliott M. *Emile Zola*. New York: Twayne Publishers, 1966.

Gray, Francine du Plessix. *Madame de Stael, The First Modern Woman*. New York: Atlas & Co., 2008.

Groot, Jerome de. *The Historical Novel*. London and New York: Routledge, 2010.

Grossman, Jonathan. *The Art of Alibi: English Law Courts and the Novel*. Baltimore and London: Johns Hopkins University Press, 2002.

Hayden John O., ed. *Walter Scott: The Critical Heritage*, 2nd edition. London and New York: Routledge, 1995.

Hazlitt, William. "Sir Walter Scott," in *The Spirit of the Age*, 4th edition. London: George Bell and Sons, 1886.

Hegel, G.W.F. *Lectures on the Philosophy of History*, translated by John Sibree and Ruben Alvarado (www.wordbridge.net, print, 2011).

Herman, Arthur. *How the Scots Invented the Modern World*. New York: Random House, 2001.

Hill, Christopher. *The Century of Revolution 1603–1714*. London: Thomas Nelson and Sons, 1966.

——. *God's Englishman: Oliver Cromwell and the English Revolution*. New York: The Dial Press, 1970.

Hingley, Ronald. *Pasternak: A Biography*. New York: Alfred A. Knopf, 1983.

Hobsbawm, Eric. *The Age of Revolution: 1789–1848*. New York: Random House, 1996. First published 1962.

Hobsbawm, E.J. *Nations and Nationalism since 1780*. Cambridge: Cambridge University Press, 1990.

Hochman, Baruch. *Character in Literature*. Ithaca: Cornell University Press, 1985.

Holmes, Robert L. *War and Morality*. Princeton: Princeton University Press, 1989.

Howe, Irving. *Politics and the Novel*, Introduction by David Bromwitch. Chicago: Ivan R. Dee, 2002. First published 1957.

Howard, Richard ed. *Gone With the Wind as Book and Film*. n.p: University of South Carolina Press, 1983.

Hugo, Victor. *Quatrevingt-treize (Ninety Three)*, translated by Frank Lee Benedict, Introduction by Graham Robb, 2nd edition. New York: Carroll & Graf, 1998.

———. *Quatrevingt-treize*, Présentation by Judith Wulf. Paris: Flammarion, 2002.

———. "The French Revolution" (1844) in *Victor Hugo's Intellectual Autobiography: Postscriptum de Ma Vie, Being Late Uncollected Works*, translated by Lorenzo O'Rourke. New York: Haskell House, 1971.

Hume, David. *Political Essays*, edited by Knud Haakonssen. Cambridge: Cambridge University Press, 1994.

———. *The History of England*, Foreword by W.B. Todd, 6 vols. Indianapolis: Liberty Fund, 1983.

Hunt, Lynn. *Politics, Culture and Class in the French Revolution*. Berkeley: University of California Press, 1984.

James, Henry. "Hugo's *Ninety-Three*" in *Literary Reviews and Essays by Henry James*, ed. Albert Mordell. New York: Twayne Publishers, 1957. First published in *The Nation* 1874.

———. "Nassau Senior" in *North American Review*, vol. 100, 1864.

———. Preface to *The Tragic Muse* in *The Art of the Novel*, Foreword by R.W.B. Lewis, Introduction by R.P. Blackmur. Boston: Northeastern University Press, 1984.

———. "The Art of Fiction" in *Henry James: The Future of the Novel*, edited by Leon Edel. New York: Vintage Books, 1956.

———. *The Art of the Novel*, Foreword by R.W.B. Lewis, Introduction by R.P. Blackmur. Boston: Northeastern University Press, 1984.

Jameson, Fredric. *Marxism and Form: Twentieth Century Dialectical Theories of Literature*. Princeton, NJ: Princeton University Press, 1971.

———. *The Antinomies of Realism*. London and New York: Verso, 2013.

———. *The Political Unconscious: Narrative as a Socially Symbolic Act*. Ithaca: Cornell University Press, 1981.

Jewett, Sarah Orne. *Letters of Sarah Orne Jewett*, edited by Annie Fields. Boston and New York: Houghton Mifflin Co., 1911.

———. *Sarah Orne Jewett Letters*, edited by Richard Cary. Waterville, ME: Colby College Press, 1956.

Johnson, Edgar. *Sir Walter Scott: The Great Unknown*, 2 vols. New York: The Macmillan Co., 1970.

Johnson, Paul. *Napoleon, A Life*. New York: Penguin, 2002.

Joyce, James. *A Portrait of the Artist as a Young Man*, edited by Seamus Deane. New York: Penguin Group, 1992.

Kalyvas, Andreas and Ira Katznelson. *Liberal Beginnings: Making a Republic for the Moderns*. Cambridge: Cambridge University Press, 2008.

Kaplan, Fred. *Gore Vidal: A Biography*. New York: Doubleday, 1999.

Katz, Michael R. *Dreams and the Unconscious in Nineteenth Century Russian Fiction*. Hanover and London: University Press of New England, 1984.

Keats, John. *Complete Poems and Selected Letters*. New York: Odyssey Press, 1935.

Keegan, John and Richard Holmes. *Soldiers: A History of Men in Battle*. New York: Viking Press, 1986.

Kermode, Frank. *The Sense of an Ending*, 2nd edition. Oxford and New York: Oxford University Press, 2000.

Lampedusa, Giuseppe Tomasi di. *The Leopard*, translated by Archibald Colquhoun, Foreword by Gioacchino Lanza Tomasi. New York: Pantheon Books, 2007.

Laws and Articles of War For the Government of his Majesties Forces Within the Kingdom of Scotland. Edinburgh: Evan Tyler, 1667.

Leavis, F.R. *The Great Tradition*. Garden City, N.Y: Doubleday Anchor, 1948.

Lenin, V.I. *The State and Revolution*. London and New York: Penguin, 1992.

Lenman. Bruce. *The Jacobite Risings in Britain, 1689–1746*. Aberdeen: The Scottish Cultural Press, 1995.

Lukacs, Georg. *Studies in European Realism*. London: Hillway Publishing Co., 1950. Reissued Merlin Press 1972.

———. *The Historical Novel*, translated by Hannah and Stanley Mitchell. Lincoln: University of Nebraska Press, 1983. First published 1937.

———. *The Theory of the Novel*, Introduction by Fredric Jameson. Cambridge, Mass: The M.I.T. Press, 1971. First published P. Cassirer, Berlin, 1920.

Lutwack, Leonard. *The Role of Place in Literature*. Syracuse, NY: Syracuse University Press, 1984.

Lynch, John. *Simon Bolivar: A Life*. New Haven and London: Yale University Press, 2006.

Lynn, John A. *Battle: A History of Combat and Culture*. Boulder, Colorado: Westview Press, 2003.

Maggach, Douglas and Paul Leduc Browne. *The Social Question and the Democratic Revolution: Marx and the Legacy of 1848*. Ottawa: University of Ottawa Press, 2000.

Macaulay, Lord. *The History of England*, edited by Hugh Trevor-Roper. London and New York: Penguin Books, 1968, First published 1848–1861.

Malraux, André. *Man's Fate*. New York: Random House, 1961.

Mantel, Hilary. *A Place of Greater Safety*. New York: Henry Holt and Co., 2006.

———. *Giving Up the Ghost*. New York: Henry Holt and Company, 2003.

———. interview by Mona Simpson, *Paris Review Interviews*, vol. 212, 2015]. http://www.theparisreview.org/interviews/6360/art-of-fiction-no-226-hilary-mantel

———. interview, *The Guardian*, October 16, 2009, http://www.guardian.co.uk/books/2009/oct/17/hilary-mantel-author-booker

———. Review of *Robespierre*, eds. Colin Haydon and William Doyle, in *London Review of Books*, vol. 22, #7, 2000.

G.E. Manwaring and Bonamy Dobreé, *The Floating Republic: An Account of the Mutinies at Spithead and The Nore in 1797*. London: Penguin, 1935.

Manzoni, Alessandro. *On The Historical Novel*. Lincoln and London: University of Nebraska Press, 1984.

Marcuse, Herbert. *Reason and Revolution: Hegel and the Rise of Social Theory.* New York: Humanities Press, 1968.

Marquez, Gabriel Garcia. *The General in His Labyrinth: A Novel,* translated by Edith Grossman. New York: Random House, 1990.

Marx, Karl. *Economic and Philosophic Manuscripts of 1844,* translated by Martin Milligan. Amherst, NY: Prometheus Books, 1988.

———. *The Eighteenth Brumaire of Louis Bonaparte.* Rockville, Maryland: Serenity Publishers, 2009. First published 1852.

Marx, Karl and V.I. Lenin. *Civil War in France: The Paris Commune,* supplementary essay by Nikita Fedorovsky. New York: International Publishers, 2008.

———. *Revolution and War,* articles first published in *The New York Tribune* 1853–1862. London and New York: Penguin Books, 2009.

Maxwell, Richard. *The Historical Novel in Europe, 1650–1950.* Cambridge and New York: Cambridge University Press, 2009.

May, Larry Rovie and Eric and Viner, Steve. *The Morality of War: Classical and Contemporary Readings.* Upper Saddle River, NJ: Pearson Prentice-Hall, 2006.

McMaster, Graham. *Scott and Society.* Cambridge: Cambridge University Press, 1981.

McWilliams, John. *New England's Crises and Cultural Memory.* Cambridge: Cambridge University Press, 2004.

———. *Political Justice in a Republic: James Fenimore Cooper's America.* Berkeley: University of California Press, 1972.

———. "Progress without Politics: *A Tale of Two Cities,*" *Clio* 7 (1977): 19–31.

———. "The Rationale for the American Romance," *Boundary II* 17 (1990): 71–82.

Melville, Herman "Hawthorne and His Mosses" (1850) in *Herman Melville: Representative Selections,* ed. Willard Thorp. New York: American Book Co., 1938.

———. *Israel Potter: His Fifty Years of Exile.* Evanston, IL: Northwestern University Press, 1982.

Merriman, John. *Massacre: The Life and Death of the Paris Commune.* New York: Basic Books, 2014.

Michelet, Jules. *History of the French Revolution,* translated by C. Cocks. London: H.G. Bohn, 1847.

Millgate, Jane. *Walter Scott: The Making of the Novelist.* Toronto: University of Toronto Press, 1987.

Mitchell, Margaret. *Gone with the Wind.* New York: Scribner, 2011.

Monod, Paul Kléber. *Jacobitism and the English People.* Cambridge: Cambridge University Press, 1989.

Moretti, Franco. *Atlas of the European Novel 1800–1900.* London and New York: Verso, 1998.

———. *The Way of the World: The Bildungsroman in European Culture.* London: Verso, 1987.

Morpurgo, J.E. *Treason at West Point: The Arnold-André Conspiracy.* New York: Mason Charter, 1975.

Nagel, Gwen L. ed. *Critical Essays on Sarah Orne Jewett.* Boston: G.K. Hall, 1984.

Orr, Linda. *Headless History: 19th Century French Historiography of the Revolution.* Ithaca: Cornell University Press, 1990.

Orwell, George. "Charles Dickens" in *Orwell: A Collection of Essays.* New York: Doubleday and Co., 1954. First published in 1939.

O'Toole, G.J.A. *Honorable Treachery: A History of U.S. Intelligence, Espionage, and Covert Action from the American Revolution to the C.I.A.* New York: Atlantic Monthly Press, 1991.

Palmer, R.R. *A History of the Modern World,* 2nd edition. New York: Alfred A. Knopf, 1960.

Palmer, R.R. *Twelve Who Ruled: The Year of the Terror in the French Revolution.* Princeton: Princeton University Press, 1940.

Parini, Jay. *Empire of the Self: A Life of Gore Vidal.* New York: Doubleday, 2015.

———. ed. *Gore Vidal: Writers Against the Grain.* New York: Columbia University Press, 1992.

———. ed. *The Selected Essays of Gore Vidal.* New York: Doubleday, 2008.

Parker, Hershel. *Reading Billy Budd.* Evanston, Illinois: Northwestern University Press, 1990.

Pasternak, Boris. *Doctor Zhivago,* translated by Max Hayward and Manya Harari, Introduction by John Bailey. New York: Pantheon Books, 1991.

Payne, Robert. *Marx.* New York: Simon and Schuster, 1968.

Pickering, James. Introduction to *The Spy.* New York: College and University Press, 1971.

Pincus, Steve. *1688: The First Modern Revolution.* New Haven: Yale University Press, 2009.

Pocock, J.G.A. ed. *Three British Revolutions: 1641, 1668, 1776.* Princeton: Princeton University Press, 1980.

Polloszek, Dieter. *Literature and Legal Discourse: Equity and Ethics from Sterne to Conrad.* Cambridge: Cambridge University Press, 1999.

Porte, Joel. *The Romance in America: Studies in Cooper, Poe, Hawthorne, Melville and James.* Middletown Conn: Wesleyan University Press, 1969.

Posner, Richard A. *Law and Literature,* 3rd edition. Cambridge, Mass: Harvard University Press, 2009.

Prawer, S.S. *Karl Marx and World Reading.* Oxford: Oxford University Press, 1978.

Prebble, John. *The King's Jaunt.* Edinburgh: Birlinn, Ltd, 2000.

Price, Martin. *Character and Moral Imagination in the Novel.* New Haven: Yale University Press, 1983.

Proffer, Carl R. editor and translator. *The Critical Prose of Alexander Pushkin.* Bloomington: Indiana University Press, 1969.

Pushkin, Alexander. *Complete Prose Fiction,* translated by Paul Debreczeny. Stanford: Stanford University Press, 1983. This edition includes Pushkin's *A History of Pugachev* (1833).

———. *Letters of Alexander Pushkin,* 3rd edition, translated by J. Thomas Shaw. Los Angeles: Charles Schlacks, Jr., 1997.

———. *The Captain's Daughter and Other Stories,* translated by Natalie Duddington. New York, Random House, 1936.

Pyron, Darden Asbury. *Southern Daughter: The Life of Margaret Mitchell.* New York and Oxford: Oxford University Press, 1991.

Ramsay, David. *The History of the American Revolution* (1789), 2 vols. Indianapolis: Liberty Fund, 1990.

Ricoeur, Paul. *The Rule of Metaphor: Multi-Disciplinary Studies of the Creation of Meaning in Language,* translated by Robert Czerny with Kathleen McLaughlin and John Costello. London: Routledge and Kegan Paul, 1978.

———. "The Metaphorical Process as Cognition, Imagination and Feeling" in *On Metaphor,* ed. Sheldon Sacks. Chicago: University of Chicago Press, 1978.

Rigney Ann. *Imperfect Histories: The Elusive Past and the Legacy of Romantic Historicism.* Ithaca and London: Cornell University Press, 2001.

———. *The Rhetoric of Historical Representation: Three Narrative Histories of the French Revolution.* Cambridge: Cambridge University Press, 1990.

Robb, Graham. *Victor Hugo.* New York: W.W. Norton, 1997.

Robespierre, Maximilien. "Rapport sur les Principes du Gouvernement Revolution-naire," December 25, 1793.

Rosenberg, Brian. *Little Dorrit's Shadows: Character and Contradiction in Dickens.* Columbia: University of Missouri Press, 1996.

Rousseau, Jean-Jacques. *The Social Contract and the First and Second Discourses,* ed. Susan Dunn. New Haven: Yale University Press, 2002.

Rules and Articles of War for the Better Government of his Majesties Army in the Kingdom of Scotland. Edinburgh: Andrew Anden, 1686.

Rose, Alexander. *Washington's Spies.* New York: Bantam Books, 2014.

Sale, Roger. *Closer to Home: Writers and Places in England, 1780–1830.* Cambridge: Harvard University Press, 1986.

Schama, Simon. *Citizens: A Chronicle of the French Revolution.* New York: Random House, 1989.

Schom, Alan. *Napoleon Bonaparte.* New York: HarperCollins, 1997.

Schramm, Jan-Melissa. *Testimony and Advocacy in Victorian law, Literature and Theology.* Cambridge: Cambridge University Press, 2000.

Scorza, Thomas J. *In the Time Before Steamships: Billy Budd, the Limits of Politics, and Modernity.* Dekalb, IL: Northern Illinois University Press, 1979.

Scott, Walter. *A Legend of the Wars of Montrose,* edited by J.H. Alexander. Edinburgh: Edinburgh University Press, 1995.

———. "An Essay on Romance," in vol. 6 *of Sir Walter Scott: Miscellaneous Prose Works.* Edinburgh: Cadell and Co., 1827.

———. *Ivanhoe,* edited by A.N. Wilson. London and New York: Penguin Publishing, 1985.

———. *Old Mortality,* edited by Jane Stevenson and Peter Davidson. Oxford and New York: Oxford University Press, 1993.

———. *Redgauntlet,* edited by Kathryn Sutherland. Oxford and New York: Oxford University Press, 1985.

———. *Rob Roy,* edited by Ian Duncan. Oxford and New York: Oxford University Press, 1998.

———. *Tales of a Grandfather* Second Series, Volume II. Boston: Sanborn, Carter and Bazin, 1855.

———. *The Bride of Lammermoor*, edited by Fiona Robertson. Oxford and New York: Oxford University Press, 1991.

———. *The Heart of Mid-lothian*, edited by Tony Inglis. London and New York: Penguin, 1994.

———. *The Life of Napoleon Buonaparte, Emperor of the French, with a Preliminary View of the French Revolution*, 3 vols. Philadelphia: Carey, Lea & Carey, 1827.

———. *Waverley; or, 'Tis Sixy Years Since*, edited by Andrew Hook. London and New York: Penguin Books, 1985.

———. *Woodstock: Or, the Cavalier.* Boston, Mass: IndyPublish.com, 2011. ISBN 1-4142-7529-3.

Semmel, Stuart. *Napoleon and the British.* New Haven: Yale University Press, 2004.

Shakespeare, William. *King Henry the Fourth, Part One.* London and New York: Penguin, 2008.

Shaw, Harry E. ed. *Critical Essays on Sir Walter Scott.* New York: The Gale Group, 1996.

———. *The Forms of Historical Fiction: Sir Walter Scott and His Successors.* Ithaca: Cornell University Press, 1983.

Skocpol, Theda. *States & Social Revolutions: A Comparative Analysis of France, Russia & China.* Cambridge: Cambridge University Press, 1979.

Soboul, Albert. *The Sans-Culottes*, translated by Rémy Inglis Hall. Princeton: Princeton University Press, 1980, first published 1968.

Stael, Germaine De. *Considerations on the Principal Events of the French Revolution*, with an introduction by Aurelian Craiu. Indianapolis: Liberty Fund, Inc., 2008.

Steele, Ian K. *Betrayals: Fort William Henry and the 'Massacre.'* Oxford: Oxford University Press, 1990.

Stendhal. *The Charterhouse of Parma*, translated by Richard Howard. New York: Random House, 2000.

Stewart, Paul Henderson. *Honor.* Chicago and London: University of Chicago Press, 1994.

Sutherland, John. *The Life of Walter Scott: A Critical Biography.* Oxford: Blackwell, 1995.

Swift, Jonathan. *Gulliver's Travels and Other Writings*, ed. Louis Landa. Cambridge: Houghton Mifflin Company, 1960.

Taylor, Helen. *Scarlett's Women: Gone With the Wind and Its Female Fans.* New Brunswick: Rutgers University Press, 1989.

Thomas, Brook. *Cross Examinations of Law and Literature: Cooper, Hawthorne, Stowe and Melville.* Cambridge: Cambridge University Press, 1987.

Tindall, Gillian. *Countries of the Mind: The Meaning of Place to Writers.* Boston: Northeastern University Press, 1991.

Tocqueville, Alexis de. *The Ancien Regime and the French Revolution*, translated and edited by Gerald Bevan, Introduction by Hugh Brogan. London and New York: Penguin Books, 2008, first published 1856).

Tolstoy Leo. *Anna Karenina*, translated by Richard Pevear. London and New York: Penguin Books, 2000.

————. *War and Peace*, the Maude translation, ed. George Gibian. London and New York: W.W. Norton & Co., 1996.

Trumpener, Katie. *Bardic Nationalism*. Princeton: Princeton University Press, 1997.

Tucker, Robert C. ed. *The Marx-Engels Reader*, 2nd edition. New York and London: W.W. Norton and Co., 1978.

Torgovnick, Marianna. *Closure in the Novel*. Princeton: Princeton University Press, 1981.

Van Ghent, Dorothy. *The English Novel: Form and Function*. New York: Harper and Row, 1953.

Vidal, Gore. *Burr: A Novel*. New York: Random House, 1973.

————. *Empire: A Novel*. New York: Random House, 2000.

————. *Lincoln: A Novel*. New York: Random House, 1984.

————. "The State of the Union" (1975) in *Essays 1952–1992*. New York: Random House, 1993.

Vigny, Alfred de. "Reflexions Sur La Verité Dans L'Art," "Preface" to *Cinq-Mars* Paris: Louis Conard, 1914.

Wallace, Diana. *The Woman's Historical Novel: British Women Writers, 1900–2000*. New York: Palgrave Macmillan, 2005.

Wallace, James D. *Early Cooper and His Audience*. New York: Columbia University Press, 1986.

Wall, Geoffrey. *Flaubert: A Life*. New York: Farrar, Straus and Giroux, 2001.

Walzer, Michael. *Just and Unjust Wars: A Moral Argument with Historical Illustrations*. New York: Basic Books, 1977.

Warner, Sylvia Townsend. *Summer Will Show*. New York: New York Review of Books, 2009.

Waswo, Richard. "Scott and the Really Great Tradition," in *Critical Essays on Sir Walter Scott; The Waverley Novels*, ed. Harry E. Shaw. New York: G .K. Hall, 1996,

Watson, Nicola. *Revolution and the Form of the British Novel 1790–1825*. Oxford: Oxford University Press, 1994.

Welsh, Alexander. *Strong Representations: Narrative and Circumstantial Evidence in England*. Baltimore: Johns Hopkins University Press, 1992.

————. *The Hero of the Waverley Novels*. New Haven: Yale University Press, 1963.

————. *What is Honor: A Question of Moral Imperatives*. New Haven and London: Yale University Press, 2008.

Wharton, Edith. *The Valley of Decision*. New York: Charles Scribner's Sons, 1902.

White, Hayden. *Metahistory: The Historical Imagination in Nineteenth Century Europe*. Baltimore and London: Johns Hopkins University Press, 1973.

Williams,Joan ed. *Sir Walter Scott on Novelists and Fiction*. London: Routledge and Kegan Paul, 1968.

Wilson, A.N. *Tolstoy*. New York: W.W. Norton, 1988.

Woolf, Virginia. "Sir Walter Scott," (1940) in *The Moment and Other Essays*. N.Y: Harcourt Brace and Company, 1948.

Worden, Blair. *The English Civil Wars 1640–1660*. London: Orion House, 2009.

Wordsworth,William. *Selected Poems and Prefaces*, ed. Jack Stillinger. Boston: Houghton Mifflin, 1965.

Wright, D. L, ed. *The French Revolution: Introductory Documents.* St. Lucia: University of Queensland Press, 1974.

Wulf, Judith. "Le Role de la Fiction," *Présentation* for Hugo's *Quatrevingt- treize.* Paris: GF Flammarion, 2002.

Zola, Emile. *La Débacle,* translated by E.P. Robbins. New York: Mondial, 2008.

Index

Adams, Henry, 7, 200
Agulhon, Maurice, 277n3
Alison, Archibald, 21
Anderson, Perry, xvii, xxxn1, 277
André, Major John, 161–63
Arac, Jonathan, 88
Arendt, Hannah, xxx, xli–xliii
Argyle, John, Second Duke of, 193–95
Aristotle, 1, 3, 6
Articles of War, 156, 158, 162, 171
Ashley, Maurice, 54n39
Augustine, Saint, 125, 152n9

Bagehot, Walter, 22, 50n4
Bailyn, Bernard, lvn3
Bakhtin, M.M., xxv, xxxiin12, 61
Balzac, Honoré de, xviii, xx, 27, 48–50,
    52n17, 275–76
Beccaria, Cesare, 155, 160
Berlin, Isaiah, 217n13
Berman, Sandra, xxxin8
Bismark, Otto von, 86n25, 123
Bloom, Harold, 81
Bolivar, Simon, 18, 200, 265n17
Bonaparte, Napoleon, xlviii–lii, 29, 42,
    84n7, 103–7, 135–36, 215
Bowman, James, 153n14
Brinton, Crane, xvi, xxx, xli–xliii, 34,
    111
Brombert, Victor, xxx, 278n9

Brown, David, 118n11, 217n7
Buchan, John, 38
Buell, Lawrence, 220n33
Burke Edmund, xliv–xlvi, 83n1
Bury, J.B., 199

Camus, Albert, 155
Carlyle, Thomas, 3, 84n10, 120n27
Cather, Willa, xxix, 204–6, 219n23
Chase, Richard V., 218n1
Chiaromonte Nicola, xxx, 220n35
Christiansen, Rupert, 154n35
Cixous, Helene, 87
Clausewitz, Carl Von, 123, 136–37
Cocteau, Jean, 145
Cole, Thomas, 3
Coleridge, Samuel Taylor, 2, 18n1,
    25–26, 124, 156. 201
Condorcet, Antoine-Nicolas de, xxxv,
    xxxviii, 200
Conrad, Joseph. xxviii, xxxiin15,
    265n17
Cooper, James Fenimore. xvii–xviii,
    48, 57, 198–99, 217n14, 219n19,
    224–25;
    The Last of the Mohicans, 48–49,
    126–27, 130–35;
    *The Spy: A Tale of the Neutral
    Ground,* 65–71, 163–66, 181–82,
    198, 229

Copernicus, xxxiii–xxxiv
Crane, Stephen, 146
Croker, John Wilson, xxxin10
Cromwell, Oliver, 28, 29, 39–45, 54n39,
    82

Daiches, David, 50n1
Danton, Georges, xxxviii, 145, 260–62
David, Jacques Louis, 11, 105
Debreczeny, Paul, 119n14
Decembrists, 234, 246n15
Dekker, George, xxx, 83n3, 84n6,
    85n12, 117n7, 218n1
Desmoulin, Camille, 109, 262–64
Dickens, Charles, xvii, 112;
    A Tale of Two Cities, xxi, 4–6.
    71–72, 100–103, 120n27, 151,
    175–77, 181–82, 230–32
Donoghue, Denis, 2, 18
Dos Passos, John, 65n6
Duncan, Ian, 51n8, 53n25, 54n32

Eagleton, Terry, 87–88
Eco, Umberto, 3
Edgeworth, Maria, xxiv, 51n12
Emerson, Ralph Waldo, 121n34
Eugenides, Jeffrey, 221

Fast, Howard, 78
Faulkner, William, 206
Feltrinelli, Giangiacomo, 211
Ferguson, Adam, 31–32, 53n20, 187,
    198
Ferguson, Niall, 120n29
Ferguson, Priscilla Parkhurst, 85n20
Ferris, Ina, lviiin33, 51n10, 118n9
Fielding, Henry, xxiv, 106
Flaubert, Gustave, xxiii, xxx, 186, 269,
    278n6, 278n8, 269–73, 276,
    278n6, 278n9;
    Sentimental Education, 271–73
Fleishman, Avrom, xxx, 51n9, 127n28,
    245n11
Foner, Eric, lviiin25
Forbes, Duncan, 53n20

Forster, E.M., 50n1, 87–88, 200,
    218n16, 246n18
Foucault, Michel, 181–82
France, Anatole, xvii, 11, 17;
    *The Gods Will Have Blood (Les
    Dieux Ont Soif)*, 11–14, 78,
    109–11, 177–81, 195, 238–39
Franco-Prussian War, 72–73
Franklin, Wayne, 85n12, 85n15, 217n14
Friedman, Barton, 120n28
Frye, Northrop, xxv
Furet, Francois, xxxi, xxxix, lviin23,
    266n25

Garibaldi, Giuseppe, 213, 214
Gilpin, William, 83n1
Godinineau, Dominique, 120n30
Goodwin, Doris Kearns, 86n24
Gorki, Maxim, 274
Graves, Robert, 211
Great Mutiny (Spithead and Nore),
    269–70
Groot, Jerome de, xxxin8, 218n17
Grotius, Hugo, 125–26, 152n11, 152n10

Hayford, Harrison, 167–72
Hazlitt, William, 47–48
Hegel, G.W.F., xv, xix, xxxin1, xxxviii–
    xxxix, 29, 35, 274, 275
Hill, Christopher, 35, 39, 53n28
historical novel, xxiii–xv, 5, 25–29,
    51n6, 186–87
Hobsbawm, E.J., xxx
Hochman, Baruch, 88
honor, 123–51
Howe, Irving, xxx, xxxviin16, lviiin30
Hugo, Victor, xvii, 8–9, 17, 80, 173;
    "The French Revolution" [1844],
    3–4, 225;
    Quatrevingt-treize (Ninety Three),
    9–11, 141–45, 154n26, 154n29,
    181–82, 195, 236–37
Hume, David, 84n8
Hunt, Lynn, 5
hybridity, xxxiii, 51n5

James, Henry, xxv, 22, 28. 50n2, 145,
203–4, 235
Jameson, Fredric, xvi–xx, xxvi, xxx,
249, 274–77
Jefferson, Thomas, xxxv, 197, 200
Jewett. Sarah Orne, xxix, 201–4,
219n19, 219 n21, 235
Johnson, Edgar, 28
Johnson, Paul, xxx, 103–4
Joyce, James, 22
justice, military vs. civilian, 174–75,
181

Kalyvas Andreas, lvin8
Katz, Michael R., 119n20, 119n23
Katznelson, Ira, lvin8
Keats, John, 243
Kermode Frank, 222, 224, 243
Kutuzov, General Michel Ilarenovich,
195–97

Lafayette, Madame de, xxix
Lampedusa, Giuseppe Tomasi di, xxi,
211;
The Leopard, 211–15, 241–43, 277
Leavis, F.R., 50n1
Lenin, V.I., xl–xlii, 14, 112, 113,
122n39
Lenman, Bruce, 54n35, 118n10
Lincoln, Abraham, 79–82, 86n24, 86n25
Locke, John, 1–2
Lukacs, Georg, xvii–xxviii, xxx, 3,
51n9, 77, 78, 186, 200, 267–70,
273–74, 278n9
Lynn, John, 129, 153n14

Macaulay, Lord, 84n8
Madison, James, xxxvi, xliii
Malraux, André. xxviii
Mantel, Hilary, xxix, xxxviii, 259,
266n19, 266n21;
A Place of Greater Safety. 249,
260–64
Manzoni, Alessandro, xxiv, 88
Marat, Jean-Paul, 145

Marcuse, Herbert, xxxviii, 274
Marquez, Gabriel Garcia, 18;
*The General in His Labyrinth: A
Novel*, xxi, 18, 249. 255–59
marriage, 221–44
Martinez, Padre Antonio José, 204,
219n28
Marx, Karl, xxvi. xxxiin14, xxxix–xli,
xlv, 114, 115–16, 148–49, 186,
249. 267–69, 275, 278n4
Maxwell, Richard, xx–xxi, xxx, 119n19,
153n.23
McWilliams, John, 85n15, 120n28,
218n1, 217n14
Melville, Herman, 124, 214n19;
*Billy Budd Sailor (An Inside
Narrative)* 151, 156, 157, 167–73
Michelet, Jules, xxxix, 217n10, 269
Millgate, Jane, 51n9, 84n5, 118n11,
216n4
Mitchell, Margaret, xxix, 206–11, 216,
220n34
Moretti, Franco, xxx, lviiin31, 55n43

Napoleon, Louis, (Napoleon III), xvii, 8,
154n32, 268
neutral ground, xxii, 27, 57–83, 142

Orr, Linda, xxxviii, xliii, lvin11. lvin21
Orwell, George, lvin18, 114, 246n12
O'Toole, G.J.A., 183n12

Paine, Thomas, xlvi–xlviii, lviin25
Palmer, R.R., xxx, 266n23
Parini, Jay, 250
Parker, Hershel, 183n15
Pasternak, Boris, xvii, 17, 121n38,
122n39;
Doctor Zhivago, 14–17, 111–17,
122n40, 149–51, 211–12, 216,
239–41
Pincus, Steve, lvn2
Pocock, J.G.A., 35
Porte, Joel, 216n1
Posner, Richard A., 182n3, 184n24

About the Author

John McWilliams is author of *Political Justice in a Republic: James Fenimore Cooper's America* (California, 1972), *Hawthorne, Melville and the American Character* (Cambridge 1984), *The American Epic* (Cambridge 1989) and *New England's Crises and Cultural Memory* (Cambridge 2004) as well as many articles and reviews. He has been awarded four Fellowships from the National Endowment of the Humanities. He has taught at The University of California, Berkeley, the University of Illinois, Chicago, and since 1978 at Middlebury College, where he is now College Professor of Humanities, Emeritus.

Lightning Source UK Ltd.
Milton Keynes UK
UKOW06n0804061217
313927UK00001B/59/P